Michael Wheeler challenges critical orthodoxy by arguing that John Ruskin's writing is underpinned by a sustained trust in divine wisdom, a trust nurtured by his imaginative engagement with King Solomon and the temple in Jerusalem, and with the wisdom literature of the Old Testament.

In *Modern Painters*, *The Seven Lamps of Architecture* and *The Stones of Venice*, belief in the wisdom of God the Father informed Ruskin's Evangelical natural theology and his celebration of Turner's landscape painting, while the wisdom of God the Son lay at the heart of his Christian aesthetics. Whereas 'the author of *Modern Painters*' sought to teach his readers how to see architecture, paintings and landscapes, the 'Victorian Solomon' whose religious life was troubled, and who created various forms of modern wisdom literature in works such as *Unto this Last*, *The Queen of the Air* and *Fors Clavigera*, wished to teach them how to live.

Michael Wheeler is Director of Chawton House Library, Hampshire, and Professor of English Literature at the University of Southampton. While writing this book he was Professor of English Literature, and Director of the Ruskin Programme and Ruskin Collection Project, Lancaster University. His main publications include *The Art of Allusion in Victorian Fiction* (1979), *English Fiction of the Victorian Period, 1830–1890* (1985), *Death and the Future Life in Victorian Literature and Theology* (1990; winner of the Conference on Christianity and Literature Award, USA, 1991–2); and its paperback abridgement *Heaven, Hell and the Victorians* (1994). In addition he has edited and contributed to *The Lamp of Memory: Ruskin, Tradition and Architecture* (1992) and *Ruskin and Environment: The Storm Cloud of the Nineteenth Century* (1995), among other volumes and journals.

CAMBRIDGE STUDIES IN NINETEENTH
CENTURY LITERATURE AND CULTURE 24

RUSKIN'S GOD

Nineteenth-century British literature and culture have been rich fields for inter-disciplinary studies. Since the turn of the twentieth century, scholars and critics have tracked the intersections and tensions between Victorian literature and the visual arts, politics, social organization, economic life, technical innovations, scientific thought – in short, culture in its broadest sense. In recent years, theo-retical challenges and historiographical shifts have unsettled the assumptions of previous scholarly syntheses and called into question the terms of older debates. Whereas the tendency in much past literary critical interpretation was to use the metaphor of culture as 'background', feminist, Foucauldian, and other analyses have employed more dynamic models that raise questions of power and of circulation. Such developments have reanimated the field.

This series aims to accommodate and promote the most interesting work being undertaken on the frontiers of the field of nineteenth-century literary studies: work which intersects fruitfully with other fields of study such as history, or literary theory, or the history of science. Comparative as well as interdisci-plinary approaches are welcomed.

A complete list of titles published will be found at the end of the book.

RUSKIN'S GOD

MICHAEL WHEELER

CAMBRIDGE
UNIVERSITY PRESS

PUBLISHED BY THE PRESS SYNDICATE OF THE UNIVERSITY OF CAMBRIDGE
The Pitt Building, Trumpington Street, Cambridge CB2 1RP, United Kingdom

CAMBRIDGE UNIVERSITY PRESS
The Edinburgh Building, Cambridge CB2 2RU, UK http://www.cup.cam.ac.uk
40 West 20th Street, New York, NY 10011-4211, USA http://www.cup.org
10 Stamford Road, Oakleigh, Melbourne 3166, Australia

© Michael Wheeler 1999

First published 1999

Printed in the United Kingdom at the University Press, Cambridge

Typeset in Monotype Baskerville 11/12½ [SE]

A catalogue record for this book is available from the British Library

Library of Congress cataloguing in publication data
Wheeler, Michael, 1947–
Ruskin's god / Michael Wheeler
p.   cm. – (Cambridge studies in nineteenth-century literature
and culture: 24)
Includes index.
ISBN 0 521 57414 5 (hardback)
1. Ruskin, John, 1819–1900 – Religion.   2. Christianity and
literature – History – 19th century.   3. Religion and literature –
History – 19th century.   4. Christianity and art – History – 19th
century.   5. Art and religion – History – 19th century.   6. God in
literature.   7. God – Art.   I. Title.   II. Series.
PR5267.R4W47   1999
828'.809 – dc21   99-11996   CIP

ISBN 0 521 57414 5 hardback

To Linda Murray
and in memory of
Peter Murray (1920–1992)

And Solomon stood before the altar of the Lord in the presence of all the congregation of Israel, and spread forth his hands toward heaven:

And he said, Lord God of Israel, there is no God like thee, in heaven above, or on earth beneath, who keepest covenant and mercy with thy servants that walk before thee with all their heart.

I Kings 8.22–3

I do not write my foolish jesting letters without a very solemn sense of the approach to you of one of those periods of life which are intended to make us look with closer trust to Him in whom we live, and move, and have our Being.

Letter from John Ruskin to Joan Severn, Brantwood,
28 September 1873

I trust in the Living God, Father Almighty, Maker of heaven and earth, and of all things and creatures visible and invisible.

I trust in the kindness of His law, and the goodness of His work.

And I will strive to love Him, and keep His law, and see His work, while I live.

John Ruskin, Article I from St George's Creed, 1875

Contents

Plates

Preface

Ruskin is so multi-faceted and polymathic that later generations have been able to appropriate those elements of him that are to their taste and ignore the rest. Ruskin's religion, which had an enormous impact upon his life and work, has often been either ignored or misunderstood in the twentieth century. Although several contemporaries wrote substantial essays on Ruskin's religious teaching, the editors of the great Library Edition of *The Works of John Ruskin* (1903–12) – E. T. Cook and Alexander Wedderburn – seem to have had no real interest in or sympathy for Ruskin's religious life, and seized every opportunity to quote Ruskin's own later commentary, written in old age, on his early Evangelicalism. Yet here was one of several great Victorians, including George Eliot and Gladstone, Newman and Manning, whose intellectual lives were grounded in the Evangelicalism of their youth which they then left behind them. As in other areas of his personal life, Ruskin's self-styled 'un-conversion' from Evangelicalism occurred later in life than usual, and although there are similarities between his position in his troubled middle years and George Eliot's agnosticism, he later returned to a simple if somewhat unorthodox Christian faith. Ruskin certainly wrestled with what his generation called 'difficulties' throughout his adult life, but in 1877 and again in 1887 he had to make it clear that he had not converted to Roman Catholicism, so strong were the rumours circulating in England. On the first occasion he stated that he was a 'Catholic' of 'those Catholics, to whom the Catholic Epistle of St. James is addressed – "the Twelve Tribes which are scattered abroad" – the literally or spiritually wandering Israel of all the Earth'.

Numerous critical books on Ruskin have, however, perpetuated the myth of Ruskin's catastrophic and irrecoverable 'loss of faith', a myth which he himself invented in a sense in his descriptions of the 'Queen of Sheba crash' in Turin in 1858. Such a crisis of faith in a Victorian intellectual is generally taken to typify the 'secularization of the

European mind'. More often than not, however, this conclusion also reflects the agnostic liberalism of the twentieth-century mind, and several critics, such as R. H. Wilenski in the 1930s and Francis G. Townsend in the early 1950s, have written off Ruskin's Evangelical upbringing as unrelievedly damaging.

There have been some notable exceptions. Van Akin Burd offers the best overview of Ruskin's religious life in the introductions to *The Winnington Letters* (1969) and *Christmas Story* (1990). George Landow, in *The Aesthetic and Critical Theories of John Ruskin* (1971), explains the relevance of Evangelical Anglican typology for Ruskin, and goes on to show how Ruskin moved away from it to his own peculiar kind of allegory. (Landow broadens his canvas in *Victorian Types, Victorian Shadows* (1980).) David Downes, in *Ruskin's Landscape of Beatitude* (1980), argues that Ruskin's standpoint was more consistently and durably Christian than is suggested by his own account in *Præterita*, and finds a continuity in Ruskin's perception of the divine within the transitory. Tim Hilton, Ruskin's biographer (1985 and forthcoming), alerts us to the significance of the Ruskin family's church- and chapel-going in the South London of the 1830s and 1840s, while Stephen Finley, in *Nature's Covenant* (1992), places Ruskin's early work in a Reformed tradition and documents his religious reading and reflection. In *The Poison Sky: Myth and Apocalypse in Ruskin* (1982), Raymond E. Fitch relates Ruskin's mythography to his reading of signs of a great cosmic battle between life-giving and death-dealing forces. More subtly, Dinah Birch's study on *Ruskin's Myths* (1988) demonstrates that, for Ruskin, myth was primarily a religious phenomenon, with an unchanging spiritual message, founded on an ancient understanding of the natural world: 'pagan' religion could thus be valued without devaluing Christianity. The late Peter Fuller's *Theoria: Art, and the Absence of Grace* (1988) places religion at the centre of a highly personal, often brilliant and sometimes wayward reading of Ruskin and modern art. Philip Davis relates what Arnold would call Ruskin's Hebraic puritanism to his 'Romantic risk of the personal' (*Literature & Theology*, 6, 4 (December 1992)). Very little indeed has been said about what I consider to be a central aspect both of Ruskin's religious life and of his writings, namely his spiritual and imaginative response to Old Testament wisdom literature, and particularly the teaching and symbolism associated with Solomon and the temple. The theologian John Drury, however, offers some of the best insights into the nature of Ruskin's spirituality in his essay 'Ruskin's Way: *Tout a Fait Comme un Oiseau*', in the forthcoming *Festschrift* for John Burrow.

Ruskin's God addresses for the first time the whole question of Ruskin and the Christian religion, and its impact upon his work, the richness and variety of which can be more fully appreciated today by recovering an understanding of the religious beliefs and ideas on which much of that work is based. For while Ruskin's life and work are in many ways unique, his internalization of debates which raged in the mid-nineteenth century – on biblical criticism, Church authority, sacred art, church architecture and Darwin – also makes him the quintessential Victorian. His beliefs underwent many changes, susceptible as they were to his own sharpened critical awareness. What never left him, however, and what proved to be least susceptible to the application of new critical tools by the scientists and biblical scholars of the day, was belief in divine wisdom and a God of peace.

Early on, in *Modern Painters*, *The Seven Lamps of Architecture* and *The Stones of Venice*, belief in the wisdom of God the Father informs Ruskin's Evangelical natural theology and his celebration of natural beauty and Turner's landscape painting, while the wisdom of God the Son lies at the heart of his Christology and his interpretation of paintings such as Tintoretto's *Crucifixion* and Holman Hunt's *The Light of the World*, and his Protestant reading of St Mark's, Venice. Whereas the 'Author of *Modern Painters*' sought to teach his readers how to see architecture, paintings and landscapes, the 'Victorian Solomon' who wrote on political economy and created the Guild of St George wished to teach them how to live. The result is a Victorian version of wisdom literature. Ruskin's most familiar maxim – 'There is no wealth but life' (*Unto this Last*) – was inspired by Solomon's Proverbs. In his attacks upon modern science in *The Queen of the Air* and *The Eagle's Nest* Ruskin traces the threads that connect wisdom in the Old Testament and the Holy Spirit in the New Testament with the cults of Athena and Neith – the Greek and Egyptian goddesses of wisdom. In his critique of modernity in *Fors Clavigera* he frequently invokes the wisdom tradition, exposing the ephemeral by juxtaposing it with the eternal. The fascinating and ambiguous figure of Solomon – the subject of Veronese's painting which Ruskin copied in Turin in 1858 – becomes increasingly important in the late work, where Ruskin attempts to rewrite his earlier cultural histories of Venice (*St. Mark's Rest*) and of France (*The Bible of Amiens*), and challenges late Victorian society to respond to his version of apocalyptic wisdom (*The Storm Cloud of the Nineteenth Century*). Ruskin's application of his foundational beliefs is prophetic, and his whole project seems even more relevant today than it did in the industrial age.

In exploring such a wide field for so long I have incurred many debts. The dedicatees have been much-loved mentors and friends, who long ago helped a student of literature to think about art and architecture (even though my cousin Peter held Ruskin in low esteem!). My wife Viv has been unfailingly generous in her support and encouragement, as ever. Professor David Carroll, my long-time friend and collaborator on many projects, has continued to listen with the acutest of ears. Dr Dinah Birch, Dr James S. Dearden, Professor Robert Hewison and Dr Chris Walsh were all kind enough to read the book in its final draft and to make helpful suggestions. Jim Dearden initiated me into the mysteries of Bembridge and the arcana of Ruskin scholarship, and, with his wife Jill, was a welcoming host. Dr Andrew Brown of Cambridge University Press encouraged me to write the book, and his colleagues Josie Dixon and Linda Bree have been splendid editors. The British Academy Humanities Research Board awarded me a grant under their Research Leave Scheme, to which Lancaster University added research leave in 1997–98. I have enjoyed and benefited from conversations with Professor Michael Alexander, the Very Revd John Drury, Professor Stephen Finley, Professor Ray Haslam, Howard Hull, Professor George Landow and Dr Andrew Tate, as well as a galaxy of Ruskin scholars too numerous to mention. Ruth Hutchison, Secretary to the Ruskin Programme, has been a strength and stay to its Director. Members of the Ruskin Programme's weekly research seminar, without whom the whole project at Lancaster would not have been possible, have explored Ruskin with me, and Robert Hewison has been an inspiring colleague. Stephen Wildman has achieved wonders in setting up the Ruskin Library at Lancaster, and Rebecca Finnerty, Deputy Curator, has been unstinting in her support in the Reading Room there. Tony Cann has always been generosity and kindliness personified.

I am also grateful to the following institutions in which I have worked: Lancaster University Library, and its Librarian Jacqueline Whiteside; Abbot Hall Art Gallery, Kendal; Record Office, Kendal; Ruskin Museum, Coniston; Brantwood, Coniston; Guild of St George Ruskin Gallery, Sheffield; Armitt Library, Ambleside; British Library, London; Bodleian Library, Oxford; Ashmolean Museum Library, Oxford; National Library of Scotland, Edinburgh; Manchester University John Rylands Library; St Deiniol's Library, Hawarden, and its Librarian, Patricia Williams; Pierpont Morgan Library, New York, and its Curator of Manuscripts, Robert Parks; New York Public Library; Houghton Library and Fogg Art Museum, Harvard; Beinecke Library and Mellon

Center for British Art, Yale; Huntington Library, San Marino; Humanities Research Center, Austin; Rosenbach Museum & Library, Philadelphia; University of California at Los Angeles Library; Notre Dame University Library; Stanford University Library; Cornell University Library.

Work in progress towards this book is reflected in the following publications: 'Ruskin Among the Ruins: Tradition and the Temple', in *The Lamp of Memory: Ruskin, Tradition and Architecture*, ed. Michael Wheeler and Nigel Whiteley (Manchester University Press, 1992); 'Environment and Apocalypse', in *Ruskin and Environment: The Storm-Cloud of the Nineteenth Century*, ed. Michael Wheeler (Manchester University Press, 1995); *Keble, Ruskin, and The Light of the World: Lecture delivered in Keble College Chapel on Sunday 28 January 1996* (Oxford: Keble College, 1996); '"Inscribed upon its visionary sides": on Reading Mountains', in *Sublime Inspiration: The Art of Mountains from Turner to Hillary* (Kendal: Abbot Hall Art Gallery, 1997); 'Gladstone and Ruskin', in *Gladstone*, ed. Peter J. Jagger (London and Rio Grande: Hambledon, 1998); 'Ruskin's Christian Theory of Art', in *English Literature and Theology*, ed. Liam Gearon (London: Cassell, 1999).

I am grateful to owners for permission to reproduce the plates (their names are given in the list of illustrations); to the Revd M. L. Malleson for permission to quote a letter from the Revd F. A. Malleson; and to The Ruskin Literary Trustees, The Guild of St George, and also those mentioned in the list of short references given below, for permission to quote from unpublished Ruskin manuscripts.

MDW Lancaster, October 1998

Abbreviations

References to Ruskin's published works are taken from *The Works of John Ruskin*, Library Edition, edited by E. T. Cook and Alexander Wedderburn, 39 vols. (London: Allen; New York: Longmans, Green, 1903–12), unless otherwise stated, and are indicated by volume and page numbers in the text, thus: 12.123. (It should be noted that they and Ruskin's earlier editors habitually capitalized pronouns and possessives associated with the Trinity, even when Ruskin did not in the manuscripts.) Another short form of reference in the main text and footnotes is *D*, 123, signifying *The Diaries of John Ruskin*, ed. Joan Evans and John Howard Whitehouse, 3 vols. (Oxford: Clarendon, 1956–9), p. 123. (The numbering runs straight through the three volumes.) This edition is unreliable and incomplete, and where possible and relevant I have quoted from the originals, most of which are at Lancaster. I have retained the original punctuation in extracted quotations. Short forms of reference to sources of manuscripts are as follows:

Ashmolean	Ashmolean Museum, Oxford
Berg	Berg Collection, New York Public Library
Brantwood	Brantwood Trust
HRC	Harry Ransom Humanities Research Center, University of Texas at Austin
Lancaster	Ruskin Foundation (Ruskin Library, Lancaster University)
Morgan	Pierpont Morgan Library, New York
Rosenbach	Rosenbach Museum & Library, Philadelphia
Rylands	John Rylands University Library of Manchester
Yale	Yale Center for British Art, New Haven

Ruskin's deletions in manuscripts are indicated as <deletions> and superscript as ^superscript^.

Introduction

CHAPTER I

'To enlighten a People by your Wisdom': the divine commission

> You are blessed with a fine Capacity & even Genius & you owe it as
> a Duty to the author of your Being & the giver of your Talents to
> cultivate your powers & to use them in his Service & for the benefit
> of your fellow Creatures.
> You may be doomed to enlighten a People by your Wisdom & to
> adorn an age by your Learning. It would be sinful in you to let
> the powers of your mind lie dormant through idleness or want of
> perseverance when they may at their maturity aid the cause of
> Truth & of Religion & enable you to become in many ways a
> Benefactor to the Human Race. I am forced to smile when I figure
> to myself the very little Gentleman to whom I am addressing such
> Language . . .
> Letter from John James Ruskin to John Ruskin, 6 November 1829[1]

I

These are extraordinary words for a father to write to his ten-year-old
son; but then neither father nor son was ordinary. As was often the case
in his middle years, John James Ruskin (1785–1864) was engaged in an
extensive business trip away from home in November 1829, visiting his
customers in the wine trade, when he wrote to inform young John that
there were signs in his latest Latin exercise of a special providence and
a divine commission. The smile that he records when thinking of the
'very little Gentleman', living at home with his mother in Herne Hill,
suggests embarrassed parental pride, ambition and affection in this
latter-day David, whose infant Solomon might one day build the temple
which he himself can never raise, being tied to the business.[2]

---

[1] *The Ruskin Family Letters: The Correspondence of John James Ruskin, his Wife, and their Son, John,
1801–1843*, ed. Van Akin Burd, 2 vols. (Ithaca and London: Cornell University Press, 1973), I,
209–10.

[2] Solomon's 'father, knowing that he was to build the temple, made great preparations for it, and
trained him up with great care': Thomas Brown, *Brown's Edition of the Proverbs of Solomon; or,
Wisdom Revived . . . to which are added, Memoirs of David and Solomon; and a Vocabulary* . . . (Edinburgh:
Brown, 1835), p. 71.

3

This study will show the extent to which John James's words were prophetic in terms of Ruskin's writings, from *Modern Painters* (his *magnum
opus*, written partly for his father, to 'aid the cause of Truth & of
Religion'), through the middle period in which the call to 'enlighten a
People' by his wisdom manifests itself in a modern form of wisdom literature, to the late work which reflects both Ruskin's broader religious
sympathies and his devout wish to be a 'Benefactor to the Human Race'.
In this introductory chapter the focus is upon the religious context which
made John James's letter possible, and which shaped his son's early religious life and later reaction against it – the dynamic Evangelical revival
which had such a profound effect on a whole generation of early
Victorians. Many of the works quoted here as examples of Evangelical
doctrine and moral teaching were published in 1829, and are contrasted
with Ruskin's later, much altered views, summarized at the end of this
chapter and examined in later chapters, where it is argued that a trust in
divine wisdom and the God of peace, nurtured by his imaginative
engagement with Solomon and the temple in Jerusalem, and with Old
Testament wisdom literature, not only remains through all the vicissi-
tudes of Ruskin's tormented private life and prophetic public role, but
also underpins the vast corpus of his published work.

The recipient of the letter was born on 8 February 1819 at 54 Hunter
Street, Brunswick Square, London, the same year as Princess Victoria,
Charles Kingsley, George Eliot, and Arthur Hugh Clough. Twelve days
later he was baptized at Hunter Street by the Revd James Boyd,
Presbyterian Minister of the Caledonian Chapel, Hatton Garden,
although it was not until 8 December 1837 that his birth was finally
'Entered, Filed, and Registered, according to the custom in use among
Protestant Dissenters', in a style that is redolent both of the family's
Dissenting tradition and of the ledgers at John James's offices in Billiter
Street in the City.[3] The Ruskins attended the Episcopalian Chapel in
Long Acre and sat under the Revd William Howels, a Welshman of
'extraordinary inability & not a little eccentricity' according to a source
described by Ruskin's biographer as typical of much that was said of him
at the time.[4] Their choice seems more understandable, however, when

---

[3] The birth certificate has in recent years been on deposit from the Ruskin Museum Coniston at
   Kendal Record Office, Cumbria: MS WDSo 106/1. As no register was kept at the Caledonian
   Chapel in Boyd's day, he sent John James this certificate on request, with a covering letter of
   explanation. It is cited in Helen Viljoen, *Ruskin's Scottish Heritage: A Prelude* (Urbana: University of
   Illinois Press, 1956), p. 216, n.10.
[4] Tim Hilton, *John Ruskin: The Early Years, 1819–1859* (New Haven and London: Yale University
   Press, 1985), p. 20.

viewed in the light of the later description by Ruskin's friend Henry Edward Manning, Cardinal Archbishop of Westminster, of this 'cracked-voiced Welshman in Longacre' as 'a wonderful and original thinker' who 'greatly arrested' him as an earnest young Anglican.[5] For the infant Ruskin, Howels provided splendid material for his party-piece – a sermon in imitation of the minister, preached 'over the red sofa cushions' at home, to the admiration of his mother's 'dearest friends', being some eleven words long and beginning with the lisped admonition, 'People, be good' (35.26).

The tutor under whom Ruskin wrote the Latin exercise that inspired the letter comes into the picture when the family moves to 28 Herne Hill, Camberwell, to the south of London, in March 1823, and worships at Beresford Chapel (further from their house than the local parish church),[6] under the Revd Dr Edward Andrews, a leading Evangelical Congregationalist who was famous for his 'ornate sermons, his energy, and his ambition', and was described as 'a sort of Pope' by his fellow Congregationalists.[7] The young Ruskin also had lessons in Classics and Hebrew three times a week from Andrews, one of the best Greek scholars of his day, and seems greatly to have admired his minister and tutor, commenting to his father on 'What a nice man doctor Andrews is', 'What nice sermons he preaches', and 'What a nice face he has' in a letter of May 1829[8] – the year in which he first went into print with his 'Lines Written at the Lakes in Cumberland: *Derwentwater*' in Andrews's short-lived magazine entitled *The Spiritual Times*.[9]

The letter would also have been read, and no doubt reread, by Margaret Ruskin (1781–1871), famed for her devoted, but also obsessive vigilance during Ruskin's childhood and early manhood, and a most powerful influence upon him well into his middle years. Whereas John

[5] Edmund Sheridan Purcell, *Life of Cardinal Manning, Archbishop of Westminster*, 2 vols. (London: Macmillan, 1896), i, 68. Manning misremembers Howels's name as 'Howell', as Ruskin does in *Præterita*. The Revd Charles Bowdler described Howels's sermons as 'didactic, sententious, aphoristic, familiarly pastoral, not drily logical': William Howels, *Sermons, &c. &c.*, 2 vols. (London: Hatchard, 1834, 1833), i, cxxviii. Howels suffered from what he himself described as 'a very violent dyspepsy', a 'heavy cross' which he bore for more than twenty years: *The Evangelical Magazine and Missionary Chronicle*, ns 9 (1831), 11.
[6] See James S. Dearden, *John Ruskin's Camberwell* (St Albans: Guild of St George/Brentham, 1990), p. 27. [7] Hilton, *John Ruskin*, p. 20.
[8] Burd, *Ruskin Family Letters*, i, 200. Hanson argues that Ruskin's 'sudden engagement with religious topics' in his poetry and prose 'can now be exactly correlated with the arrival in early 1829 of his new tutor, the Reverend Edward Andrews': David C. Hanson, 'The Psychology of Fragmentation: A Bibliographic and Psychoanalytic Reconsideration of the Ruskin Juvenilia', *Text*, 10 (1997), 237–58 (p. 249).
[9] *The Spiritual Times: A Monthly Magazine*, i, 4 (August 1829), 150.

James, whose own mother had been a daughter of the manse,[10] was a moderate man in religious matters and later warned his son against excessive zeal, Margaret Ruskin was deeply invested in Calvinist Evangelicalism. She was baptized into the Church of England as a child and was taught 'evangelical principles' in a day-school in Croydon (35.18). Her Scottish Presbyterian inheritance from her Aunt Catherine (John James's mother), with whom she lived in Edinburgh as a young woman, gave a firmer shape to her adult religious life, and helps to explain her family's attendance at Beresford Chapel on a Sunday.[11] (It was not until she reached middle age, and both the family's fortunes and her own clerical ambitions for her son had risen, that she again became a practising member of the Established Church.) Having dedicated her boy to God at his birth, she later insisted that he read aloud two or three chapters from the Bible each day, and also learnt several verses daily – a habit that stayed with him into adult life, by which time he knew the Bible better than the bishops.[12] In *Præterita* (1885–9), the autobiography written at the end of his career, he was to record his gratitude to his mother for the lessons, continued until he was fourteen, which had made every word of the 'Scriptures' familiar to his ear 'in habitual music, – yet in that familiarity reverenced, as transcending all thought, and ordaining all conduct' (35.40, 189). He learned the whole of 1 Kings 8 and Deuteronomy 32 by heart, for example, and, as he noted in *Præterita*, 'the lower corners of the pages' of his oldest Bible in use were 'worn somewhat thin and dark' at these chapters as a result, the learning of Solomon's prayer at the dedication of the temple – a passage also loved by other Evangelicals[13] – and the last song of Moses having cost him 'much pains' (35.42). (Significantly, he also learned four chapters from Proverbs and Psalm 32 – part of the wisdom tradition of the Old Testament.[14]) It would also have been at his mother's instigation that

[10] On 30 October 1807, Catherine Tweddale Ruskin had written to her son in terms not dissimilar from John James's own to Ruskin twenty-two years later: 'thy God will give thee Wisdom, and lead thee on with the spirit of truth to Eternal Joy and happiness' (Burd, *Ruskin Family Letters*, 1, 10). [11] See Viljoen, *Ruskin's Scottish Heritage*, p. 85.

[12] He was still learning passages from the Bible by heart at the age of thirty-four (12.lxxviii).

[13] John Cumming, the popular preacher, wrote, 'I do not know a more sublime, spiritual, and comprehensive litany in any language than that which was offered at the dedication of the temple of Solomon': *Expository Readings on the Book of Kings* (London: Hall, Virtue, [1859]), p. 57.

[14] The subjects of the chapters which Ruskin claims in *Præterita* to have learnt by heart and to have 'established [his] soul in life' are as follows: Exodus 15 and 20 (Moses' song after crossing the Red Sea; the ten commandments); 2 Samuel 1.17–end (David's lament over Saul and Jonathan); 1 Kings 8 (Solomon's prayer at the dedication of the temple); Psalms 23 ('The Lord is my shepherd'), 32 ('Blessed is he whose trangression is forgiven'), 90 ('Lord, thou has been our dwelling place'), 91 ('He that dwelleth in the secret place'), 103 ('Bless the Lord, O my soul'), 112 ('Praise

Ruskin, in his own words in *Præterita* (35.490), 'received' his religion from Bunyan and from Isaac Ambrose, the Puritan divine whose standard work was entitled *Looking unto Jesus* (1658).[15]

Yet it would be a mistake to think of Mrs Ruskin as a Mrs Clennam, Dickens's life-denying sabbatarian Calvinist in *Little Dorrit*. Although her favourite chapters of the Bible are largely from the Old Testament, many are expressions of thanksgiving and blessing, and the only chapter which dwells upon the wrath of God – Deuteronomy 32 – was omitted from Ruskin's list of what he regarded as his most significant inheritance from her.[16] Her reference to 'receiving' *The Evangelical Magazine and Missionary Chronicle* in 1823,[17] offers some clue to her religious position during the Herne Hill years, when she was training up her child in the way he should go (Proverbs 22.6).[18] Calvinist doctrine is vigorously defended in the magazine,[19] and Byron's *Letters and Journals* are said to 'present a melancholy picture of the human mind in its unregenerate state'.[20] Yet Byron was read and admired in the Ruskin household, and it appears that it was not only towards the end of her life that Margaret Ruskin, in a manner inherited by her son, could

ye the Lord'), 119 ('Blessed are the undefiled'), 139 ('O Lord, thou hast searched me'); Proverbs 2, 3, 8, 12 (the benefits of obedience and wisdom); Isaiah 58 (the benefaction of true godliness); Matthew 5, 6, 7 (the Sermon on the Mount); Acts 26 (Paul tells the story of his conversion to Agrippa); 1 Corinthians 13, 15 (on 'charity' and on the resurrection of the dead); James 4 (on sanctification and judgment); Revelation 5, 6 (the book sealed with seven seals, the four horses, the opening of the sixth seal). Ruskin also had the versified Scottish paraphrases of the Bible to learn (35.41).

[15] See p. 101 below. Ruskin also records that in boyhood he read Walter Scott's novels and the *Iliad* (in Pope's translation) on weekdays, and *Robinson Crusoe* and the *Pilgrim's Progress* on Sundays (35.13). When Mary Richardson joined the family in 1828, the diet on Sunday evenings included the sermons of Hugh Blair, Bunyan's *Pilgrim's Progress* and *Holy War*, Quarles's *Emblems*, Foxe's *Book of Martyrs*, Mrs Sherwood's *Lady of the Manor* and *Henry Milner*, the *Youth's Magazine*, Mrs Hofland's *Alfred Campbell the Young Pilgrim* and the Revd W. Bingley's *Animal Biography* (35.72–3).

[16] See Viljoen, *Ruskin's Scottish Heritage*, p. 162. On Margaret Ruskin's more earthy and 'Smollettesque' side, see Jeffrey L. Spear, *Dreams of an English Eden: Ruskin and his Tradition in Social Criticism* (New York: Columbia University Press, 1984), p. 16.

[17] Burd, *Ruskin Family Letters*, I, 121. We also know that she took the *Christian Treasury* in the mid-1850s (see p. 100 below).

[18] Another favourite Evangelical text: see, for example, Thomas Dale, *Heavenly Wisdom the only Sound Principle of Education: A Sermon, preached at Christ-Church, Newgate Street, before the Right Hon. the Lord Mayor, and the Governors of the Royal Hospitals, &c., &c., &c. . . . on St. Matthew's Day, Sept. 21, 1837* (London: Richardson, 1837), p. 13. The Book of Proverbs emphasizes the importance of sons receiving 'correction' from fathers (3.12), and refers not only to the father's instruction but also to that of the mother (1.8): see John Day, 'Foreign Semitic Influence on the Wisdom of Israel and Its Appropriation in the Book of Proverbs', in *Wisdom in Ancient Israel: Essays in Honour of J. A. Emerton*, ed. John Day, Robert P. Gordon and H. G. M. Williamson (Cambridge University Press, 1995), pp. 55–70 (p. 66).

[19] See, for example, *The Evangelical Magazine and Missionary Chronicle*, NS 2 (1824), 518, 528.

[20] *The Evangelical Magazine and Missionary Chronicle*, NS 9 (May 1831), 190–1.

soften her hard line on a topic in the face of particular practical cases.[21]

John James's letter to his son was written towards the end of a momentous year for Evangelical Protestants, who had been profoundly disturbed by the Catholic Emancipation legislation brought in by Wellington's Tory government. Indeed the more radical among them had read it as an ominous 'Sign of the Times', in the eschatological sense of heralding the end of the established world order.[22] On 14 February Margaret Ruskin had written hesitantly to her husband in Chester:

I cannot rely on my own judgment for I may be prejudiced but it seems to me that all that is urged by the R Catholics and their favourers is weak equivocal underhand equally devoid of sincerity or honesty & integrity in short they appear to me not to care what they do or say to gain their end I believe they would take Satan himself into their cabals to further their purposes to bring every thing under their subjection.[23]

Significantly, however, the Ruskins chose not to worship at the Episcopalian Chapel, Hatton Garden, during the ministry of the far from hesitant Edward Irving,[24] the most charismatic preacher (in every sense) in London, who in 1829 wrote an impassioned plea against bringing in the legislation entitled *The Signs of the Times*, in which he applied the language of the Book of Revelation, or Apocalypse, to Roman Catholicism: 'The "dragon" describes the spirit of the Roman empire before Christianity was established in it, while it sought to devour the woman, which is the Church, and her man child, which is the faithful progeny of the church.'[25] Irving and *The Morning Watch* frequently denounced the so-called 'Clapham Sect' for their indifference to wage-slavery at home, but it seems likely that, for all Margaret's more extreme

---

[21] In March 1871, following the death of Ruskin's old nurse, Ann Strachan, Margaret Ruskin commented: 'one must hope there are intermediate kinds of places where people get better'. Malcolm Hardman writes, 'Like his mother, Ruskin tended towards the absolute, but also possessed a willingness to demolish it in the face of experience': *Ruskin and Bradford: An Experiment in Victorian Cultural History* (Manchester and Dover, NH: Manchester University Press, 1986), p. 31. Margaret's choice of a Congregational chapel also reflects a moderate rather than an extreme Calvinism; many used an abridged version of the Anglican liturgy: see C. Stephen Finley, *Nature's Covenant: Figures of Landscape in Ruskin* (University Park, PA: Pennsylvania State University Press, 1992), p. 55.

[22] Thomas Carlyle adopts rather than invents the year's catch-phrase (from Matthew 16.3) in the title of his well-known essay, 'Signs of the Times', published in the *Edinburgh Review* in 1829.

[23] Burd, ed., *Ruskin Family Letters*, I, 177. [24] Hilton, *John Ruskin*, p. 20.

[25] Edward Irving, *The Signs of the Times* (London: Panton, 1829), p. 19; compare his *Babylon and Infidelity Foredoomed of God: A Discourse on the Prophecies of Daniel and the Apocalypse which relate to these Latter Times, and until the Second Advent*, 2nd edn (Glasgow: Collins, 1828), pp. 81–2. The reviewer of the first edition of *Babylon and Infidelity* (1826) in *The Evangelical Magazine and Missionary Chronicle* was pained to 'pronounce a dissentient opinion': NS 4 (1826), 292–4 (p. 292).

views, the Ruskins would not have associated themselves with the pre-millenialist, pentecostal, adventist and revivalist Irvingites, who believed in God's direct intervention in the world and therefore supported direct human intervention in social affairs.[26]

Dr Andrews himself pronounced on the crisis in the opening words of the first number of his monthly magazine, *The Spiritual Times*, in May 1829:

> The last month or two have been distinguished by changes and agitations unparalleled in the history of this or any other country . . . we have seen at home, and within a few weeks, a total and unexpected reversion of certain arrangements and habits, in reference to a distinction which has long been deemed sacred between two Churches, essentially hostile to and destructive of each other . . .
> May it please Almighty God to make this awful visitation a means of stirring up our church clergy to greater zeal.[27]

What the young Ruskin described as Dr Andrews's 'nice face' had appeared as the frontispiece to the *Evangelical Magazine* for June 1828 (plate 1).[28] He thus joined the magazine's hall of fame at a time when the more popular Evangelical preachers of the day were treated as celebrities. Engravers made preachers look as appealing as possible to readers, especially, one suspects, lady readers: their coats and stocks are presented as generously cut, and their hair luxuriously coiffured.[29] Popular preachers attracted large congregations when they gave charity sermons, and raised substantial sums. (W. E. Gladstone and John James Ruskin were to be among the subscribers when the Revd Thomas Dale and the Revd Henry Melvill – both of whom ministered to the Ruskins – preached on 'Spiritual Destitution of the Parish of Bethnal-Green' on 29 December 1839, in Melvill's case before the Lord Mayor and Sheriffs.) The omnibus conductors used to call out 'Melvill' on their way to Camberwell on Sundays (1.490n), and the *Evangelical Magazine* reported that the crush in the parish church of Kirkcaldy on 17 June 1828, when it was falsely rumoured that Irving was to preach, was so great that twenty-six members of the congregation were killed following the

---

[26] See Boyd Hilton, *The Age of Atonement: The Influence of Evangelicalism on Social and Economic Thought, 1795–1865* (Oxford: Clarendon, 1988), pp. 10, 15–16, and Christopher Tolley, *Domestic Biography: The Legacy of Evangelicalism in Four Nineteenth-Century Families*, Oxford Historical Monographs (Oxford: Clarendon, 1997), p. 58, *et passim*. John James Ruskin was to disapprove of his son's writing on political economy in the early 1860s, thus causing a rift between them.

[27] *The Spiritual Times: A Monthly Magazine*, no.1 (May 1829), 2.

[28] Andrews's *Sermons Delivered at Beresford Chapel, Walworth* (1827) also includes a portrait.

[29] In his diary for 31 March 1840 Ruskin records Dr Shuttleworth's account of 'Sydney Smith's intense dislike of fashionable preachers', those 'dandy saints' (*D*, 76).

Plate 1. 'Revd. Dr. Andrews, Walworth', *The Evangelical Magazine and Missionary Chronicle*, NS 6 (June 1828), frontispiece

collapse of the gallery.[30] The magazine responded angrily to the methods employed by *The Preacher*, which, unlike *The British Preacher* (published 'under the sanction of the Ministers whose Discourses appear in its pages'), sent its reporters 'from chapel to chapel, to pirate the sermons of ministers, without their consent'.[31] It was in the context of lively activity and fervent belief among Evangelicals, when sermons were news and preachers were pin-ups, that John James wrote to his son in November 1829. The young Ruskin was already copying Andrews's sermons for his father, with the help of his cousin Mary Richardson, who now lived with the family, and was soon to write sermons of his own.[32]

It was probably between September 1832 and some time in 1834 that Ruskin carefully inscribed eighteen sermons on the Pentateuch in five small manuscript booklets, hand-made, like the Brontës' juvenilia, and with pages neatly arranged so as to look as much like printed books as possible. The sermons' systematic commentary on the Pentateuch reveals their author's early interest in religious themes that were to be taken up in the mature published writings, and lays special emphasis upon prayer, obedience to the Law (for Ruskin the key to religion (28.156)), church attendance, observance of the Sabbath and benevolence. While exceptional in their precocity, the sermons follow a conventional Evangelical plan of interpreting the Bible as revealing 'the process of conversion: conviction of sin, justification by faith, and sanctification of the justified sinner'.[33] One passage should be cited here, however, as it touches upon beliefs which were later to be central to Ruskin's religious life. The more we examine and meditate upon the Bible, he argues, 'the

---

[30] *The Evangelical Magazine and Missionary Chronicle*, NS 6 (June 1828), 312. Later in the century, in 1856, a malicious false alarm of fire caused panic at the Surrey Gardens Music Hall, where Spurgeon was preaching to a congregation of 12,000, causing seven fatalities: see C. H. Spurgeon, *Autobiography*, vol. 1: *The Early Years, 1834–1859*, rev. edn, originally compiled by Susannah Spurgeon and Joseph Harrald (Edinburgh and Carlisle, PA: Banner of Truth, 1962), p. 435. When Spurgeon toured the country preaching in 1858, a large temporary structure built to accommodate an audience of 8,000 in Halifax collapsed, but not, providentially it was thought, during the service: see William Walters, *Life and Ministry of the Rev. C. H. Spurgeon* (London and Newcastle-on-Tyne: Scott, [1882]), p. 82.

[31] *The Evangelical Magazine and Missionary Chronicle*, NS 6 (June 1828), 245–6.

[32] The abstracts that Ruskin and Mary Richardson compiled of sermons heard at Beresford Chapel (35.72) were little more than fragmentary notes (Beinecke MS 11), and are not to be confused with Ruskin's 'Sermons on the Pentateuch': see Van Akin Burd, 'Ruskin's Testament of His Boyhood Faith: *Sermons on the Pentateuch*', in *New Approaches to Ruskin: Thirteen Essays*, ed. Robert Hewison (London: Routledge, 1981), pp. 1–16 (p. 2), where Helen Viljoen's unpublished notes on the sermons are summarized.

[33] David C. Hanson, '"Out of the Same Mouth Proceedeth Blessing and Cursing": Ruskin as the "Strange Disciple"', *Modern Philology*, 90, 3 (February 1993), 360–80 (p. 363). Hanson has carried out the most exhaustive research to date on Ruskin's childhood religion.

more we shall believe in the sanctity of its origin and the wisdom of its author'.[34]

Theological and devotional writings of the late eighteenth and early nineteenth centuries placed considerable emphasis upon wisdom, discernible in creation as a hypostasis of God.[35] Ruskin absorbed this teaching in boyhood. His mother made him learn Proverbs 2, 3, 8 and 12 by heart, and on Sunday evenings his father would sometimes read a sermon by the Revd Dr Hugh Blair, Professor of Rhetoric and Belles Lettres at Edinburgh in the previous century, several of which addressed the subject of wisdom (35.42,72). In a sermon on 'The Wisdom of God', for example, Blair spoke for his generation in proclaiming that it is 'difficult to say, whether the natural or the moral world afford the most conspicuous and striking displays of the wisdom of God'; that 'in the smallest and most inconsiderable, as well as in the most illustrious works of God, equal marks appear of profound design and consummate art'; and that 'a great, a wise, and beneficent Mind continually superintends every event'.[36]

In 1834 Ruskin enrolled at the 'Academy' in Grove Lane, Camberwell, under the Revd Thomas Dale, described by the *Dictionary of National Biography* as an 'old-fashioned high church evangelical', thus distinguishing him from Tractarians in his commitment to the Reformation principles of the sole authority of Holy Scripture and justification by grace through faith.[37] Six years earlier the *Evangelical Magazine* had made the following announcement under the heading 'Religious Intelligence – London – London University': 'To the sons of members of the Church of England, the Rev. Dr. Lardner and the Rev. Mr. Dale have engaged to deliver Lectures; and to the children of Protestant Dissenters, the Rev. Dr. Cox and the Rev. Joseph Fletcher.'[38] Ruskin's studies under Dale – in 1834 at the Grove Lane school, in 1835 in central London, when Dale

---

[34] See Burd, 'Ruskin's Testament', in Hewison, *New Approaches to Ruskin*, p. 4.

[35] Theissen and Merz provide a modern summary of the Old Testament teaching: 'The period of early Judaism was the heyday of wisdom. At this time Wisdom became a hypostasis of God, i.e. an independent aspect of God which opens up direct access to him. As Wisdom was at work in creation (Prov. 8; Sir. 24; Wisdom 6–8, especially 7.22), it can be recognized in creation.' Gerd Theissen and Annette Merz, *The Historical Jesus: A Comprehensive Guide* (London: SCM, 1996), p. 373. In manuscript, Ruskin was very casual in his use of the capital initial letter for the divine name and divine attributes; his various editors tended to capitalize the former but not the latter.

[36] Hugh Blair, *Sermons*, 5 vols, new edn (London: Sharp, 1822), iv, 369, 370, 386.

[37] See Peter Toon, *Evangelical Theology, 1833–1856: A Response to Tractarianism*, Marshalls Theological Library, ed. Peter Toon (London: Marshall, 1979), pp. 4–5.

[38] *The Evangelical Magazine and Missionary Chronicle*, NS 6 (1828), 354. Of the almost seventy works published by Dale, Ruskin's library was to include *A Memorial of Pastoral Ministrations* (1837) and *Sermons, Principally on Points of Christian Experience, Delivered in St Matthew's Chapel, Denmark Hill*

moved to St Bride's, Fleet Street, and finally in 1836 at King's College, London, in preparation for Oxford – marks his transition from a child who had been 'Entered, Filed, and Registered, according to the custom in use among Protestant Dissenters' to a son of the Church of England. His parents' ambition that he should enter the ordained ministry of the Church of England – and perhaps, as Ruskin was wryly to observe, become 'at forty, Bishop of Winchester, and at fifty, Primate of England' (35.185) – was bound up in this transition, and in the 'three crosses crosslets' incorporated in the family crest his father ordered at the 'Heralds' College' in 1835 (35.390–1). John James chose as his motto 'Age quod agis', based upon what his son described in a sermon the following year as 'advice of Solomons' [*sic*]: 'Whatsoever thy hand findeth to do, do it with thy might; for there is no work, nor device, nor knowledge, nor wisdom, in the grave, whither thou goest' (Ecclesiastes 9.10).[39] (This was the text that dominated the life of W. E. Gladstone – like Ruskin a leading public figure whose every minute had privately to be accounted for to St Peter, and whose roots were also Evangelical.[40]) Ruskin was to change the wording on his own seal to '"To-day," tacitly underlined to [himself] with the warning, "The night cometh, when no man can work"' (1.xi; John 9.4; plate 2) – a favourite Evangelical text.[41]

These two mottoes have a common, hitherto unrecognized literary source in Carlyle's *Sartor Resartus* (1833–4);[42] but they were also staples of Ruskin's regular Evangelical diet throughout his most formative years in Camberwell, along with texts such as that cited by Melvill in his charity sermon of 1839 mentioned earlier: 'There is no offer in the Bible for to-morrow: the message always is, "To-day, if ye will hear His voice, harden not your hearts"' (Psalms 95.7–8, Hebrews 3.7).[43] By this time Ruskin's diet had become more varied, through his exposure to the views of a

---

(1836). An equally important legacy was the training in the cut and thrust of debate which Ruskin received at Dale's hands, and which is reflected in Ruskin's 'Essay on Literature', written in opposition to Dale's views in 1836.

[39] Morgan MA 1704, second sermon of 1836, note on sheet following p. 6. Compare, for example, 18.175.

[40] See Sir Wemyss Reid, *The Life of William Ewart Gladstone* (London: Cassell, 1899), p. 601; Michael Wheeler, 'Gladstone and Ruskin', in *Gladstone*, ed. Peter J. Jagger (London and Rio Grande: Hambledon, 1998), pp. 177–95.

[41] See, for example, William Wilberforce's letter of 2 August 1797 to Hannah More, quoted by Tolley, *Domestic Biography*, p. 38.

[42] They round off the famous climactic chapter entitled 'The Everlasting Yea': see *Carlyle's Works*, Edition de Luxe, 20 vols. (Boston: Estes, Lauriat, 1884), I, 149 . Ruskin knew *Sartor* well, and greatly admired it (17.287).

[43] Henry Melvill and Thomas Dale, *Spiritual Destitution of the Parish of Bethnal-Green, London* (London: Smith, Elder, 1840), p. 16.

Plate 2. Ruskin's seal, showing 'three crosses crosslet', 1835

wide range of ordained clergy and fellows at Oxford, at a time when the Oxford Movement confronted undergraduates of all religious complexions with the major historical questions of Church authority and practice.[44] Moreover, in the early 1840s his upwardly mobile Ultra-Tory parents transferred their allegiance from Thomas Dale, now at St Bride's, Fleet Street, to Henry Melvill, the fifth son of the Lieutenant-Governor of Pendennis Castle in Cornwall, and in the last years of his

---

[44] Ruskin was up at Christ Church from January 1837 to April 1840, when he left through ill health, returning to Oxford (but not to Christ Church) to take his examinations in April 1842. Among the ordained clergy and fellows he encountered as an undergraduate were: the Rt Revd Richard Bagot, Bishop of Oxford, who confirmed him on 22 April 1837; the Revd Walter Lucas Brown, his college tutor, who urged him to be confirmed and later put him up at Wendlebury in October

incumbency at Camden Church.[45] Said to be the most popular preacher in London at the time, Melvill was famous for his rapid delivery, and delivered his Evangelical sermons in the comparatively short time of three-quarters of an hour.[46] As we will see, Ruskin was to praise those he heard during the composition of the first volume of *Modern Painters* in 1842–3, and continued to seek them out after Melvill became Principal of the East India College that year.

II

For the moment, however, we should consider those Evangelical doctrines and moral teachings which Ruskin largely accepted in his youth, but which he either rejected in the 1850s or continued to wrestle with until the end of his active life in the late 1880s – in his private diaries and correspondence, in his published and unpublished writings which specifically engaged with religious matters, such as the 'Essay on Baptism' (1850–1), *Notes on the Construction of Sheepfolds* (1851), *The Nature and Authority of Miracle* (1873), and *Letters to the Clergy on the Lord's Prayer and the Church* (1879–80), and in the major works. Much of that doctrine developed from Calvinist teaching on 'the total depravity of man', one of Ruskin's themes in his precocious 'Sermons on the Pentateuch',

1841 following his stay at Leamington; the Revd Osborne Gordon, see pp. 54–7 below; the Revd Dr William Buckland, Canon of Church Church and Oxford's first Reader in Geology, whose geology and natural theology engaged Ruskin's close attention; Dean Thomas Gaisford of Christ Church, Regius Professor of Greek, who admired Ruskin's undergraduate drawings; the Revd Walter Kerr Hamilton, vicar of St Peter in the East, whose services were attended by Margaret Ruskin; the Revd John Keble, Vicar of Hursley and a leading Tractarian, whose verse in *The Christian Year* Ruskin admired, and who as Professor of Poetry corrected Ruskin's Newdigate Prize poem, 'Salsette and Elephanta'; the Revd Henry Liddell (later Dean) of Christ Church, who admired Ruskin's undergraduate drawings; the Revd John Owen Parr, Fellow of Brasenose, whose Evangelical sermon of 1839 against Newman Ruskin liked 'much', according to his mother; the Revd Dr Edward Bouverie Pusey, Regius Professor of Hebrew, Canon of Christ Church, and a leading Tractarian, who gave his 'Lectures on Types and Prophecies of the Old Testament' in 1836–7, and never spoke to Ruskin; the Revd Philip Nicholas Shuttleworth, Warden of New College, the titles of whose books, *Not Tradition but Scripture* (1838) and *Justification through Faith* (1840), neatly summarize the Evangelical response to the Oxford Movement, and whose family Ruskin knew. Ruskin's Oxford contemporaries who went on to be ordained included Edward Clayton, the 'College Friend' to whom he wrote letters in the 1840s (published in 1894), and Frederick William Robertson, who debated with Ruskin at Oxford, and later become a famous preacher at Trinity Chapel, Brighton.

45 Robert Hewison points out that both Dale and Melvill were Ultra-Tories like John James Ruskin: 'Notes on the Construction of *The Stones of Venice*', in *Studies in Ruskin: Essays in Honor of Van Akin Burd*, ed. Robert Rhodes and Del Ivan Janik (Athens, Ohio: Ohio University Press, 1982), pp. 131–52 (p. 139). Hewison cites G. S. Simes, 'The Ultra-Tories in British Politics 1824–1834', unpublished doctoral dissertation, University of Oxford, 1974.

46 *Dictionary of National Biography*; compare 35.386–8.

where he argues that the rejection of the warning contained in the building of the ark is 'among the very strongest proofs on record, of the utter wickedness of the human soul'.[47] One of the most eloquent preachers on the subject was the Revd Dr John Cumming, Minister of the National Scottish Church in Covent Garden, whose first sermon in his published *Occasional Discourses* (1850) is on 'Fallen Humanity'. The heart, he declares, 'is the seat of our moral depravity – the ever overflowing cistern from which our corruptions come':

If man's thoughts are evil to the very core, where is the foundation of that superstructure of human merit or deservings which the Roman Catholic has reared? . . . If we would but carry with us what we are by nature, we should feel that every good we achieve springs from above, and that little else than sin and ungodliness naturally originate from ourselves.[48]

In the light of teaching such as Cumming's, it is not difficult to see why Evangelicals laid great emphasis upon the urgent need for conversion. Ruskin learned at his mother's knee Acts 26, in which Paul tells the story of his conversion to Agrippa, and he may well have been in Beresford Chapel in 1829 (the year of John James's letter) to hear Dr Andrews say to his flock: 'I speak to you now as the regenerated elect, – the converted, – the called by divine grace.'[49] Whereas in 1850/1 Ruskin's own contribution to the debate on baptism that raged at the time of the Gorham crisis was still broadly Evangelical in its emphasis upon conversion, by 1858 he had undergone his self-styled 'un-conversion' at Turin.

It was also in 1829 that Bishop John Bird Sumner, later to become the first Evangelical Primate of England, delivered a Charge to the clergy of the Diocese of Chester which was reported rapturously by the *Evangelical Magazine*: 'He represented forcibly the absolute necessity of holding Christ as the only author of the way, the truth, and the life, and of dwelling upon the great and vital doctrines of justification by faith, sanctification by the Spirit, and salvation by grace and mercy alone.'[50] In the early 1840s Melvill began a sermon which Ruskin may well have heard, or seen in print, with the words: 'It was a saying of Luther, and

---

[47] Cited by Burd, 'Ruskin's Testament', in Hewison, *New Approaches to Ruskin*, p. 5.

[48] John Cumming, *Occasional Discourses*, 2 vols, new edn (London: Hall, Virtue, 1852), I, 5, 15.

[49] Edward Andrews, *Spiritual Lethargy: A Sermon, delivered at Beresford Chapel, Walworth* (London: Palmer, 1829), p. 5.

[50] *The Evangelical Magazine and Missionary Chronicle*, NS 7 (1829), 443–4 (p. 443). The article ends: 'We cannot but rejoice to read such a charge as this from the lips of a Bishop. How unlike diocesan charges in general!'

one which is often quoted amongst ourselves, "that the doctrine of justification by faith is the doctrine of a standing or a falling church".[51] Cumming's uncompromising Pauline statement in one of his *Occasional Discourses* that 'No man can be justified by works' reflects Evangelicalism's assault on Roman Catholic doctrine at mid-century.[52] Article XI of the Church of England (one of the 39 Ruskin learned and studied at Oxford, probably with the help of Tomline's *Elements of Christian Theology* (1799)[53]) affirms justification by faith alone, and Jeremy Taylor had attempted to find a doctrine of justification which mediated between the positions of Roman Catholics and Puritans.[54] Indeed, Ruskin's careful reading of Taylor and Hooker, both leading Anglican divines of earlier centuries, was motivated partly by a need to resolve to his own satisfaction this and other issues relating to Evangelical doctrine. His diary entry of 26 November 1843, recording 'a good sermon from Melville [*sic*] on the promise of Eternal life "before the world began," showing that all the promises in the Bible were made not to us but to Christ – and their fulfilment, of course, independent of our worthiness' (*D*, 250), would seem to cast doubt on the claim that he always opposed justification by faith alone.[55] There can be no doubt, however, that the doctrine became a stumbling-block for him, and that it was partly in his reaction against it that his foundational thinking on work and works in the 1850s prepared the ground for the socio-economic writings of the 1860s.

Ironically, an equally problematic Evangelical doctrine for Ruskin the critic and interpreter was the authority of the 'Word', in the sense of 'the scriptures'. In 1829 Edward Irving wrote in *The Signs of the Times*,

[51] Henry Melvill, *Sermons on certain of the less prominent Facts and References in Sacred Story*, 2 vols. (London: Rivington, 1843–5), I, 31.

[52] Cumming, *Occasional Discourses*, I, 79. Litton, one of only two Evangelicals who wrote treatises on the Church at this period, commented, 'In the Romish System, the idea of the Church gives a shape to all other doctrines: in Protestantism this governing influence belongs to its doctrine of Justification': Edward Arthur Litton, *The Church of Christ, in Its Idea, Attributes, and Ministry: with a particular reference to the Controversy on the subject between Romanists and Protestants* (London: Longman, 1851), p. xiii; see Toon, *Evangelical Theology*, pp. 173–4.

[53] George Tomline, *Elements of Christian Theology*, 9th edn of vol. I, 7th edn of vol. II, 2 vols. (London: Cadell, Davies, 1812), II, 256–65. Ruskin's reference to Tomline on Article XVIII in his diaries suggests that the book was on his shelves: see Lancaster MS 5c, Diaries, fol. 156.

[54] See Toon, *Evangelical Theology*, p. 146. The Evangelical G. S. Faber, in *The Primitive Doctrine of Justification Investigated* (1837), 'attempted to prove, against Alexander Knox . . . and against Joseph Milner . . . that the Protestant doctrine of justification by Faith was actually taught by the early Fathers, before its corruption in the medieval period': see Toon, *Evangelical Theology*, p. 141.

[55] See Finley, *Nature's Covenant*, p. 82. Also compare Ruskin's criticism in *Modern Painters* II (1846) of 'the effort of men to earn, rather than to receive, their salvation', and his characteristic editorial intervention of 1883 contradicting his earlier position (4.217).

'the book before me is the infallible word of God'; and this is what
Ruskin was brought up to believe, like most practising Christians in the
first half of the nineteenth century.[56] Thomas Dale's reminder to his
congregation at St Bride's, that the Bible should be their 'companion'
and 'counseller' [*sic*] 'twice in the day at least' was typical of
Evangelical teaching, and Margaret Ruskin's drilling of the scriptures
into her son was unusual only in being more thorough than in most
Evangelical households, there being at Herne Hill ample time available
to the deeply committed teacher, and exceptional ability in the young
pupil.[57] Thomas Brown of Musselburgh considered that the whole of
Proverbs 8 should be 'committed to memory in small parts';[58] Ruskin
learned this and three other chapters.[59] Ruskin naturally became a
'Bible Christian', in the sense that he turned to scripture as his prime
authority and, in his middle years, loosened his affiliation to any specific
sect or tradition.[60] Evidence from the unpublished material in his diary
notebooks indicates that in the late 1840s he was turning to the Revd
Thomas Scott's famous Bible commentary (1788–92) for explanatory
notes on texts which he was studying.[61] Scott, a Calvinist, argues in the
Preface that

The Bible alone, and such books as make it their basis, introduce the infinite
God speaking in a manner worthy of himself, with simplicity, majesty, and
authority. His character, as there delineated, comprises all possible excellence

---

[56] Edward Irving, *The Signs of the Times* (London: Panton, 1829), p. 8. On the widespread belief in
the inerrancy of the Bible in this period see Stephen Neill, *The Interpretation of the New Testament,
1861–1961*, The Firth Lectures, 1962 (Oxford University Press, 1966), p. 31.

[57] Thomas Dale, *Sermons, Doctrinal and Practical, Preached in the Parish Church of St. Bride, Fleet Street*
(London: Richardson, 1831), p. 307.

[58] Brown, *Proverbs of Solomon*, p. 23. Brown helps his pupils to recite the text by 'marking the sounds'
in this pocket edition (p. 3).

[59] Chapters 2, 3 and 8 are from the first part of Proverbs, which are 'chiefly confined to the conduct
of early life': see C[harles] Bridges, *An Exposition of the Book of Proverbs*, 2 vols. (London: Seeley,
1846), I, viii. Bridges considered that the whole book had a '*distinctive character, as a Book for the
Young*': I, xix.

[60] He writes to Dale from Leamington on 22 September 1841: 'Scripture of course must be the ultimate appeal . . . our fellows are departing every instant into eternal pain' (1.395–7).

[61] See Lancaster MS 5C, Diaries, fol. 94, where Ruskin casually quotes Scott on Matthew 5.3 in his
notes. The accessibility and clarity of Scott's commentary made it hugely popular. In the
opening chapter of his *Apologia*, when describing his Evangelical upbringing, Newman recorded
that he almost owed his soul to Scott, whose commentary he bought as an undergraduate:
Apologia Pro Vita Sua: Being a History of his Religious Opinions, ed. Martin J. Svaglic (Oxford:
Clarendon, 1967), pp. 18–19. Bishop Colenso of Natal commented in 1863 that 'no commentary
on the *Old* Testament [had] yet taken the place of that of the excellent THOMAS SCOTT, – a work
admirable for the age in which it was written, but including, of course, none of the remarkable
results of modern criticism': John William Colenso, *The Pentateuch and Book of Joshua Critically
Examined*, 7 parts (London: Longman, 1862–79), IV, x. Scott was widely cited by other commentators: see, for example, Bridges, *Exposition*, I, vi.

without any intermixture; his laws and ordinances accord to his perfections; his works and dispensations exhibit them; and all his dealings with his creatures bear the stamp of infinite wisdom, power, justice, purity, truth, goodness, and mercy, harmoniously displayed.[62]

Indeed, Ruskin's approach to his habitual and formative Sunday reading and study, often written up in the diaries, was not dissimilar to Scott's, again described in the Preface:

the Author having, for many years, made the Bible his daily and principal study; and having bestowed great pains to satisfy his own mind, as to the meaning of most parts of Scripture, and the practical use which should be made of them; and supposing also that his talent chiefly lies, in speaking plainly and intelligibly to persons of ordinary capacity and information; he adopts this method of communicating his views of divine truth, in connexion with the Scriptures themselves, from which he has deduced them.

Working in a similar way, Ruskin's habit was to read the Bible largely unaided by earlier commentaries[63] and to arrive at conclusions only after careful analysis, in the same way that his youthful studies in geology, architecture and painting were based upon patient and careful observation.[64] His instinct was to examine primary source material in all these domains, to which he brought an unswerving literalism (e.g. 17.461). Towards the end of his career Ruskin was 'entirely disposed to concur' with Mazzini's comment that he had 'the most analytic mind in Europe' (35.44).

Ruskin's analytic mind was to take him far from the Evangelical position on biblical authority that he espoused in early manhood.[65] Before leaving questions of Evangelical doctrine for the moment, however,

---

[62] *The Holy Bible*, with explanatory notes, practical observations, and copious marginal references by Thomas Scott, 9th edn, 6 vols. (London: Seeley, 1825), I, Preface (n.p.).

[63] According to Collingwood, who worked closely with Ruskin later in his career, he 'read neither commentaries nor modern critics', but kept by him Smith's *Bible Dictionary*, Cruden, the *Englishman's Greek Concordance*, Sharpe's *Translation of the Hebrew Scriptures*, and two copies of Finden's *Landscape Illustrations of the Bible* – 'But even these few were little used': W. G. Collingwood, 'Ruskin's Bibles', in his *Ruskin Relics* (London: Ibister, 1903), pp. 195–211 (pp. 210–11); compare 34.702. Benjamin Jowett considered that 'any one who, instead of burying himself in the pages of the commentators, would learn the sacred writings by heart, and paraphrase them in English, will probably make a nearer approach to their true meaning than he would gather from any commentary': 'On the Interpretaton of Scripture', in Frederick Temple, *et al.*, *Essays and Reviews*, 12th edn (London: Longmans, 1869), pp. 399–527 (p. 466).

[64] Ruskin started to create a mineralogical dictionary in 1831, the year in which Darwin began his observations on the voyage of the Beagle.

[65] On Evangelicalism's 'non-essential' doctrines of eternal punishment, millenarianism, special providence, and assurance see Elisabeth Jay, *The Religion of the Heart: Anglican Evangelicalism and the Nineteenth-Century Novel* (Oxford: Clarendon, 1979), p. 82; compare George P. Landow, *The Aesthetic and Critical Theories of John Ruskin* (Princeton University Press, 1971), pp. 248–9, where Ryle's 'five distinctive doctrinal marks' are cited.

we must briefly note the centrality of Atonement theology to Evangelicalism, and to Ruskin's religion.[66] For Ruskin's interest in the temple and in wisdom literature can be explained at least partly by Solomon's status for Evangelicals as a type of Christ the prophet, priest and king, who in his death on the cross, 'for our redemption', 'made there (by his one oblation of himself once offered) a full, perfect, and sufficient sacrifice, oblation, and satisfaction, for the sins of the whole world'.[67]

The wisdom books of the Old Testament – Proverbs, Job and Ecclesiastes, together with the apocryphal Ecclesiasticus and Wisdom of Solomon, and several of the Psalms – provided suitable texts for Victorian preachers when addressing the subject of education, and a Broad Churchman like the Revd Julius Charles Hare could apply the typology of the temple broadly when preaching 'in Behalf of the Chichester Central Schools' in 1841:

> the great purpose for which Solomon was endowed with all his wisdom, was, that he might build the temple of God in the beauty of holiness: and we should tell our children that they too have the same glorious work to accomplish, – that they too have a temple of God to build, even in their own hearts and souls . . . and that, poor and lowly as it may seem, if it be but clean and simple, the Holy Ghost will dwell in it, and it will endure for ever.[68]

In contrast, the Evangelicals, like their High Church brethren,[69] adhered more closely to the rich scriptural tradition associated with the tabernacle, the temple and the revelation of the Christ which unfolds typologically through the old covenant into the new, and from the historical and physical sphere to the eternal and spiritual. George Offor, a Baptist book-seller and biographer who built up an unrivalled collection of Bunyaniana, summarized that tradition in his editor's 'advertisement' to Bunyan's *Solomon's Temple Spiritualized; or, Gospel Light fetched out of the Temple at Jerusalem, to let us more easily into the Glory of New Testament Truths* (1688), in the edition of the collected works that he published in 1853:

[66] Following a walk with Ruskin on 22 September 1877, the Revd F. A. Malleson wrote to his wife: 'I went clearly & plainly into the doctrine of the atonement with him – in wh. he is as sound and believing as you or I . . . he was rejoiced that I was not a *stiff* evangelical': Brantwood, Letters of John Ruskin to the Revd F. A. Malleson. Finley argues that the Atonement is 'the central tenet of Ruskin's faith, the reiterated point of his sermons, even as it will become the most resonant element of Reformed theology to survive into his extended readings of the sacred text of nature' (p. 65). Later, however, Ruskin's 'Catholic' theology is Incarnational in emphasis: see p. 000 below.   [67] Holy Communion, Book of Common Prayer.

[68] Julius Charles Hare, 'The Worth of Knowledge, or the Judgement of the Queen of Sheba: A Sermon Preacht in the Cathedral Church of Chichester, on Thursday, June 9th, 1841, in Behalf of the Chichester Central Schools', in *Sermons* (London: Parker, 1846), pp. 299–319 (p. 317).

[69] See, for example, Christopher Wordsworth's commentaries on the wisdom books of the Old Testament, cited in chapter 3 below.

Of all the wonders of the world, the temple of Solomon was beyond comparison the greatest and the most magnificent. It was a type of that temple not
made with hands, eternal in the heavens, of that city whose builder and maker
is God, and which, at the consummation of all things, shall descend from
heaven with gates of pearl and street of pure gold as shining glass, and into
which none but the ransomed of the Lord shall enter. Jesus, the Lamb of God,
shall be its light and glory and temple; within its walls the Israel of God, with
the honour of the Gentiles, shall be brought in a state of infinite purity. No
unclean thing will be able to exist in that dazzling and refulgent brightness
which will arise from the perfection of holiness in the immediate presence of
Jehovah; and of this, as well as of the whole Christian dispensation, the temple
of Solomon was a type or figure.[70]

An aspect of King Solomon's ambiguity, however, was his fall into
idolatry, the fear of which shaped the Evangelical culture in which
Ruskin was brought up. In Dr Andrews's Beresford Chapel sermon of
1829, quoted earlier, he preached against 'spiritual lethargy', declaring
on the subject of 'company': 'Let us be anxious to associate only with
those who are truly pious.'[71] Ruskin drew on his experience of living in
such company when he wrote in 1846: 'men in high state of moral
culture are often insensible to the influence of material beauty' (4.210;
cf. 10.124). Poetry, Ruskin's first literary form, was acceptable, and was
published in the Evangelical journals. A survey of the *Evangelical
Magazine* of the period, however, reveals no references to painting, architecture or the decorative arts; and a book which it reviews in 1828 entitled *Evangelical Beauties* turns out to be a volume of extracts from the
works of Archbishop Leighton.[72] Idolatry, a loathsome subject for
Evangelicals, was to be one of Ruskin's themes.

If, as Cumming argued in a passage quoted earlier, the heart is 'the
seat of our moral depravity – the ever overflowing cistern from which
our corruptions come', then those corruptions reveal themselves
through the 'members'. Here again, Solomon is an ambiguous figure,
and for Ruskin a troubling one, having 'loved many strange women'
who 'turned away his heart after other gods' (1 Kings 11.1,4). Whether
Ruskin's personal identification with the Solomon who built the
temple and, by tradition, wrote the Proverbs, was also associated with
the legend that the king ordered the Queen of Sheba's body hair to

---

[70] *The Works of John Bunyan*, ed. George Offor, 3 vols. (Glasgow: Blackie, 1853), III, 460. The
Waldenses, or Vaudois, who were idealized by the Evangelicals, included only the wisdom books
of the Old Testament with the New Testament in their ancient Bible.
[71] Andrews, *Spiritual Lethargy*, p. 27.
[72] *The Evangelical Magazine and Missionary Chronicle*, NS 6 (1828), 353.

be removed before they lay together, must remain a matter of specu-lation.[73] Certainly Ruskin's denial of the body, which helps to explain not only the agonies of his private life but also his negative reading of the architecture of the Renaissance and much of its art, has its origins in an Evangelical world of physical concealment and linguis-tic circumlocution. Confronted, for example, with the task of giving an eye-witness account of the tragic circumstances surrounding the death of Bishop Heber of Calcutta in his plunge pool at Trichinopoly, the Revd J. W. Doran resorted to the kind of euphe-mism which was characteristic of the 'truly pious': 'alas! mine was the awful task to drag, together with Mr. Robinson, his mortal remains from the water . . . The immortal inhabitant had forsaken its tene-ment of clay.'[74]

At greatest risk to temptation and to idolatry was the eye, an organ which for Evangelicals was associated with 'spiritual sight'.[75] Ruskin himself wrote on Luke 2.13–14, in a Christmas sermon of 1836, 'Man can only realize – or try to realize the Unseen by his experience of the Seen',[76] and commented much later in life: 'You do not see *with* the lens of the eye. You see *through* that, and by means of that, but you see with the soul of the eye' (22.194). A clear link can be made between his failing eyesight on the Italian tour of 1840–1 and his morbid sensibility;[77] and the cardinal importance of eyesight to him is epitomized in that frequently quoted statement, taken from *Modern Painters* III (1856): 'Hundreds of people can talk for one who can think, but thousands can think for one who can see. To see clearly is poetry, prophecy, and religion, – all in one' (5.333). Also familiar, however, is the anguished comment in a letter to Lady Mount-Temple, dated 16 January 1875: 'The worst of me is that the Desire of my *Eyes* is so much to me! Ever so much more than the desire of

---

[73] For the legend see Lou H. Silberman, 'The Queen of Sheba in Judaic Tradition', in *Solomon & Sheba*, ed. James B. Pritchard (London and New York: Phaidon / Praeger, 1974), pp. 65–84 (p. 71).

[74] *The Evangelical Magazine and Missionary Chronicle*, NS 4 (1826), 483. For further examples of euphe-misms associated with death and the body, see Michael Wheeler, *Death and the Future Life in Victorian Literature and Theology* (Cambridge University Press, 1990), pp. 18–19, 57–8.

[75] 'Our spiritual eyesight is so blinded by the darkness and the contagion of guilt, and so accus-tomed to its lines, that we do not see it in its real magnitude or fearful heinousness': Cumming, *Occasional Discourses*, I, 74.   [76] Morgan MA 1704.

[77] See Finley, *Nature's Covenant*, p. 146. Compare Ruskin's own link between his depression and his need for spectacles in 1872: *The Correspondence of John Ruskin and Charles Eliot Norton*, ed. John Lewis Bradley and Ian Ousby (Cambridge University Press, 1987), p. 254. The case of Tennyson is similar.

my mind.'[78] Only a few months after his lengthy discussions on Roman Catholic doctrine in the 'Sacristan's Cell' at Assisi, and shortly before he plunged into experiments with Spiritualism, following the death of Rose la Touche, Ruskin can still write privately like an anxious English Evangelical.

III

Ruskin's first extended period of acute mental illness in 1878 – often described as the 'first madness' – can be explained by his genetic inheritance, by manic overwork, by his need to escape from the pain of bereavement, by his confusion over the great question of life after death, or by other immediate problems relating to his spiritual life. Alternatively, or rather additionally, the biographer seeking an 'environmental' explanation in his boyhood could turn to John James's description of his divine commission, in the letter written almost fifty years earlier: 'You may be doomed to enlighten a People by your Wisdom & to adorn an age by your Learning.' It would be mistaken, however, to regard Ruskin's Evangelical inheritance as being wholly negative in its effect upon him. Evangelicalism not only equipped Ruskin with habits of Bible study and worship which were to remain with him for the rest of his life.[79] It also provided him, as it has so many others before and since, with a system of belief and morality against which an alert critical mind could test alternative views before finally breaking away from the tradition.

On his troubled spiritual journey away from Evangelicalism, through what he called the 'religion of Humanity' (29.90), to a broadly defined 'Catholicism' in later years, Ruskin's beliefs underwent many changes, susceptible as they were to his own sharpened critical awareness. From the 1850s onwards his private biblical notes, while still reminiscent of Thomas Scott's commentary in their directness and their application to daily life, often focus upon his study of the original Greek in the New Testament and problems of translation, and upon the need to establish accurate chronologies of Old Testament history.[80] Indeed, the awkward

---

[78] *The Letters of John Ruskin to Lord and Lady Mount-Temple*, ed. John Lewis Bradley ([Columbus]: Ohio State University Press, 1964), p. 358. Finley compares Ruskin and Wesley to Augustinian *concupiscentia oculorum*: see p. 79, n.99.

[79] In *Fors*, Letter 41 (May 1874) Ruskin wrote: 'My good wiseacre readers, I know as many flaws in the book of Genesis as the best of you, but I knew the book before I knew its flaws, while you know the flaws, and never have known the book, nor can know it' (28.85).

[80] See, for example, Lancaster MS 9, Diaries, fol. 38. He also cites the Vulgate in the 1850s: see, for example, Lancaster MS 11, Diaries, fols. 30, 32.

questions raised by Ruskin's search for what he called 'the facts' anticipate those addressed by the controversial Bishop Colenso of Natal in
the 1860s. By 1867, when spelling out the four 'possible Theories
respecting the Authority of the Bible' in *Time and Tide*, he could sweep
aside the theory that every word of the Bible was 'dictated by the
Supreme Being, and is in every syllable of it His "Word"' as being 'of
course tenable by no ordinarily well-educated person' (17.348), and later
to describe calling any book, or collection of books, 'the Word of God'
a 'heresy' (27.669).

Ruskin's interpretation of the gospel places particular emphasis upon
the Sermon on the Mount (Matthew 5–7) – which he learnt as a child
and which includes the Beatitudes and the Lord's Prayer – and Christ's
summary of the commandments (Matthew 22.37–40). His most strongly
held religious tenet seems to have crystallized from a conversation in
October 1848 on matters of faith with the father of his friend Edmund
Oldfield, who believed that 'there is but One great Difference, and that
is, between him that serveth God, and him that serveth him not
[Matthew 6.24]'.[81] Three years later Ruskin stated in *Notes on the
Construction of Sheepfolds* that he wished the issue of baptismal regeneration could be laid to rest, as 'the great question for every man' – easily
answered, though rarely asked – is, 'Whether he be Now serving God
or not?' (12.576). As Ruskin applied this simple test to the clergy and
laity of different sects in the 1850s, his respect for organized religion
diminished, so that he could write to the Brownings in March 1858 as
follows:

I am all at sea myself – all that I am sure of is that we live in very 'dark ages'
compared with ages which will be; and that most churches are in a sad way
because they all keep preaching the wrong way upwards, and say 'Know and
you shall do' instead of 'Do and you shall know.' [John 7.17.][82] As I read the
Bible my main result in way of belief is that those people are to be exalted in
eternity who in this life have striven to do God's will, not their own. And so very
few people appear to me to do this in reality that I don't know what to believe
– the truth as far as I can make it out seems too terrible to be the truth. All
churches seem to me mere forms of idolatry. A Roman Catholic idolizes his
saint and his relic – an English High Churchman idolizes his propriety and his
family pew – a Scotch Presbyterian idolizes his own obstinacy and his own opin-

---

[81] The entry ends: 'and that is implied by what St Paul says, "Grace, mercy & peace, be to all them
   that love our Lord Jesus, in sincerity". "If any man love *not* the Lord Jesus, let him be anathema
   maranatha': Lancaster MS 5c, Diaries, fol. 127; compare *D*, 370.
[82] Thomas Scott wrote, 'all, who desire earnestly and seek diligently to know the will of God, in
   order to reduce it to practice, shall be guided through every labyrinth of uncertainty, and past
   every precipice of error, into the ways of truth and peace': Scott, *The Holy Bible*, V, 'Practical
   Observations' on John 7.11–18.

ions – a German divine idolizes his dreams, and an English one his pronunciation . . . (36.279–80)

Although Ruskin, like most of his intelligent contemporaries, encountered what were known as 'difficulties' with aspects of Christian faith,
his quarrel was not with the teaching of Christ but with its interpretation and application by the Church.[83]

Take, for instance, one of the most thorny and divisive subjects in the
history of the Victorian Church – everlasting damnation. Ruskin's tutor,
Dale, wrote in a sermon of 3 September 1837, designed to stir up the
consciences of his respectable congregation at St Bride's, and entitled
'Escape from the Path of the Destroyer':

[God] will bring every work into judgment, and every secret thought, whether
it be good or evil; and to doubt of his omniscience, would be the equivalent to
the denial of his existence . . .
He who lives for a whole day without a personal, individual remembrance of
God, is for that day at least an unbeliever . . . [84]

Whereas in 1841 Ruskin could write to Dale of their fellows 'departing
every instant into eternal pain' (1.396–7), by 1856 he was confessing to
Thomas Lupton that even heaven was 'unconceivable' [*sic*] to him.[85]
Like Dean Farrar, he was to question the 'common view' of judgment,
in which the majority of mankind await an 'irreversible doom to endless
tortures' after death.[86]

Ruskin's rebellion against his Evangelical upbringing came later in life
than usual: he himself dated the final break in 1858, his fortieth year. It
had only been through a willed act of faith in 1852, when he assured his
father by letter that he would act 'as if the Bible *were* true' (10.xxxix), that
he had been able to sustain a faith which, as he had put it to his friend
Henry Acland the previous year, fluttered in 'weak rags' of gold leaf
'from the letter of its old forms':

If only the Geologists would let me alone, I could do very well, but those dreadful Hammers! I hear the clink of them at the end of every cadence of the Bible
verses – and on the other side, these unhappy, blinking Puseyisms; men trying
to do right and losing their very Humanity. (36.115)

---

[83] Compare Browning's narrator in *Easter-Day* (1850): 'How very hard it is to be / A Christian! Hard
for you and me, / – Not the mere task of making real / That duty up to its ideal . . .' (1–4). 'Ruskin
never became a true agnostic, let alone an atheist, but without doubt he lost faith in the promised end – personal salvation and eternal life': Spear, *Dreams*, p. 46.

[84] Thomas Dale, *Escape from the Path of the Destroyer: A Sermon Preached . . . at St. Bride's Church, on Sunday
Morning, September 3rd, 1837, The Church of England Preacher*, vol. 1, no. 13 (London: Harding, 1837),
pp. 208–9.   [85] See chapter 2, note 29.

[86] Frederic W. Farrar, *Eternal Hope: Five Sermons Preached in Westminster Abbey, November and December,
1877* (1904), p. xxii.

The last part of this statement, on the Tractarians, is seldom quoted, and stands as a warning against trying to explain Ruskin's difficulties in terms of a single cause. The fact is that he applied his 'analytic mind' to every aspect of religious debate, and found more and more evidence that while Utilitarianism, modern science and German thought brought no new light into the world, Christ's teaching was not being followed in the nineteenth century, not least because his gospel was not being preached in church or chapel.

Ruskin thus wandered in the wilderness in the 1860s and early 1870s, years that coincide with his doomed relationship with Rose La Touche. In both the socio-economic and scientific writings, however, where Ruskin's reflections on the Greek Athena and the Egyptian Neith are of central importance, it is the threads that connect these deities with Judæo-Christian wisdom that fascinate him. Indeed, from the period of *Unto this Last* (1860) Ruskin became a 'Victorian Solomon' and his writings a modern form of wisdom literature. The 'Catholic' position which became possible for him after the formative stay in the Sacristan's Cell at Assisi in 1874 inspired his attempt to rewrite his earlier, Evangelical interpretations of Venice and of French Gothic in the late work, and to write the history of Christendom. Here too, Solomon is present. Susceptible as Ruskin's beliefs were to his own sharpened critical awareness, what never left him, and what proved to be least susceptible to the application of new critical tools by the scientists and biblical scholars of the day, was a belief in divine wisdom and the God of peace; and what came closest to resolving the conflict between the desire of his physical eye and the claims of his spiritual eye was a nexus of symbols and traditions associated with wisdom, the temple and Solomon – types of the Holy Spirit, the sanctified Christian soul and the Christ whose bequest to the world, and to Ruskin, was peace. Solomon, whose name is based on the word *shalom*, came to represent for Ruskin the antithesis of Evangelical philistinism. The wisdom books – traditionally associated with King David's son – provided the basis for Ruskin's writing on socio-economic issues in the 1860s, not only in terms of content but also of form and style; and Solomon's role as judge – again he is a type of Christ – is often referred to when Ruskin believes most strongly that he and the rest of the world are under judgment. By tracing his deepening interest in wisdom literature and identification with Solomon in the course of his career as a Victorian writer and thinker, we can see more clearly the nature of Ruskin's God.

PART ONE

The Author of Modern Painters

CHAPTER 2

'The Shechinah of the blue': in God's temple

Where Poussin or Claude has three similar masses, nature has fifty pictures, made up each of millions of minor thoughts; fifty aisles, penetrating through angelic chapels to the Shechinah of the blue; fifty hollow ways among bewildered hills, each with its own nodding rocks, and cloven precipices, and radiant summits, and robing vapours, but all unlike each other, except in beauty, all bearing witness to the unwearied, exhaustless operation of the Infinite Mind.

'Of Truth of Clouds: – Secondly, of the Central Cloud Region',
Modern Painters I (3.381)

I

'Shechinah', or Shekinah, derives from the Hebrew *shakhan*, and means 'dwelling' or 'that which dwells'.[1] The word is not used in the Old Testament but occurs frequently in other Jewish literature, applied solely to God. In reaction against the anthropomorphism of much of the Old Testament, where God is described, for example, as dwelling in a place or being seen, the Targums – later Aramaic paraphrases – use the terms 'the Word', or 'Spirit', or 'Wisdom' in place of the divine name. Similarly, 'the Shekinah rests' stands for 'God dwells', and 'the house of Shekinah' for 'the temple of God'. The Shekinah was the source and centre of the glory manifested in the cloud in the tabernacle (*mishkan*, from the same root) and later in Solomon's temple in Jerusalem (I Kings 8.11); and in the New Testament the word 'glory' (Greek *doxa*) can refer to the Shekinah, most significantly in John 1.14: 'And the Word was made flesh, and dwelt among us ['sojourned' or 'tabernacled' in us], (and we beheld his glory, the glory as of the only begotten of the Father,) full of grace and truth.'[2] Ruskin used both Bishop Tomline's standard manual

---

[1] See C. W. Emmet, 'Shekinah', in James Hasting, *Dictionary of the Bible*, 2nd edn, rev. Frederick C. Grant and H. H. Rowley (Edinburgh: Clark, 1963), pp. 904–5.

[2] See *The Greek Testament*, ed. Henry Alford, 4 vols, 7th edn (London: Rivingtons, 1874), I, 685–6.

for ordinands, *Elements of Christian Theology* (1799), and Thomas Scott's Bible commentary (1788–92), and could have found an explanation of 'Shechinah' (with that spelling) in either of them.[3]

Ruskin's description of the 'Shechinah of the blue' in *Modern Painters* I (1843) is characteristic of that volume's oxygenated prose in praise of nature, of its creator and sustainer (the 'Infinite Mind'), and of its some-what improbable chief prophet – J. M. W. Turner. Seventeen years later, when, in response to pressure from his father, Ruskin finally brought out the fifth and final volume, he could state that in 'the main aim and prin-ciple of the book, there is no variation, from its first syllable to its last. It declares the perfectness and eternal beauty of the work of God; and tests all work of man by concurrence with, or subject to that' (7.9). Yet by 1860 his ideas on nature, his religious beliefs, and his interpretation of Turner had changed, and he had published two other major works – *The Seven Lamps of Architecture* (1849) and *The Stones of Venice* (1851–3).[4] This chapter examines the use of language and symbolism associated with Solomon's temple and the wisdom tradition in *Modern Painters* – an aspect of the coherence and continuity which Ruskin himself claimed for the work – as Ruskin moves from seeing Turner as the true prophet of divine wisdom, truth and love as manifested in nature, to regarding him as a genius who was 'without hope', the product of an irreligious England whose national Church had failed him and his generation. Whereas nature is regarded as God's temple in the first four volumes, the empha-sis in the fifth falls upon the temple of the human body (I Corinthians 3.16). The chapters that follow in part I demonstrate the centrality of this biblical tradition to the major works of the 1840s and 1850s by the 'Author of *Modern Painters*', arguing that in *Modern Painters* II, where Ruskin presents his Christian aesthetic, his God is the God of peace who lives in heaven and in the 'temple of the heart'; that in *The Stones of Venice* he interprets St Mark's as a 'Book-Temple', accessible to the English

---

[3] George Tomline, *Elements of Christian Theology*, 9th edn of vol. I, 7th edn of vol. II (London: Cadell, Davies, 1812), I, 183–4, 214. *The Holy Bible*, with explanatory notes, practical observations, and copious marginal references by Thomas Scott, 9th edn, 6 vols. (London: Seeley, 1825), v, John 1.14. An example of the alternative spelling is: 'The ling'ring train in sacerdotal vest, / Scarce left the precincts of the Holiest, / Ere the Shekinah roll'd its streaming light / In snow-white volume, and in radiance bright / To bless the work with God's approving eye, / By this pure emblem of Divinity': Charles J. Champneys, *The Temple of Solomon, and Poems on Scriptural and other Subjects* (Glasgow: Smith, 1848), pp. 9–10.

[4] See George P. Landow, *The Aesthetic and Critical Theories of John Ruskin* (Princeton, NJ: Princeton University Press, 1971); Robert Hewison, *John Ruskin: The Argument of the Eye* (London: Thames & Hudson; Princeton, NJ: Princeton University Press, 1976); Elizabeth K. Helsinger, *Ruskin and the Art of the Beholder* (Cambridge, Mass., and London: Harvard University Press, 1982).

Protestant reader via the Baptistery rather than the Virgin's side chapel; that his heralding of the era of the birth of 'true sacred art' in Turner and the Pre-Raphaelites finds its true subject in Holman Hunt's *The Light of the World*; and finally that in Ruskin's several accounts of his 'un-conversion' of 1858, Veronese's *The Presentation of the Queen of Sheba to Solomon* actually offers him a way forward, both in his religious quest and in his work.

In 1843, the year of George Richmond's portrait entitled 'The Author of "Modern Painters"' (plate 3), Ruskin set out to prove that 'the truth of nature is a part of the truth of God' (3.141), with the corollary that 'the truths of nature are one eternal change – one infinite variety' (3.145) – evidence that she is 'constantly doing something beautiful for us' (3.156). The broad theological argument had been elaborated with a variety of emphases over the centuries,[5] and was familiar enough in the pulpits of South London. The Revd Thomas Dale, for example, Ruskin's former tutor, preached in St Matthew's Chapel, Denmark Hill:

The works of God in nature are constantly symbolical of the works of God in grace; and they who are acute to discern and diligent to explore the correspondence, may 'read sermons in stones, and find good in every thing.' . . . whatever is now a law was a miracle when first ordained.[6]

On this foundation the anonymous young 'Graduate of Oxford' raised an elaborate edifice in defence of Turner which emulated Locke, as the 'Synopsis of Contents' in *Modern Painters* 1 immediately indicates. The reference to 'the Shechinah of the blue' suggests that the implied reader is widely read, while the accuracy of its application to the sky beyond the 'central cloud region' and to the source of its 'glory', and the metaphor of 'fifty aisles penetrating through angelic chapels', typifies Ruskin's use of biblical and ecclesiastical sources – particularly those associated with

[5] See, for example, Hooker on 'the great phenomena of nature', quoted on p. 57 below; Richard Baxter: 'Compare also the excellencies of heaven, with those glorious works of creation, which our eyes now behold. What wisdom, power, and goodness, are manifested therein!': *The Saint's Everlasting Rest* (London: Caxton, n.d.), p. 278; John Ray, *The Wisdom of God as Manifested in the Works of the Creation* (1691); the eight Bridgewater Treatises (four of them by clergymen) 'On the Power, Wisdom, and Goodness of God, as manifested in the Creation', published in the 1830s; and Berkeleyan Christian Platonism, to which Coleridge was heir – see R. L. Brett, *Faith and Doubt: Religion and Secularization in Literature from Wordsworth to Larkin* (Cambridge and Macon: Clarke / Mercer University Press, 1997), p. 23.

[6] Thomas Dale, *A Memorial of Pastoral Ministrations: Sermons, principally on Points of Christian Experience, delivered in St. Matthew's Chapel, Denmark Hill* (London: Richardson, 1837), pp. 93–4. The contrary view was also expressed by Evangelicals such as the Revd Hugh McNeile, who stated that 'what fallen man can now read in himself, or in the book of nature, conveys no true and adequate information concerning God': *The Church and the Churches; or, The Church of God in Christ, and the Churches of Christ Militant here on Earth* (London: Hatchard, 1846), p. 110.

Plate 3. George Richmond, *The Author of 'Modern Painters'*, 1843

Solomon's temple and the wisdom books of the Old Testament[7] – which present nature as an artifact. The argument that when Ruskin quotes from the Bible he relies on 'holy writ to save him further thought' is simply incorrect.[8] For Ruskin, nature is God's culture, so that art and architecture – his subjects in the major early works – provide the very language with which also to describe the creation: nature has 'fifty pictures' and 'fifty aisles', and reveals the work of divine wisdom – 'the unwearied, exhaustless operation of the Infinite Mind'.

Four years earlier, when Ruskin was still an undergraduate at Oxford, his 'Remarks on the Present State of Meteorological Science', published in the *Transactions of the Meteorological Society*, had ended with an appeal for data to be sent in from all quarters, so that the 'vast multitude of beautiful and wonderful phenomena, by which the wisdom and benevolence of the Supreme Deity regulates the course of the times and the seasons' could be reduced to 'principle and order' (1.210). Now, in Part II of *Modern Painters* I – 'Of Truth' – his analysis 'Of Truth of Skies' (Section III), 'Earth' (IV), 'Water' (V), and 'Vegetation' (VI) finds in nature the same 'principle and order' as that described in the Book of Proverbs, traditionally ascribed to Solomon, where wisdom 'crieth at the gates':

> When he prepared the heavens, I was there: when he set a compass
>   upon the face of the depth:
> When he established the clouds above: when he strengthened the
>   fountains of the deep:
> When he gave to the sea his decree, that the waters should not pass his
>   commandment: when he appointed the foundations of the earth;
> Then I was by him . . .
>
> (Proverbs 8.27–30)

While clerical members of the Meteorological Society, and indeed of the Geological Society,[9] including Evangelicals, would have understood the structure of *Modern Painters* I, and been at home with Ruskin's comments on 'the grace and infinity of nature's foliage, with every vista a cathedral, and every bough a revelation' (3.169), they would also have recognized the danger of analogies drawn from architecture – and even more those from painting – tending towards idolatry and thus Tractarianism or,

---

[7] The examples he offers from Turner are Old Testament subjects: the *Babylon* (1832–4) – 'Now this is nature!' (3.383) – and *Jerusalem: Solomon's Pools* (c.1832–4), both from Finden's *Landscape Illustrations of the Bible*, which Ruskin consulted regularly.

[8] *Ruskin Today*, ed. Kenneth Clark (London: Murray, 1964), p. xv.

[9] Ruskin became a Fellow in 1840.

God forbid, the Scarlet Woman of Rome.[10] Ruskin was himself accused by the Revd John Eagles in *Blackwood's* of 'somewhat blaspheming the Divine attributes' when he described Turner in the first edition as 'sent as a prophet of God to reveal to men the mysteries of His universe, standing, like the great angel of the Apocalypse, clothed with a cloud, and with a rainbow upon his head, and with the sun and stars given into his hand' (3.254; Revelation 10.1). (The charge of blasphemy becomes more pointed if the angel is either 'Christ himself, or an emblematic display of his glory', as the author of the commentary consulted by Ruskin believed.[11]) The barb prompted Ruskin to omit the passage from the second edition. It was what he later called the 'young-mannishness' of volume I (3.668) that made him vulnerable to criticism, as he became over-enthusiastic on the theme which was to remain at the heart of *Modern Painters* – that of mediation, between God and man, heaven and earth, through divine revelation, through natural phenomena and through human agency.

In the fifth and final volume of *Modern Painters*, Ruskin stated that 'perhaps the best and truest piece of work done' in volume I was the 'account given in it of the rain-cloud' (7.175). Having described in that account the 'legitimate rain-cloud, with its ragged and spray-like edge, its veily transparency, and its columnar burden of blessing', Ruskin argues that 'neither it, nor anything like it or approaching it, occurs in any painting of the old masters' that he has ever seen (3.396–7), and that it is beyond the powers currently possessed by engravers (3.400). The demonstration that follows of Turner's superiority in his treatment of the rain-cloud over Gaspar Poussin, among others, is unremarkable, until the long final paragraph that is, where Ruskin describes the ever-changing wonders of nature and, in the manner of a preacher, demands repeatedly of his reader: 'Has Claude given this?' (3.415–19). 'Stand upon the peak of some isolated mountain at daybreak', he urges, and watch the effects of cloud and light by day and by night: 'Has Claude given this?' Finally, after the dawn,

wait yet for one hour, until the east again becomes purple, and the heaving mountains, rolling against it in darkness, like waves of a wild sea, are drowned

---

[10] See chapter 4 below. One reviewer thought that the author's 'enthusiastic admiration' approached, if it did not 'absolutely touch upon idolatry of Turner': '*Modern Painters*', *The Church of England Quarterly Review*, 15 (January 1844), 213–21 (p. 221). Compare the reviewer of volume II who commented that the painter who is a 'student of Nature' with a 'want of purity of heart' may be punished by his being permitted to 'bow in sensual adoration of his model': '*Modern Painters*, Vol.II', *The Ecclesiastic*, 3 (April 1847), 212–22 (p. 222).

[11] Scott, *The Holy Bible*, VI, Revelation 10.1.

one by one in the glory of its burning: watch the white glaciers blaze in their winding paths about the mountains, like mighty serpents with scales of fire: watch the columnar peaks of solitary snow, kindling downwards, chasm by chasm, each in itself a new morning; their long avalanches cast down in keen streams brighter than the lightning, sending each his tribute of driven snow, like altar-smoke, up to the heaven; the rose-light of the silent domes flushing that heaven about them and above them, piercing with purer light through its purple lines of lifted cloud, casting a new glory on every wreath as it passes by, until the whole heaven, one scarlet canopy, is interwoven with a roof of waving flame, and tossing, vault beyond vault, as with the drifted wings of many companies of angels: and then, when you can look no more for gladness, and when you are bowed down with fear and love of the Maker and Doer of this, tell me who has best delivered this His message unto men! (3.418–19)

This *tour de force* has a specific provenance in contemporary hymnody which Ruskin's first readers would have recognized, but which twentieth-century commentators have not. Ruskin echoes four famous hymns, all written between 1826 and 1834, when 'literary hymns', strongly influenced by the Romantic movement, featured in a great revival of hymnody within the Church of England:[12] '*New* every *morning* is the love', by Keble; 'Praise, my soul, the King of Heaven, / To His feet thy *tribute* bring', by Henry Francis Lyte; 'O worship the King All-glorious above . . . Whose robe is the light, Whose *canopy* space', by Sir Robert Grant; and 'Holy, Holy, Holy! Lord God Almighty!', by Bishop Heber:

> Holy, Holy, Holy! all the Saints adore Thee,
>   *Casting down* their golden crowns around the glassy sea;
> Cherubim and Seraphim *falling down* before Thee,
>   Which wert, and art, and evermore shalt be.[13]

In 1839, Ruskin's winning Newdigate prize poem, in which he referred to Heber's *Narrative of a Journey . . . from Calcutta to Bombay* (1828; 2.100), had been edited by Keble, then Professor of Poetry at Oxford (2.xxvi) and a leading Tractarian; and Keble's *The Christian Year*, which opens with 'New every morning', was later to accompany Ruskin to the Alps, like the poems of George Herbert (*D*, 498). Heber's morning hymn is based on Revelation 4, in which the throne of God is described (here there is no need of a temple[14]), and ends with praise of the 'Blessed

---

[12] See Ian Bradley, *Abide with Me: The World of Victorian Hymns* (London: SCM, 1997), pp. 15, 19, 21–2. Ruskin quotes the first verse of 'Addison's well-known hymn' – 'The spacious firmament on high' – in a footnote to 'The Firmament' in volume IV (6.112).

[13] See *Hymns Ancient and Modern, for Use in the Services of the Church*, standard edn (London: Clowes, 1916), nos. 4, 298, 167, 160.

[14] 'There is no temple in [the New Jerusalem]; for the Lord God Almighty, and the Lamb, are the temple of it': Baxter, *The Saint's Everlasting Rest*, p. 268.

Trinity' which anticipates both this particular Ruskin passage and the sectional organization of *Modern Painters* I: 'All Thy works shall praise Thy Name, in earth, and sky, and sea.' Some of Grant's key words – 'power', 'splendour', 'girded', 'robe', as well as 'canopy' – are also Ruskin's (3.93, 287, 469, 416), and his last verse, ending, 'And sweetly distils in the dew and the rain', would have made a fitting epigraph for the chapter on the rain-cloud.

In the early nineteenth century, full use was made of the performative nature of hymns, emphasizing the belief that acts of worship in church or chapel are also going on simultaneously in heaven, as in Lyte's 'Pleasant are Thy courts above', for example. In 'Holy! Holy! Holy!', the rhyming of the durative 'casting' and 'falling' epitomizes this sense of synchronic worship, here 'below' and there 'above'.[15] In the Ruskin passage the present tense is also durative ('heaving', 'rolling', 'kindling'), while the offering of a song of praise by the creation itself echoes the *Benedicite* from the Book of Common Prayer ('O ye Mountains and Hills, bless ye the Lord'). In God's vast temple of nature, with its purple curtains, columns, altar-smoke, domes, canopy, roof, vault, and companies of angels (the cherubim), a constant but every-varying series of mediations between heaven and earth is enacted.[16] In the description of the feast of the dedication of the temple in Jerusalem (1 Kings 8), which Ruskin learnt by heart as a boy, the cloud fills the house of the Lord, and Solomon says: 'Then hear thou in heaven, and forgive the sin of thy servants, and of thy people Israel, that thou teach them the good way wherein they should walk, and give rain upon thy land, which thou hast given to thy people for an inheritance' (v.36).

Thus far Ruskin is on safe ground, as nature is incapable of idolatry or blasphemy. It is in the final words of the passage that he makes himself vulnerable to accusations of blasphemy, where he presents Turner, seemingly translated in being unnamed, as a messenger of God. Like Moses in Exodus, Solomon in 1 Kings, and the angel in the Revelation, Turner's role is, for Ruskin, that of an intermediary between God and

---

[15] See Michael Wheeler, *Death and the Future Life in Victorian Literature and Theology* (Cambridge: Cambridge University Press, 1990), pp. 144–7.

[16] In a cancelled passage of the chapter 'Of Truth of Vegetation' in the first and second editions, Ruskin wrote of the 'sensation of absolute impotence ... which comes over the artist in his forest walks, as he sees the floor, and the pillars, and the roof of the great temple, one labyrinth of loveliness, one wilderness of perfection, with the chequering sunbeams dancing before him like mocking spirits' (3.574). Compare *The Woods were God's First Temple* (1867), a painting by Thomas Moran, one of Ruskin's American followers, and William Cullen Bryant's poem, 'A Forest Hymn' (1824): Nancy K. Anderson, *Thomas Moran* (Washington: National Gallery of Art; New Haven and London: Yale University Press, 1997), pp. 29–30.

man, through his representation of the creation, itself full of signs of mediation and the covenant between God and man – whether it be the rain-cloud's 'columnar burden of blessing', or the 'pure and holy hills, treated as a link between heaven and earth' (3.449), or the 'rejoicing trees of La Riccia', 'purple, and crimson, and scarlet, like the curtains of God's tabernacle', 'every separate leaf quivering with buoyant and burning life' (3.279). In the chapter on 'The Region of the Cirrus', Ruskin describes the 'neglected upper sky' as Turner's 'peculiar and favourite field: he has watched its every modification, and given its every phase and feature; at all hours, in all seasons, he has followed its passions and its changes, and has brought down and laid open to the world another apocalypse of Heaven' (3.363).

II

Eagles, a harsh critic of Turner, was one of Ruskin's main targets in *Modern Painters* I, as he may have detected when reading Ruskin's allusion to I Corinthians: 'Precisely as we are shallow in our knowledge, vulgar in our feeling, and contracted in our views of principles, will the works of this artist be stumbling-blocks or foolishness to us' (3.610).[17] Perhaps it was Eagles's criticism of him for 'somewhat blaspheming the Divine attributes' that prompted Ruskin to pay such close attention to them in *Modern Painters* II (1846).[18] Ruskin rarely left a subject alone, however, even after the publication of his most thorough treatment of it,[19] and in the following year we find him thinking further, in a Sunday diary entry: 'In the reading of the psalms this morning, I was struck by the 5th & 6th verses of the v, where the abhorrence or contrarity [sic] of God to evil is expressed as regards his three attributes of wisdom, truth, and love.'[20] The first two divine attributes are particularly important to Ruskin during the period of *Modern Painters*, as, for example, in *The Seven Lamps of Architecture* (1849), where he writes, in 'The Lamp of Truth': 'The Divine Wisdom is, and can be, shown to us only in its meeting and con-tending with the difficulties which are voluntarily, and *for the sake of that*

---

[17] 'But we preach Christ crucified, unto the Jews a stumblingblock, and unto the Greeks foolish-ness; But unto them which are called, both Jews and Greeks, Christ the power of God, and the wisdom of God' (I Corinthians 1.23–4).   [18] See chapter 3 below.

[19] On 7 August 1847, for example, he notes in his diary a reference that is 'useful' to his 'chapter on penetrative imagination', published the previous year: Lancaster MS 5c, Diaries, fol. 75; *D*, 359. The reference duly appeared as a footnote to the second edition of 1849 (4.251).

[20] Diary for Sunday evening, 1 August 1847: Lancaster MS 5c, fol.69; compare *D*, 354. Note the verse that follows: 'But as for me, I will come into thy house in the multitude of thy mercy: and in thy fear will I worship toward thy holy temple' (Psalms 5.7).

contest, admitted by the Divine Omnipotence' (8.71). Ruskin had studied Proverbs on the subject of truth on the French tour of 1849 (*D*, 442), and was to make extensive notes on Proverbs in relation to wisdom, teaching and authority in the autumn of 1850, taking his favourite description of wisdom as his point of departure for notes towards an unpublished essay on 'The Principles of Religion', and for a section of his published *Notes on the Construction of Sheepfolds* (1851):

as I opened the Bible to day I was peculiarly struck with the well known – never enough known, passage Prov. II. 3. 4. "If thou seekest her as silver, and searchest for her, as for hid treasures", showing that we must indeed do this – in order to understand at all, and how few do it: In the Bible itself, probably the poorest & simplest readers do it the most – for more learned readers raise cavilling question, but not earnest & longing question, and so the simplest understand the best.[21]

Ruskin was to be confirmed in this belief in December 1853, in discussions with Beveridge, his 'comparatively unlearned' doctor in Edinburgh, whose 'pure Bible reading' set a new standard for his own, so that he felt a sense of shame in noticing, as far as he recollected for the first time,

that "Solomon" meant peaceable. How beautifully is this connected with, 'The wisdom that cometh from above is first pure, then peaceable' [James 3.17]
I have hitherto endeavoured too much to learn the Bible by heart, (more, I fear from vanity than any other feeling) instead of diving into it as I read.
I always begin things too eagerly and carelessly, but have prayed I may go on with this.[22]

Thus Solomon figured prominently not only in Ruskin's early learning of passages from the Bible,[23] but also in his recognition in his mid-thirties of the need to 'dive into it' as he read. From the mid-1850s Solomon became an increasingly important presence in his reflections and writing, and finally one of his most powerful *alter egos*.

In the *Modern Painters* period, Solomon's traditional identification as

---

[21] Lancaster MS 5c, Diaries, fol. 152 (compare *D*, 466–7 and 12.542–4); he re-examines the text on fol.159; see also fols 158–9 on wisdom, Solomon and the 'Fear of the Lord'. For Ruskin's further notes on Proverbs in 1850, see Beinecke MS, Architecture note-book, Italy, 1850–1 [i.e. 1849–50], fols. 57–9, 65. (In an appendix to *Modern Painters* III Ruskin argued that 'the Proverbs of Solomon' were more useful to the person who wants philosophy '*for use*' than the 'German metaphysicians and divines' (5.425).) He also wrote a 90-page commentary on Job in Venice in 1850 (10.xxxviii).

[22] Lancaster MS 8, Diaries, fol. 77; compare *D*, 481. Scott's commentary on *The Holy Bible* gives a cross-reference from James 3.17 to 1 Chronicles 22.9, and there glosses 'Solomon': 'That is, *Peaceable*'. Solomon's 'first measure concerned the maintenance of *salom*': Leonidas Kalugila, *The Wise King: Studies in Royal Wisdom as Divine Revelation in the Old Testament and its Environment*, Coniectanea Biblica, Old Testament Series, 15 (Lund: Gleerup, 1980), p. 107.

[23] See p. 6 above.

the first naturalist is as significant to Ruskin as the prophet king's divinely inspired wisdom. In Ruskin's lecture on 'Turner and his Works', for example, delivered in Edinburgh in November 1853, he argues that the language of the Bible is distinguished from that of other early literature by its delight in nature imagery:

Then at the central point of Jewish prosperity, you have the first great natural-ist the world ever saw, Solomon; not permitted, indeed, to anticipate, in writing, the discoveries of modern times, but so gifted as to show us that heavenly wisdom is manifested as much in the knowledge of the hyssop that springeth out of the wall [1 Kings 4.33] as in political and philosophical speculation. (12.106)[24]

In the lecture that follows, on 'Pre-Raphaelitism', Ruskin's characteris-tically dramatic account of the moment at which Raphael wrote upon the walls of the Vatican the *'Mene, Tekel, Upharsin* of the Arts of Christianity' – 'And from that spot, and from that hour, the intellect and art of Italy date their degradation' (12.148) – is followed by commentary in which he argues that Raphael wrongly placed the Athenian philoso-phers above Solomon and St Paul, those 'greater masters by the last of whom that school was rebuked, – those who received their wisdom from heaven itself, in the vision of Gibeon, [1 Kings 3.5–9] and the lightning of Damascus [Acts 9.3, 17.15–23]' (12.149–50). And in *Modern Painters* III (1856) Ruskin relates Ezekiel's vision in exile of the 'Temple of God' to the three virtues associated with the meadow grass, the reed and flax, in one of his more complex passages of biblical interpretation (5.292–3).

In volume IV (1856), which contains Part V of *Modern Painters* ('Of Mountain Beauty'), Ruskin turns to the symbolism associated with Solomon's temple for analogies with which to describe the works of 'the great Architect of the mountains' (6.180) as signs of divine wisdom, truth and love, and of the covenant between God and his people. Following Ruskin's explanation that he is going to have to 'trace, with more obser-vant patience, the ground which was marked out in the first volume', and that this time his analysis of Turner will take the truth of earth, skies, water and vegetation in a different sequence (6.104–5), the chapter enti-tled 'The Firmament' contains commentary on Genesis 1.6[25] with which Ruskin was later to remain content (6.106), and which was reprinted in

---

[24] The identification of the hyssop plant referred to in the Bible was the subject of fresh research in the 1840s, reported in *The Pictorial Bible*, standard edn rev., ed. John Kitto, 4 vols. (London: Knight, 1847–9), I, 198.

[25] 'And God said, Let there be a firmament in the midst of the waters, and let it divide the waters from the waters'. For Ruskin's first puzzled notes on verse 7, in 1849, see Lancaster MS 6, Diaries, fol. 264; on the verso Ruskin has scribbled, years later: 'My first thought of Firmament'. See his further notes in Edinburgh in November 1853: Lancaster MS 8, Diaries, fols 77–8, 82v; *D*, 481–2.

two of the later anthologies of selected passages from *Modern Painters* – *Frondes Agrestes* (1875) and *Cœli Enarrant* (1885). In a less impressionist account of the mediating function of the rain-cloud than that offered in volume I – dividing 'water in its collective and tangible state, from water in its divided and aerial state' (6.108) – he argues that 'the most simple and natural interpretation' of the words 'firmament' (expansion)[26] and heaven is 'the likeliest in general to be the true one':

> Next, if we try this interpretation in the theological sense of the word *Heaven*, and examine whether the clouds are spoken of as God's dwelling-place, we find God going before the Israelites in a pillar of cloud; revealing Himself in a cloud on Sinai; appearing in a cloud on the mercy seat; filling the Temple of Solomon with the cloud when its dedication is accepted [I Kings 8.10] . . .
> understand by the "Heavens" the veil of clouds above the earth, and the expression is neither hyperbolical nor obscure; it is pure, plain, and accurate truth . . . By accepting the words in their simple sense, we are thus led to apprehend the immediate presence of the Deity, and His purpose of manifesting Himself as near us whenever the storm-cloud stoops upon its course . . . (6.108–10)

The tabernacle and the temple provide the key to Ruskin's characteristically literalist biblical interpretation that follows, where he brings out the vivid immediacy of texts describing God's covenant with man, and what he calls the 'mediatorial ministries' of the clouds:

> This, I believe, is the ordinance of the firmament; and it seems to me that in the midst of the material nearness of these heavens God means us to acknowledge His own immediate presence as visiting, judging, and blessing us. "The earth shook, the heavens also dropped, at the presence of God." [Psalms 68.8] "He doth set His bow in the cloud", [Genesis 9.13] and thus renews, in the sound of every drooping swathe of rain, His promises of everlasting love. "In them hath He set a *tabernacle* for the sun"; [Psalms 19.4] whose burning ball, which without the firmament would be seen but as an intolerable and scorching circle in the blackness of vacuity, is by that firmament surrounded with gorgeous service, and tempered by mediatorial ministries; by the firmament of clouds the golden pavement is spread for his chariot wheels at morning; by the firmament of clouds the temple is built for his presence to fill with light at noon; by the firmament of clouds the purple veil is closed at evening round the sanctuary of his rest; by the mists of the firmament his implacable light is divided, and its separated fierceness appeased into the soft blue that fills the depth of distance with its bloom, and the flush with which the mountains burn as they drink the overflowing of the dayspring. And in this tabernacling of the unendurable sun with men, through the shadows of the firmament, God would seem to set

---

[26] Compare 'The word, translated *firmament*, and *expansion* . . . is used for the whole space which surrounds the earth': Scott, *The Holy Bible*, I, Genesis 1.6.

forth the stooping of His own majesty to men, upon the *throne* of the firmament.
As the Creator of all the worlds, and the Inhabiter of eternity, we cannot behold
Him; but, as the Judge of the earth and the Preserver of men, those heavens are
indeed His dwelling-place. "Swear not, neither by heaven, for it is God's throne;
nor by the earth, for it is His footstool." [Matthew 5.34–5] And all those pass-
ings to and fro of fruitful shower and grateful shade, and all those visions of
silver palaces built about the horizon, and voices of moaning winds and threatening thunders, and glories of coloured robe and cloven ray, are but to deepen
in our hearts the acceptance, and distinctness, and dearness of the simple
words, "Our Father, which art in heaven." [Matthew 6.9] (6.113–14)

Whereas in his Alpine *Benedicite* in volume I, discussed earlier, Ruskin
maps nature on to the Bible, describing the mountains in terms of the
tabernacle and the temple, and echoing contemporary hymnody, here
he maps the Bible on to nature, treating the workings of the God of
wisdom, truth and love more directly and prophetically.

'The Firmament' serves as an introduction to Ruskin's main religious
theme in volume IV, spelled out in the subsequent chapter on 'The Dry
Land': 'it is necessary for all men to consider . . . the depth of the wisdom
and love which are manifested in the ordinances of the hills' (6.117).
Sensitive to the fact that he could be criticized for presuming to
comment on the divine attributes, as he had been thirteen years earlier,
or on God's purpose in not making the mountains permanent, for
example, he adds a telling footnote in which he argues that 'Wisdom can
only be demonstrated in its ends . . . He who in a morbid modesty sup-
poses that he is incapable of apprehending any of the purposes of God,
renders himself also incapable of witnessing His wisdom' (6.134). Time
and decay are part of the divine plan, he believes, 'and the Builder of
the temple for ever stands beside His work, appointing the stone that is
to fall, and the pillar that is to be abased' (6.180–1). The 'present
confirmation of the earth appears dictated . . . by supreme wisdom and
kindness' (6.177), as for example in the 'provision for the safety of the
inhabitants of the high mountain regions' (6.208). To those with eyes to
see, there is 'wealth in every falling rock, and wisdom in every talking
wave' (6.385).

When he turns to the question of the influence of mountain landscape upon human beings, he argues in 'The Mountain Gloom' that
'where the beauty and wisdom of the Divine working are most manifested, there also are manifested most clearly the terror of God's wrath,
and inevitableness of His power' (6.416). In the closing pages of 'The
Mountain Glory', however, he writes of the mountains as the earth's

'natural cathedrals, or natural altars, overlaid with gold, and bright with broidered work of flowers, and with their clouds resting on them as the smoke of a continual sacrifice' (6.457); and he ends the chapter, and thus the book, in typically homiletic mode, with a haunting type with which to send the reader out into the world:

Nor, perhaps, should we have unprofitably entered into the mind of the earlier ages, if among our other thoughts, as we watch the chains of the snowy mountains rise on the horizon, we should sometimes admit the memory of the hour in which their Creator, among their solitudes, entered on His travail for the salvation of our race; and indulge the dream, that as the flaming and trembling mountains of the earth seem to be the monuments of the manifesting of His terror on Sinai, [Exodus 19.16–18] – these pure and white hills, near to the heaven, and sources of all good to the earth, are the appointed memorials of that Light of His Mercy, that fell, snow-like, on the Mount of Transfiguration. [Luke 9.28–9] (6.465–6)

We will return to 'The Mountain Gloom' and 'The Mountain Glory' in chapter 6, as it was only two years after the publication of *Modern Painters* IV, in 1858, that Ruskin's religious crisis in Turin coincided with a radical change in his views on the relationship between 'Romanism' and 'Mountain Gloom'. For the moment the focus is to be upon the final volume of *Modern Painters* (1860), published a further two years after the 'Queen of Sheba crash' (35.497), where Ruskin's references to Solomon's temple and the wisdom tradition reflect his current estimate of Turner's genius, altered in the light of his exhaustive (and exhausting) work on the Turner Bequest in the National Gallery in 1858, and his positive response to Veronese in Turin later the same year.

III

The first half of volume V – containing Part VI, 'Of Leaf Beauty', and Part VII, 'Of Cloud Beauty' – completes what Ruskin calls the 'second division' of *Modern Painters*, in which he examines how far art may be and has been 'obedient to the laws of physical beauty' (7.203). It is hardly surprising, then, to find continuities between Parts VI and VII and earlier volumes; but there are also signs of a sea-change in Ruskin's religious views. In his description of the Bay of Uri, for example, in the penultimate chapter of Part VI, he again likens a mountain scene to a cathedral, writing of the shore:

Steepest there on its western side, the walls of its rocks ascend to heaven. Far in the blue of evening, like a great cathedral pavement, lies the lake in its darkness;

and you may hear the whisper of innumerable falling waters return from the hollows of the cliff, like the voices of a multitude praying under their breath. From time to time the beat of a wave, slow lifted, where the rocks lean over the black depth, dies heavily as the last note of a requiem. (7.114)

The fact, however, that God's natural temple can now be Catholic indicates the distance that Ruskin has travelled since writing 'The Mountain Gloom', where the anti-Romanist prejudice instilled in him in childhood was still in evidence. Now it is the Protestant tourist, encoded as 'the stranger', who is contrasted unfavourably with the pastoral Catholic of Uri:[27]

> I have seen that it is possible for the stranger to pass through this great chapel, with its font of waters, and mountain pillars, and vaults of clouds, without being touched by one noble thought, or stirred by any sacred passion; but for those who received from its waves the baptism of their youth, and learned beneath its rocks the fidelity of their manhood, and watched amidst its clouds the likeness of the dream of life, with the eyes of age – for these I will not believe that the mountain shrine was built, or the calm of its forest-shadows guarded by their God, in vain.

In the last chapter of Part VII, 'The Angel of the Sea', Ruskin comments that he has little to add descriptively to the chapter on the rain-cloud in volume I: 'But the question before us now is, not who has drawn the rain-cloud best, but if it were worth drawing at all' (7.175). In answering his own question, Ruskin still turns to the Psalms when explaining how Turner's drawings of Sinai and Lebanon for Finden's Bible show 'the opposite influences of the Law and the Gospel' (7.191–2); and he still ends the chapter, and thus the 'second division' of *Modern Painters*, with detailed commentary on Psalm 19 ('The heavens declare the glory of God'), glossing the 'tabernacle for the sun' (v.4) as 'literally, a tabernacle, or curtained tent, with its veils and its hangings; also of the colours of His desert tabernacle – blue, and purple, and scarlet' (7.197), and reading 'the testimony of the Lord is sure' (v.7) as further teaching on the nature of wisdom, as he understand it: 'Bright as the sun beyond all the earth-cloud, [the testimony] makes wise the simple; all wisdom being assured in perceiving it and trusting it; all wisdom brought to nothing which does not perceive it' (7.198). Yet earlier in the chapter, where Ruskin discusses his central theme of mediation, his religious perspective is much broader, encompassing what he formerly regarded as pagan gods:

---

[27] Twenty years later, Ruskin's projected history of Christendom entitled *Our Fathers Have Told Us* was to have included a book on the pastoral forms of Catholicism entitled 'The Bay of Uri' (33.lxv).

It would be strange, indeed, if there were no beauty in the phenomena by which this great renovating and purifying work is done. And it is done almost entirely by the great Angel of the Sea – rain; – the Angel, observe, the messenger sent to a special place on a special errand . . . Far away in the south the strong river Gods have all hasted, and gone down to the sea. Wasted and burning, white furnaces of blasting sand, their broad beds lie ghastly and bare; but here in the moss-lands, the soft wings of the Sea Angel droop still with dew, and the shadows of their plumes falter on the hills . . . (7.178)

And the discussion in the middle of the chapter focuses upon Greek rather than Christian religion, leading to the important observation that to Turner (who knew 'most of the great Greek traditions'), 'as to the Greek, the storm-clouds seemed messengers of fate' (7.189). For Turner, Ruskin now implies, Christian and pagan religious sources were of equal importance: the drawings of Salisbury and Stonehenge, for example, reflect Turner's being struck by these 'monuments of the two great religions of England – Druidical and Christian' (7.190).[28]

Thus the ground is prepared for Ruskin's tactical withdrawal in the 'last division' of *Modern Painters*, where he has to consider 'the relations of art to God and man: its work in the help of human beings, and service of their Creator' (7.203), from his construction of a Christian Turner which had seemed so essential to the project in 1843, but is now untenable. Although Ruskin's own spiritual depression in the second half of the 1850s, and his loss of belief in a future life, contributed to this change of view,[29] his despair at the failure of the Church to preach the gospel of Christ had an even more profound effect upon his interpretation of Turner's life and work at this time. On his way to the Continent in May 1859, he states in a letter to the Revd Daniel Moore, Melvill's successor at Camden Church, that he believes the 'entire modern church system to be a dream – & worse';[30] and the following August he writes to his friend Charles Eliot Norton of Harvard, from Thun in Switzerland: 'I don't believe in Evangelicalism – and my Evangelical (once) friends now look upon me with as much horror as on one of the possessed Gennesaret pigs – Nor do I believe in the Pope – and some Roman Catholic friends, who had great hopes for me, think I ought to be

[28] Compare Holman Hunt's *A Converted British Family Sheltering a Christian Missionary from the Persecution of the Druids* (RA 1850).

[29] See, for example, Ruskin's letter to Thomas Lupton dated 4 December 1856, in which he explains that the 'next world' is 'inconceivable' to him (Yale ALS). Helsinger goes so far as to read Ruskin on Turner's loss of hope as pseudo-autobiography: 'The "Alas, for Turner" is an "Alas" for Ruskin too' (p. 235).

[30] Morgan MA 2186 (3); compare Ruskin's letter to Browning of 29 March 1858 (36.280).

burned.'[31] His jaundiced view of the Church of England shapes one of his most effective pairings in *Modern Painters*, 'The Two Boyhoods', in which the contrasts between the art of Giorgione and Turner are explained partly in terms of the religious life that they *saw* in fifteenth-century Venice and nineteenth-century London. Giorgione grew up where there was a religion 'towering over all the city – many-buttressed – luminous in marble stateliness, as the dome of our Lady of Safety shines over the sea', whereas the young Turner saw 'faith, of any national kind, shut up from one Sunday to the next, not artistically beautiful even in those Sabbatical exhibitions; its paraphernalia being chiefly of high pews, heavy elocution, and cold grimness of behaviour'; St Mark ruled over life, in St Mark's Place, but the 'Saint of London' ruled over death, in St Paul's Churchyard (7.381–3).

In 'The Nereid's Guard' Ruskin examines the 'gloomy tendency of mind' in Turner's early work (7.389), arguing that in *The Goddess of Discord choosing the apple of contention in the Garden of Hesperides* (1806), 'our English painter's first great religious picture' and 'exponent of our English faith', the 'Mammon dragon' on the hill-top 'is our British Madonna', it appears (7.407–8, 420). This analysis sets the agenda for Ruskin's social writing of the 1860s, and his satire of the national worship of the 'Goddess of Getting-on' (18.447–8).[32] It is grounded, however, in his views on religion in modern Europe. In volume III he claimed that 'there never yet was a generation of men . . . who, taken as a body, so woefully fulfilled the words "having no hope, and without God in the world," [Ephesians 2.12] as the present civilized European race' (5.322); and in 'The Wings of the Lion' in volume V he contrasts Venetian Catholicism with English Protestantism, pointing out that Venetians usually choose to be portrayed on their knees, whereas an English gentleman 'will assuredly not let himself be painted praying' (7.288). Now he moves on in 'The Hesperid Ægle' to take *Apollo and Python* (1811; plate 4) as the last major Turner to receive detailed critical attention in *Modern Painters*. And the source of Turner's spiritual malaise is brought starkly into view when the outward and visible signs of the Church of England, familiar from his childhood, are uncomfortably juxtaposed with the artist's lack of hope:

The Mammon dragon was armed with adamant; but this dragon of decay is a mere colossal worm: wounded, he bursts asunder in the midst, and melts to

---

[31] *The Correspondence of John Ruskin and Charles Eliot Norton*, ed. John Lewis Bradley and Ian Ousby (Cambridge University Press, 1987), p. 53.
[32] See Landow, *Aesthetic and Critical Theories*, p. 422.

Plate 4 J. M. W. Turner, *Apollo and Python*, 1811

pieces, rather than dies, vomiting smoke – a smaller serpent-worm rising out of his blood.

Alas, for Turner! This smaller serpent-worm, it seemed, he could not conceive to be slain. In the midst of all the power and beauty of nature, he still saw this death-worm writhing among the weeds. . .

How this sadness came to be persistent over Turner, and to conquer him, we shall see in a little while. It is enough for us to know at present that our most wise and Christian England, with all her appurtenances of school-porch and church-spire, had so disposed her teaching as to leave this somewhat notable child of hers without even cruel Pandora's gift.

He was without hope. (7.420–1)

The impact of this indictment of the Church in the late eighteenth and early nineteenth centuries is all the greater in its context in 'The Hesperid Æglé', where it follows Ruskin's theological analysis of colour, reserved for this climactic moment in the final volume of *Modern Painters* and awkwardly spilling over into an enormous footnote in which he anthologizes passages on the subject from his other works. For here Ruskin presents a Turner whose spirituality could have flourished if he had been nurtured in a truly Christian country, and by a Church which taught the true gospel of Love – the third of the divine attributes we have been considering.

Had Turner died early, Ruskin suggests, he would have been 'spoken of, popularly, as a man who had no eye for colour' (7.410). After 1820, however, he becomes, 'separately and without rival, the painter of the loveliness and light of the creation' – that is, the Turner whom Ruskin originally set out to defend in *Modern Painters* 1. Claude and Cuyp had painted the 'sun*shine*', Turner alone, the 'sun *colour*'. Even in the *Apollo and Python*, a work which predates 1820, he 'must paint the sun in his strength': 'there is rose colour and blue on the clouds, as well as gold' (7.411). Moreover, only Turner perfected the 'colour chord' by means of scarlet, daring to paint the scarlet and purple sky tones, and discovering the 'scarlet *shadow*' – for Ruskin 'the glory of sunshine' (7.413). In the famous La Riccia passage from volume 1, quoted earlier, Ruskin had described the 'conflagration' of the autumnal trees as 'purple, and crimson, and scarlet, like the curtains of God's tabernacle' (3.279). Now, through a heavily weighted reference to Leviticus, he encourages the reader to study the laws associated with sacrifice (some of which took place at the door of the tabernacle) and to reflect upon their typological significance:

colour generally, but chiefly the scarlet, used with the hyssop, in the Levitical law, is the great sanctifying element of visible beauty, inseparably connected with purity and life.

I must not enter here into the solemn and far-reaching fields of thought which it would be necessary to traverse, in order to detect the mystical connection between life and love, set forth in that Hebrew system of sacrificial religion to which we may trace most of the received ideas respecting sanctity, consecration, and purification. This only I must hint to the reader – for his own following out – that if he earnestly examines the original sources from which our heedless popular language respecting the washing away of sins has been borrowed, he will find that the fountain, in which sins are indeed to be washed away, is that of love, not of agony. (7.414–17)

Ruskin's lecture on 'Turner and his Works' (1853), in which he admired Solomon's 'knowledge of the hyssop that springeth out of the wall' (I Kings 4.33), has already been cited. Now he refers to the laws regarding sacrifice for the cleansing of the leper: 'Then shall the priest command to take for him that is to be cleansed two birds alive and clean, and cedar wood, and scarlet, and hyssop; And the priest shall command that one of the birds be killed in an earthen vessel over running water' (Leviticus 14.4–5).[33] Thomas Scott explains that the two birds 'may signify Christ shedding his blood for sinners, and then rising and ascending into heaven, there to appear in the presence of God'.[34] Hyssop was the plant used for purification, as in the rite of the passover (Exodus 12.22), and in the crucifixion, when they filled a sponge with vinegar and 'put it upon hyssop, and put it to his mouth' (John 19.29). According to Christopher Wordsworth, scarlet was the colour of 'royalty and victory, the colour of joy and health as contrasted with the whiteness of the leper'; and it was 'the colour with which Christ was robed at His Passion'. Thus the Church Fathers were not fanciful in recognizing in these verses from Leviticus 'a type of the blood of Christ triumphing as a Royal Conqueror in His suffering'.[35] Ruskin's deprecatory reference to the Evangelicals' favourite phrases such as 'washed in the blood of the lamb' perhaps reflects his recent discussions with Spurgeon,[36] from which he seems to have emerged with a soteriology grounded in sanctification and redemption, and an understanding of baptism based upon texts such as Psalm 51.7: 'Purge me with hyssop, and I shall be clean: wash me, and I shall be whiter than snow.'[37]

---

[33] 'Note how *Scarlet* is emblem of Purity in cleansing with hyssop. Leviticus 14,4, &c', Lancaster MS 9, Diaries, fol. 116v – autumn 1854.   [34] Scott, *The Holy Bible*, I, Leviticus 14.4.

[35] *The Holy Bible*, with Notes and Introductions by Chr[istopher] Wordsworth, 6 vols. (London: Rivingtons, 1864–70), I, Pt. II, pp. 42–3.   [36] See pp. 127–31 below.

[37] In *Præterita* Ruskin comments on 'the too common Evangelical phrase, "washed in the blood of Christ" [Revelation 7.14], being, it seemed to me, if true at all, true of the earth and her purest snow, as well as of her purest creatures' (35.474).

Significantly, at this crucial point near the end of *Modern Painters*, Ruskin now draws together the divine attributes of wisdom, truth and love, explaining his theologically based colour theory through his favourite symbol of mediation – the cloud:[38]

But, without approaching the presence of this deeper meaning of the sign, the reader may rest satisfied with the connection given him directly in written words, between the cloud and its bow. [Genesis 9.13] The cloud, or firmament, as we have seen, signifies the ministration of the heavens to man. That ministration may be in judgment or mercy – in the lightning, or the dew. But the bow, or colour of the cloud, signifies always mercy, the sparing of life; such ministry of the heaven as shall feed and prolong life. And as the sunlight, undivided, is the type of the wisdom and righteousness of God, so divided, and softened into colour by means of the firmamental ministry, fitted to every need of man, as to every delight, and becoming one chief source of human beauty, by being part of the flesh of man; – thus divided, the sunlight is the type of the wisdom of God, becoming sanctification and redemption. Various in work – various in beauty – various in power.

Colour is, therefore, in brief terms, the type of love. (7.416–19)

Here, then, is the context in which Ruskin satirizes the 'wise and Christian England' that left Turner without hope: a theology which affirms sunlight as the type of divine wisdom and righteousness, and colour as the type of Love.[39]

Ruskin discussed the divine attribute of Love earlier in volume v, in 'The Dark Mirror', where his gloss on 'God is love' (1 John 4.16) – 'Look into the mirror, and you will see' – flows from his observation that 'the soul of man is still a mirror, wherein may be seen, darkly, the image of the mind of God' (7.260–1; 1 Corinthians 13.12). In sharp contrast to his position in volume 1, he can now write, in Carlylean or Arnoldian mode:

that flesh-bound volume is the only revelation that is, that was, or that can be. In that is the image of God painted; in that is the law of God written; in that is the promise of God revealed. Know thyself; for through thyself only thou canst know God . . .

Man is the sun of the world; more than the real sun. (7.262)

---

[38] For a detailed discussion of clouds in Ruskin see Caroline M. Blyth, 'The Art of Clouds: An Account of the Origins of *Cœli Enarrant* (1885) with Reference to the Wider Significance of Clouds in Ruskin's Work', unpublished doctoral dissertation, University of Oxford, 1995.

[39] For detailed discussion on these themes see Dinah Birch, '"The Sun is God": Ruskin's Solar Mythology', in *The Sun is God: Painting, Literature and Mythology in the Nineteenth Century*, ed. J. B. Bullen (Oxford: Clarendon Press, 1989), pp. 109–23, and Stephen Bann, 'The Colour in the Text: Ruskin's Basket of Strawberries', in *The Ruskin Polygon: Essays on the Imagination of John Ruskin*, ed. John Dixon Hunt and Faith M. Holland (Manchester University Press, 1982), pp. 122–36.

Indeed, at the beginning of 'The Lance of Pallas', he can state that man is 'the light of the world' (7.263). Christian art, he argues, 'erred by pride in its denial of the animal nature of man; and, in connection with all monkish and fanatical forms of religion, by looking always to another world instead of this' (7.264) – the opposite of the argument he put forward in volume III (5.72). He now states that 'the right faith of man is not intended to give him repose, but to enable him to do his work'; he should 'look stoutly into this world' (7.267). Many of Ruskin's religious 'difficulties' which he shared with other Victorian intellectuals in the 1850s were associated with the otherworldly perspective of orthodox Christianity. In the wisdom literature of the Old Testament, however, on which his whole critique of Victorian political economy was to be based in the 1860s, he could draw upon teaching with an anthropocentric viewpoint[40] which was less susceptible to modern criticism than other parts of the Bible such as the Pentateuch, as he does in the concluding chapter of *Modern Painters* v, entitled 'Peace', to which we finally turn.[41]

Developing the theme of the preceding chapters – the 'infidelity of England' (7.445) – Ruskin claims that 'this form of unbelief in God is connected with, and necessarily productive of, a precisely equal unbelief in man' (7.448). In its neglect of William Holman Hunt, England almost did not get the *The Finding of the Saviour in the Temple* (1860; 7.451); and Ruskin can hardly trust himself to imagine 'What Turner might have done for us, had he received help and love, instead of disdain' (7.454). 'So far as in it lay', he believes,

this century has caused every one of its great men, whose hearts were kindest, and whose spirits most perceptive of the work of God, to die without hope: – Scott, Keats, Byron, Shelley, Turner. Great England, of the Iron-heart now, not of the Lion-heart; for these souls of her children an account may perhaps be one day required of her. [Luke 11.49–50]

She has not yet read often enough that old story of the Samaritan's mercy. [Luke 10.30–7] (7.455)

The affirmation of faith that follows challenges the infidelity of England, and England's Established Church:

So far as *they* are concerned, I do not fear for them; – there being one Priest [Hebrews 7] Who never passes by [Luke 10.31]. The longer I live, the more clearly I see how all souls are in His hand – the mean and the great. Fallen on the earth in their baseness, or fading as the mist of morning in their goodness;

---

[40] See J. C. Rylaarsdam, 'Hebrew Wisdom', in *Peake's Commentary on the Bible*, ed. Matthew Black and H. H. Rowley (London: Nelson, 1962), pp. 386–90.

[41] Ruskin's father was pleased with this final chapter (17.xxi).

– still in the hand of the potter as the clay [Jeremiah 18.6; Romans 9.21], and in the temple of their master as the cloud [I Kings 8.10]. It was not the mere bodily death that He conquered – that death had no sting [1 Corinthians 15.55]. It was this spiritual death which He conquered, so that at last it should be swallowed up – mark the word – not in life; but in victory [1 Corinthians 15.54]. As the dead body shall be raised to life, so also the defeated soul to victory, if only it has been fighting on its Master's side, has made no covenant with death; nor itself bowed its forehead for his seal. Blind from the prison-house [Judges 16.25; Isaiah 42.7], maimed from the battle [Luke 14.13], or mad from the tombs [Luke 8.27], their souls shall surely yet sit, astonished, at His feet Who giveth peace [John 14.27]. (7.456)

In *Modern Painters* I Ruskin had celebrated the 'Shechinah of the blue' and placed the reader in nature's temple. Some reviewers criticized him, however, for his lack of interest in and concern for human beings.[42] (Ruskin's descriptions of landscape, unlike Turners' pictures, are reminiscent of many of his drawings of streets and market squares: they are deserted.) Seventeen years later his concern is for the great men of his Age, and Christ's promise of entry to the kingdom that is foreshadowed in I Kings 8 – the Shekinah 'in the temple of their master as the cloud'. Ruskin emphasizes that he himself is not 'hopeless', though his 'hope may be as Veronese's: the dark-veiled' (7.457; compare 7.291).[43] The kingdom for which 'we are bid to ask' it is 'not in our power to bring; but it is, to receive' (7.459). Reminding the reader that God calls us to our labour, as Christ to our rest, Ruskin ends the volume, and thus *Modern Painters* as a whole, with a passage which, in the manner of preachers, and of Dickens at the end of *Hard Times*,[44] presents the reader with a challenge:

I leave you to judge, and to choose, between this labour, and the bequeathed peace; these wages, and the gift of the Morning Star; this obedience, and the doing of the will which shall enable you to claim another kindred than of the earth, and to hear another voice than that of the grave, saying, 'My brother, and sister, and mother'. (7.460)

The reader, too, must become as wise as Solomon.

---

[42] See, for example, the *Quarterly Review*, 98 (March 1856), 384–433 (p. 405).

[43] In 1861 he was to write to his father: 'It is a difficult thing, to live without hope of another world, when one has been used to it for forty years' (17.xxxviii).

[44] A novel dedicated to Carlyle and much admired by Ruskin (17.31).

CHAPTER 3

'The Peace of God' and a Christian theory of art

> the mighty pyramids stood calmly – in the very heart of the high
> heaven – a celestial city with walls of amethyst and gates of gold –
> filled with the light and clothed with the Peace of God.
>
> Cancelled passage from *Modern Painters* II (4.364)

I

The sight of the Aiguilles standing quietly above the storm like the heavenly Jerusalem (Revelation 21) had, Ruskin claimed, first taught him
'the real meaning of the word Beautiful' – the subject of *Modern Painters*
II.[1] Yet the substantial passage in the manuscript describing the inspirational moment 'before, and in the Presence of, the manifested Deity' at
his beloved Chamonix in July 1842 (*D*, 230), from which this epigraph is
taken, was not incorporated in the printed text.[2] Ruskin may have felt
that its youthful effusiveness and its confessional quality would have been
more in tune with the 'young-mannishness' of volume I (1st edn 1843,
2nd edn 1844), in which he had written of 'adorable manifestations of
God's working' in mountain rock and heather (3.198), than with the
'serious, quiet, earnest, and simple' manner he strove for in volume II,
published in April 1846 (3.668). Furthermore, the Italian tour of 1845 –
the first made without his parents – changed the whole direction of the
project, so that instead of continuing the discussion of landscape from
volume I, as envisaged by Ruskin, his father, his publisher (George
Murray Smith), his 'literary master' (W. H. Harrison) and, interestingly,
an engraver (John Cousen) in January 1844 (4.xxi), it became a theoretical study (without plates) which focused upon the religious art of the

---

[1] The volume contains Part III of *Modern Painters* – 'Of Ideas of Beauty'.
[2] For a detailed analysis of the passage and its omission see C. Stephen Finley, *Nature's Covenant: Figures of Landscape in Ruskin* (University Park, PA: Pennsylvania State University Press, 1992), pp. 177–9.

Italian old masters. Thus the omission of the passage on the Aiguilles may also reflect Ruskin's new aim of bringing the reader before and in the presence of a quite different kind of revelation of the 'Peace of God': namely, the divine 'manifested' in art.

Ruskin's feverish 'gathering together' of a 'mass of evidence from a number of subjects' which he described to his mother in a letter from Florence dated 26 June 1845 (4.xxxiii), and which provided rich material for the new volume, followed two years – based mainly at Denmark Hill – of picture research, drafting and desultory reading, including the art criticism of Alexis François Rio and Gustav Friedrich Waagen, the philosophy of Aristotle and Plato and the Anglican writings of Richard Hooker, Jeremy Taylor and George Herbert. It was in September 1845, however, that Ruskin's overwhelming encounter with Tintoretto's huge religious paintings in the Scuola di S. Rocco in Venice – then neglected and little valued – finally provided the focus that the book needed, and material with which to illustrate 'Ideas of Beauty' and theories of the imagination which had been incubating ever since an earlier visit to Venice in 1841 (1.451). This chapter examines the way in which Ruskin's interpretation of both 'Tintoret' – the artist who temporarily displaces Turner as his chief focus of attention in his critical writing – and Fra Angelico is shaped by a theology which emphasizes divine attributes such as symmetry and repose, and a Christian aesthetic which celebrates beauty rather than the sublime as the true manifestation of divine wisdom and sign of the hope of heaven. It argues that in *Modern Painters* II Ruskin comes closer to a mainstream Anglican position than at any other time, while remaining an Evangelical in doctrine and a Dissenter in independence of mind;[3] that his concepts of Theoria and the Imagination Penetrative enabled him to publish Protestant readings of Catholic art which even his Evangelical English readers could accept;

---

[3] The specifically Evangelical content of a work which describes humanity as 'creatures in probation' (4.61) was to embarrass Ruskin later in life, although the harshness of some of the self-deprecating notes on his youthful 'insolence' which he added to the 're-arranged' edition of 1883 also reflects the effect upon his judgment of several major mental breakdowns from 1878. One reviewer of the first edition detected a 'serious spirituality about it; a *wresting*, if we may be permitted the expression, of all things in Nature to the glory of Nature's God, which would win for it the title of *Religio Pictoris* – for it is in very truth the religion of painting': '*Modern Painters*. Vol. II', *The Church of England Quarterly Review*, 20 (July 1846), 205–14 (p. 206). Another went further, saying that in volume II Ruskin 'still assumes art to be nothing but an auxiliary to the Church and to the Religious Tract Society': '*Modern Painters*, Second edition, and Vol. II', *The Foreign Quarterly Review*, 37 (July 1846), 380–416 (p. 403). This last reference to 'the Church', however, gives the clue to what is in fact a broader Anglican background to Ruskin's Evangelicalism in *Modern Painters* than has previously been recognized.

and that already Ruskin's religious beliefs – unusually, perhaps, for one so young – centre upon the God of peace.

Whereas the frequent retelling of the story of Ruskin and J. D. Harding reeling under the impact of the Tintorettos – Harding feeling 'more like a flogged schoolboy than a man' (4.xxxviii, 354) – has encouraged careful analysis of Ruskin's work on the paintings in S. Rocco,[4] his reminiscence in *Præterita* concerning his Oxford tutor, Gordon, encouraging him to read Hooker's *Ecclesiastical Polity* 'both for its arguments and its English' (35.414) has inspired only fleeting references to the stylistic influence of the work,[5] and one sustained piece of commentary, seldom cited, on the significance of its arguments.[6] The Revd Osborne Gordon (1813–83) rose to be Censor of Christ Church and University Reader in Greek.[7] In the autumn of 1839, only three years after taking a double First in Classics and Mathematics, he stayed at Herne Hill in order to prepare Ruskin for his Oxford finals (35.249–52), and remained a steadying influence and faithful mentor – including on some Continental tours – until his death, when Ruskin wrote the epitaph for his memorial in Easthampstead parish church in Berkshire, where he served as Rector for the last twenty-three years of his life (34.648). A moderate High Churchman who actively opposed 'Romanism' in 1850, preached a sermon denying the necessity of conversion in 1868 and, as a young tutor, steered Ruskin away from sectarian extremism, Gordon provided the brilliant but vulnerable

[4] For example, George P. Landow explains the typology of the 'Headstone of the Corner' (Psalms 118.22) in the *Annunciation: Victorian Types, Victorian Shadows: Biblical Typology in Victorian Literature, Art, and Thought* (Boston and London: Routledge, 1980), p. 122. Gary Wihl argues that Ruskin's discussion of typology in the *Crucifixion* circles back to his concern with the 'proper degrees of unity and proportion' earlier in the volume: *Ruskin and the Rhetoric of Infallibility*, Yale Studies in English, 194 (New Haven and London: Yale University Press, 1985), pp. 47–8. J. B. Bullen discusses the fact that Ruskin can 'keep separate in his mind the Renaissance in painting and the Renaissance in architecture': *The Myth of the Renaissance in Nineteenth-Century Writing* (Oxford: Clarendon Press, 1994), p. 131.

[5] Ruskin himself was later embarrassed by the complexity of his Hookerian sentence structure in the volume. Tennyson, however, included both Hooker and Ruskin in his list of authors in whom the stateliest English prose was to be found (3.xxxviii).

[6] Malcolm MacKenzie Ross, 'Ruskin, Hooker, and the "Christian Theoria"', in *Essays in English Literature from the Renaissance to the Victorian Age, presented to A. S. P. Woodhouse*, ed. Millar MacLure and F. W. Watt (University of Toronto Press, 1964), pp. 283–303, argues that Ruskin's response to Hooker's 'Thomist structure of Law' enabled him to 'propose a theory of art in its essentials consonant with a Christian sacramentalism' (p. 284). This excellent article (which does not examine the contested appropriation of Hooker in England in the 1840s) is seldom quoted or recognized. Thus Ruskin's biographer can argue that the author of *Præterita* perhaps exaggerated the influence of Hooker: Tim Hilton, *John Ruskin: The Early Years, 1819–1859* (New Haven and London: Yale University Press, 1985), p. 99.

[7] See *Osborne Gordon: A Memoir, with a Selection of his Writings*, ed. Geoffrey Marshall (Oxford and London: Parker, 1885).

undergraduate with solid Anglican foundations during the controversial period in the later 1830s and early 1840s when the Oxford Movement was at its height.[8] While *Modern Painters* I and II were in gestation, Tractarian sacramentalism shaped the aesthetics of Keble and Newman, some pages of whose 'curious essay' on the ecclesiastical miracles Ruskin read during Gordon's stay at Herne Hill in January 1843, finding them to be 'full of intellect but doubtful in tendency. I fear insidious – yet I like it' (*D*, 240).[9] Considering the intensity of Margaret Ruskin's vigilance, not only with regard to her son but also to his tutor,[10] John James's generous donation of £5,000 as a tribute to Gordon for the augmentation of poor Christ Church livings was probably richly deserved.[11]

When Gordon advised Ruskin to read Hooker in preparation for the writing of *Modern Painters* II, debate was raging in Oxford and throughout the country on questions such as the Church of England's historic identity as part of the 'holy Catholick Church', and the meaning of the 'real presence' of Christ in the eucharist. Hooker in fact represented safe middle ground, as Gordon would have known, in that his Anglican classic of the *via media*, *Of the Laws of Ecclesiastical Polity*,[12] originally designed to justify the episcopacy in the face of Puritan opposition, had been appropriated in the 1830s by opposing camps. In April 1830 *The Evangelical Magazine and Missionary Chronicle*, favoured by Margaret Ruskin, printed a positive review of a three-volume edition of *Ecclesiastical Polity*, gleefully pointing out that it was edited by a 'non-conforming layman' – Benjamin Hanbury, the historian of Congregationalism.[13] Six years later, however, in 1836, John Keble, a leading Tractarian, argued

---

[8] Compare the Revd Walter Lucas Brown, another of Ruskin's tutors, who encouraged him to read Isaac Taylor's *Natural History of Enthusiasm* (1829): see Lancaster MS 5c, Diaries, fol. 175; Hilton, *John Ruskin*, p. 47.

[9] J. H. Newman, 'The Miracles Recorded in Ecclesiastical History', in his translation of Fleury's *Ecclesiastical History* (1842). For an outrageously High Anglican statement, see Ruskin's letter to Acland dated 27 December 1844 (Bodley MS Acland 4 b–c), which, as Hilton points out, is difficult to take at face value: Hilton, *John Ruskin: The Early Years*, pp. 83–4.

[10] She wrote to her son in a letter dated 12 June 1843 from Denmark Hill: 'What strange whims even men of first-rate talents get into their heads. Does Mr. Gordon forget that we have an Almighty Intercessor? . . . I am sorry, very sorry, that such differences should take place anywhere, but more especially that they should have arisen in Oxford. What are the real doctrines of what is termed Puseyism? . . . Any time I have heard Mr. Newman preach, he seemed to me like Oliver Cromwell to talk that he might not be understood . . . I thank God I have his Word to go to; and I beseech you to take nothing for granted that you hear from these people, but think and search for yourself. As I have said, I have little fear of you, but I shall be glad when you get from among them' (36.xxii).   [11] See 35.249 and Marshall, ed., *Osborne Gordon*, p. 71.

[12] Bks I–IV were published c.1594 (printed in London by John Windet), Bk V in 1597, Bks VI and VIII posthumously in 1648, and Bk VII in 1662.

[13] *The Evangelical Magazine and Missionary Chronicle*, NS 8 (April 1830), 150.

in the preface to his own famous edition of Hooker that Hanbury's had been executed 'with considerable spirit and industry, but in some parts with a degree of haste, and in many with an expression of party feeling, tending to lessen its usefulness greatly'.[14] Inevitably Keble's own editorial commentary was to be criticized in its turn, in this case a further six years later by William Goode the younger, probably the most learned Evangelical on the subjects of historical theology and ecclesiastical history and law, who disputed this 'Tractator's' reading of Hooker on scripture and tradition.[15]

In guiding Ruskin towards Hooker's *Of the Laws of Ecclesiastical Polity*, Osborne Gordon would also have been sensitive to the fact that the argument of *Modern Painters* i had been grounded upon those God-given 'laws' which govern the creation, or, as Ruskin himself describes them, 'universal laws' (3.432, 451). Indeed, it was in his reply to Gordon's letter of March 1844, where he was asked 'if the cultivation of taste be a proper "ergon" [work] of a man's life', that Ruskin explained the purpose of *Modern Painters* most clearly: 'to spread the love and knowledge of art among all classes', this love and knowledge being 'of the universal system of nature' (3.665). In Hooker, Ruskin could find authoritative arguments which supported his own method of reading both scripture and nature, predicated on the working of divine wisdom:

The bounds of wisdom are large, and within them much is contained. Wisdom was Adam's instructor in Paradise; wisdom endued the fathers who lived before the law with the knowledge of holy things; by the wisdom of the law of God David attained to excel others in understanding; and Solomon likewise to excel David by the self-same wisdom of God teaching him many things besides the law . . .

Some things she openeth by the sacred books of Scripture; some things by the glorious works of Nature: with some things she inspireth them from above by spiritual influence; in some things she leadeth and traineth them only by worldly experience and practice [our emphasis].[16]

---

[14] *The Works of that Learned and Judicious Divine Mr. Richard Hooker: With an Account of his Life and Death by Isaac Walton*, ed. John Keble, 3 vols. (Oxford University Press, 1836), i, li.

[15] William Goode, *The Divine Rule of Faith and Practice; or, A Defence of the Catholic Doctrine that Holy Scripture has been, since the Times of the Apostles, the sole Divine Rule of Faith and Practice to the Church: Against the Dangerous Errors of the Authors of the Tracts for the Times and the Romanists, as, particularly, that the Rule of Faith is "Made up of Scripture and Tradition together;" etc.; In which also the Doctrines of the Apostolical Succession, the Eucharistic Sacrifice, &c. are fully Discussed*, 2nd edn, 3 vols. (London: Jackson, 1853), ii, 110–11, 244, 279, 379, 384–5; compare ii, 380.

[16] Hooker, *Works*, i, 363–4. Internal evidence indicates that this is the edition Ruskin used, although his quotations from Hooker are, characteristically, slightly inaccurate. In 1842, when working on *Modern Painters* i, Ruskin had written the following stanza in a poem entitled 'Charitie': 'When first He stretched the signèd zone, / And heaped the hills, and barred the sea, / Then Wisdom sat beside His throne; / But His own Word was Charitie' (2.212). For an example of Ruskin's deprecatory remarks on Hooker's ideas on the Church, see Lancaster MS 10a, fol. 53.

Ruskin could also quote from Hooker when providing a more developed answer to Gordon's question, in the chapter in which he considers
the last, and in his view 'the most essential of all' typical beauty (that is,
beauty 'in some sort typical of the Divine attributes', 4.64) – 'Of
Moderation, or the Type of Government by Law':

> finish, exactness, or refinement . . . are commonly desired in the works of men,
> owing both to their difficulty of accomplishment and consequent expression of
> care and power . . . and from their greater resemblance to the working of God,
> whose "absolute exactness", says Hooker, "all things imitate, by tending to that
> which is most exquisite in every particular."[17](4.136)

In the chapter on the 'law whereby man is in his actions directed to the
imitation of God', from which Ruskin quotes here, Hooker's treatment
of the religious impulse would also have interested, and possibly
inspired, the author of *Modern Painters* II: 'With Plato what one thing
more usual, than to excite men unto love of wisdom, by shewing how
much wise men are thereby exalted above men; how knowledge doth
raise them up into heaven; how it maketh them, though not gods, yet as
gods, high, admirable, and divine?'[18] Compare Ruskin's conception of
Theoria, from which everything else in *Modern Painters* II flows:

> Now the mere animal consciousness of the pleasantness I call Æsthesis; but the
> exulting, reverent, and grateful perception of it I call Theoria. For this, and this
> only, is the full comprehension and contemplation of the Beautiful as a gift of
> God; a gift not necessary to our being, but added to, and elevating it, and
> twofold: first of the desire, and secondly of the thing desired. (4.47)

Ruskin quotes from Hooker again in his chapter 'Of Moderation, or
the Type of Government by Law', when explaining the nature and value
of moderation:

> this restraint or moderation (according to the words of Hooker, "that which
> doth moderate the force and power, that which doth appoint the form and
> measure of working, the same we term a Law,") is in the Deity not restraint,
> such as it is said of creatures, but, as again says Hooker, "the very being of God
> is a law to His working," so that every appearance of painfulness or want of
> power and freedom in material things is wrong and ugly . . . (4.138–9)[19]

Ruskin's call for 'self-command' in the artist (4.140) is related to his argument, early in the volume, that we must acknowledge and work within
the God-given limits of our intellects – an argument again buttressed by
a reference to Hooker:

> it is ordained . . . that all the great phenomena of nature, the knowledge of
> which is desired by the angels only, by us partly, as it reveals to farther vision the

[17] Compare Hooker, *Works*, I, 269.   [18] Hooker, *Ibid.*, 269–70.   [19] Compare *Ibid.*, 249.

being and the glory of Him in whom they rejoice, and we live, dispense yet such kind influences, and so much of material blessing, as to be joyfully felt by all inferior creatures, and to be desired by them with such single desire as the imperfection of their nature may admit . . . †

† Hooker, *Eccl. Pol.*, book ii. Chap. ii. § 2. (4.34)

In fact the more important source is to be found a few pages beyond the passages he quotes from Hooker on moderation, where the subject is 'Eternal law':

That part of it which ordereth natural agents we call usually Nature's law; that which Angels do clearly behold and without any swerving observe is a law Celestial and heavenly; the law of Reason, that which bindeth creatures reasonable in this world, and with which by reason they may most plainly perceive themselves bound; that which bindeth them, and is not known but by special revelation from God, Divine law; Human law, that which out of the law either of reason or of God men probably gathering to be expedient, they make it a law. (1, 255)

The angels also 'clearly behold' God, and it is towards Fra Angelico's representations of angels that *Modern Painters* ii finally moves, as Ruskin explores the significance to painting, and to art criticism, of what he calls 'the written promise, "Blessed are the pure in *heart*, for they shall see God"' (4.50; Matthew 5.8).

II

Ruskin declares early in *Modern Painters* ii that 'Man's use and function . . . are, to be the witness of the glory of God, and to advance that glory by his reasonable and resultant happiness' (4.28–9).[20] Characteristically, however, the writing gains energy and momentum as an enraged Ruskin sets against this eternal ideal the present reality of a time when neglect and 'restoration' are destroying the monuments of Europe, and when 'the honour of God is thought to consist in the poverty of His temple' (4.31–2). In arguing in the first edition that God did not teach men of old how to 'build for glory and for beauty' that 'we, *foul and sensual as we are,*

---

[20] A. S. Mories regards Ruskin's words as 'almost a transcript of the time-honoured and masterly answer to the first question of our [Scottish] Shorter Catechism, with which he had been familiar. "Man's chief end is to glorify God and to enjoy Him for ever"': 'The Sophia of Ruskin: What Was It? and How Was It Reached?', *Saint George: The Journal of the Ruskin Society of Birmingham*, 4, 14 (January 1901), 150–71 (p. 157). In Finley's view, Ruskin 'became perhaps the nineteenth century's foremost "theologian" of the *Deus gloriosus*, practicing the *theologia gloriae* with lavish gifts of heart and hand and eye': *Nature's Covenant*, p. 44.

might give the work of their poured-out spirit to the axe and the hammer' (4.32), Ruskin is carried to extremes of impassioned pulpit oratory, as the removal in the second edition of the words italicized here indicates. Although the phrase 'the axe and the hammer' is to be taken up later in the work, where Ruskin relates a Tintoretto to the ideal architecture of Solomon's temple, for the moment his invective against the restorers is set aside until his next book, *The Seven Lamps of Architecture*, as he turns to a discussion of 'the Christian Theoria' (4.42–50) – later approvingly explained by Ruskin himself, in the language of seventeenth-century Protestant divines,[21] as being '"Contemplation" – seeing within the temple of the heart' (29.576).

In print, Ruskin answers his tutor's query about the 'cultivation of taste' being a fit life's work for a person on Gordon's own ground, through an argument which underpins all his later art teaching:

true taste is for ever growing, learning, reading, worshipping, laying its hand upon its mouth because it is astonished, lamenting over itself, and testing itself by the way that it fits things. And it finds whereof to feed, and whereby to grow, in all things. The complaint so often heard from young artists, that they have not within their reach materials or subjects enough for their fancy, is utterly groundless, and the sign only of their own blindness and inefficiency; for there is that to be seen in every street and lane of every city, – that to be felt and found in every human heart and countenance, – that to be loved in every roadside weed and moss-grown wall which, in the hands of faithful men, may convey emotions of glory and sublimity continual and exalted. (4.60) [22]

A statement which would have appealed to Charles Kingsley's Alton Locke, as further evidence of the democratization of Victorian culture,[23] also offered comfort to Tory High Churchmen like Osborne Gordon in its emphasis upon 'faithful men'. In *The Temple* – surely a resonant title for Ruskin, who cites the collection frequently – the moderate Anglican George Herbert finds his divine analogies in commonplace experience:

Let therefore the young artist beware of the spirit of Choice;* it is an insolent spirit at the best, and commonly a base and blind one too, checking all progress and blasting all power, encouraging weaknesses, pampering

---

[21] 'seeing thy enjoyment of God in this contemplation much depends on the capacity and disposition of thy heart, seek him here, if ever, with all thy soul . . . thrust those thoughts from the temple of thy heart, which have the badge of God's prohibition upon them': Richard Baxter, *The Saint's Everlasting Rest* (London: Caxton, n.d.), p. 253.

[22] Cook and Wedderburn, *Works*, miss the hyperbolic variant reading in the 1st edn:'astonished, casting its shoes from off its feet because it finds all ground holy, lamenting' (omitted in the 2nd edn).   [23] See Charles Kingsley, *Alton Locke: Tailor and Poet* (1850), chapter 9, 'Poetry and Poets'.

partialities, and teaching us to look to accidents of nature for the help and the joy which should come from our own hearts.

> * "Nothing comes amiss,
> A good digestion turneth all to health." – G. HERBERT. (4.60)

Ruskin had used the metaphor of digestion himself, in correspondence with his mother on the tour of 1845. She packed Bunyan's *Grace Abounding* for him to read, when in fact he preferred Herbert – just as vigorous in his 'imagination' and 'communings', but having a 'well bridled & disciplined mind'; taught by God, not 'through his liver', like Bunyan, but 'through his brains'; and 'full of faith & love, regardless of himself'.[24] The 'Author of *Modern Painters*' is often sarcastic in his analysis of certain features of his early manhood that he wishes to leave behind, including the self-centred introspection that can characterize ultra-Protestant belief and practice.[25] Similarly, in volume II he expresses his embarrassment at having in volume I attributed 'too much community and authority' to his own taste for 'scenery inducing emotions of wild, impetuous, and enthusiastic characters, and too little to those which I perceive in others for things *peaceful*, humble, meditative, and solemn' (4.75; our emphasis). Whereas the youth sympathizes more with the 'gladness, fulness, and magnificence of things', he continues, 'grey hairs' sympathizes with their 'completion, sufficiency, and repose'. The 'signature of God' is 'upon His works', but we 'see not all'.

In turning to what he considers to be the six most significant kinds of Typical Beauty, Ruskin seems to align himself with the wisdom of 'grey hairs' several years before the appearance of his first, literal grey hair,[26] while at the same time asking the reader to 'enter upon the subject with [him], as far as may be, as a little child' (4.77), like those who wish to enter the kingdom of God (Mark 10.15). In the mid-1840s, a period in which he often expresses a sense of profound weariness,[27] Ruskin's God is the

---

[24] See *Ruskin in Italy: Letters to His Parents, 1845*, ed. Harold I. Shapiro (Oxford: Clarendon, 1972), pp. 17–18, 33; see also Ruskin's comment on a view of religion as a 'particular phase of indigestion', p. 34. Compare 35.344–5. John Brown wrote of 'repose' in volume II, 'The theology, natural and revealed, as well as the poetry of this, we have in George Herbert', quoting 'The Pulley': John Brown '*Modern Painters*. 2 vols.', *The North British Review*, 6 (February 1847), 401–30 (p. 424).

[25] In *Præterita* Ruskin states that he 'received' his religion from Bunyan and Isaac Ambrose, the Puritan divine (35.490).

[26] On the morning of 2 September 1850 – his mother's birthday: Lancaster MS 5C, Diaries, fols 151–2; compare *D*, 466.

[27] See, for example, 4.134n and *D*, 258. Symptoms akin to those of manic depression, or bipolar disorder, are present from Ruskin's adolescence onwards, including the period following the completion of *Modern Painters* I.

God of wisdom and of peace, whose home is in heaven and in the temple of the pure heart. The Typical Beauty of Hookerian 'Moderation, or the Type of Government by Law', has already been discussed. 'Infinity, or the Type of Divine Incomprehensibility', is exemplified in the 'calm and luminous distance', and the 'still small voice of the level twilight behind purple hills' (4.80; I Kings 19.12). In defining 'Unity, or the Type of the Divine Comprehensiveness', Ruskin turns to Hooker's statement that 'All things, God only excepted, besides the nature which they have in themselves, receive externally some perfection from other things' (4.92),[28] and to Christ's farewell discourses in John's gospel:

the only unity which by any means can become grateful or an object of hope to men, and whose types therefore in material things can be beautiful, is that on which turned the last words and prayer of Christ before His crossing of the Kedron brook, "Neither pray I for these alone, but for them also which shall believe on Me through their word; that they all may be one, as Thou, Father, art in Me, and I in Thee." (4.92; John 17.20)

A natural progression from Christ's last words to his disciples is to Stephen's 'apology' before his martyrdom, echoed when Ruskin argues that 'the unity of matter is, in its noblest form, the organization of it which builds it up into temples for the spirit' (4.93; Acts 7.48); the unity of 'earthly creatures' is 'their power and their peace'. 'Symmetry, or the Type of Divine Justice' is swiftly dealt with, and exemplified in Tintoretto's *Crucifixion*, 'where not only the grouping, but the arrangement of light, is absolutely symmetrical': 'When there is no symmetry, the effects of passion and violence are increased, and many very sublime pictures derive their sublimity from the want of it, but they lose proportionally in the diviner quality of beauty' (4.127). In discussing 'Purity, or the Type of Divine Energy', Ruskin reminds the reader that the 'ocular delight in purity is mingle . . . with the love of the mere element of light, as a type of wisdom and of truth' (4.130); in colour, 'pureness is made to us desirable, because expressive of that constant presence and energizing of the Deity by which all things live and move, and have their being' (4.133; Acts 17.28); in the 'Apocalyptic descriptions' it is the 'purity of every substance that fits it for its place in heaven' (4.134). Whereas the eschatological endings of so many chapters in later works by Ruskin emphasize divine judgment, 'Of Purity' is characteristic of *Modern Painters* II in its closing emphasis upon the hope of heavenly peace, as described in the Revelation.

---

[28] See Hooker, *Works*, I, 317.

It is in the chapter entitled 'Of Repose, or the Type of Divine Permanence', however, that Ruskin's emphasis upon divine peace is most clearly revealed. First, the theological groundwork is carefully laid, with references to the '"I am" of the Creator opposed to the "I become" of all creatures', to the divine wisdom ('the supreme knowledge which is incapable of surprise'), and to the 'labour' inflicted upon mankind at the fall, from which a profound longing for rest originates: 'Hence the great call of Christ to men, that call on which St. Augustine fixed as the essential expression of Christian hope, is accompanied by the promise of rest [Matthew 11.28]; and the death bequest of Christ to men is peace [John 14.27]' (4.114).[29] In subsequent paragraphs, which Ruskin was later to regard as some of his best, he argues that repose 'demands for its expression the implied capability of its opposite, Energy', and cites as an example the faithful 'standing still' of the Israelites on the Red Sea shore – 'the quietness of action determined, of spirit unalarmed, of expectation unimpatient' (4.116; Exodus 14.13). Here is the Old Testament type of Christ's peace before 'crossing the Kedron brook', cited in the chapter on 'Unity' – a peace which in Ruskin's view is to be consummated in the crucifixion, as we will see in his discussion of Tintoretto. For the moment it is the wisdom attributed to Solomon in Proverbs – itself the type of Christ's teaching in Matthew – to which Ruskin refers in his comment that the 'paths of wisdom are all peace' (4.118; Proverbs 3.17, Matthew 11.29–30).[30]

Turning to examples in art, Ruskin compares 'the convulsions of the Laocoon with the calmness of the Elgin Theseus' (4.119) – the result of research carried out in the British Museum when, in the autumn of 1844, he found himself 'necessarily thrown on the human figure' for many of his illustrations (4.xxiii). The chapter concludes, however, with the fruits of a visit to the cathedral at Lucca the following year. In a famous passage he chooses the monument by Jacopo della Quercia to Ilaria di Caretto as 'furnishing an instance of the exact and right mean between the rigidity and rudeness of the earlier monumental effigies, and the morbid imitation of life, sleep, or death, of which the fashion has taken place in modern times' (4.122–3; plate 5). Many of Ruskin's

---

[29] Compare the commentary which Ruskin used: 'Our Lord being about to die, and leave his disciples, bequeathed to them "his peace" as a legacy': *The Holy Bible*, with explanatory notes, practical observations, and copious marginal references by Thomas Scott, 9th edn, 6 vols. (London: Seeley, 1825), v, John 14.27. The last words of Ruskin's pamphlet, *Notes on the Construction of Sheepfolds* (1851) are those of Christ to his Church: 'My peace I leave with you' (12.558).

[30] Thomas Scott offers the cross-reference in his marginal notes: see Scott, *The Holy Bible*, III, Proverbs 3.17. Not until 1853 did Ruskin notice that Solomon meant 'peaceable': see p. 38 above.

Plate 5. Jacopo della Quercia, monument to Ilaria di Caretto, Cathedral at Lucca

later histories of architecture, sculpture and painting are to turn upon such moments of equipoise, which are always explained with reference to the moral and religious climate in which the work was produced. Here, however, another kind of equipoise is emphasized, for about the lips there is 'something which is not death nor sleep, but the pure image of both' (4.123). Writing at a time when poets and novelists were interested in the deathbed as an ambiguous site of interpretation – is this sleep or death? Is death itself a 'sleep' from which there will be an awakening?[31] – Ruskin's own meditation on Ilaria is at once aesthetic and moral: 'If any of us, after staying for a time beside this tomb, could see, through his tears, one of the vain and unkind encumbrances of the grave, which, in these hollow and heartless days, feigned sorrow builds to foolish pride, he would, I believe, receive such a lesson of love as no coldness could refuse, no fatuity forget, and no insolence disobey' (4.124). Whereas at the end of Gray's Elegy the reader participates in the act of reading an imagined epitaph, Ruskin concludes his chapter with an imagined act of seeing, distorted through tears, which teaches the difference between the peace of God and man's foolish pride – for Ruskin the root

---

[31] See Michael Wheeler, *Death and the Future Life in Victorian Literature and Theology* (Cambridge University Press, 1990), pp. 35–41.

cause of the 'fall' in the Renaissance. Poised between sleep and death, the effigy of Ilaria exhibits the power of repose that comes from a sense of former life and movement, but which for Ruskin remains, like the 'forms of the limbs', safely 'concealed'. Shunning studio life drawings, he makes his own private studies – written and graphic – in peace, from the draped figure of the classical and medieval sculptor.

In the last chapters of Section I, 'Of the Theoretic Faculty', where Ruskin defines varieties of 'Vital Beauty', he adumbrates a number of themes – redemption, the ministry of angels, the wisdom of Solomon – which are to be developed in his interpretation of Tintoretto and Fra Angelico later in the volume. Vital beauty in man is discussed in the light of the fall (4.177) – the subject of a sermon by Melvill on Ash Wednesday 1844 that Ruskin found 'valuable' (*D*, 266). The results of the 'Adamite curse', Ruskin argues, can be seen not only in the human frame and face, but also in the 'suffering of Christ himself' and the 'uncomprehended pain' of the angels, as they 'try and try again in vain, whether they may not warm hard hearts with the brooding of their kind wings' (4.186). Solomon, whom Thomas Scott describes as being 'deeply versed in all the branches of natural philosophy', and who 'discoursed in an admirable manner upon the nature, properties, and uses of the several species of plants and animals',[32] is identified as the type of Christ in his writing on the lower creatures:

And so what lesson we might receive for our earthly conduct from the creeping and laborious things, was taught us by that earthly King who made silver to be in Jerusalem as stones [I Kings 10.27] (yet thereafter was less rich toward God).[33] But from the lips of a heavenly King, who had not where to lay His head [Matthew 8.20], we were taught what lesson we have to learn from those higher creatures who sow not, nor reap, nor gather into barns, for their Heavenly Father feedeth them [Matthew 6.26]. (4.156–7)

Towards the end of chapter XIV, 'Of Vital Beauty in Man', however, Ruskin quotes Hooker on the penetrative nature of the wisdom of Solomon: he was 'eminent above others, for he gave good heed, and *pierced* everything to the very ground' (4.206, our emphasis). The section ends with a resonant piece of apocalyptic where the final emphasis is upon the promise that his servants shall see God:

but this we know, that there will come a time when the service of God shall be the beholding of Him; and though in these stormy seas where we are now

---

[32] Scott, *The Holy Bible*, II, I Kings 4.30–4.
[33] On Ruskin's note of 1883 on Dante's Solomon, see p. 257 below.

driven up and down, His Spirit is dimly seen on the face of the waters [Genesis 1.2], and we are left to cast anchors out of the stern, and wish for the day [Acts 27.29], that day will come, when, with the evangelists on the crystal and stable sea, all the creatures of God shall be full of eyes within [Revelation 4.6, 8], and there shall be "no more curse, but His servants shall serve Him, and shall see His face [Revelation 22.3–4]." (4.218)

In closing section I, Ruskin opens up ideas and metaphors with which he is going to work in that echo chamber of a chapter entitled 'Of Imagination Penetrative' – the longest and the most remarkable in section II, and indeed in the book.

III

Ruskin's reference at the beginning of the chapter to Milton's Leviathan in Book I of *Paradise Lost* (4.249–50) not only echoes the nautical biblical references at the end of Section I but also, through its whaling associations, prepares for the metaphor of 'piercing' through which the Imagination Penetrative – 'the highest intellectual power of man' – is to be described and illustrated. First the (startling) description: 'There is no reasoning in it; it works not by algebra, nor by integral calculus; it is a piercing pholas-like[34] mind's tongue, that works and tastes into the very rock heart; no matter what be the subject submitted to it, substance or spirit; all is alike divided asunder, joint and marrow, whatever utmost truth, life, principle it has, laid bare' (4.251). Following a number of literary examples of fancy and imagination, Ruskin invites the reader to compare a passage from 'Solomon's Song, where the imagination stays not at the outside, but dwells on the fearful emotion itself': 'Who is she that looketh forth as the morning; fair as the moon, clear as the sun, and terrible as an army with banners?' (4.257; Song of Solomon 6.10). The Authorized Version gives as a running head to this chapter, 'The church professeth her faith in Christ'; and Christopher Wordsworth, who finds in the enigmatic qualities of the Song 'a striking resemblance to its Christian counterpart, the Book of Revelation', comments that the question 'seems to be asked by a chorus of faithful friends, who behold the Bride coming': 'The question denotes wonder and admiration . . . at her glorious appearance, after the ill-treatment to which she had been exposed in searching for Christ'; her banner is 'the blood of the Lamb (Rev.xii.11), shed on the cross'.[35]

---

[34] Like a sea mollusc that makes holes in stones.
[35] *The Holy Bible*, with Notes and Introduction by Chr[istopher] Wordsworth, 6 vols. (London: Rivingtons, 1864–70), IV, Pt III, 125, 148.

Plate 6. J. M. W. Turner, 'Jason' (LXVIII), *Liber Studiorum*

The pacific nature of Ruskin's Christian aesthetic is then brought to bear upon the contrast between fancy and imagination, which he figures as 'being at the heart of things' as she 'poises herself there, and is still, quiet, and brooding, comprehending all around her with her fixed look' (4.258). Yet the things comprehended by that fixed look are often violent. Whereas in Retzsch's fanciful illustrations to Schiller's *Der Kampf mit dem Drachen* we have the dragon 'from the beginning of his career to the end' and yet 'have never got into the dragon heart', in Turner's 'Jason' in the *Liber Studiorum* (plate 6) we 'have the dragon, like everything else, by the middle', through a kind of *ars negativa*: 'No far forest country, no secret path, nor cloven hills . . . No flaunting plumes nor brandished lances, but stern purpose in the turn of the crestless helmet, visible victory in the drawing back of the prepared right arm behind the steady point' (4.259–60). In this, the first of a series of interpretations in which Ruskin employs in his descriptive prose the same Imagination Penetrative that he is analysing in a picture, the series of negatives and the synecdochic 'steady point' represent linguistically the engraving's absences – the former balanced by the trunks of the trees on the right in which Turner is said to address 'that morbid and fearful condition of mind which he has endeavoured to excite in the spectator, and which in reality would

Plate 7. Jacopo Tintoretto, *The Annunciation*

have seen in every trunk and bough, as it penetrated into the deeper thicket, the object of its terror'.

Tintoretto's *Annunciation* (plate 7) is also first described through a series of negatives, in this case in contrast with Fra Angelico's *Annunciation*. The Virgin is portrayed 'not in the quiet loggia, not by the green pasture of the restored soul' as in Fra Angelico's 'pure vision', but 'houseless, under the shelter of a palace vestibule ruined and abandoned, with the noise of the axe and the hammer in her ears' (4.264). The biblical echo suggests a further contrast between this ruin and Solomon's temple, 'built of stone made ready before it was brought thither: so that there was neither hammer nor axe nor any tool of iron heard in the house, while it was in building' (1 Kings 6.7),[36] which in turn prepares for the clinching evidence of Tintoretto's Imagination Penetrative in the foreground detail: the 'stone which the builders refused is become the Headstone of

[36] Compare 'No hammer's clang, nor axe's pond'rous din, / Disturbs the Temple's majesty within, / In silent dignity the grand design / Starts into beauty, from deep wisdom's mine . . .': Charles J. Champneys, *The Temple of Solomon, and Poems on Scriptural and other Subjects* (Glasgow: Smith, 1848), p. 3.

the Corner' (Psalm 118.22), a text which Christ quotes in his teaching to his disciples (Mark 12.10).

Tintoretto's 'wild thought' might seem, then, to be the perfect demonstration of Ruskin's earlier observation that 'the Theoretic faculty takes out of everything that which is beautiful, while the Imaginative faculty takes hold of the very imperfections which the Theoretic rejects; and, by means of these angles and roughnesses, it joints and bolts the separate stones into a mighty temple, wherein the Theoretic faculty, in its turn, does deepest homage' (4.241). Yet the 'force of the thought hardly atones for the painfulness of the scene and the turbulence of the feelings' (4.265), and the picture is set aside in favour of the *Baptism of Christ*. But the most 'exquisite instance of this imaginative power', Ruskin argues, occurs in an incident in the background of the *Crucifixion* (4.270; plate 8). Even when, in the first flush of enthusiasm, Ruskin had described the work in its own dynamic terms when writing home in September 1845 – Tintoretto 'lashes out like a leviathan, and heaven and earth come together' – he felt that the true 'master's stroke' was his 'touch of quiet thought': 'there is an *ass* in the distance, feeding on the remains of strewed palm leaves'.[37] In the text the emphasis falls even more heavily upon two touches of quiet thought. Having first eschewed his own powers of rhetoric – 'I will not insult this marvellous picture by an effort at a verbal account of it' – he approaches the core of his subject by establishing what it is not ('the common and most Catholic treatment of the subject'), and then dramatizing in his prose the painter's use of the Imagination Penetrative in the displacement of muscular exertion from the crucified to the crucifying:

penetrating into the root and deep places of his subject, despising all outward and bodily appearances of pain, and seeking for some means of expressing, not the rack of nerve or sinew, but the fainting of the deserted Son of God before His Eloi cry, and yet feeling himself utterly unequal to the expression of this by the countenance, has, on the one hand, filled his picture with such various and impetuous muscular exertion, that the body of the Crucified is, by comparison, in perfect repose, and, on the other, has cast the countenance altogether into shade. But the Agony is told by this, and by this only; that, though there yet remains a chasm of light on the mountain horizon where the earthquake darkness closes upon the day, the broad and sunlike glory about the head of the Redeemer has become wan, *and of the colour of ashes*. (4.270–1)[38]

[37] Shapiro, ed., *Ruskin in Italy*, p. 212.
[38] The capitalized '*His* Eloi cry' was not substituted for 'his' until 1883, in the edition 're-arranged in two volumes, and revised by the author'.

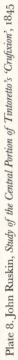

Plate 8. John Ruskin, *Study of the Central Portion of Tintoretto's 'Crucifixion'*, 1845

Here is the 'manifested Deity' in the 'perfect repose' of the Atonement. At the heart of his chapter on the Imagination Penetrative, defined as that which pierces to the middle of a subject, dividing asunder, 'joint and marrow', Ruskin focuses upon the restraint and moderation of Tintoretto's treatment of the crucified Christ before he is pierced by the spear, where divine power and glory are signified, not through the coming earthquake darkness, but through a divine repose which also figures its harrowing 'opposite, Energy' in the saving agony of the cross.

A sudden rhetorical turn then draws our attention to 'something more' the 'great painter' felt he had to do yet, as Ruskin again uses negative constructions: 'Not only that Agony of the Crucified, but the tumult of the people . . . Not only the brutality of the soldier . . . but the fury of His own people, the noise against Him of those for whom He died, were to be set before the eye of the understanding, if the power of the picture was to be complete.' After the rhetorical fire, a still small voice, as the reader, already reflecting on the penitential colour of ashes, is directed to the palm-leaves which the 'multitude' – common humanity – had strewed in Christ's path on his entry to Jerusalem:

In the shadow behind the cross, a man, riding on an ass colt, looks back to the multitude, while he points with a rod to the Christ crucified. The ass is feeding on the *remnants* of *withered palm-leaves.*

With this 'master's stroke' – also privately recorded in a careful copy of the original – Ruskin believes he may 'terminate all illustration of the peculiar power of the imagination over the feelings of the spectator'. He has not, however, 'sufficiently dwelt on the fact from which this power arises, the absolute truth of statement of the central fact as it was, or must have been' (4.272). Thus in the *Massacre of the Innocents* there is 'no blood, no stabbing or cutting, but there is an awful substitute for these in the chiaroscuro': 'It is a woman, sitting quiet, – quite quiet, – still as any stone; she looks down steadfastly on her dead child, laid along on the floor before her, and her hand is pressed softly upon her brow' (4.273). And only in Tintoretto's *Last Judgment* has this 'unimaginable event been grappled with in its Verity; not typically nor symbolically, but as they may see it who shall not sleep, but be changed' (4.277; 1 Corinthians 15.51) – a power also evident in Michelangelo, who in the Sistine Chapel would 'pierce deeper yet' and 'see the indwelling angels' (4.280–1).

Angels are also Ruskin's subject in the final chapter of *Modern Painters* II, 'Of the Superhuman Ideal', in which he defines four ways in which

'Beings supernatural may be conceived as manifesting themselves to human sense' – always in the 'form of some creature to us known' (4.314–15). Fra Angelico is valued for his 'reserve and subjection' (4.317) and for his 'purity of colour almost shadow less' in painting angel forms (4.323).[39] And it is with his angels that the final paragraph concludes:

> With what comparison shall we compare the types of the martyr saints; the St. Stephen of Fra Bartolomeo, with his calm forehead crowned by the stony diadem, or the St. Catherine of Raffaelle looking up to heaven in the dawn of the eternal day, with her lips parted in the resting from her pain; or with what the Madonnas of Francia and Pinturicchio, in whom the hues of the morning and the solemnity of eve, the gladness in accomplished promise, and sorrow of the sword-pierced heart, are gathered into one human Lamp of ineffable love? or with what the angel choirs of Angelico, with the flames on their white foreheads waving brighter as they move, and the sparkles streaming from their purple wings like the glitter of many suns upon a sounding sea, listening in the pauses of alternate song, for the prolonging of the trumpet blast, and the answering of psaltery and cymbal, throughout the endless deep, and from all the star shores of heaven? (4.331–2)

Ruskin was later to be embarrassed by this 'honest canticle', which read 'more like a piece of Mrs Jameson' than of him (4.331). It is true that celebratory comparisons between a number of artists in their representations of one subject are frequent in *Sacred and Legendary Art* by Anna Jameson, whose *Early Italian Painters* had appeared in 1845.[40] Unlike her, however, Ruskin has prepared for his Dantesque evocation of heavenly peace – '*calm* forehead', '*resting* from her pain', '*solemnity* of eve', '*pauses* of alternate song' – through the painstaking writing of a Christian aesthetic and detailed analysis of religious art in the main body of his text. And even in this last canticle, the power of the Penetrative Imagination is suggested in what Ruskin would call the 'central fact' of the Madonna's 'sword-*pierced* heart'.

Furthermore, Ruskin's remarkable knowledge of the Bible, and his already long experience of hearing biblical exegesis delivered from a variety of pulpits in South London, the fashionable West End and Oxford, equipped him with critical tools which were far more sophisticated that Anna Jameson's, and which were now applied to religious art that repaid his attention, in that they actually emulated the richness of

[39] See also p. 58 above.
[40] Having met her in Venice in September 1845, Ruskin tells his father that Anna Jameson 'has some tact & cleverness, & knows as much of art as the cat': Shapiro, ed., *Ruskin in Italy*, pp. 215–16.

the Bible.[41] Thus it was that Ruskin could justify his work on Italian Catholic art, not only to his father and to himself, but also to his Protestant English readers. Whereas the 'turbulence' of Tintoretto might prove to be too strong for English tastes, one of the master's 'quiet thoughts' could speak clearly of the peace of God which passes all understanding. For, crucial as the glory and the power are to Ruskin's understanding of the nature of God and of his signature upon the creation throughout *Modern Painters*, it is the peace of God – 'the death bequest of Christ to men' – and the hope of heaven – in which Fra Angelico's paintings strengthened his belief[42] – that inform the theology of *Modern Painters* II.

---

[41] Ruskin sensed this when he wrote to his father from Pisa on 15 May 1845: 'I have been drawing from Benozzo's life of Abraham, which is as full & abundant as the scripture itself – *nothing* missed, though a good deal added': Shapiro, ed., *Ruskin in Italy*, p. 65.

[42] Ruskin wrote to his mother from Florence on 9 June 1845: 'the fact is, I really *am* getting more pious than I was, owing primarily to George Herbert, who is the only religious person I ever could understand or agree with, and secondarily to Fra Angelico & Benozzo Gozzoli, who make one believe everything they paint, be it ever so out of the way' (Shapiro, ed., *Ruskin in Italy*, p. 108).

CHAPTER 4

'The Book-Temple': a Protestant beholder of St Mark's

Never had city a more glorious Bible. Among the nations of the North, a rude and shadowy sculpture filled their temples with confused and hardly legible imagery; but, for her, the skill and the treasures of the East had gilded every letter, and illumined every page, till the Book-Temple shone from afar off like the star of the Magi.

'St. Mark's', *The Stones of Venice* II (10.141)

I

During the years of his marriage to Effie Gray, from 1848 to 1854, Ruskin's research, drawing and writing focused upon architecture: northern and southern Gothic in *The Seven Lamps of Architecture* (1849) – the title of which is based on the seven lamps of the menorah in the temple in Jerusalem[1] – and Venetian Byzantine, Gothic and Renaissance in *The Stones of Venice* (1851–3). Apologizing to his readers for the delay thus caused to the publication of *Modern Painters* III, he asked them to appreciate the urgency of his project to create a written and visual record of ancient buildings in France and Italy which in his view were in imminent danger of destruction at the hand of the 'Restorer, or Revolutionist' (8.3). Meanwhile, Ruskin and his English Protestant readers were acutely aware that these were also years of turmoil in the religious life of their own nation, when the authority of the Church of England was being challenged through the Gorham case (1848–50), which turned on the doctrinal question of baptismal regeneration, and through the 'Papal Aggression' associated with the restoration of the Roman Catholic hierarchy in England in 1850.

---

[1] See Samuel Lee, *Orbis Miraculum; or, The Temple of Solomon, Pourtrayed by Scripture-Light: Wherein All its famous Buildings, the pompous Worship of the Jewes, with its attending Rites and Ceremonies; the several Officers employed in that Work, with their ample Revenues: and the Spiritual Mysteries of the Gospel vailed under all; are treated of at large* (London: Streater, 1659), p. 66; Margaret Barker, *The Gate of Heaven: The History and Symbolism of the Temple in Jerusalem* (London: SPCK, 1991), pp. 90–5.

73

What is the relationship, at this stage of Ruskin's career, between his inner or spiritual eye, trained in the Evangelical tradition, and his exceptionally acute critical eye for architectural decoration; and to what extent does his own position on specific religious issues of the day in England shape the highly selective 'views' of a Protestantized Venice that he provides for his reader, whom he assumes to be a 'Protestant beholder' (10.27)? Chapters such as 'St. Mark's' in *The Stones of Venice* II have always been admired for the richness of their descriptive prose. What has not been recognized, however, is that much of the tense energy of this writing derives from his mapping of his own understanding of Baptism and the nature of the Church, worked out after the Gorham judgment in England, on to this Venetian Byzantine version of Solomon's temple, in an attempt to make the saving message of its mosaics accessible to Victorian Protestants; and that he celebrates the mosaics of St Mark's – for him midway between the idolatrous waxen image on the one hand and the great painting which distracts the viewer from the religious subject on the other – as 'illuminations' of biblical history, originally designed for the common Catholic worshipper in Venice. First, however, we must consider Ruskin's thinking and writing on the religious controversies that raged in Britain between 1846 (the year of *Modern Painters* II) and 1853, when *The Stones of Venice* II was published.

II

In 1846, the year after Newman had 'gone over' to Rome, the Revd William Gresley, the prolific Prebendary of Lichfield, wrote:

The Church of England has just passed through a process of fermentation, a fever has raged in her veins, a storm has troubled her atmosphere; and now that these symptoms have subsided, a great change is found to have taken place within her. The Church is not what she was.[2]

The symptoms were soon to return, however, and with even greater violence. In December 1847 and March 1848 the High Church Bishop Phillpotts of Exeter interviewed the Revd George Cornelius Gorham at length in order to ascertain whether he was sound on baptismal regeneration, and, finding him wanting, refused to institute him to the living of Brampford Speke. Here began a controversy which, like so many of its kind before and since, was really about authority in the Church, important though the specific doctrinal issues were. Although Gorham's

---

[2] W. Gresley, *The Real Danger of the Church of England* (London: Burns, 1846), p. 3.

particular doctrinal position on Baptism was not shared by most of his fellow Evangelicals,[3] the Evangelical wing of the Church of England took his side against the High Church party when the case went first to the Court of Arches, which found for the bishop in August 1849, and then to a judicial committee of the Privy Council, which found for Gorham in March 1850, thus traumatizing High Churchmen who believed that Church authority in matters of doctrine had been undermined by a secular power.[4] Meanwhile Evangelical hostility towards both the 'Papists', who seemed intent on reclaiming England for Rome, and the 'Tractarians', who continued to foster a lively Catholic revival within Anglicanism, intensified year by year.[5]

In August 1848, four months after their wedding, John and Effie Ruskin set off for a tour of Normandy which was to provide material for *The Seven Lamps of Architecture*. Ruskin's comments in his diary for 15 October on a service he attended in Rouen Cathedral are deeply ambiguous, reflecting both the powerful anti-Catholic sentiment which he shared with the majority of English Protestants at the time, and a lively recognition of the dramatic power of the service:

I felt convinced, that freed from abuses, this *mode* of service was the right one, and that if bishops were bishops indeed – & priests priests indeed – if the doctrines of purgatory and bought absolution, of Mariolatry, and of the vicarianism of the Pope – above all – if dishonesty & doing evil that good might come, and doctrines of salvation by works, were cast out of the Church, & the Bible made free to the people, that all these proud pillars & painted casements – all these burning lamps and smoking censers, all these united voices and solemn organ peals, had their right and holy use in this their service – and that all these white robed priests and young troops of novice or chorister, could be – and ought to be – devoted to their lofty duties and separated from the common world without offence, yes – & with high honour, before God. As I never before felt so assured of all this – so on the other hand, I never more strongly felt the nonimportance of all these things as subjects of dispute or of law. In some respects they are little other than matters of taste in religion, certainly not to be enforced upon those whose vulgarity they offend, but still less to be refused to, or blamed in, those whom they edify.[6]

In his boyhood Ruskin had found High Mass at Rouen Cathedral aesthetically attractive – a striking 'change' from morning service in Dr Andrews's

[3] See Peter J. Jagger, *Clouded Witness: Initiation in the Church of England in the Mid-Victorian Period, 1850–1875*, Pittsburgh Theological Monographs, new series (Allison Park, PA: Pickwick, 1982), p. 19.
[4] See Owen Chadwick, *The Victorian Church*, Part I, 3rd edn, Ecclesiastical History of England, vol. VII (London: Black, 1971), pp. 250–71.   [5] See ibid., pp. 271–309.
[6] Lancaster MS 6, Diaries, fols 258–9; compare *D*, 370.

Beresford Chapel (35.132–3). Now he noted the 'abuses' and 'dishonesty' of modern Catholicism, while musing on the possibility of something akin to this mode of service becoming a channel for true religion.

In print, however, Ruskin reversed the sequence and thus the emphasis of his thoughts on contemporary Roman Catholicism, when, in the first edition of *The Seven Lamps*, published on 10 May 1849, he supplemented his comparison between the 'idolatrous Romanist' and the 'idolatrous Egyptian' in chapter 1 – 'The Lamp of Sacrifice' – with an authorial note, printed at the back of the book:[7]

No man was ever more inclined than I, both by natural disposition and by many ties of early association, to a sympathy with the principles and forms of the Romanist Church; and there is much in its discipline which conscientiously, as well as sympathetically, I could love and advocate. But in confessing this strength of affectionate prejudice, surely I vindicate more respect for my firmly expressed belief, that the entire doctrine and system of that Church is in the fullest sense anti-Christian; that its lying and idolatrous Power is the darkest plague that ever held commission to hurt the Earth . . . (8.267–8)

In Ruskin's view the Romanist must be 'expelled' from the place 'impiously conceded' to him by the legislators of 1829, and he expresses unequivocal solidarity with the position of the Revd Dr Croly – an Orangeman and a friend of the Ultra-Tory John James Ruskin – whose essay on 'England the Fortress of Christianity' he cites and earnestly recommends 'to the meditation of those who doubt that a special punishment is inflicted by the Deity upon all national crime, and perhaps of all such crime, most instantly on the betrayal, on the part of England, of the truth and the faith with which she has been entrusted' (8.269).[8] Ruskin's statement of 'confidence in the central religious body of the English and Scottish people, as being not only untainted with Romanism, but immoveably adverse to it' (8.267) is typical of Protestant opinion at the time, anticipating, for example, Sir Robert Peel's words in his maiden speech in the Commons on the Papal Aggression in March 1851.[9] It

---

[7] Printed in the 1st (1849) and 2nd (1855) editions, but omitted in the 3rd (1880) as a 'piece of rabid Protestantism' (8.267).

[8] On the Ultra-Toryism of the Ruskins and their clerical friends, see Robert Hewison, 'Notes on the Construction of *The Stones of Venice*', in *Studies in Ruskin: Essays in Honor of Van Akin Burd*, ed. Robert Rhodes and Del Ivan Janik (Athens, Ohio: Ohio University Press, 1982), pp. 131–52. Hewison cites G. S. Simes, 'The Ultra-Tories in British Politics 1824–1834', unpublished doctoral dissertation, University of Oxford, 1974.

[9] See *The Maiden Speech of Sir Robert Peel, delivered In the House of Commons, on Friday Evening, March 15th, 1851, on the Papal Aggression* (Manchester: Pratt, [1851]), pp. 7, 8. For a Roman Catholic riposte to Ruskin's 'gospel according to Dr. Croly', see *Ruskin: The Critical Heritage*, ed. J. L. Bradley (London: Routledge, 1984), p. 113.

served for the time being as Ruskin's modest, almost parenthetical contribution to the anti-Catholic literature published in 1849, significantly
the three-hundredth anniversary of the first Act of Uniformity, which
had imposed upon churches the exclusive use of the Book of Common
Prayer. It also doubtless pleased his father.

This end-note, set up in smaller type than the main text, offered those
of Ruskin's first readers who cared to consult it a caveat to his Protestant
celebration of medieval Catholic architecture, at a time when the fears
of what George Eliot called 'English Puritanism'[10] were more intense
than they had been since 1829, the year of Catholic emancipation – a
'national crime' deserving of divine punishment. Note 1 is appended to
a passage in 'The Lamp of Sacrifice' in which Ruskin offers a Protestant
typological reading of the 'Mosaical system' of sacrifice as anticipating
the New Testament, and in which he contradicts Catholic teaching on
'acceptable' and 'necessary' sacrifice: 'Was the glory of the tabernacle
necessary to set forth or image His divine glory to the minds of His
people? What! purple or scarlet necessary, to the people who had seen
the great river of Egypt run scarlet to the sea, under His condemnation?'
(8.35–6). For Ruskin, sacrifice occurs on the fleshy altar of the believer's
heart,[11] not on the stone altar of the Catholic's church.[12] The tenth part
of what is 'sacrificed in domestic vanities' would, he argues, 'build a
marble church for every town in England'; but he does not want such
churches for their own sake, rather 'for the sake of the spirit that would
build them': 'It is not the church we want, but the sacrifice; not the
emotion of admiration, but the act of adoration; not the gift, but the
giving' (8.39–40). Ruskin's view of human motivation here is profoundly
religious, and it prepares for the ending of the chapter in which he celebrates the elaborate stone-carving on the 'central gate' of Rouen
Cathedral: the cathedral builders have, he states, 'taken with them to the
grave their powers, their honours, and their errors; but they have left us
their adoration' (8.53).

What, then, is the relationship in *The Seven Lamps* between Ruskin's
inner, spiritual eye and his outer eye for Gothic architecture? In 'The
Lamp of Life' he moves round to the south transept door of Rouen
Cathedral (the famous Portail des Libraires) to examine the sculptural

---

[10] George Eliot, *Middlemarch*, ed. David Carroll, Clarendon edn (Oxford: Clarendon, 1986), p. 188
(ch.20).   [11] Compare 8.227.
[12] Compare Cumming's Protestant argument that 'now we have no atoning sacrifices which we
need or dare to offer in the house of God; for all atonement has ceased': John Cumming,
Expository Readings on the Book of Kings (London: Hall, Virtue, [1859]), p. 58.

decoration, and describes the tiny figures carved in relief – so enticingly that Proust is later to make a special pilgrimage to Rouen to see them for himself.[13] Ruskin believes that the 'right question to ask, respecting all ornament, is simply this: Was it done with enjoyment?' (8.218). He then describes a neo-Gothic church, Notre Dame de Bonsecours, built in 1840–2 only 2 miles from Rouen in the style of the thirteenth century,

vile enough, indeed, in its general composition, but excessively rich in detail; many of the details are designed with taste, and all evidently by a man who has studied old work closely. But it is all as dead as leaves in December; there is not one tender touch, not one warm stroke on the whole façade. The men who did it hated it, and were thankful when it was done. (8.218)

Ruskin would have the reader believe that all this can be read in the ornament. He does not, however, address the issue of the preconceptions that the 'Protestant beholder' – both author and reader – brings to the act of beholding. Did his comparative analysis of Rouen Cathedral and Notre Dame de Bonsecours reinforce his respect for medieval Catholicism and his abomination of modern Catholicism and French Republicanism; or was it the other way round?[14]

In either case, there runs through Ruskin's critical architectural judgments in *The Seven Lamps* a thin but hard vein of reference to divine judgment. Chapter II, 'The Lamp of Truth', for example, has the ring of an Evangelical sermon or tract, as in this passage:

Do not let us lie at all. Do not think of one falsity as harmless, and another as slight, and another as unintended. Cast them all aside: they may be light and accidental; but they are an ugly soot from the smoke of the pit, for all that; and it is better that our hearts should be swept clean of them, without over care as to which is largest or blackest. (8.56)

For the Protestant Victorian reader the terrifying events that follow the sounding of the fifth trumpet and the fall of a star from heaven to earth were all too familiar: 'And he opened the bottomless pit; and there arose a smoke out of the pit, as the smoke of a great furnace; and the sun and the air were darkened by reason of the smoke of the pit' (Revelation 9.2). Ruskin's God was a God of judgment, but also of wisdom. Solomon's famous judgments reflected his God-given wisdom, and his sculpture on

---

[13] See Marcel Proust, *On Reading Ruskin*, trans. and ed. Jean Autret, *et al.* (New Haven and London: Yale University Press, 1987), pp. xxiv-v.

[14] Clive Wainwright has kindly suggested that there is a further question: To what extent was Ruskin's reading of Bonsecours tainted by his knowledge that its architect was involved in the restoration of Rouen Cathedral, of which Ruskin strongly disapproved? (Personal communication).

the Ducal Palace – used as the palace of justice and consciously modelled on Solomon's palace – was important to Ruskin. His reference to
the sculpture in 'The Lamp of Memory', where he conveniently ignores
the fact that it is work of the despised Renaissance period, anticipates his
later commentary on Solomon as a type of Christ:

> every capital of its arcades was filled with meaning. The large one, the corner
> stone of the whole, next the entrance, was devoted to the symbolisation of
> Abstract Justice; above it is a sculpture of the Judgment of Solomon, remark-
> able for a beautiful subjection in its treatment to its decorative purposes. (8.230)

It is in the closing paragraph of 'The Lamp of Obedience', however,
and thus of the whole work, that Ruskin most clearly allies himself with
Evangelical tradition, adopting the rhetorical convention beloved of his
Camberwell pastors of reminding their hearers that they are under judgment, and opening up an eschatological perspective with a final thun-
derclap:

> I have paused, not once nor twice, as I wrote, and often have checked the
> course of what might otherwise have been importunate persuasion, as the
> thought has crossed me, how soon all Architecture may be vain, except that
> which is not made with hands [2 Corinthians 5.1]. There is something ominous
> in the light which has enabled us to look back with disdain upon the ages among
> whose lovely vestiges we have been wandering. I could smile when I hear the
> hopeful exultation of many, at the new reach of worldly science, and vigour of
> worldly effort; as if we were again at the beginning of days. There is thunder
> on the horizon as well as dawn. The sun was risen upon the earth when Lot
> entered into Zoar [Genesis 19.23]. (8.265–6)

In the winter of 1848–9, as he works on *The Seven Lamps*, Ruskin is not
only acutely aware, as he writes in Note 1, of how 'strongly and swiftly
the heresy of the Protestant and the victory of the Papist . . . seem to be
extending among us' (8.267). He also recognizes in himself and his contemporaries a recurrence of that apocalyptic sense of an ending of the
old world order which accompanied the 'national crime' of 1829, and of
what both Irving and Carlyle then described as 'Signs of the Times'.[15]

III

When the judicial committee of the Privy Council announced its judgment for Gorham on 9 March 1850, the face of William Goode – a
leading Evangelical – shone with bliss, while the Tractarians Robert

[15] See p. 8 above.

Wilberforce and James Hope (Scott) walked silently down the steps, heads drooping.[16] 'Here, for the first time during three hundred years', Wilberforce wrote in his Archidiaconal Charge to the Clergy of the East Riding, 'we have the decision, on appeal, of a great doctrinal case; conflicting elements have come into collision; and we are enabled to estimate the exact nature of that system under which we live, to ascertain its laws, and appreciate its tendencies'.[17] Wilberforce, soon to convert to Rome, was one of a group of High Churchmen who, on 19 March, issued a series of ominous resolutions protesting at the judgment. Towards the end of the month, Bishop Phillpotts published a letter repudiating the judgment and threatening to withhold communion from Archbishop Sumner – an Evangelical, and himself in attendance at the deliberations of the judicial committee of the Privy Council.

On 31 March Ruskin, who had been in Venice all winter gathering masses of material – measurements, drawings, memoranda – for *The Stones of Venice*, read about Phillpotts's protest in an English-language newspaper in Avignon on his way home:

I read to-day in Galignani part of an acrimonious and of what I fear will become an indecent controversy between the Arch of Canterbury and the B of Exeter, respecting Infant Regeneration by Baptism. I am induced to set down what seems to me to be principles of right judgment in this case which a man of candour belonging by Education to neither party could hardly fail to acknowledge. (*D*, 464)

This private intention was to be fulfilled when Ruskin wrote his unpublished 'Essay on Baptism', in 1850–1. Meanwhile, the Church of England was rocked by a further challenge to its authority. Among those present at the announcement of the Gorham judgment was Dr Nicholas Wiseman, the figure chiefly responsible for the drive to 'Romanize' the old English Catholics. Four months later, in July 1850, Wiseman gleefully twisted the tail of Anglicanism in a discourse delivered before a large congregation of Catholics and Protestants in Salford, saying:

The trial has come, and what has that church [of England] proved itself to be? Why, strange enough, instead of her power, instead of her energy being called forth into existence, on the contrary her powerlessness and complete subjection to the dominion of this world have been demonstrated both by word and by act.[18]

---

[16] See Baroness Bunsen's *Memoir of Bunsen*, cited in Chadwick, *Victorian Church*, p. 262.

[17] Robert Isaac Wilberforce, *The Practical Effect of the Gorham Case: A Charge, to the Clergy of the East Riding, Delivered at the Ordinary Visitation, A. D. 1850* (London: Murray, [1850]), p. 5.

[18] [Nicholas] Wiseman, *A Discourse Delivered at St. John's, Catholic Church, Salford, on Sunday, July 28th., 1850 . . . on the Gorham Controversy* (np: np, nd), p. 7.

Gorham gave his first sermon at Brampford Speke on 15 September, choosing as his subject justification by faith, that cornerstone of Evangelical doctrine; and a fortnight later Wiseman became Cardinal Archbishop of Westminster, following Pius IX's 'Letters Apostolical', issued from Rome on 29 September. Wiseman's famous Pastoral Letter, 'Out of the Flaminian Gate of Rome', of 7 October further infuriated senior Churchmen, and there were anti-popery riots in November, the month in which Dr Cumming, full of strange prophecies, gave two inflammatory anti-Catholic lectures in Hanover Square rooms which were rapturously received.[19] The following February a more sober gathering, convened by the Evangelical Alliance at Exeter Hall, heard a more reasoned response to Papal Aggression by the Revd Dr Steane, who carefully listed 'those doctrines of our common Protestantism' which in his view the tenets of Romanism subvert:

1. 'the sufficiency and exclusive authority of the Bible'
2. 'the perfect Atonement made for sin by the once offered sacrifice of the cross, and the sole mediation and intercession, founded upon it, of the glorified Son of God'
3. 'justification by faith only, through the blood and righteousness of Christ'
4. 'the work of the Holy Spirit in regeneration and sanctification'
5. 'the unity of all true believers of every communion in the One True and Spiritual Church of the living God, evidenced by their agreement in all saving truth, and their conformity to the requirements of the Word of God in all practical holiness'[20]

And during this troubled winter of 1850–1 Ruskin was himself attempting to define and defend 'our common Protestantism', while also writing the first volume of *The Stones of Venice*, in Camberwell.

'The Quarry' – the opening chapter of volume 1 (published on 3 March 1851) – immediately establishes a sense of prophetic urgency:

Since first the dominion of men was asserted over the ocean, three thrones, of mark beyond all others, have been set upon its sands: the thrones of Tyre, Venice, and England. Of the First of these great powers only the memory remains; of the Second, the ruin; the Third, which inherits their greatness, if it forget their example, may be led through prouder eminence to less pitied destruction. (9.17)

---

[19] See *The Roman Catholic Question: A Copious Series of Important Documents, of Permanent Historical Interest, on the Re-establishment of the Catholic Hierarchy in England, 1850–1* (London: Gilbert, 1851), 6th ser., p. 1.
[20] *Evangelical Protestantism: Report of a Meeting Convened by The Evangelical Alliance . . . Exeter Hall, on Thursday, February 27, 1851* (London: Partridge, Oakey, 1851), pp. 5–6.

What distinguishes this passage from eighteenth-century 'ruin sentiment'[21] is the extraordinary rhetorical power derived from Ruskin's characteristic use of biblical allusion: 'three thrones' ('and behold, a throne was set in heaven' (Revelation 4.2)); 'set upon its sands' ('a foolish man, which built his house upon the sand' (Matthew 7.26)); 'Tyre . . . ruin . . . destruction' ('Thy riches . . . shall fall into the midst of the seas in the day of thy ruin', 'What city is like Tyrus, like the destroyed in the midst of the sea?' (Ezekiel 27.27, 32)).

In reality Tyre's ruin was only one of several disasters from which the city has always risen again. For Ruskin, however, we are left with 'only a memory'. Generations of visitors to modern Tyre had gloried in the myth of the inundation of the old city, quoting Ezekiel's words with relish. But Ruskin believed that his generation read them 'as a lovely song', and felt he should remind his readers of their 'sternness'. He does not draw their attention to the fact that 'God's judgment upon the prince of Tyrus', in the words of the running head in the Authorized Version, is followed by the prophet's vision of the 'Restoration of Israel'. For God is, of course, on 'our' – or Israel's – 'side' in this Old Testament song.

Ruskin's aim is to trace the faint image of the once great 'throne' of Venice, 'before it be for ever lost', and to record the 'warning' which seems to him to be 'uttered by every one of the fast-gaining waves, that beat like passing bells, against the STONES OF VENICE' (9.17) – a warning specifically directed at English readers whose nation is in danger of 'less pitied destruction'. The parallel between Venice and England, and of their histories, is strengthened by Ruskin's Protestantizing of Venice from the outset, as he emphasizes the Venetians' historic defiance of Rome (9.29), to which 'the Romanist will attribute their irreligion, and the Protestant their success', here adding a long appendix on the subject entitled 'Papal Power in Venice'. Appendix 5, which is mainly made up of quotations from a variety of sources, including his own father, offers Ruskin the opportunity to expand upon that first note he appended – 'not,' he states, 'without deliberation' – to *The Seven Lamps,* and to draw parallels between Church–state relations in the Venice of the Doges and in nineteenth-century England, lamenting the work of 'the English parliament of 1829' (8.419–24).

In subsequent chapters of *The Stones of Venice* i, Ruskin painstakingly analyses and categorizes architectural features which provide 'The

---

21 For a fuller account of this theme see Michael Wheeler, 'Ruskin among the Ruins: Tradition and the Temple', in *The Lamp of Memory: Ruskin, Tradition and Architecture,* ed. Michael Wheeler and Nigel Whiteley (Manchester and New York: Manchester University Press, 1992), pp. 77–97.

Foundations' – the volume's title – upon which the superstructure of subsequent volumes is to be erected. If the main text of 'The Quarry' offers, as *its* title suggests, raw material for all three volumes, so too do its appendices, which include analysis of the foundations upon which English Protestantism is based, and which are now being shaken. In the final paragraph of the chapter, for example, Ruskin implicitly draws a further parallel between Venetian and English history which would have been noticed by his first English Protestant readers, but is easily over-looked today:

if I should succeed, as I hope, in making the Stones of Venice touch-stones . . . and if thus I am enabled to show the baseness of the schools of architecture and nearly every other art, which have for *three centuries* been predominant in Europe, I believe the result of the inquiry may be serviceable for proof of a more vital truth than any at which I have hitherto hinted . . . He [the Romanist] boasts that it was the papacy which raised the arts; why could it not support them when it was left to its own strength? How came it to yield to the Classicalism which was based on infidelity . . . ? Shall we not rather find that Romanism, instead of being a promoter of the arts, has never shown itself capable of a single great conception since the separation of Protestantism from its side.* [our emphasis] (9.57–8)

As his fellow English Protestants wrestle with the irony of the fact that the restoration of the English Catholic hierarchy followed hard upon the three-hundredth anniversary of the Act of Uniformity, Ruskin goes further, applying their arguments to the history of art and architecture. Again, as in *The Seven Lamps*, he relegates to the back of the book material that has the familiar shrill tone of anti-Catholic polemic at mid-century, when he annexes to this part of his final paragraph (marked by an asterisk) Appendix 12, 'Romanist Modern Art':

It is of the highest importance, in these days, that Romanism should be deprived of the miserable influence which its pomp and picturesqueness have given it over the weak sentimentalism of the English people . . . Fatuity . . . to talk of the authority of the Church . . . Fatuity! to talk of a separation of Church and State, as if a Christian State, and every officer therein, were not necessarily a part of the Church, † . . . Fatuity! to seek for the unity of a living body of truth and trust in God, with a dead body of lies and trust in wood . . . But of all these fatuities, the basest is the being lured into the Romanist Church by the glitter of it, like larks into a trap by broken glass . . . (9.436–7)

and so on. While in Appendix 12 itself Ruskin goes on to train his guns upon Pugin – his antagonist in the fevered religious politics of early Victorian architectural criticism – a note directs the reader towards his

own treatment of the more important subject of the Church, in the form
of a supplementary text he has written:

† One or two remarks on this subject, some of which I had intended to have
inserted here, and others in Appendix 5 ['Papal Power in Venice'], I have
arranged in more consistent order, and published in a separate pamphlet,
"Notes on the Construction of Sheep-folds," for the convenience of readers
interested in other architecture than that of Venetian palaces. (9.437)

Ruskin's complex web of cross-reference between his main text and
appendices and notes is completed in this pamphlet, published three
days after *The Stones of Venice* I and famous for the bemusement its scriptural title caused to hill farmers who mistakenly bought it as a practical
farming guide. The original aim, he explains, had been to support 'an
assertion made in the course of the inquiry' in *The Stones of Venice* that
'the idea of separation of Church and State was both vain and impious
– to limit the sense in which it seemed to me that the word "Church"
should be understood' (12.524). In producing his first religious pamphlet
at a time when a torrent of such publications was pouring from the
presses, Ruskin publicly enters the lists as a concerned Protestant
layman, signalling his affiliations by quoting from 'a sermon lately published at Oxford, by an anti-Tractarian divine' (12.524),[22] and demon-
strating his biblical scholarship by informing the reader that the word
'church' occurs 114 times in the New Testament, meaning 'a congregation or assembly of men', but that it 'bears this sense under four different
modifications' (12.525).[23] These are then analysed, leading to the important conclusion that 'the Church is a body to be taught and fed, not to
teach and feed' (12.534).

Ruskin's main aim, however, in *Notes on the Construction of Sheepfolds* is to
disabuse those who have come to believe that the Church is the clergy,
some of whom should be called 'priests' (12.537). A minister of religion,
he argues, is God's 'Messenger', not His 'Representative' (12.550), and,
as so often, he chooses Solomon as one of his illustrative Old Testament
types:

Aaron is always subject to Moses. All solemn revelation is made to Moses, the
civil magistrate . . . Nor is anything more remarkable throughout the whole of
the Jewish history than the perfect subjection of the Priestly to the Kingly

[22] A long list of 'Anglican Evangelical Writings against Tractarianism' can be found in Peter Toon,
Evangelical Theology 1833–1856: A Response to Tractarianism, Marshalls Theological Library (London:
Marshall, 1979), pp. 232–5.

[23] Ruskin lists these uses of εκκλησια at the end of Lancaster MS 5c, Diaries.

Authority. Thus Solomon thrusts out Abiathar from being priest, 1 Kings ii.27 ... (12.555)

In concluding with commentary on 'the schism between the so-called Evangelical and High Church Parties in Britain', which is 'enough to shake many men's faith in the truth or existence of Religion at all' (12.556), Ruskin argues that the 'sin lies most at the High Church door', as Evangelicals are at least willing to work with High Churchmen (12.557). If, however,

the Church of England does not forthwith unite with herself the entire Evangelical body, both of England and Scotland, and take her stand with them against the Papacy, her hour has struck. She cannot any longer serve two masters; not make courtesies alternately to Christ and Antichrist. That she *has* done this is visible enough by the state of Europe at this instant. Three centuries since Luther – three hundred years of Protestant knowledge – and the Papacy not yet overthrown! (12.557)

Ruskin writes in this pamphlet as a Bible Christian who answers his own question, 'But how to unite the two great sects of paralyzed Protestants?', thus: 'By keeping simply to Scripture' (12.557).

Ruskin's argument in his contemporaneous but unpublished 'Essay on Baptism' is also grounded, first, in the authority of scripture, rather than that of the Church, and, secondly, in an understanding of Christianity as a faith to be embraced and lived out 'To-day', in the world, rather than disputed upon by opposing religious parties. Challenging with typical directness both 'you Churchmen' and 'you Evangelicals' to set this dispute to one side and 'put Christ to the fair trial', he concludes: 'See if He will not, at your prayer, bless the Child which you baptize in His name, and whether those whom their Lord has blessed, shall not be Blessed for Ever' (12.589). At the beginning of the essay he defamiliarizes the current debate associated with the Gorham judgment by imagining how strange this world of sectarian warfare would seem to one of the angels of God if he were 'this day to descend from His presence' (12.573). He accuses 'Low Church Christians' and 'High Church Christians' alike of hypocrisy in failing to obey the divine commandments, as set out in the Bible, while continuing to preach them (12.576). As for baptismal regeneration, he wishes the issue could be laid to rest, as the really great question – easily answered, though rarely asked – is, 'Whether he be Now serving God or not?' (12.576). Nevertheless, he does address the question himself, and defines three distinct ways in which the 'Church's words' may be understood (12.577).

Whereas High Churchmen of the period emphasize the sacramental relationship between Baptism and the Incarnation, Ruskin, with his Evangelical background, relates it to conversion. Directly addressing an Evangelical in the text, however, he seeks common, non-sectarian ground in suggesting that just as we say a person is dying, so we can say that a person is 'converting', and that in God's eyes the beginning of that converting process – of which the individual and those around him or her may be unaware – could be as important as the moment of conversion itelf. That beginning, he argues, 'may more properly be termed Regeneration' (12.583) – the term that High Churchmen related to Baptism. Again, in his private writing Ruskin is more moderate than in print, pursuing a line of argument that is not dissimilar from those of contemporaries such as the 'Catholic Evangelical' George Howard Wilkinson, or the Evangelical controversialist Frederick Meyrick.[24]

Nevertheless, Ruskin is far from liberal, and always returns to the theme of the awful reality of divine judgment. For example, the 'unhappy parent' who comes to doubt the efficacy of Baptism is asked to reflect on whether his or her 'treatment of the lost child was wise as well as religious, consistent as well as holy': 'when His judgment is set, and the books are opened, you will perhaps discover that while no soul was ever lost but by the determined counsel and Foreknowledge of God, yet a strange account of Secondary Causes has been kept against those who dealt with them upon the Earth, and that many and many a one of those condemned Spirits has been lost for want of a single quiet word spoken at the right time' (12.588).

It is upon these theological foundations which Ruskin laid in the winter of 1850–1 – the sternness of God's judgment, the Church defined as God's people, the need for Protestants to unite by 'keeping simply to Scripture', baptismal regeneration defined as the beginning of the converting process – that the early chapters of *The Stones of Venice* II were to be built during the subsequent 'long winter' in Venice.

IV

Having guided the reader through narrow paved alleys and into the great square of 'St Mark's' – the title of chapter 4 in volume II – Ruskin describes the façade of the cathedral in one of the most frequently anthologized of his set-pieces of poetic prose:

[24] See Jagger, *Clouded Witness*, pp. 22–3.

there rises a vision out of the earth . . . a treasure-heap, it seems, partly of gold, and partly of opal and mother-of-pearl, hollowed beneath into five great vaulted porches, ceiled with fair mosaic, and beset with sculpture of alabaster, clear as amber and delicate as ivory, – sculpture fantastic and involved, of palm leaves and lilies, and grapes and pomegranates, and birds clinging and fluttering among the branches, all twined together into an endless network of buds and plumes; and in the midst of it, the solemn forms of angels . . . And round the walls of the porches there are set pillars of variegated stones, jasper and por-phyry, and deep-green serpentine spotted with flakes of snow, and marbles, that half refuse and half yield to the sunshine, Cleopatra-like, "their bluest veins to kiss" [*Antony and Cleopatra*, II.v.29] . . . their capitals rich with interwoven tracery, rooted knots of herbage, and drifting leaves of acanthus and vine, and mystical signs, all beginning and ending in the Cross . . . (10.82–3)[25]

The tension here between the sensuousness of the exotic ('Cleopatra-like') and the chaste solemnity of the traditional Christian symbolism ('mystical signs') reflects events in Ruskin's spiritual life during his extended visit to Venice from September 1851 to June 1852, when he drafted the 'greater part' of volumes II and III, sending chapters home to W. H. Harrison (10.xxxiv). In his correspondence with his father, for example, we find him writing from Verona and describing the 'strong instinct' in him to 'draw and describe' the things he loves – 'a sort of instinct like that for eating and drinking': 'I should like to draw all St. Mark's, and all this Verona stone by stone, to eat it all up into my mind, touch by touch' (10.xxvi). Meanwhile, soon after writing a 90–page com-mentary on Job in Venice, Ruskin focuses his inner or spiritual eye upon questions of prophecy, comparing notes with his father on their different areas of 'difficulty' within their shared Christian faith (10.xxxviii; 36.126–9); and on Good Friday 1852 he commits himself to acting 'as if the Bible *were* true' (10.xxxix).

For the Victorian Protestant reader who knew the Bible well, the passage conflates Old and New Testament prophecy – visions of earth and heaven, of physical and spiritual temples – in a manner reminiscent of seventeenth-century works such as Samuel Lee's *Orbis Miraculum; or, The Temple of Solomon* (1659; plate 9).[26] Through biblical allusion, the *raising* of Solomon's temple in 1 Kings 6 – built with cedars of Lebanon supplied by Hiram, king of Tyre – is folded into the description in

---

[25] The passage is inspired partly by Milton's description of the temple in *Paradise Regained*, which Ruskin had been reading in January 1852: see 10.112.

[26] In the background of the frontispiece St John the Divine sees the New Jerusalem descending in a cloud and speaks prophetically, saying, 'I am the holy City, the new Jerusalem coming down from God out of heaven Rev: 21.2.'

Plate 9. Samuel Lee, *Orbis Miraculum; or, The Temple of Solomon, Pourtrayed by Scripture-Light*, (London: Streater, 1659), frontispiece

Revelation 21 of the heavenly Jerusalem which came *down* from God out
of heaven, when 'the first heaven and the first earth were passed away;
and there was no more sea'.[27] (Ruskin's earlier prophetic references to
'how soon all Architecture may be vain, except that which is not made
with hands', and to 'other architecture than that of Venetian palaces',
are quoted above, p. 79). In his reading of the capitals ('rich with interwoven tracery, rooted knots of herbage, and drifting leaves of acanthus
and vine, and mystical signs, all beginning and ending in the Cross')
Ruskin leads the reader's eye to the universal sign of Dr Steane's second
'doctrine of our common Protestantism' – 'the perfect Atonement made
for sin by the once offered sacrifice of the cross, and the sole mediation
and intercession, founded upon it, of the glorified Son of God'. This
strategy of guiding the reader's eye towards particular images and away
from others is prepared for in earlier chapters of 'The Sea-Stories', and
is to be used most powerfully as he takes the reader around the interior
of St Mark's.

In chapter II, 'Torcello', for example, Ruskin adopts the analogy of
sight and blindness as he positions the 'Protestant beholder' where he or
she can 'see' what the first Christian worshippers would have seen there:

> For observe this choice of subjects . . . I am rather inclined to believe that at
> any rate the central division of the building was originally decorated, as it is
> now, simply by mosaics representing Christ, the Virgin, and the Apostles, at one
> extremity, and Christ coming to judgment at the other. And if so . . . observe
> the significance of his choice . . . The mind of the worshipper was fixed entirely
> upon two great facts, to him the most precious of all facts, – the present mercy
> of Christ to His Church, and His future coming to judge the world. That
> Christ's mercy was, at this period, supposed chiefly to be attainable through the
> pleading of the Virgin, and that therefore beneath the figure of the Redeemer
> is seen that of the weeping Madonna in the act of intercession, may indeed be
> matter of sorrow to the Protestant beholder, but ought not to blind him to the
> earnestness and singleness of the faith with which these men sought their sea-
> solitudes . . . (10.26–7)

Unlike in *The Seven Lamps*, Ruskin now makes due allowance for the prejudices which his Protestant reader brings to such images of the
Madonna. In focusing upon images of divine mercy and judgment

---

[27] Some of the exquisite marble revetment was stripped from Hagia Sophia, the church of the
wisdom of God, in Constantinople, while the Pillars of Acre came from the great church of St
Polyeuctus, itself probably intended to emulate the Temple of Solomon. In the twelfth century
it was believed that St Mark's had been modelled upon 'the temple of our Lord in Jerusalem':
Patricia Fortini Brown, *Venice & Antiquity: The Venetian Sense of the Past* (New Haven and London:
Yale University Press, 1996), pp. 17, 24.

which speak to Protestant as well as Catholic tradition, he opens up a
space in which he can re-educate the Protestant eye, as in his treatment
of the pulpit, for example, where he argues that 'if once we begin to
regard the preacher, whatever his faults, as a man sent with a message to
us . . . we shall look with changed eyes upon that frippery of gay furni-
ture about the place from which the message of judgment must be delivered' (10.32).

Ruskin's guided tour of the interior of St Mark's in chapter 4 is not
only more detailed than those of Torcello and Murano (chapter 3), but
also, for those Protestant beholders who had eyes to see in July 1853,
more closely related to the doctrinal issues that had troubled them in
England in recent years. First he must manoeuvre the reader inside; but
how? Here, 'in front of the church', are cafés, Austrian bands and, 'in
the recesses of the porches', Venetian layabouts and 'unregarded children'; and 'the images of Christ and His angels look down upon it continually' (10.84–5). Ostensibly in order to avoid entering the church 'out
of the midst of the horror of this', Ruskin invites the reader to turn
southwards: 'let us turn aside under the portico which looks across the
sea, and passing round within the two massive pillars brought from St.
Jean d'Acre, we shall find the gate of the Baptistery; let us enter there'
(10.85). This small external area adjacent to the Baptistery door (today
fastened as a window) was of great personal significance to Ruskin, who
drew it from all angles and seems to have regarded it almost as an interior.[28] As his earliest Venetian drawings indicates, he had long been aware
that the sculpture of the Judgment of Solomon on the Ducal Palace –
admired, as we have seen, in 'The Lamp of Memory' – directly faces the
door of the Baptistery (plate 10).[29] As in his unpublished 'Essay on
Baptism', where the 'unhappy parent' who comes to doubt the efficacy
of Baptism is warned of future divine judgment, the connection remains
mute in 'St. Mark's', as the 'heavy door' of the Baptistery 'closes behind
us instantly, and the light and the turbulence of the Piazzetta are
together shut out by it'.

Other reasons for Ruskin's taking the reader into the church via the
Baptistery present themselves. First, and most obviously, he can focus
there upon the tomb of Doge Andrea Dandalo, 'a man early great
among the great of Venice', which is an important 'touch-stone' in
Ruskin's cultural history of the city. Secondly, he thus avoids entering

---

[28] See John Unrau, *Ruskin and St. Mark's* (London: Thames & Hudson, 1984), p. 127.

[29] Also compare John Ruskin, *St. Mark's from the Southwest*, 1835 (Smith College Museum of Art),
reproduced in Unrau, *Ruskin and St Mark's*, p. 14.

Plate 10. John Ruskin, *The Piazzetta and St. Mark's*, 1835

through the north ('Arabian') porch, as most nineteenth-century Venetians do in order to worship in their favourite side chapel, which is dedicated to the Virgin and vulgarly decorated with 'silver hearts' (10.91). Thirdly, he softens the impact of the extraordinary interior of St Mark's upon the untrained English Protestant eye by repeating the familiar route taken by a visitor to a church at home – through the door, past the font, and into the main body of the building. That route symbolizes the passage of an individual soul into membership of 'Christ's holy Church' through Baptism (Book of Common Prayer) – the subject of the recent controversy in England during which Evangelicals such as Gorham reaffirmed Dr Steane's third doctrine of 'our common Protestantism': 'justification by faith only, through the blood and righteousness of Christ'. Here in the Baptistery of St Mark's, Ruskin's emphasis falls upon the first doctrine – 'the sufficiency and exclusive authority of the Bible' – as he encourages the reader to 'look round at the room in which he [Dandalo] lies' (10.86). The dimness of the place allows the eye of the Protestant beholder – both author and reader – to dwell, not on the Catholic altar, but on the surrounding biblical iconography, which is legimated through reference to England's greatest Puritan writer:

> The light fades away into the recess of the chamber towards the altar, and the eye can hardly trace the lines of the bas-relief behind it of the baptism of Christ: but on the vaulting of the roof the figures are distinct, and there are seen upon it two great circles, one surrounded by the 'Principalities and power in heavenly places,' [Ephesians 3.10] of which Milton has expressed the ancient division in the single massy line,
>   "Thrones, Dominations, Princedoms, Virtues, Powers," [*Paradise Lost*, v, 601] and around the other, the Apostles; Christ the centre of both: and upon the walls, again and again repeated, the gaunt figure of the Baptist, in every circumstance of his life and death; and the streams of the Jordan running down between their cloven rocks; the axe laid to the root of a fruitless tree that springs up on their shore. "Every tree that bringeth not forth good fruit shall be hewn down, and cast into the fire." [Matthew 3.10] Yes, verily: to be baptized with fire, or to be cast therein; it is the choice set before all man. The march-notes still murmur through the grated window, and mingle with the sounding in our ears of the sentence of judgment, which the old Greek has written on that Baptistery wall. Venice has made her choice.
>   He who lies under that stony canopy would have taught her another choice, in his day, if she would have listened to him; but he and his counsels have long been forgotten by her, and the dust lies upon his lips. (10.87–8)

Ruskin chooses to spell out to an endangered England the 'warning' which a now ruined Venice embodies here in the Baptistery, where, in contradistinction to Catholic doctrine, his Protestant interpretation of its iconography emphasizes choice, and the convert's Baptism by fire, in a passage crammed with favourite Evangelical types of Baptism and appropriate biblical texts.

As on the capitals of the pillars of the external façade and on the internal vaulting of the Baptistery, Christ crucified presides in the main body of the church to which Ruskin now leads us, as long as the eye is directed away from the altars to which nineteenth-century Venetians turn their gaze. The church is 'lost in still deeper twilight, to which the eye must be accustomed for some moments before the form of the building can be traced; and then there opens before us a vast cave, hewn out into the form of a Cross, and divided into shadowy aisles by many pillars' (10.88). Ruskin's main theme is the saving message of the mosaics of St Mark's – the 'mystery of the redemption': for the 'mazes of interwoven lines and changeful pictures' lead 'always at last to the Cross, lifted and carved in every place and upon every stone', but 'conspicuous most of all on the great rood that crosses the church before the altar, raised in bright blazonry against the shadow of the apse'. It is not the Madonna but the Cross that is 'first seen, and always, burning in the centre of the temple; and every dome and hollow of its room has the figure of Christ in the utmost height of it, raised in power, or returning in judgment' (10.88–9).

Unlike the first worshippers in St Mark's, Venetians in Ruskin's day focus upon the building's remarkable collection of 'stage properties of superstition', and never in his experience 'regard for an instant' the 'Scripture histories on the walls' (10.90–1). Thus the crowded church of St Mark's stands, 'in reality, more desolate than the ruins through which the sheep-walk passes unbroken in our English valleys' (10.92). It is in the light of this perception that Ruskin sets out to judge the building, first as a piece of architecture. Here he concentrates upon its 'incrusted' quality and consequent richness of colour, to appreciate which those familiar with northern European cathedrals have to set aside their prejudices (10.113). He then considers St Mark's as a place of worship. Having tackled the thorny issue (in Protestant circles) of 'whether richness of ornament be right in churches at all', arguing that it is in the case of medieval churches which were originally surrounded by decorated domestic buildings (10.117–23), he discusses whether 'the ornament of St. Mark's be truly ecclesiastical and Christian', concentrating here on the 'essentially pictorial character' of its Byzantine decoration (10.123).

It is in this last-mentioned section that Ruskin confronts most directly the gap between the Protestant beholder and this alien Catholic building which earlier in the chapter he has striven so hard to close, and in the process enunciates the tension between the spiritual and the aesthetic eye. Having stated that he has 'never yet met with a Christian whose heart was thoroughly set upon the world to come, and, so far as human judgment could pronounce, perfect and right before God [Colossians 4.12], who cared about art at all', he goes on to mock the artistic tastes of the 'ordinary Protestant Christian mind' and to assert that 'all truly great religious painters have been hearty Romanists' (10.124–5). As he returns to the subject of the mosaics in St Mark's, however, the gap closes again, for he now repeats his earlier description of the 'whole church as a great Book of Common Prayer', adding that the mosaics were 'illuminations' through which, he pointedly reminds the Protestant reader, the 'common people of the time were taught their Scripture history'

(10.129).[30] The importance of the mosaics as religious art, he argues, lies in their standing 'exactly midway between the debased manufacture of wooden and waxen images which is the support of Romanist idolatry all over the world, and the great art which leads the mind away from the religious subject to the art itself' (10.130). Stating in the main text that on the one hand no great religious painting by Leonardo or Raphael 'has ever been worshipped, except by accident', while on the other idolatry is 'no encourager of the fine arts', Ruskin adds an important appendix (10) on the 'Proper Sense of the word Idolatry', where he takes his fellow Protestants to task for their lazy and prejudiced judgments on questions of individual faith that are hidden with God (10.451). These great mosaics were 'before the eyes of the devotee at every interval of his worship', he writes in the main text – 'vast shadowings forth of scenes to whose realization he looked forward, or of spirits whose presence he invoked' (10.132). In his treatment of the mosaics of St Mark's Ruskin invites the Victorian Protestant beholder to share the experience of those old Venetian Catholics who first read their biblical history on the walls and ceilings of this church.

The ground is thus prepared for the final, analytical section of this long chapter on St Mark's, where Ruskin attempts to 'form an adequate conception of the feelings of its builders, and of its uses to those for whom it was built', by showing the Protestant reader how to 'take some pains' to 'read all that is inscribed' in the building. By showing the reader first the atrium or portico reserved for 'unbaptized persons and new converts', and then the mosaics over the main entrance which the newly baptized saw when they were first permitted to pass into the church (10.134), Ruskin makes him or her repeat the same spiritual journey completed earlier, although physically in another part of the building. Yet again he asks the Protestant reader to 'now observe' – this time to attend to particular aspects of mosaics in which Christ is represented with appropriate texts such as 'I am the door' (John 10.9):

Now observe, this was not to be seen and read only by the catechumen when he first entered the church; every one who at any time entered was supposed to look back and to read this writing; their daily entrance into the church was thus made a daily memorial of their first entrance into the spiritual Church; and we shall find that the rest of the book which was open for them upon its walls con-

---

[30] Ruskin's metaphor was taken up by the Revd Dr Alexander Robertson, the Presbyterian chaplain at Venice, in *The Bible of St. Mark: St. Mark's Church – The Altar & Throne of Venice* (London: Allen, 1898), pp. 16–17. When Ruskin was visited by Robertson in Venice in September 1888 he said: 'What a blessed thing it is to be able to do anything for the cause of Christ!' (35.xxxii).

tinually led them in the same manner to regard the visible temple as in every part a type of the invisible Church of God. (10.134–5)

As in his unpublished 'Essay on Baptism', quoted earlier, where Ruskin sought common, non-sectarian ground by emphasizing the 'converting *process*', the beginning of which 'may more properly be termed Regeneration', he now wants the Protestant reader to believe that the makers of these physical mosaics in a physical Catholic church of the twelfth and thirteenth centuries understood that Baptism was an initiation into the spiritual Church, daily brought to mind in the process of re-entering the building. Therefore the mosaic of the first dome, he points out, 'which is over the head of the spectator as soon as he has entered by the great door (that door being the type of Baptism), represents the effusion of the Holy Spirit, as the first consequence and seal of the entrance into the Church of God' (10.135). None of this diverges from Dr Steane's doctrines of 'our common Protestantism', the fourth and fifth of which – 'the work of the Holy Spirit in regeneration and sanctification' and 'the unity of all true believers of every communion in the One True and Spiritual Church of the living God, evidenced by their agreement in all saving truth, and their conformity to the requirements of the Word of God in all practical holiness' – inform Ruskin's interpretation of the words from Matthew 21.9 that are inscribed around the border of the dome, where he ignores the fact that they also figure in the Mass:

> HOLY, HOLY, HOLY, LORD GOD OF SABAOTH:
>   HEAVEN AND EARTH ARE FULL OF THY GLORY.
>   HOSANNA IN THE HIGHEST:
>   BLESSED IS HE THAT COMETH IN THE NAME OF THE LORD.

And observe in this writing that the convert is required to regard the outpouring of the Holy Spirit especially as a work of *sanctification*. It is the *holiness* of God manifested in the giving of His spirit to sanctify those who had become His children, which the four angels celebrate in their ceaseless praise . . . (10.135–6)

To focus upon 'the convert' in this context is to Protestantize indeed, and the further analysis of mosaics which follows concludes with Ruskin hoping that the reader will now be disposed 'to look with some change of temper upon the gorgeous building and wild blazonry of that shrine of St. Mark's':

He now perceives that it was in the hearts of the old Venetian people far more than a place of worship. It was at once a type of the Redeemed Church of God, and a scroll for the written word of God. It was to be to them, both an image of the Bride, all glorious within, her clothing of wrought gold [Psalms 45.13]; and the actual Table of the Law and the Testimony, written within and without. (10.140)

Earlier tensions between the sacred and the profane, mystical signs and sensuous exoticism, in both the public domain of cultural and religious differences between northern Protestantism and southern Catholicism, and the private domain of Ruskin's competing spiritual and aesthetic eyes, are resolved through his interpretation of the 'temple' of St Mark's as a Bible, open to all, and warning of divine judgment, in a reprise of the Baptistery section discussed earlier:

Not in the wantonness of wealth, not in vain ministry to the desire of the eyes or the pride of life, were those marbles hewn into transparent strength, and those arches arrayed in the colours of the iris. There is a message written in the dyes of them, that once was written in blood; and a sound in the echoes of their vaults, that one day shall fill the vault of heaven, – "He shall return to do judgment and justice." [Genesis 18.19] The strength of Venice was given her, so long as she remembered this: her destruction found her when she had forgotten this; and it found her irrevocably, because she forgot it without excuse. Never had city a more glorious Bible. Among the nations of the North, a rude and shadowy sculpture filled their temples with confused and hardly legible imagery; but, for her, the skill and the treasures of the East had gilded every letter, and illumined every page, till the Book-Temple shone from afar off like the star of the Magi. (10.141)

The Old Testament type of the journey of the Magi to find the Saviour is the journey made by the Queen of Sheba to test the wisdom of Solomon and see his great temple. As Solomon's temple was built with cedars of Lebanon, supplied by Hiram, king of Tyre, so St Mark's was built with exotic materials from Byzantium, including a column reputed to have 'graced the temple of Solomon'.[31] In Ruskin's view, Venice, like Tyre, was now a ruin; but he rescued St Mark's for the Protestant beholder by presenting it as a 'Book-Temple' to which the Magi – the acceptable religious face of orientalism, appropriated by Christianity – are drawn in wonder.

The sins of Venice, Ruskin concludes, were 'done with the Bible at her right hand', and 'through century after century of gathering vanity and festering guilt, that white dome of St. Mark's had uttered in the dead ear of Venice, "Know thou, that for all these things God will bring thee into

---

[31] 'the magnificent marble Basilica . . . the winding amber-looking columns from Constantinople, that graced the temple of Solomon, . . . delighted me in a high degree': Andrew Clarke, *Tour in France, Italy, and Switzerland, during the Years 1840 and 1841* (London: Whittaker, 1843), p. 243.

judgment"' (10.142; Ecclesiastes 11.9). By the time he published the Travellers' Edition of *The Stones of Venice* in 1879, Ruskin was acutely aware of and embarrassed by his ignorance of Catholic doctrine in the early 1850s. Nevertheless, in the first edition of volume II – Ruskin's first work as a cultural historian – he does already show an awareness of the prejudice which both he and his English Protestant readers bring to their reading of a city, the faint image of which contains a warning for an England ravaged by sectarian division. In presenting St Mark's as a 'Book-Temple', however, and thus making it accessible to the Protestant beholder, he reveals the continued strength of his affiliations to Evangelicalism and to his father, for whom he must still fulfil his divine commission to 'aid the cause' of truth and of (Protestant) religion.

CHAPTER 5

'True sacred art' and Christ the great high priest

All the histories of the Bible are, in my judgment, yet waiting to be painted. . . . religious art, at once complete and sincere, never yet has existed.

It will exist: nay, I believe the era of its birth has come, and that those bright Turnerian imageries . . . and those calm Pre-Raphaelites studies . . . form the first foundation that has been ever laid for true sacred art.

'Of the False Idea; – First, Religious', *Modern Painters* III (5.87)

I

Ruskin's provocative statement on religious art, couched in Adventist tones ('the era of its birth has come'), follows his demolition of Raphael's cartoon of *Christ's Charge to Peter* and his praise of Orcagna and Angelico as 'faithful religious masters' who portrayed important eschatological subjects, and of William Holman Hunt who, in *The Light of the World* (1854), represents Christ as 'a living presence among us now' (5.86). Since the publication of Ruskin's last major statement on the subject of religious paintings – *Modern Painters* II (1846) – Anna Jameson had appropriated the term 'sacred art' in her two-volume study on *Sacred and Legendary Art* (1848), where she offered a fairly orthodox, if inaccurate reading of Raphael's cartoon in the very year in which the Pre-Raphaelite Brotherhood was formed: hence Ruskin's pointed reference to '*true* sacred art'.[1] Earlier in *Modern Painters* III (1856) he declared that *The Light of the World* was 'the most perfect instance of expressional purpose with technical power, which the world [had] yet produced' (5.52), and argued that in Hunt's 'great poetical picture' the 'whole thought and arrangement being imaginative, the several details of it are

---

[1] [Anna] Jameson, *Sacred and Legendary Art*, new edn, 2 vols. (London: Longmans, Green, 1891), I, 199.

wrought out with simple portraiture' (5.65). He need say no more, particularly as his famous defence of the painting in a letter to *The Times* in May 1854 took the form of a detailed description and analysis of its symbolism.

But why was this painting, ridiculed by art critics and public alike when it was first exhibited in the Royal Academy, so very important to Ruskin? As we have seen in earlier chapters, and will see again in the next, Ruskin draws the reader into interpreting as he interprets by devoting a special kind of sustained attention to a particular building, such as St Mark's Venice, or painting, such as Tintoretto's *Crucifixion*, Turner's *Apollo and Python*, or Veronese's *Solomon and the Queen of Sheba*. In his treatment of the Hunt and the Veronese he emphasizes the need to stand in front of a work for long enough to contemplate that to which the artist himself devoted so much time and labour. Like the Imagination Penetrative, Theoria – 'the full comprehension and contemplation of the Beautiful as a gift of God' (4.47) – must be given time to work upon the highest of subjects; and what subject could be higher than that of Christ himself? In considering why Ruskin made so much of *The Light of the World* and so little of Hunt's later *The Finding of the Saviour in the Temple* (1860), we must examine the tensions between his role as an art critic who defended Turner and the Pre-Raphaelites and the Evangelical tradition which he inherited of 'looking upon Christ', or 'looking unto Christ', in which paintings played only a very minor role, if any; between his sense that he lived in the era of the birth of religious art and his uneasiness concerning the recent burgeoning of popular illustrated Bibles; between his plea for 'histories of the Bible' in modern art and his deprecation of *The Finding of the Saviour*; and between his own sectarian bias (deplored in others) and the special status he accords to *The Light of the World* – a painting which defeats narrow sectarian readings, thus making it possible for it to become, as an engraving, the most popular Protestant icon of all time.[2] Hunt's figure of the risen Messiah, standing in an English orchard, bears the symbols of what Ruskin, echoing his Evangelical spiritual fathers, called Christ's 'everlasting offices of prophet, priest, and king' (12.329) – a visual representation of the kind of Christology on which Ruskin himself had been reflecting earlier in the 1850s. In contrast to Christ the great high priest, who knocks at the door of the temple of the human heart in an eternal present, Hunt's youthful, Jewish Jesus among the doctors at the newly rebuilt temple in Jerusalem is caught in

---

[2] See Jeremy Maas, *Holman Hunt and The Light of the World* (London and Berkeley: Scolar, 1984).

the time-warp of biblical archaeology to which the artist devoted so much energy – in Ruskin's view as misplaced as that expended on different types of project by the German philosophers and divines, such as Strauss, on whom he wrote an appendix in *Modern Painters* III.

In his chapter 'Of the False Idea; – First, Religious', Ruskin makes a characteristic defamiliarizing move when he comments that he does not think 'that any man, who is thoroughly certain that Christ is in the room, will care what sort of pictures of Christ he has on its walls' (5.84). By presenting this scenario in the present tense ('Christ *is* in the room'), he avoids the issue of historicism ('What *did* Jesus, the son of man, look like?') to which he only pays lip-service in the chapter. Instead the emphasis falls upon what Jesus and the apostles did not look like, as Ruskin relates the problem of representing sacred subjects in art to the problem of faith itself. Raphael is the chief culprit, and 'to this day, the clear and tasteless poison of the art of Raphael infects with sleep of infidelity the hearts of millions of Christians', so that the 'pre-eminent *dulness* which characterises what Protestants call sacred art' leads to our feeling instinctively 'that the painted Christ and painted apostle are not beings that ever did or could exist' (5.83).

Ruskin's animus against 'what Protestants call sacred art' has biographical and theological, as well as aesthetic, origins. In returning to the subject of painting after six years of marriage and of writing on architecture, Ruskin has also returned (one might say, regressed) to the family home at Denmark Hill, graphically described by James Smetham, his pupil at the Working Men's College, on 5 February 1855. Ruskin's mother, a 'ruddy, dignified, richly dressed old gentlewoman of 75, who knows Chamounix better than Camberwell', presides. She is 'evidently a *good* old lady', this devout Methodist notes, 'with the *Christian Treasury* tossing about on the table'.[3] Had Ruskin picked up the issue for December 1854, he would have found there a short closing piece entitled 'Looking upon Christ':

He who looks upon Christ through his graces, is like one that sees the sun in water; which wavers and moves as the water doth. Look upon Christ only as shining in the firmament of the Father's grace and love; and then you will see him in his own genuine glory and unspeakable fulness. – *Wilcox*.[4]

[3] *The Letters of James Smetham, with an Introductory Memoir*, ed. Sarah Smetham and William Davies (London and New York: Macmillan, 1891), p. 53.

[4] *The Christian Treasury, Containing Contributions from Ministers and Members of Various Evangelical Denominations* (1854–5), 456. Thomas Wilcox (1549?-1608), the Puritan divine, became a martyr figure when he was imprisoned for his opposition to episcopacy; he published numerous works on a wide range of religious subjects.

The passage comes from a Protestant tradition that was familiar to Ruskin, in which the inner or spiritual eye of the believer is taught to focus upon Jesus Christ. Isaac Ambrose – with Bunyan the major influence on Ruskin's religious life in boyhood, according to Ruskin himself (35.490) – wrote a standard devotional work entitled *Looking unto Jesus; or, The Soul's Eyeing of Jesus, as Carrying on the Great Work of Man's Salvation* (1658). 'Looking unto Jesus [Hebrews 12.2]', Ambrose argues, 'is the epitome of a Christian's happiness, the quintessence of evangelical duties.'[5] The adult Ruskin would not have quarrelled with this. The problem for him, however, was that while the spiritual eye of Evangelicalism was highly trained in looking upon Christ, the physical eye was not trained in looking at religious paintings.[6]

Consider, for example, the Revd Dr John Cumming, the famous Minister of the Scottish National Church, Covent Garden, whose sermons Ruskin heard from time to time in the 1850s, and who published a volume entitled *Scripture Illustrations; Chiefly from the Old Masters* in 1844. The naïvety of his approach to the subject in the introduction is similar to that displayed by him and many of his fellow Evangelicals in discussing issues of biblical criticism, such as the transmission of Christ's original words through the editorial work of the gospel writers. 'In recent times,' Cummings writes, 'much new and valuable light has been thrown upon the manners, customs, and facts recorded in Sacred Scripture', adding that the 'glory of the sacred volume, like the glory of its Author, needs only to be seen as it really is, in order to be felt as no earthly emanation'.[7] 'Seen as it really is' begs the very question we are considering here, and it is not surprising to find that Cumming rarely comments on the illustrations as art, saying nothing, for example, about the aesthetic qualities of Veronese's *The Judgment of Solomon*, but offering instead a moral analysis of motherhood and the education of their children.[8]

Scripture Illustrations epitomizes, in Ruskin's terms, 'what Protestants call sacred art', with Raphael (8) and four eighteenth-century artists –

---

[5] Isaac Ambrose, *Works* (London: Tegg, 1835), p. 142. Victorian devotional works included titles such as W. Poole Balfern's *Glimpses of Jesus*, much admired by Spurgeon: see C. H. Spurgeon, *Autobiography*, vol. I: *The Early Years, 1834–1859*, rev. edn, originally compiled by Susannah Spurgeon and Joseph Harrald (Edinburgh and Carlisle, PA: Banner of Truth, 1962), p. 414.

[6] The painter James Smetham, the son of a Wesleyan minister, was one of the exceptions that proved the rule, which may have contributed to the enthusiasm with which Ruskin responded to his work.

[7] *Scripture Illustrations; Chiefly from the Old Masters*, with historical and descriptive notes, by the Rev. John Cumming (London: Virtue, [1844]), p. i.   [8] Ibid., pp. 112–13.

Hamilton (10 – plate 11[9]), Loutherbourg (6), Stothard (4) and Artaud (4) – most heavily represented. Several of the works reproduced here were originally commissioned for Macklin's *Bible and Poetic Gallery* series (1788–93), and were the kind of thing that Ruskin had in mind when he wrote that the 'group calling themselves Evangelical ought no longer to render their religion an offence to men of the world by associating it only with the most vulgar forms of art', adding in a footnote that he does not know 'anything more humiliating to a man of common sense, than to open what is called an "Illustrated Bible" of modern days', and offering as an example 'the plates in Brown's Bible (octavo: Edinburgh, 1840), a standard evangelical edition' (5.88).[10] In Brown's Bible and some of the other illustrated Bibles published in the 1830s and 1840s, not only were many of the original works hateful to Ruskin, but the poor quality of some of the engravings compounded the offence.

Ruskin is silent, however, on the important subject to which Cumming refers when he writes of new light being thrown upon the 'facts recorded in Sacred Scripture'. Recent research carried out in the Holy Land made it possible for engravers to exploit new print technology at home in producing numerous illustrations of landscapes, plants, animals, artifacts and so on, and for biblical commentators to write more detailed explanatory notes on such matters.[11] It was Charles Knight's *Pictorial Bible* of 1836 that caught the imagination of Holman Hunt,[12] who was later to set out for the Near East himself, against Ruskin's advice, in January 1854, several months before *The Light of the World* was exhibited at the Royal Academy, in order to fulfil his strong desire to use his powers, as he put it to Augustus Egg, 'to make more tangible Jesus Christ's history and teaching'.[13] Hunt was in tune with his contemporaries in this desire, as the many depictions of Christ in paintings of the 1850s testify. Carlyle, in responding negatively to *The Light of the World* on a second visit to

---

[9] Hamilton's biblical subjects are typified by this plate from the Revd John Fleetwood, *The Life of Our Blessed Lord & Saviour Jesus Christ* (London: Virtue, 1842[?]), p. 254.

[10] A journal published by the Religious Tract Society reprinted a short extract on the self-taught Scottish shepherd, in 1851: 'John Brown, the Commentator', *The Visitor, or Monthly Instructor*, NS (1851), 56.

[11] The prospectus of the standard edition of the *Pictorial Bible* (1847), recorded that it was 'now ten years since this universally popular work began to be published. The principal feature of this edition of the Bible was defined by its title – to make the objects described or referred to in the Holy Scriptures familiar to the eye of the general reader.' The more lavish plates of the original edition had now been removed but more notes added, reflecting 'the immense increase in our stores of biblical information': *The Pictorial Bible*, standard edn, ed. John Kitto, 4 vols. (London: Knight, 1847–9), I, 1.   [12] See Maas, *Holman Hunt*, pp. 2–4.

[13] W[illiam] Holman Hunt, *Pre-Raphaelitism and the Pre-Raphaelite Brotherhood*, 2 vols. (London and New York: Macmillan, 1905), I, 349.

Plate 11. William Hamilton, 'Mary Anointing Jesus' Feet', in the Revd John Fleetwood, *The Life of Our Blessed Lord & Saviour Jesus Christ* (London: Virtue, [1842?]), plate 35

Hunt's studio, told him that he would give a third of his modest savings for a 'veritable contemporary representation of Jesus Christ, showing Him as He walked about'.[14] Ironically, however, such a representation could never come to light, as the early Christians, realizing 'how repulsive to the Gentile world would appear the idea of worshipping a crucified Jew', presented 'the Saviour in a form which was familiar and attractive'.[15] Ruskin dismissed both the 'familiar and attractive' images of the Saviour which appealed to his fellow Evangelicals and the historicist images produced by artists who travelled to the Holy Land in search of the facts. These antipathies, however, only partly explain his responses to Hunt's paintings, to which we now turn.

II

At the Royal Academy summer exhibition of 1850, two months after reading of the Gorham crisis on his way back from Venice and four months before the restoration of the Catholic hierarchy in England, Ruskin was 'dragged' back to look more closely at Millais's *Christ in the Carpenter's Shop (Christ in the House of his Parents)* by William Dyce (12.xlv). One sign of Tractarian sympathies in the painting is the separation of the sheep in the background from the figures in the foreground, hinting at the separation of the laity from the clergy in High Church practice that was anathema to Ruskin, who would also have seen Hunt's more obviously Tractarian *A Converted British Family Sheltering a Missionary from the Persecution of the Druids* at the exhibition.[16] The following winter saw Ruskin writing *The Stones of Venice* I and *Notes on the Construction of Sheepfolds*, published on 3 and 6 March 1851 respectively, only days before Sir Robert Peel addressed the House of Commons on the Papal Aggression and as preparations for the Great Exhibition in Hyde Park reached fever pitch – the two main topics in the current *Illustrated London News*.[17] On 1 May, the day of the official opening of the exhibition, Ruskin's diary entry was a restatement of his divine commission:

Morning: All London is astir – & some part of all the World. I am sitting in my quiet room – hearing the birds sing: and about to enter on the true beginning of the second part of my Venetian Work. May God help me to finish it to His glory, and mans good. J. Ruskin.[18]

---

[14] Ibid., 356.   [15] James Burns, *The Christ Face in Art* (London: Duckworth, 1907), p. 6.

[16] See Alastair Grieve, 'The Pre-Raphaelite Brotherhood and the Anglican High Church', *Burlington Magazine*, III, 794 (May 1969), 294–5.

[17] See *Illustrated London News*, 18, 472 (1 March 1851) and subsequent numbers.

[18] Lancaster MS 8, Diaries, front end-paper; compare *D*, 468.

Twelve days later Ruskin again wrote against the grain of Victorian culture, but this time in the public form of a letter to *The Times*, defending the young Pre-Raphaelites against the critique of their works in the Academy exhibition published on 7 May (12.319). Yet on the religious content of their paintings he wrote with the grain, mocking the 'idolatrous toilet-table' in *Mariana* and the 'lady in white' in Collins's *Convent Thoughts*, and reminding the British establishment of his own position on such matters: 'No one who has met with any of my writings,' he insisted, 'will suspect me of desiring to encourage them in their Romanist and Tractarian tendencies' (12.320).

Soon after this, Holman Hunt started work on both *The Light of the World* and *The Hireling Shepherd*, the latter painting reflecting a deeply felt response to the ecclesiastical issues of the day, and specifically to Ruskin's *Sheepfolds* pamphlet. In July Millais, Hunt's companion at Ewell, corresponded with the wife of his patron, the High Church Thomas Combe, printer to Oxford University, thanking her for sending Dyce's printed reply to Ruskin, which both of them were keen to read.[19] Sheepfolds, shepherds and sheep seemed to be everywhere, first in debates on the great religious issues of the day, and then in the art world; they even figured prominently in the foreground of one of the views of 'The Great Exhibition Building' in the *Illustrated London News* in April 1851.[20] Hunt's *The Hireling Shepherd* was exhibited at the Academy in 1852 (the same year as Ford Madox Brown's *'The Pretty Baa-Lambs'*, when Ruskin was in Venice) and *Our English Coasts, 1852 (Strayed Sheep)* in 1853.

The following year, on 10 June 1854, the opening of the Crystal Palace at Sydenham – close enough to Denmark Hill to spoil the view – again attracted enormous publicity. While the *Illustrated London News* celebrated the event, Ruskin again absented himself, this time in

---

[19] John Guille Millais, *The Life and Letters of Sir John Everett Millais, President of the Royal Academy*, 2 vols. (London: Methuen, 1899), I, 120–1. The 'domestic altar' in *Mariana* was probably based on one in Combe's house: see Grieve, 'Pre–Raphaelite Brotherhood', p. 295. In his *Notes on Shepherds and Sheep: A Letter to John Ruskin, Esq., M. A.* (London: Longmans, 1851), William Dyce concentrates upon Ruskin's use of the term 'Visible' Church, which is non-biblical; in fact it comes from Hooker: see, for example, *The Works of that Learned and Judicious Divine Mr. Richard Hooker: With an Account of his Life and Death by Isaac Walton*, ed. John Keble, 3 vols. (Oxford: Oxford University Press, 1836), I, 428; for Ruskin's notes on Hooker and the 'visible Church', see, for example, Lancaster MS 10a, Diaries, fol. 54.

[20] See *Illustrated London News*, 18, 479 (19 April 1851), 310. Millais's aversion to sheep – reportedly caused by his having to eat so much mutton and help Hunt by holding down his models in the fields – may have been shared by others in the months and years that followed: see Millais, *Life and Letters*, I, 121, 130. The interpenetration of religion and the arts at the time is epitomized in Millais's diary entry for 19 November 1851: 'Read Tennyson and the Thirty-nine Articles. Discoursed on religion' (Millais, ibid., I, 133).

Switzerland, where he could recover his spirits after the breakdown of his marriage and the public scandal that ensued. In his pamphlet on *The Opening of the Crystal Palace*, published in London on 22 July, he contrasted the haughtiness of this glittering 'mighty palace' with the quiet humility of the 'low larch huts' of the mountains that surrounded him, and the 'fourteen acres of ground' covered with glass with the 'true and noble Christian architecture' currently being destroyed all over Europe (12.417, 421). 'Must this little Europe,' he asked, 'this corner of our globe, gilded with the blood of old battles, and grey with the temples of old pieties . . . be utterly swept and garnished for the masque of the Future?' (12.429).

Before Ruskin's departure for the Continent on 10 May, the build-up to the opening of the Crystal Palace had been overshadowed by the Crimean War, which began in March. On the Sunday before Ruskin stood in front of Hunt's *The Light of the World* (plate 12) at the Royal Academy summer exhibition, a 'Day of Humiliation' had been marked by 'Fast-Day Sermons', and among the leading preachers on 26 April whose portraits accompanied those of Archbishop Sumner and Dean Milman in the *Illustrated London News* were the Ruskins' friends, the Revd George Croly and the Revd Daniel Moore, Melvill's successor at Camden Church, with whom Ruskin corresponded on religious matters.[21] Not all visitors to the exhibition, however, saw the spiritual significance of Hunt's painting at this time of national crisis. On 13 May the *Illustrated London News* reported that

Mr. Hunt's cold allegory of our Saviour is viewed with a devotional feeling by some, by others with a gaze of ill-stifled wonderment, and by too many as a piece of medieval barbarity. Nor does his smaller picture fare much better, though the attempt to discover its actual meaning has too often proved abortive, for "the Awakening Conscience" of this clever painter is now familiarly known as "the Loose Lodging".[22]

Ruskin described his own experience of watching the effect that *The Light of the World* produced 'upon the passers-by' – 'Few stopped to look at it, and those who did almost invariably with some contemptuous expression'[23] – in his third letter to *The Times* (5 May) in defence of Pre-Raphaelite art, five days before his departure for the Continent, stating that, with Hunt already 'travelling in the Holy Land', it was important

---

[21] See the *Illustrated London News*, 24, 680 (29 April 1854), 401. For the Ruskin–Moore correspondence see Morgan MA 2186.   [22] *Illustrated London News*, 24, 682 (13 May 1854), 438.

[23] Maas wonders whether Ruskin, who was notoriously naïve in such matters, might have mistaken some of the contemptuous stares that were actually directed at him: Maas, *Holman Hunt*, p. 64.

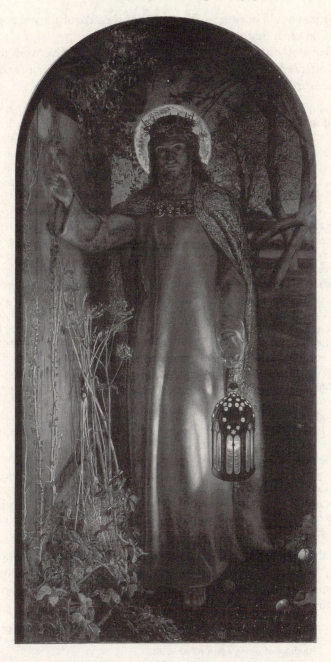

Plate 12. William Holman Hunt, *The Light of the World*, 1854

that 'justice should be done to his work', for the sake of the many people who would see it that year (12.328).[24]

Having stated that Holman Hunt never explained his work to him, Ruskin offers what appears to him 'its palpable interpretation', and starts with the words painted at the bottom of the frame:

The legend beneath it is the beautiful verse, – "Behold, I stand at the door and knock. If any man hear my voice, and open the door, I will come in to him, and will sup with him, and he with me." – Rev.iii.20. On the left-hand side of the picture is seen this door of the human soul. It is fast barred: its bars and nails are rusty; it is knitted and bound to its stanchions by creeping tendrils of ivy, showing that it has never been opened. A bat hovers about it; its threshold is overgrown with brambles, nettles, and fruitless corn, – the wild grass, "whereof the mower filleth not his hand, nor he that bindeth the sheaves his bosom". [Psalms 129.7] Christ approaches it in the night-time, – Christ, in his everlasting offices of prophet, priest, and king. He wears the white robe, representing the power of the Spirit upon him; the jewelled robe and breastplate, representing the sacerdotal investiture; the rayed crown of gold, inwoven with the crown of thorns; not dead thorns, but now bearing soft leaves for the healing of the nations.

Now, when Christ enters any human heart, he bears with him a twofold light: first, the light of conscience, which displays past sin, and afterwards the light of peace, the hope of salvation. The lantern, carried in Christ's left hand, is this light of conscience. Its fire is red and fierce; it falls only on the closed door, on the weeds which encumber it, and on an apple shaken from one of the trees of the orchard, thus marking that the entire awakening of the conscience is not merely to committed, but to hereditary guilt.

The light is suspended by a chain wrapt about the wrist of the figure, showing that the light which reveals sin appears to the sinner also to chain the hand of Christ.

The light which proceeds from the head of the figure, on the contrary, is that of the hope of salvation; it springs from the crown of thorns, and, though itself sad, subdued, and full of softness, is yet so powerful that it entirely melts into the glow of it the forms of the leaves and boughs, which it crosses, showing that every earthly object must be hidden by this light, where its sphere extends. (12.329–30)

Ruskin then states his belief that there are very few people on whom the picture, 'thus justly understood', will not 'produce a deep impression', and adds: 'For my own part, I think it one of the very noblest works of sacred art ever produced in this or any other age.'

---

[24] The editor had not printed an earlier, longer letter, in which Ruskin also commended pictures by Leslie and Inchbold. Ruskin therefore substituted this shorter letter dealing only with Hunt's picture, in the hope of seeing it printed: see 12.xlix.

Ruskin is always a hyperbolic writer, and he describes numerous paintings as the best he has ever seen, or one of the very noblest works of sacred art ever produced. In this case, however, further comments he makes reinforce his first stated view on the importance of *The Light of the World*. As we have seen, two years later he told his readers in *Modern Painters* that 'Hunt's great poetical picture' was in his view 'the most perfect instance of expressional purpose with technical power, which the world [had] yet produced' (5.65, 52). One explanation for Ruskin's high opinion of the picture is its evident strength of feeling, reflected not least in the labour which went into its making. We saw in *The Seven Lamps* that for Ruskin it is 'not the church we want, but the sacrifice; not the emotion of admiration, but the act of adoration; not the gift, but the giving' (8.39–40).[25] In his chapter 'Of the False Ideal; – First, Religious', written not long after the letter to *The Times*, Ruskin associates Hunt's representation of 'Christ as a living presence among us now' in *The Light of the World* with 'pictures of the *passionate* ideal which present imaginary beings of another world' [our emphasis] (5.85). As a later critic was to comment on the challenge of portraying Christ visually, 'however sure the touch, or wise the hand, one thing still is needed more': 'Heart counts more than hand, and soul than touch.'[26] The nurturing of religious feeling was an area in which Evangelicalism was strong.[27] Cumming, for example, in a published lecture entitled 'The Appeal of Love', took Revelation 3.20 as his text, evoking the image of 'our Lord . . . standing all night, the dark, weary, dismal, wintry, stormy night, at the door, asking for admission, and, in innumerable instances, the response being, I will not'.[28] For Ruskin, Hunt's portrayal of Christ seeking admission to 'the human heart' demands a heartfelt response from the viewer.

Secondly, Ruskin greatly admired the technique of the painting, writing in his commentary on Hunt's *The Scapegoat*, which he disliked: 'No one could sympathize more than I with the general feeling displayed in the "Light of the World"; but unless it had been accompanied with

[25] See p. 77 above.   [26] J. R. Aitken, *The Christ of the Men of Art* (Edinburgh: Clark, 1915), p. xxi.

[27] An anonymous reviewer considered that where 'religious *feeling* only is concerned', Ruskin himself was 'almost without exception, right', and argued that 'it is *heart* religion that lives and grows': 'John Ruskin as a Religious Writer', *The Christian Observer*, 62 (Sept. 1862), 658–78 (pp. 674, 678).

[28] John Cumming, *Apocalyptic Sketches; or, Lectures on the Seven Churches of Asia Minor*, 8th thousand (London: Hall, Virtue, 1851), pp. 532–3. Three series of the *Sketches* were first published in 1848–50.

perfectly good nettle painting, and ivy painting, and jewel painting, I should never have praised it' (14.65).[29]

Thirdly, the representation of Christ in the painting not only failed to offend the hypersensitive Ruskin on sectarian grounds, or further to erode his already severely tested faith, but actually confirmed him in his own Christology, the subject of Sunday reflections earlier in the decade, as recorded both in his unpublished notes and the published *Notes on the Construction of Sheepfolds*. For, contrary to the view of one modern critic, that the whole quality of the work forced Ruskin to dwell on the barred door overgrown with brambles,[30] it is the lantern and its light – discussed in detail by Ruskin – and the Christ figure itself that receive both the viewer's and Ruskin's fullest attention – 'Christ, in his everlasting offices of prophet, priest, and king'. Let us consider these three 'offices' in turn.

Christ the prophet is of special interest, as Hunt himself referred only to Christ as priest and king when commenting on the painting.[31] Isaiah's words, 'the Spirit of the Lord God is upon me; because the Lord hath anointed me to preach good tidings unto the meek' (Isaiah 61.1), have been read by Christian commentators as a prophecy of Christ's assuming the prophetical office at his Baptism, when a voice from heaven says, 'This is my beloved Son, in whom I am well pleased' (Matthew 3.16–17).[32] Ruskin's reference, however, to Christ's wearing 'the white robe, representing the power of the Spirit upon him', would seem to point to that later repetition of the Father's owning of his Son, when Jesus is transfigured before Peter, James and John, and his raiment is 'white as the light' (Matthew 17.2; Luke 9.29).[33] Following Christ's death and

[29] One reviewer commented in *The Guardian*, 16 July 1856: 'Let any one realise his own state of mind if he believed the Light of the world to be, indeed, before him; and if he thinks in that Blessed Presence he could have any eye for nettles, he will tolerate Mr. Ruskin's criticism, admire the temper of his mind, and think him a sound art critic: not otherwise' (14.xxvi). For further references to *The Light of the World* in Ruskin, see 20.63, 409; 21.75,105; 22.203; 32.220–1; 33.270; 34.169; 37.83,428.

[30] See Timothy Hilton, *The Pre-Raphaelites* (London: Thames, Hudson, 1970), p. 92.

[31] 'The kingly and priestly dress of Christ, the sign of His reign over the body and the soul': Hunt, *Pre-Raphaelitism*, I, 350–1.

[32] See, for example, Matthew Henry, *An Exposition of the Old and New Testament*, stereotype edn, 3 vols. (London: Robinson, 1828), II, 857. Also compare lines from Bishop Christopher Wordsworth's hymn, 'Songs of thankfulness and praise' – 'Manifest at Jordan's stream, / Prophet, Priest and King supreme': *Hymns Ancient and Modern*, standard edn, with accompanying tunes (London: Clowes, 1916), no. 81.

[33] Thomas Scott comments on Matthew 17.1–2, ' "the Light of the world," shone forth': *The Holy Bible*, with explanatory notes, practical observations, and copious marginal references by Thomas Scott, 9th edn, 6 vols. (London: Seeley, 1825), v. See 5.82–3 for Ruskin's note on the Transfiguration, ending, 'And, then, look at Raphael's kicking gracefulnesses' (compare original version in Lancaster MS 9, Diaries, fol.78).

Resurrection, two of these witnesses – Peter and John – heal the lame man in the temple in his name. Peter then preaches to the people who have gathered to see the spectacle 'in the porch that is called Solomon's', citing Deuteronomy: 'The Lord thy God will raise up unto thee a Prophet from the midst of thee, of thy brethren, like unto me; unto him ye shall hearken' (Deuteronomy 18.15; Acts 3.22). Ruskin cited the text in *Notes on the Construction of Sheepfolds*, when pouring scorn on the parallel made by the Tractarians between the Christian and Levitical churches, and specifically the threat of judgment fire on the rebellious Korahs, Dathans and Abirams of the day (Numbers 16), in Keble's poem in *Lyra Apostolica* (1836):

There are indeed such fires. But when Moses said, "a Prophet shall the Lord raise up unto you, like unto me", did he mean the writer who signs γ in the *Lyra Apostolica*? (12.538–9)[34]

Ruskin's reference to Christ's prophetical office is compatible with the tradition in which he was brought up. Isaac Ambrose, for example, describes Christ as 'the publisher of the gospel covenant; and in this respect he is called a Prophet, Acts iii.22. whose office it was to impart God's will unto the sons of men, according unto the name, angel'.[35] Matthew Henry, author of a famous commentary (1708–10) favoured by non-conformists in the nineteenth century, explains the typology of the verse before drawing out its eschatological significance:

a greater than Moses is here where Christ is. He is a *Prophet of God's raising up*, for he took not this honour of himself, but was *called of God* to it. He was raised up unto Israel in the first place; he executed this office in his own person among them only . . .
There is a future state, another life after this . . . *Behold, the Judge standeth before the door* . . . (Rev. xxi.1) . . .
They must hear Christ, *the great Prophet* . . .
Repent, for the kingdom of heaven is at hand . . . [36]

The Light of the World is Adventist in its symbolism and atmosphere,[37] and the origin of the theme text in the Revelation ('Behold, I stand at the door and knock') places it firmly in the realm of Christian eschatology.
    Ruskin's reference, however, to Christ's 'everlasting' office of prophet

---

[34] [J. W. Bowden, *et al.*], *Lyra Apostolica*, 2nd edn (Derby: Mozley, 1837), pp. 201–3. In contrast, Thomas Scott wrote on Hebrews 7.26–8: 'the Levitical priesthood was intended to typify, and prepare the way for that of Christ; which was pre-ordained in due time to supersede and disannul it': Scott, *Holy Bible*, VI.

[35] Ambrose, *Works*, p. 263. Also compare p. 145, where Ambrose writes of 'the offices of Christ'.

[36] Henry, *Exposition of the Old and New Testament*, III, 738–9.

[37] See Michael Wheeler, *Keble, Ruskin, and The Light of the World: A Lecture Delivered in Keble College Chapel on Sunday 28 January 1996* (Oxford: Keble College, 1996).

not only points forward to judgment and glory in the end-time, but also back to the Old Testament, and to prophecy through which, he believed, Christ himself spoke. In one of his Venice notebooks, Ruskin wrote the following entry in November or December 1851:

Prophecy of David. I wonder the 69th Psalm is not used on Good Friday instead of the 40th or 54th, it, with the 22nd, being the clearest speakings in the person of Christ. The 5th & 6th verse however are most clearly in his own person – and most beautiful [38]

Ruskin goes beyond a typological reading here: he reveals his orthodox and literalist understanding of inspired prophecy in two of what Churchmen called the 'Passion-Psalms' – 'My God, my God, why hast thou forsaken me?' (Psalm 22) and 'Save me, O God; for the waters are come in unto my soul' (Psalm 69) – and echoes Thomas Scott's headnote to Psalm 22 – 'David, prophetically speaking in the person of Christ'.[39] Thus the visual similarity between Hunt's Christ figure and traditional representations of King David can be read not only as genealogical and typological signs, but also, according to Ruskin's higher reading, of Christ's office of prophet through all eternity.[40]

Turning to Christ in his office of priest, Hunt's Messiah wears a version of the robe and breastplate which God instructed Moses to prepare for Aaron and his sons as signs of their authority as priests – their 'sacerdotal investiture', as Ruskin calls it. Hunt excitedly marked Exodus 28 in the richly illustrated Pictorial Bible which inspired so much of his work.[41] The breastplate of the Jewish priest, illustrated in Hunt's Bible, is faithfully reproduced on a smaller scale as the square ouch of the elaborate clasp in the painting. (According to F. G. Stephens, the thirteen precious stones set in the circular ouch to the left were intended to represent 'the heathen priesthoods, some of whom bore a symbol of this kind'.[42]) Meanwhile Ruskin himself wrote private notes on the priest's breastplate in October 1852 – an uncanny example of the convergence of his interests and those of Hunt.[43]

[38] Lancaster MS 8, Diaries, fol. 28. In Psalm 69.5–6 David acknowledges his sinful nature.

[39] Scott, *Holy Bible*, III.

[40] Ruskin's difficulties with prophecy, explained to his father in a letter from Venice in January 1852, concerned his no longer enjoying its 'poetry' and instead looking for 'one or two clearer dates' (36.127). His emphasis here falls upon prophecy as the prediction of the future: '*all* our Saviour's prophecies', he writes, 'except those respecting Jerusalem, remain subjects of continual dispute' (36.128).   [41] See Maas, *Holman Hunt*, pp. 31–3.

[42] F. G. Stephens, *William Holman Hunt and his Works* (London: Nisbet, 1860), p. 26; quoted by Maas, *Holman Hunt*, p. 32.

[43] 'The Breastplate. Passing by the overlaying with gold – and vail of the Tabernacle – we come to the Breastplate – a breast plate of Judgment – the jewels, the Urim & Thummim [Exodus 28.30]': Lancaster MS 10a, Diaries, fol.146.

It is in Hebrews 7 that the doctrine of the priestly office of Christ is set in a tradition coming down from Melchizedek, king of Salem and the first high priest (Genesis 14.18):

But this man, because he continueth ever, hath an unchangeable priesthood. . . . A minister of the sanctuary, and of the true tabernacle, which the Lord pitched, and not man. (Hebrews 7.24, 8.2)

Hunt's Christ the great high priest, 'standing at midnight by a barred door', it later appeared to one viewer, 'with nineteen centuries of baffled expectation in His eyes',[44] continueth ever. When Ruskin, in *Notes on the Construction of Sheepfolds*, addressed the question, 'What should be the offices, and of what kind should be the authority, of the Clergy?' (12.535), he dismissed the 'blasphemous claim on the part of the Clergy of being *more* Priests than the godless laity' as 'altogether a Romanist heresy' (12.537). For him it was therefore utterly appropriate that the Christ be dressed in the 'jewelled robe and breastplate, representing the sacerdotal investiture', rather than the clergy.[45]

Again, Evangelical sermons and devotional literature had shaped Ruskin's beliefs and ideas.[46] Isaac Ambrose, for example, wrote in a chapter entitled 'Of the Covenant of Promise, as manifested to David':

Christ is more clearly manifested in this breaking forth of the covenant, than in any of the former. For here we see . . . That he must be Priest, as well as King; and Sacrifice, as well as Priest. *Thou art a Priest for ever, after the order of Melchisadech.* [Hebrews 7.17][47]

Later in *Looking unto Jesus*, Ambrose develops the theme of Christ as 'Sacrifice, as well as Priest', stating that 'the apostle sets forth Christ as an high priest, who was *holy, harmless, undefiled, and separate from sinners*; and in like manner saith Peter; *Ye are a chosen generation, a royal priesthood*'; and that

as the Jews had their high-priest to intercede for them, so the Lord Jesus was to be the high-priest of our profession, and to intercede for us . . . The physical symbols on the high priest are types of the spiritual attributes of Christ as high priest . . . The high-priests then interceded not without all these materials, viz. a temple, an altar, a sacrifice, a censer of burning coals taken off the altar, a putting the incense upon the fire, that the cloud of the incense might cover the

[44] G. A. Chadwick, 'The Ministry of Jesus Christ', in *The Gospels in Art*, ed. W. Shaw Sparrow, Art & Life Library (London: Hodder, Stoughton, 1904), pp. 113–22 (p. 119).
[45] In the early 1850s Ruskin made some private notes criticizing Walter Farquhar Hook's sermon, *Hear the Church* (1838) – 'as if the Office of the High Priesthood, and office of ministry, were all one!': Lancaster MS 10a, Diaries, fol. 52v.
[46] Thomas Scott wrote on Hebrews 5, 'Christ alone is qualified and authorized to be our High Priest': Scott, *Holy Bible*, VI.   [47] Ambrose, *Works*, p. 175.

mercy seat, a sprinkling the mercy-seat with the blood of the bullock and of the goat: but Jesus Christ in his intercessions now needs none of these materials; but rather he himself, and his own merits, are instead of all; as, 1. He is the temple . . . 2. He is the altar . . . Christ stands next to God, as our great high-priest . . . Christ was called to this office by God, his Father.[48]

We will return to this passage in a moment, but must first consider Hunt's Christ the king, wearing what Ruskin describes as 'the rayed crown of gold, inwoven with the crown of thorns; not dead thorns, but now bearing soft leaves for the healing of the nations'. It is in the Book of Revelation that Christ is hailed as 'Lord of lords, and King of kings' (17.14), having, as Matthew Henry expresses it, 'both by nature and by office, supreme dominion and power over all things'.[49] This king is also the eternal judge; indeed, Hunt's theme text, 'Behold, I stand at the door, and knock', comes from the passage in which the angel of Laodicea is rebuked for being neither hot nor cold, and is immediately preceded by these words: 'As many as I love, I rebuke and chasten: be zealous, therefore, and repent' (Revelation 3.19). Ruskin described Revelation 21 as 'one of the most important chapters' in the Bible, and drew upon it in *The Stones of Venice*, where, not long before the 1854 exhibition at the Royal Academy, he had written of Venice coming to judgment.[50] Indeed, he claimed to have learnt 'most of the Apocalypse' by heart (12.168)[51] and his study of it in middle age enthralled and excited him.[52] In Revelation 14.14, 'one sat like unto the Son of man, having on his head a golden crown' – the crown of victory for the risen Son of David (King David, who was anointed by Samuel (1 Samuel 16.12).) Ruskin's emphasis, however, falls upon the crown of thorns that is woven into the crown of gold, and which, like Aaron's rod (Numbers 17.8), buds,[53] producing

---

[48] Ibid., pp. 293, 416–19, 424. Similarly, Thomas Scott writes of Christ in his commentary on Exodus 27, 'He indeed is our Prophet . . . our King . . . our Example, . . . our Altar, our Priest, our Sacrifice, our Mediator': Scott, *Holy Bible*, I.

[49] Henry, *Exposition of the Old and New Testament*, III, 1408.

[50] See chapter 4 above. Revelation 21.23 is particularly relevant to *The Light of the World*: 'And the city had no need of the sun, neither of the moon, to shine in it: for the glory of God did lighten it, and the Lamb is the light [λυχνος, lamp] thereof'.

[51] In a separate statement, Ruskin recorded that Revelation 5 and 6 were on his mother's list of chapters that he committed to memory (28.101).

[52] On 24 October 1877, for example, as he prepared the December *Fors* of that year (see 29.296–304), he wrote from Brantwood to his god-daughter, Constance Oldham: 'I'm in spirits this morning because I've had a lovely little lesson myself – I never noticed before this morning that the attribute claimed by Christ in each address, in IInd chapter Apoc, – has direct reference to the promise or threatening to the several Churches and the promise to him that overcometh.' Rylands MS 12/48, fol.36.

[53] Thomas Scott writes on Numbers 17.6–11, 'This was a fit emblem of the Messiah's resurrection, as declarative . . . of his priesthood's being acceptable to God': Scott, *Holy Bible*, I.

leaves as on the tree of life described in the last chapter of the Bible: 'and the leaves of the tree were for the healing of the nations' (Revelation 22.2).

As in *Modern Painters* II, then, it is the God of peace whom Ruskin celebrates in his reading of Christ the king in *The Light of the World*, rather than the God of power and might. In his unpublished notes on 'The Headship of Christ', made as he worked on *Notes on the Construction of Sheepfolds* in the autumn of 1850, he focused upon the Greek word *pleroma*, arguing that in Ephesians 1.23 Christ is 'spoken of as over all & filling all: Then the church or whole body of his saints, is said to be his body: in the filling up and completion of Him who fills all things'.[54] It is in the fulfilment of Christ's three everlasting offices of prophet, priest and king that, for Ruskin, the true nature of this 'filling all' is revealed. And again, Solomon and his temple are important Old Testament types for Christ's ministry in the 'true tabernacle' of the new covenant.

Ruskin argued in *Notes on the Construction of Sheepfolds* that a minister of religion is God's 'Messenger', not His 'Representative' (12.550), and chose Solomon as one of his illustrative Old Testament types (12.555).[55] He referred in his working notes to Solomon putting Zadok the priest 'in the room of Abiathar' (1 Kings 2.35), and drew upon both 1 Kings and 1 Chronicles, which treat the same material from different perspectives:

The people anoint Solomon for chief governor, & Zadok to be priest as if both derived at least the Confirmation of their authority from the people 1 Chron. 29.22

Again Solomon thrusts out Abiathar from being priest I. Kings II.27 and appointed the courses of the priests to their service II. Chron. VIII 14.

Jeroboam, in leading the people astray, ordains a feast: in the month which he had devised of his own heart I. Kings 12.32 and made of the lowest of the people priests of the high places. I. Kings 13.32 [56]

Like the high priests to whom Isaac Ambrose refers in *Looking unto Jesus*, Solomon 'interceded not without all these materials' when he 'offered a sacrifice of peace offerings' in his newly dedicated temple (1 Kings 8.63), whereas Christ the king, his antitype, is the temple, is the altar, is the priest.[57] Ruskin, in the section of *Notes on the Construction of Sheepfolds* in

---

[54] Lancaster MS 5c, Diaries, fol. 164.   [55] See p. 84 above.

[56] Lancaster MS 5c, Diaries, fol. 171.

[57] Compare 'As the *Golden Candlestick* did yield a beautiful light within the Temple continually before the Lord: Accordingly, doth our Lord Jesus term himself *the light of the World* [John 8.12], that whoever followeth him, and worketh by that light, shall not walk in darknesse; but enjoy the light of eternal life': [Samuel Lee], *Orbis Miraculum; or, The Temple of Solomon* (London: Streater, 1659), p. 191.

which he attacks Keble, argues that 'the office of the Lawgiver and Priest is now for ever gathered into One Mediator between God and man; and THEY are guilty of the sin of Korah who blasphemously would associate themselves in His Mediatorship' (12.539). For Ruskin, Hunt's great high priest, dressed in the 'jewelled robe and breastplate, representing the sacerdotal investiture' and a minister of the true tabernacle, completes the work not only of King Melchizedek, but also of King David and King Solomon.

Ruskin also associated Hunt's theme text with the wisdom tradition of the Old Testament, for again, Christ *is* wisdom (1 Corinthians 1.30).[58] The description of the pulpit at Torcello in *The Stones of Venice* II (1853) anticipates his reading of *The Light of the World* in a number of ways:

> But if once we begin to regard the preacher, whatever his faults, as a man sent with a message to us, which it is a matter of life or death whether we hear or refuse; . . . if we make some endeavour to conceive how precious these hours ought to be to him, a small vantage on the side of God after his flock have been exposed for six days together to the full weight of the world's temptation, and he has been forced to watch the thorn and the thistle springing in their hearts, and to see what wheat had been scattered there snatched from the wayside by this wild bird and the other [Matthew 13.3–9]; and at last, when, breathless and weary with the week's labour, they give him this interval of imperfect and languid hearing, he has but thirty minutes to get at the separate hearts of a thousand men . . . to try by this way and that to stir the hard fastenings of those doors where the Master Himself has stood and knocked yet none opened [Revelation 3.20], and to call at the openings of those dark streets where Wisdom herself hath stretched forth her hands and no man regarded, [Proverbs 1.20, 24] – thirty minutes to raise the dead in . . . (10.32)

Later, in 'The Ducal Palace', Ruskin argues that all 'early Christians' knew that the 'believer who had Christ' had all the virtues: 'Wisdom? Christ was his light' (10.368).

Thus for Ruskin, Hunt's *The Light of the World* confirms him in an understanding of the Christ as the everlasting prophet, priest and king who is himself the light of wisdom, for 'a greater than Solomon is here' (Matthew 12.42, Luke 11.31). Moreover, the author of *Notes on the Construction of Sheepfolds* could approve a painting which, though labelled at different times Evangelical, Broad Church, and 'Papist' in orienta-

---

[58] 'Wisdom – in His incarnation, in His life of obedience, in His teaching, in His death of atonement, in His glorification and sending of the Spirit': Henry Alford, *The Greek Testament: with a Critically Revised Text*, 7th edn, 4 vols. (London: Rivingtons, 1877), II, 482.

tion,[59] in fact defeats sectarian readings by presenting a Christ who appeals to every human heart and by making no overt reference to the contentious issues of church authority or biblical authority.

It was perhaps the combination of these factors that gave Ruskin the confidence, indeed the audacity to hold the painting up for comparison with Raphael in 'Of the False Ideal; First – Religious' in *Modern Painters* III, thus flying in the face not only of the art establishment's views on Raphael and his tradition, but also of Evangelical opinion.[60] John Cumming, it was stated earlier, rarely comments on the quality of the pictures discussed in *Scripture Illustrations*. He does, however, risk this observation on Raphael's *Miraculous Draught of Fishes*:

> The figures in this Cartoon are six, well and expressively arranged. Peter's attitude of blended fear, and joy, and admiration, and our Lord's position of dignity, and grandeur, and power, are most remarkable. The only defect in the Cartoon is the small size of the boats . . . [61]

More surprising is his relaxed attitude to the content of the cartoon of *Christ's Charge to Peter* (plate 13) in the Kensington Museum: 'The keys were given to all the apostles, and all were invested with equal power and authority, though Peter, the chiefest sinner, was specially made use of to admit the Gentiles to the same privileges and promises with the Jews.'[62] In contrast, Ruskin fumes at the 'bold fallacy' of putting all the other apostles in the picture, and then in the background – 'a mere lie to serve the Papal heresy of the Petric supremacy' (5.81).[63]

Using his favourite technique of overpowering a work which he dislikes with a salvo of his own descriptive prose, Ruskin juxtaposes Raphael's 'vapid fineries' with his own evocation of the gospel scene, in which he emphasizes the 'close facts' of this post-Resurrection appearance through his references to the apostles eating their 'broiled fish' and

---

[59] Andrew Tate reads it as an Evangelical conversion painting: 'Conversion in Crisis: Ruskin and his Circle, 1850–60', unpublished doctoral dissertation, Lancaster University, 1998. P. T. Forsyth wrote of Hunt's 'Broad-Churchism which still retains its evangelical fervour': *Religion in Recent Art: Expository Lectures on Rossetti, Burne Jones, Watts, Holman Hunt and Wagner* (London: Hodder, Stoughton, 1901), p. 165. Carlyle dismissed it as as a 'mere papistical fantasy': Hunt, *Pre–Raphaelitism*, I, 355.

[60] James Smetham told Ruskin, in a letter dated 16 November 1854: 'At eleven . . . I went to a boarding-school at Woodhouse Grove, in Yorkshire, where the sons of Methodist preachers are educated, or ought to be; and where I ought to have learned more than I did. There I copied Raphael's cartoons from the *Penny Magazine*'. *Letters of Smetham*, p. 3.

[61] Cumming, *Scripture Illustrations*, p. 46.   [62] Ibid., p. 48.

[63] Thomas Scott comments on John 21.15–17, 'The arguments of the papists for the supremacy of the pope, from this passage, only prove their cause to be desperate, as to scriptural argument': Scott, *Holy Bible*, V. In a note of 1856 Ruskin writes, 'Of the "thou shalt be called Cephas", I can understand nothing particular': Lancaster MS 11, fol.32.

Plate 13. Raphael, cartoon for *The Charge to Peter*

to Peter, 'thinking a little, perhaps, of what happened by another coal fire, when it was colder' (5.80–2). This kind of literalist retelling of key biblical events was an aspect of Evangelical tradition to which Ruskin was deeply indebted. Henry Melvill, whom Ruskin much admired, may have been particularly influential in this case through his published sermon on 'The Fire on the Shore', in which he asks:

How came this fire of coals on this lonely shore? Who kindled it? Who laid out the provision, the fish and the bread? . . .
We must proceed with caution, we must proceed with prayer: the inspired historian adds no explanation; he gives nothing but the facts . . .
We consider that Christ caused a miraculous draught of fishes, to remind Peter how He had called him originally, and to produce in him a sorrowing remembrance of his grievous apostasy.[64]

Ruskin, like Melvill, observes the scene with the inner eye of faith and recreates it with what he calls an 'anxious thirst' for the facts. What disturbs him is Raphael's ability to think of the Madonna dispassionately, rejecting the 'glittering childishness of the old art' and scientifically reconstructing her, from the skeleton up, and then draping her with classical grace (5.78). The new truths of the Renaissance were not 'sought for truth's sake, but for pride's'. The result, in the case of *Christ's Charge to Peter*, is that 'we feel our belief of the whole thing taken away' (5.82).

It is a few pages after this that Ruskin writes of the works of those 'faithful religious masters', 'the more they are considered, not as works of art, but as real visions of real things, more or less imperfectly set down, the more good will be got by dwelling upon them', adding: 'The same is true of all representations of Christ as a living presence among us now, as in Hunt's Light of the World' (5.86). True sacred art is in Ruskin's view an act of faith, both in its making and in its reception. It represents that which belief apprehends as the real through the workings of the Imagination Penetrative and Theoria; and through its pursuit of truth it leads to life. Twelve years later, James Smetham, Ruskin's pupil and devotee, was to compare the Epistle to the Hebrews to a living body:

It is mighty through God. It arises and stands upon its feet. Now, no one can describe the difference between inanimation and *life*, but the whole nature echoes loudly to it. "Because I live," says the Great High Priest, "ye shall live also."[65]

---

[64] Henry Melvill, *Sermons on certain of the less prominent Facts and References in Sacred Story*, 2 vols. (London: Rivington, 1843–5), II, 25, 26, 34.   [65] *Letters of Smetham*, p. 146.

IV

If the pursuit of truth leads to life, why did Ruskin not like the picture
on which Hunt worked over a period of six years, and considered to be
his masterpiece – *The Finding of the Saviour in the Temple* (1860; plate 14)?
The irony of the fact that Ruskin neglected a painting which 'so embodies a Ruskinian programme' in its realism and use of typology has been
noted.[66] The irony deepens when his interest in the temple at Jerusalem
is taken into account. The claim, however, that by 1860 Ruskin had 'lost
his religious belief' and therefore was 'no longer interested' is not a satis-
factory explanation.[67] Ruskin's 'un-conversion' in Turin in 1858 was not
the total 'loss of faith' that most critics assume it to be; and Ruskin
remained deeply interested and engaged in biblical history and its visual
representation after 1858.[68] It is rather the historicism of the painting
that presents him with difficulties.

Ruskin's very high opinion of Hunt is not in doubt, and his reference
to this 'great picture' in 'Peace' in *Modern Painters* v (1860), where he
argued that England's 'form of unbelief in God is connected with, and
necessarily productive of, a precisely equal unbelief in man' (7.448), was
a public acknowledgment of his gratefulness to Hunt for his continued
adherence to Pre-Raphaelite and Christian principles, and regret that
the critics and the public had neglected him.[69] Privately, however,
Ruskin had always been against Hunt's going to the Holy Land after
completing *The Light of the World*. He wrote to him on 20 October 1853:

> You are not fit to do it yet – your own genius is yet *quite undeveloped* – I say so the
> more positively because I think it is a great one – and the greater it is, the longer
> it will take to mature. If you go to the Holy Land now, you will paint things that
> you will be ashamed of in seven years . . .[70]

Ruskin seems to have recognized that Hunt, whose obsessive attention
to detail drove him to work on *The Light of the World* from dusk until dawn
in an orchard in Surrey, would find too many exotic subjects in Palestine

---

[66] George P. Landow, '"Your Good Influence on Me": The Correspondence of John Ruskin and
William Holman Hunt', *Bulletin of the John Rylands University Library of Manchester*, 59 (1976–7),
95–126, 367–96 (p. 368).

[67] Landow, ibid., p. 105, 368. For evidence of Ruskin's continued close study of and interest in the
Bible, for example, see his notes on Romans made in the summer of 1859: Lancaster MS 11,
Diaries, fols. 285f. (Landow does, however, acknowledge that Ruskin rediscovered his faith later
in life.)   [68] See chapter 6 below.

[69] Great as it is, *The Finding of the Saviour in the Temple* and Hunt's other works are not 'the best he
could have done' but 'the least he could have done'; and Ruskin can hardly trust himself to
imagine 'what Turner might have done for us, had he received help and love, instead of disdain'
(7.451, 454).   [70] Landow, 'Correspondence', p. 114.

Plate 14. William Holman Hunt, *The Finding of the Saviour in the Temple* 1860

for seductively detailed treatment, and thus be diverted from his higher purpose of producing 'true sacred art'.[71] He would also be carried away with his own enthusiasm and artistic feeling. Ruskin modified his earlier statements on the importance of feeling in art when writing his critique of *The Scapegoat* (1856) in *Academy Notes*:

Now, we cannot, I think, esteem too highly, or receive too gratefully, the temper and the toil which have produced this picture for us . . . But, at the same time, this picture indicates a danger to our students of a kind hitherto unknown in any school – the danger of a too great intensity of feeling, making them forget the requirements of painting as an *art*. This picture regarded merely as a landscape, or as a composition, is a total failure. (14.64)

A further problem for Ruskin in the case of *The Finding of the Saviour* is hinted at in a letter he writes some time between October 1856 and the summer of 1857 concerning a visit to Hunt's studio to see the painting, accompanied by a minor artist of his acquaintance: 'I am going to bring a clever little lady, Mrs Blackburn, to see you & the Jews.'[72] Ruskin knew that Hunt had found it difficult to obtain Jewish models in Jerusalem, and his facetious remark reflects the fact that there are so many Jewish figures in the painting. He would also have understood, if not necessarily supported, the position of one of Hunt's fellow artists who disliked the painting as it was 'nothing less than blasphemous, seeing "it was only a representation of a parcel of modern Turks in a café"'.[73] The unnamed artist probably knew that Hunt had worked up the interior of the temple from the Alhambra Court in the Crystal Palace.[74] This information would have shocked Ruskin, confirming his worst suspicions concerning Hunt's diversion from the true path of sacred art. For not only was it Herod's recently restored temple that was represented in the painting, with perfect historical accuracy, and not Solomon's temple, which was of such profound typological significance to Ruskin; but some of Hunt's details were gleaned from that temple of glass at Sydenham to which Ruskin had directed the full force of his opposition in print only two or

[71] P. T. Forsyth took a similar line to Ruskin's, arguing that 'what the archaeology of the creeds did to the theologian [F. D. Maurice], the archaeology of the Holy Land seems to have done to the artist. It has engrossed his enthusiasm without always furthering in a proportionate degree the expression of his genius': Forsyth, *Religion in Recent Art*, pp. 165–6. Compare Ruskin's comments on *The Shadow of Death* (30.308).   [72] Landow, 'Correspondence', p. 119.

[73] Hunt, *Pre-Raphaelitism*, II, 197.

[74] 'Islamic architecture was thought to have derived from ancient sources': Judith Bronkhurst, 'William Holman Hunt, *The Finding of the Saviour in the Temple*', in *The Pre-Raphaelites* (London: Tate Gallery / Penguin, 1984), p. 158. The Alhambra Court was described as 'indescribably magnificent' when the Crystal Palace opened at Sydenham: *Illustrated London News*, 24, 688 (17 June 1854), 580.

three years earlier. Above all, however, although Hunt was unable to find a Jewish model for him, the boy Jesus is represented as a Jew, the son of Jewish parents. In terms of biblical archaeology this was of course correct, and might have been the kind of image for which Carlyle was willing to give a third of his savings. For the Jews themselves, however, it was a blasphemy, and for Ruskin it was not a representation of the living Lord.[75]

Hunt's agitated letter to Ruskin of 4 May 1858 indicates that the critic's nagging comments about the time he was devoting to the work had upset him. (Ruskin did not perhaps fully realize that Hunt was forced to break off from time to time and produce smaller works for financial reasons.) It also challenges Ruskin on his own ground of the artist's pursuit of the truth 'to its home until it is secured as a new revelation from God'.[76] For Ruskin such inspiration came not from scenes in Palestine, but from the Bible under the guidance of the Holy Spirit, and could be encouraged through the kind of alert attention to daily Bible readings that he himself maintained for most of his life. It was on these grounds that Ruskin criticized *The Finding of the Saviour* when he allowed himself a rare statement on the work in a letter to his 'Birds' at Winnington School in 1860. The girls had seen it on display in Manchester, and had been discussing it. Ruskin wrote:

I can't tell you what to look for in Hunt's picture. There are some things I don't like – others I don't understand in it. I never venture to speak about it: in many ways it is admirable – and you had better all admire it – as much as you can – unbiassed for or against. I should like much to know what you think of it.

I don't mind telling you this much – that I don't believe Christ ever spoke to a person – least of all to his mother – without wholly *thinking of them*. He never was thinking of something else – (I mean – humanly considering Him).

This is my chief fault with the picture, a radical one to my mind.

Miss Bramwell's account of the light of the world is most true & right & admirable. I hope you will soon have the engraving of it.[77]

Not for Ruskin the twentieth-century understanding of Christ's 'hard sayings' to his mother which challenge the ideal of the Holy Family as a

---

[75] Late in his career, in his first lecture on *The Art of England* at Oxford (1883), Ruskin praised Hunt's *The Triumph of the Innocents* for its imaginative realization of the flight into Egypt and its representation of 'the glorified souls of the Innocents' (33.277).

[76] Landow, 'Correspondence', p. 124. Ruskin was still complaining to the Brownings that Hunt spent 'too much time on one picture, without adequate result' in December 1859 (36.331).

[77] *The Winnington Letters: John Ruskin's Correspondence with Margaret Alexis Bell and the Children at Winnington Hall*, ed. Van Akin Burd (London: Allen, Unwin, 1969), pp. 264–5. In a note of 1856 on the 'First recorded words of Christ', Ruskin found 'mystical' significance for Christians in the 'how is it that ye sought me', but changed his mind on 11 July 1858 – 'Very absurd. Take it simply': Lancaster MS 11, Diaries, fols. 30–1.

model for Christians to follow. Ruskin's careful analysis of the gospels in the devotional manner encouraged by Thomas Scott's commentary and thousands of Evangelical sermons – and he never made a comment like this without being able to provide the evidence to support it – led him to believe that attentiveness to others during his lifetime was one of Christ's attributes, and that Hunt painted the scene without seeking the divine inspiration that would have led him to such a conclusion himself. Again, Ruskin's reading is strongly Protestant: his Methodist pupil James Smetham writes of Christ in a letter of 1863, 'How *personal* he was.'[78]

Fifteen years later, in 1875, Ruskin was to make a passing comment in one of his *Academy Notes* which summarized his view of the two paintings that have been under discussion. He argued that 'your own people, as they live, are the only ones you can understand': 'Lewis loses his animal power among the arabesques of Cairo, Turner his Yorkshire honesty at Rome, and Holman Hunt – painting the "Light of the World" in an English orchard – paints the gaslight of Bond Street in the Holy Land' (14.291). For Ruskin it was Hunt's portrayal of Christ as 'a living presence among us now' that could be described as 'true sacred art'.

---

[78] *Letters of Smetham*, p. 113.

CHAPTER 6

Solomon's 'Christian royalty': a rite of passage in Turin

> In order to show the meaning of this symbol, and that Solomon is
> typically invested with the Christian royalty, one of the elders, by a
> bold anachronism, holds a jewel in his hand in the shape of a cross,
> with which he (by accident of gesture) points to Solomon . . .
>
> 'The Wings of the Lion', *Modern Painters* v (7.293)

I

In the summer of 1858, two years after the publication of *Modern Painters*
III and IV and two years before that of volume V, Ruskin underwent a
rite of passage in his spiritual life which he later described as an un-conversion (29.89) and later still as 'the Queen of Sheba crash' (35.497).
Following an exhausting winter devoted to the Turner Bequest in the
National Gallery, and having 'set about' the last volume of *Modern
Painters* in early March (*D*, 534), he escaped from Denmark Hill and his
elderly parents on a Continental tour which allowed him breathing
space from May until September, and which proved to be as formative
as the earlier tour of 1845 (35.493). For the first time since his marriage
breakdown and his rise to fame in both Britain and America in the mid-
1850s, Ruskin was able to take a holiday from being the famous 'Author
of *Modern Painters*' and all that that implied to him, to his reading public
and to his anxious and demanding father. Mindful of his own mortality
in his fortieth year, and having lost his belief in a life after death, he went
through a classic liminal phase in his personal life, during which his emotions were unsettled, and his views on religious and artistic issues revised.
He surprised himself by being bored among the high Alps and then
enjoying the bustle of Turin, where the glorious Renaissance worldliness
of Veronese's *The Presentation of the Queen of Sheba to Solomon* captivated
him. He was less surprised at being disappointed by the Vaudois 'shepherds' idealized by English Puritanism, both in the famous Valleys of the

Waldensians and in their new church in Turin. It was when he considered the Vaudois and Veronese's painting together, in a pairing like those
in *Modern Painters* v, that the contradictions in his own life – between his
art criticism and his religion – found their 'objective correlative'.[1]

As this was the most important crisis in Ruskin's religious life, and the
most easily caricatured as another simple case of Victorian 'loss of faith',
it deserves revisiting with a closer attention to biographical detail than
in earlier chapters, with the aim of identifying the religious associations
of various elements of the tour for Ruskin. The relationship between the
mountains and the city, and between the Vaudois (inhabitants of the
mountains) and Veronese's painting (exhibited in the city) will be examined as we consider the several accounts Ruskin gives of the painting –
first privately and then in various public forms – and the symbolic
significance of Solomon and Sheba for him at this stage of his career.
First, however, we should consider the state of Ruskin's spiritual life
before he set out on the tour.

Looking back at what he called the 'breaking down' of his 'Puritan
faith' in the chapter entitled 'The Grand Chartreuse' in *Præterita*
(35.483), Ruskin describes himself in an ironic tone as a marginal figure
in London religious circles in the 1850s, and specifically in his contacts
with the 'Liberalism of Red Lion Square' and 'the Puritanism of
Belgravia' (35.490). He recalls a dispute with the Revd F. D. Maurice
at the one Bible lesson by the Principal of the Working Men's College
that he attended, when he 'sate silent' through the instruction and then
'ventured' to make an enquiry, only to creep away in disgrace and
never to return (35.486). (The fact that two pupils who were present on
this occasion wrote jointly to Ruskin in 1888 disputing his account of
the lesson (35.487) reflects the unreliability of Ruskin's memory by this
time, or his tendency to shape his reminiscences to suit himself, partly
for therapeutic reasons, or both.) He also describes himself literally
taking a back seat at a 'fashionable séance of Evangelical doctrine' in
Belgravia, where again he asked an awkward question of the presiding
clergyman, the Revd Capel Molyneux, to the horror of the 'converted
company', and again retired, never to return (35.489).[2] Ruskin's rest-
lessness and his confrontational behaviour reflect his impatience with
the Churches in the 1850s, and the urgency with which he sought

---

[1] T. S. Eliot, 'Hamlet', in *Selected Essays*, 3rd edn (London: Faber, 1951), p. 145.

[2] A series of Evangelical addresses in Geneva in the late 1850s were entitled '*Séances Historiques*':
see Henry Bristow Wilson, '*Séances historiques de Genève: The National Church*', in Frederick Temple,
et al., *Essays and Reviews*, 12th edn (London: Longmans, 1869), pp. 173–248 (p. 173).

teaching based upon what he regarded as the fundamental message of the gospel – that we are to live and work according to God's will and not our own. Ruskin was equally confrontational with the young Charles H. Spurgeon, who was fifteen years his junior, declaring during one of their many conversations at the Baptist preacher's house around 1858 that 'the apostle Paul was a liar' and that he 'was a fool!' (34.660).[3]

Both men were under strain in the early months of 1858. As well as struggling with religious difficulties, the sexually immature Ruskin had come across disturbingly explicit sketches by his Master during the work on the Turner Bequest, and had in January met for the first time the 10-year-old Rose La Touche, with whom he was to fall in love.[4] (Ironically, Rose's father, John La Touche, who played a leading role in the tragedy that ensued, also heard Spurgeon preach at this period, and was baptized by him in 1863.[5]) Spurgeon himself, whose fund-raising campaign for his Metropolitan Tabernacle was proving to be extremely demanding, seemed to be 'sad' and 'troubled' during February and March 1858, according to one eye-witness, in spite of his fame and the success of his mission.[6] Whether Spurgeon was also passing through some kind of spiritual wilderness, and, if so, whether this had anything to do with his conversations with Ruskin, we cannot tell. We do, however, have access to Ruskin's thoughts about Spurgeon, shared in correspondence with the Brownings at Casa Guidi, Florence, as friends who understood how the English Puritan tradition manifested itself in the Dissenting pulpits of South London.[7] The vulgarity of the Spurgeon phenomenon was a favourite topic among the educated classes, and the preacher even

[3] By upbringing and by inclination Ruskin always had leading figures in their fields as sparring partners: the Revd Thomas Dale, who was to become the first Professor of English Language and Literature in England, for arguments on literature in his youth; Spurgeon, the most famous Baptist preacher in England, for debates on Protestantism at forty; and his friend Henry Edward Manning, Cardinal Archbishop of Westminster, for discussions on Catholicism at fifty. He disagreed with all of them.

[4] See *John Ruskin and Rose la Touche: Her Unpublished Diaries of 1861 and 1867*, ed. Van Akin Burd (Oxford: Clarendon; New York: Oxford University Press, 1979), p. 37. Ruskin mistook her age for 9. [5] See Burd, ibid., p. 31.

[6] 'I shall never forget the way in which, about this period, he quoted those words of our Lord, "My God, My God, why hast Thou forsaken Me?" The piercing, wailing, almost shrieking cry, and the sorrowful tones of his voice, must have gone to many another heart as they did to mine': C. H. Spurgeon, *Autobiography*, vol. 1: *The Early Years, 1834–1859*, rev. edn, originally compiled by Susannah Spurgeon and Joseph Harrald (Edinburgh and Carlisle, PA: Banner of Truth, 1962), pp. 43–4.

[7] Robert Browning's mother sat under the Revd George Clayton in York Street, Walworth: see William Irvine and Park Honan, *The Book, the Ring, and the Poet: A Biography of Robert Browning* (London: Bodley, 1975), p. 4.

addressed it himself.[8] Ruskin touches upon it with characteristic humour in a letter of 24 January 1858. His main point is, however, more significant – that Spurgeon, irrespective of his style and his sectarian affiliation, is not to be criticized for preaching doctrine that is central to Christianity:

His doctrine is simply Bunyan's, Baxter's, Calvin's, and John Knox's – in many respects not pleasant to *me*, but I dare not say that the offence is the doctrine's and not mine. It is the doctrine of Romish saints and of the Church of England. Why should we find fault with it specially in Spurgeon and not in St. Francis or Jeremy Taylor? The "Turn or Burn" is merely a vulgar modernism of Proverbs i. 23 – 32, but the vulgarity of it is the precise character which makes it useful to vulgar people; and it is certainly better to save them vulgarly than lose them gracefully – as our polite clergymen do. Evangelicalism (Dissenter's Evangel at least) is, I confess, rather greasy in the finger; sometimes with train oil; but Spurgeon's is olive, with the slightest possible degradation sometimes – in the way of Castor. (36.275–6)[9]

Noting in passing that Ruskin chose Solomon's teaching as his touch-stone here, where he might have chosen a passage from the New Testament or Spurgeon's own text (Psalms 7.12),[10] the more important point is its use in defence of Spurgeon, whom he admired in spite of his doctrines and his vulgarity.

Ruskin's admiration for Spurgeon had grown over the previous twelve months, during which he frequently joined other leading members of London society among the vast throngs of all creeds and of none who flocked to the Surrey Gardens Music Hall to hear him,[11] the most popular preacher of the day (plate 15).[12] Ruskin had recorded in his diary on his birthday, Sunday 8 February 1857, 'Heard Mr. Spurgeon on

[8] 'Preaching for the Poor', 25 January 1857: 'we have long learnt that vulgarity is a very different thing from what some men suppose . . . we are willing to be even clowns for Christ's sake'. *The New Park Street Pulpit, Containing Sermons Preached and Revised by the Rev. C. H. Spurgeon, Minister of the Chapel, During the Year 1857*, vol. III (London: Alabaster, Passmore, 1858), p. 375.

[9] A reviewer in Spurgeon's house journal calls Bunyan 'Honest John': *The Sword and the Trowel* (1887), 363.

[10] C. H. Spurgeon, *Sermons*, 2nd ser. (New York: Sheldon, Blakeman, 1857), p. 426.

[11] See Spurgeon, *Autobiography*, I, 501, 543. Spurgeon explained in December 1857 that he had changed the style of his sermons (but not their doctrine) that year to suit 'a large and mixed audience': 'His anxiety for the salvation of souls leads him to select themes which are rather awakening than instructive, and therefore more adapted for the babes in grace than for strong men in Christ Jesus.' *New Park Street Pulpit*, pp. v-vi.

[12] See William Walters, *Life and Ministry of the Rev. C. H. Spurgeon* (London and Newcastle-upon-Tyne: Scott, [1882]), pp. 74–5. On 7 October 1857 Spurgeon preached in the Crystal Palace, Sydenham, to 'the largest audience that [had] assembled in modern times' – 24,654 in number – to hear a minister of the gospel, on the day of national humiliation associated with the Indian Mutiny: Walters, *Life and Ministry* p. 77.

Plate 15. J. Buckley, 'Revd. C. H. Spurgeon Preaching in the Music Hall, Royal Surrey Gardens', *The New Park Street Pulpit, containing sermons preached and revised by the Rev. C. H. Spurgeon, Minister of the Chapel, during the year 1857*, vol. 3 (London: Alabaster, Passmore, 1858), frontispiece

"Cleanse thou me from secret faults" [Psalm 29.12] – very wonderful' (*D*, 526),[13] and, after one morning service, had presented him with one hundred pounds towards the Tabernacle. (*Punch* had picked up the story from the *Morning Advertiser* and printed a satiric piece entitled 'Ruskin at the Feet of Spurgeon' with a cartoon (plate 16).[14])

By 1858, then, Ruskin could comment on Spurgeon with authority when answering the Brownings' enquiries about his own spiritual life, and when returning to his theme of obedience, in a letter of Monday, 29 March:

I've just come back from Spurgeon's – he is a little bit emptier than he was at first: he ought to be shut up with some books – or sent out into the fields. And touching that great question you put to me, I am all at sea myself – all that I am sure of is that we live in very 'dark ages' compared with ages which

---

[13] It may have been Spurgeon's delivery that was 'wonderful', although both the final section, where he repeated 'the words at which so many have cavilled – it is now or never, it is *turn or burn*', and said how earnestly he longed for the congregation 'in the bowels of Christ Jesus', and the earlier section in which he described God as a photographer and a diarist, must have been particularly memorable: 'Secret Sins', in *New Park Street Pulpit*, pp. 418–19, 424.

[14] *Punch*, 28 March 1857, p. 129. Ruskin read *Punch*; he sent the Brownings a clipping of the 'Spurgeon Quadrilles' cartoon in January 1858 (36.276).

RUSKIN AT THE FEET OF SPURGEON.

HE *Morning Advertiser* late has become gre addicted to controver points of religion. Tho circulating through Bunch of Grapes, and sorts of Lions, Red, Wh Black, and Blue, the *'T* though given to the p licans, is always ready attack the Pharisees. *A* why not? As BYRON say

"There's nought, no doubt much the spirit calms, As rum and true religion.

Porter and polemics m very strengthening half-a half. Therefore, the *'I* is the affectionate advoc of MR. SPURGEON, crowning triumph, faithf records the visits of Jud and ex-Ministers to the I of the Surrey Gard LORD JOHN is found am the congregation: straightway MR. SPURG throws him like a h

Plate 16. 'Ruskin at the Feet of Spurgeon', *Punch*, 28 March 1857, 129

will be; and that most churches are in a sad way because they all keep preaching the wrong way upwards, and say 'Know and you shall do' instead of 'Do and you shall know.' [John 7.17.][15] As I read the Bible my main result in way of belief is that those people are to be exalted in eternity who in this life have striven to do God's will, not their own. And so very few people appear to me to do this in reality that I don't know what to believe – the truth as far as I can make it out seems too terrible to be the truth. All churches seem to me mere

[15] Scott, whose commentary Ruskin used, wrote on this verse, 'all, who desire earnestly and seek diligently to know the will of God, in order to reduce it to practice, shall be guided through every labyrinth of uncertainty, and past every precipice of error, into the ways of truth and peace': *The Holy Bible*, with explanatory notes, practical observations and copious marginal references by Thomas Scott, 9th edn, 6 vols. (London: Seeley, 1825), v, 'Practical Observations' on John 7.11–18.

forms of idolatry. A Roman Catholic idolizes his saint and his relic – an English High Churchman idolizes his propriety and his family pew – a Scotch Presbyterian idolizes his own obstinacy and his own opinions – a German divine idolizes his dreams, and an English one his pronunciation . . . (36.279–80)

Ruskin's comments on the churches would have amused Robert Browning, whose narrator in the poem *Christmas-Day* (1850) finds himself in a liminal position on the thresholds of Zion Chapel, St Peter's, Rome, and the Professor's lecture room in the University of Göttingen. Unlike that narrator's journey, however, Ruskin's is not to be circular, returning him to his Evangelical roots after seeing other traditions; rather, both on the Continental tour of 1858 and in his spiritual life in the subsequent sixteen years, it is to be the journey of a wanderer.[16]

II

Ruskin's aims as he set off on 13 May 1858 were to recover from the rigours of the Turner marathon, to track down the settings of some of Turner's coloured sketches that he had seen the previous winter, and to do more work on the historic Swiss towns – a project which never came to fruition.[17] He was pleased to have got 'reluctant leave' from his father to take his old Swiss guide, Couttet, again, and to have 'all [his] own way' (35.485). The itinerary was not fixed, and it took some unexpected turns. In outline, the route was as follows: Dover to Calais, Boulogne, Paris, Bar-le-Duc, Basle (where Ruskin was joined by Couttet), Rheinfelden (where he made his first Sunday drawing, marking, he commented ten years later, 'henceforward the beginning of total change in habits of mind' (19–27 May – *D*, 535, 35.493)[18]), Laufenburg, Brugg, Bremgarten, Zug, Lake Lucerne (3–11 June), Bellinzona (12 June–8 July), the Borromean islands, Baveno, Turin (15 July–31 August), Lanslebourg, Annecy, St Gervais (to be with the Simons and visit Chamonix), Geneva, Paris, Calais, London (14 September). It was not until he had been away for seven weeks that Ruskin wrote to his father from Bellinzona, on 2 July 1858, saying that 'a glance at Paul Veronese at Turin and then a month

---

[16] Twenty-one years later, in 1879, Ruskin described himself as a 'mere wandering Arab' (24.277).

[17] See John Ruskin, *Letters from the Continent 1858*, ed. John Hayman (University of Toronto Press, 1982), pp. xiii-xiv. These letters served as Ruskin's diary, and provide a particularly detailed day-by-day account of the tour. During the Turin section of the tour they are supplemented with 'Notes on the Gallery of Turin' for Ruskin's father to keep until he returned (p. 88).

[18] See, however, note 73 below.

of Monte Viso' would 'put [him] to rights',[19] on the basis of which quantities of papers were sent from Denmark Hill to La Tour (or La Torre), the principal town of the Vaudois, to await his arrival after a brief stay in Turin, the capital of Piedmont.[20] A fortnight later, however, Turin and Veronese seized him, and did not let him go for more than six weeks.

Ruskin was in a slightly agitated state of mind when he decided to head for Turin. In a letter from Baveno of 11 July he explained to his father that he was 'a little unsettled' by his 'defeat in drawing' – an ambitious landscape at Bellinzona had failed – and by the 'strange difference in [his] own feelings about every thing': 'If I could set myself to any hard work I should be right – but to rest is difficult.'[21] He now felt differently about climbing the mountains – a change which seemed to have been going on in him for years but had now crystallized. (This pattern was to be repeated in Turin.) On 9 July Ruskin wrote to his father from Isola Bella to announce that the previous three or four years had 'completed a change' in him which had begun some ten years previously, and which enabled him to sympathize with his father almost entirely in his 'feelings about mountains': 'I have nearly given up climbing the hills . . . and – climax of all conceivable change, I am actually thinking it will be rather amusing to "see the palace" at Turin!!!'[22] He arrived in the city six days later, on Thursday 15 July.

The theme of change in his opinions and difference in his feelings continued in the first letters from Turin, with Ruskin writing to his father the day after settling into their favourite hotel:

> I assure you I do miss you very much, and especially here, where I used to grumble so at being kept sometimes: but my mind is much altered. I do not think the alteration in all respects a gain – in some it is certainly: and I hope the increased love of order and splendour is no harm . . . I enjoy . . . Paul Veronese much more than I used to do – having more sympathy with his symmetry, splendour, and lordly human life. I have been to the gallery this morning and find three Paul Veronese's of great size and intense interest . . .[23]

The 'upshot' was that his father could send things to him in Turin rather than La Tour, as he would 'certainly not stir for a week at least'.[24]

---

[19] Hayman, ed., *Letters from the Continent*, p. 68.   [20] Ibid., p. 141. Only one arrived.
[21] Ibid., p. 79. In his middle and later years Ruskin was to find that rest could lead to depression. When work, the antidote, became overwork, it could lead to mania.   [22] Ibid., p. 75.
[23] Ibid., p. 87. By 3 August Ruskin was writing to Mrs Simon announcing that he was 'certainly "translated" like Bottom': ibid., p. 192.   [24] Ibid., p. 88.

For the time being, then, mountains were to be viewed from a distance, and Ruskin's letters from Turin are peppered with references to the view of the Alps from the city.[25] Thirty years later, in *Præterita*, Ruskin was to recall of this self-indulgent period in Turin that he still had 'some purpose, even in this libertinage, namely, to outline the Alpine chain from Monte Viso to Monte Rosa' (35.494). His most vivid description of this libertinage, however, was in a letter to Lady Trevelyan, written after his return to London, in which he portrayed himself sauntering the 30 yards between his comfortable hotel and the gallery in his slippers, enjoying the music of the military band, pottering off to see what was going on on the shady side of the piazzas and attending the opera each evening, following a good dinner.[26]

The impression that Ruskin gives in this letter is of a relaxed daily routine, punctuated with two hours' work copying Veronese in the morning, when he felt like it, and a further two hours in the afternoon ('doing as little there as possible'). Augustus J. C. Hare's account, however, of Ruskin 'sitting all day upon a scaffold in the gallery, copying bits of the great picture by Paul Veronese' (16.xl) suggests that Ruskin, already sensitive about the failed Bellinzona drawing, exercised dramatic license in his letter to Lady Trevelyan, partly in reaction to his father's disappointment in the results of his work at Turin (35.497).[27] Hare's own exaggerated account of Ruskin looking at the flounce in a dress for 'five minutes' and then painting 'one thread', and his calculation that at this rate it would take ten years to paint the whole dress, provides a further explanation for the comparatively meagre results of six weeks' work.

The most notable feature of Ruskin's copying work, however, is the fact that he was so interested in the fabric of the maid of honour's dress in *The Presentation of the Queen of Sheba to Solomon* (plate 17). Only three years earlier, in a review of *Illustrations of Scripture* by 'an Animal Painter', he had solemnly stated that 'the luxury and idolatry of the reign of Solomon are hinted behind a group of "apes and peacocks" [1 Kings

---

[25] Ibid., p. 113.

[26] *Reflections of a Friendship: John Ruskin's Letters to Pauline Trevelyan, 1848–1866*, ed. Virginia Surtees (London: Allen, Unwin, 1979), pp. 132–3.

[27] Cook and Wedderburn *Works*, list 1. 'The Queen's attendants, etc., the lower r. hand portion of the picture' (the study of the negress, now in the Fogg Art Museum, may have been a piece of this larger study); 2. 'A large chiaroscuro sketch of the negress's mistress, a maid of honour'; 3. 'Solomon' (a sketch is now in the Ruskin Library, Lancaster (plate 18), of which there was 'another more finished study'); 4. 'A White Hawk', once owned by C. G. Montefiore; 5. 'The Queen's dog' (38.303).

10.22]' (34.483). Now he was luxuriating in the worldly delights of Veronese's paintings, as well as admiring the technique which he could never begin to emulate. His private comment to Hare in the gallery at Turin is reminiscent of his controversial description of Turner in *Modern Painters* I, fifteen years earlier: 'I merely think that Paul Veronese was ordained by Almighty God to be an archangel, neither more nor less; for it was not only that he knew how to cover yards of canvas with noble figures and exquisite colouring, it was that it was all *right*' (38.xl–xli).

Having 'sat out' a Mass on his first Sunday in Turin at which the priest was 'not even mumbling at the altar, merely standing there',[28] Ruskin took stock of the Veronese the next day:

> I hope to get rather a nice bit of drawing a little like my black Tintoret angels – from Veronese here – only the angel is in this case a negress – much frightened at seeing her mistress the Queen of Sheba – nearly fainting before Solomon. The Queen is on her knees – so of course are all her attendants – and everybody is in awe and consternation, except the Queen of Sheba's dog . . . I shall try and make a sketch of him. The Solomon is the most majestic and beautiful I have ever seen, a fair youth with *short* curled hair – such as Veronese only can paint.
>
> Band playing very beautifully this morning.[29]

Four years previously Ruskin had asked himself whether Veronese intended 'irony or insult' in the cats he painted in the 'great Cana picture' in the Louvre.[30] Now he celebrated this unabashed dog as a literal 'sign of life', and was pleased with his copy of it. It was the beauty of Veronese's Solomon – the young author of the Song of Solomon, or Canticles, in what one commentator called the 'spring-time' of his 'best and holiest years'[31] – rather than his wisdom, that profoundly impressed Ruskin. This emphasis upon the visual appeal of Solomon in all his glory is also true to the original Bible story: like the Magi, of whom she was an Old Testament type, the Queen of Sheba had to *see* for herself.[32]

[28] Hayman, *Letters from the Continent*, p. 91.
[29] Ibid., pp. 92–3. The reference is to *Cherubs: detail from Tintoretto's 'Adoration of the Magi'* (c.1852). John James Ruskin was fond of bands.   [30] Lancaster MS 9, Diaries, fol. 106.
[31] *The Holy Bible*, with Notes and Introductions by Chr[istopher] Wordsworth, 6 vols. (London: Rivingtons, 1864–70), IV, Pt III, ix.
[32] 'And when the queen of Sheba heard of the fame of Solomon concerning the name of the Lord, she came to prove him with hard questions. And she came to Jerusalem with a very great train, with camels that bare spices, and very much gold, and precious stones: and when she was come to Solomon, she communed with him of all that was in her heart. And Solomon told her all her questions: there was not any thing hid from the king, which he told her not. And when the queen

Plate 17. Paulo Veronese, *The Presentation of the Queen of Sheba to Solomon*

Initially Ruskin thought that his copying work would not take long, informing John Simon by letter the next day, Tuesday 20 July, that he intended to leave for the Vaudois valleys the following Monday (36.286). By Thursday 22 July, however, in the first of a series of deferrals, he was telling his father that he would leave the following Wednesday or Thursday, although he 'could stay a year with these Paul Veroneses'.[33]

On his second Sunday in Turin, Ruskin was in 'rather a worse temper than usual', having attended 'an overcrowded, ill managed, melancholy military mass in a small church'.[34] During his second full week in the city he made progress on copies of several parts of the painting, and by Friday 30 July could write to his father:

I have also got a large chiaroscuro sketch half done, which promises well – of the negro's mistress in her golden and white robe; – (not the Queen, she is much too beautiful for me to manage, – having all Veronese's glow of colour in her face) – but the maid of honour I think I shall get tolerably; and finally I mean to do Solomon himself in colour, of the size of the other coloured sketch. This last if I *can* for Solomon is in the dark and I may only make a mess of him.

. . .

I will give Mama's five pounds, as directed.[35]

Again, it was the physical beauty of Veronese's Queen of Sheba which so impressed, and indeed overawed him, with the 'glow of colour in her face'. His mother's five pounds came from another world – that of Camberwell Evangelicalism: it was intended, as Ruskin later drily put it in *Præterita*, to make his 'peace with Heaven in a gift to the Vaudois churches' (35.497). There is evidence from the early and mid-1850s, however, indicating that Ruskin, like his mother and their fellow Evangelicals, regarded the Vaudois from afar as a Protestant ideal, thus continuing a tradition in England that predated Milton's famous

---

(*cont.*)
of Sheba had *seen* all Solomon's wisdom, and the house that he had built, And the meat of his table, and the sitting of his servants, and the attendance of his ministers, and their apparel, and his cupbearers, and his ascent by which he went up unto the house of the Lord; there was no more spirit in her. And she said to the king, It was a true report that I heard in mine own land of thy acts and of thy wisdom. Howbeit I believed not the words, until I came, and *mine eyes had seen it*: and, behold, the half was not told me: thy wisdom and prosperity exceedeth the fame which I heard' (I Kings 10.1–7; our emphases). Twenty years later Ruskin was amused to hear a sermon on the Queen of Sheba in the unlikely setting of Ingleton, where the preacher said that she was a 'person who liked new impressions on the brain': Lancaster L 42, Letters from John Ruskin to Joan Severn, 17 August 1878.

[33] Hayman, *Letters from the Continent*, p. 96; Ruskin first wrote 'Tuesday' and then erased it. He was relieved when his parents approved of his staying in Turin (p. 98).

[34] Ibid., p. 101.   [35] Ibid., p. 108.

sonnet.[36] Indeed, ironically enough his positive reference to the 'struggling' Protestant Church of Piedmont in *The Stones of Venice* I (1851; 9.473) was quoted in a pro-Waldensian tract of 1854 in defence of the expenditure on the very church in Turin that Ruskin was later to describe as vulgar and larger than necessary.[37]

Although three weeks were to elapse before Ruskin delivered the gift in person to one of the Vaudois 'shepherds' in the famous valleys, the arrival of his mother's 5 pounds, combined with his disgust at the Masses in Turin, could have been the spur to his seeking out the recently completed Vaudois church on his third Sunday in the city. The first, somewhat oblique reference to the service was in an extraordinary 'Note on the Turin Gallery' to which John James Ruskin responded on 4/5 August.[38] It follows a passage in which Ruskin makes some startling new observations on art and artists, on which a passage in *Modern Painters* V was later to be based (7.264):[39]

without the least effort, merely treating their figures as pieces of decoration, Titian and Veronese are always noble and the curious point is that both of *these* are sensual painters, working apparently with no high motive, and Titian perpetually with definitely sensual aim, and yet invariably noble; while this Gentileschi is perfectly modest and pious – & yet base. – And Michael Angelo goes even greater lengths – or to lower depths – than Titian – and the lower he stoops, the more his inalienable nobleness shows itself. Certainly it seems intended that strong and frank animality, rejecting all tendency to asceticism – monachism – pietism – & so on, should be connected with the strongest intellects. Dante, indeed, is severe, at least, of all nameable great men, he is the severest I know – but Homer – Shakespeare – Tintoret – Veronese – Titian – Michael Angelo – Sir Joshua – Rubens, Velasquez – Correggio Turner – are all of them boldly Animal. Francia and Angelico and all the purists, however beautiful – are poor weak creatures in comparison. I don't understand it – one would have thought purity gave strength, but it doesn't. A good – stout – self-commanding, magnificent Animality is the <temper> make for poets & artists, it seems to me.[40]

36 'Avenge, O Lord, thy slaughtered saints, whose bones / Lie scattered on the Alpine mountains cold' ('On the late Massacre in Piedmont', 1655). For Ruskin's positive comments see 12.139, 356, and Lancaster MS 10a, Diaries, fol. 149. At the end of the nineteenth century the Vaudois legend could be summed up thus – 'Though gashed by the Savoyard spear, and scorched by the Romish fagot, they stood unflinchingly for God's Word and his honor': E. G. White, *The Great Controversy between Christ and Satan during the Christian Dispensation*, rev. edn (Watford and London: International Tract Society [c.1900]), p. 65.

37 See W. S. Gilly, *Piedmont, and the Waldenses* (London: p. p., [1854]), p. 2, and p. 139 below.

38 Lancaster L 4, Letters from John James Ruskin to John Ruskin. The letter indicates that John's letters and Notes were giving his parents pleasure.   39 See p. 50 above.

40 Lancaster MS 38, Notes on the Gallery at Turin, p. 5; compare Cook and Wedderburn's transcription, *Works* (7.xl).

(In his reply John James Ruskin writes: 'Strange notes on Sensual Painters, a source of deep thinking'.) A specific moment is then described, less as an epiphany than the starting-point for new lines of thought on the 'gorgeous' qualities of God's creation:

One day when I was working from the beautiful maid of honour in Veronese's picture, I was struck by the Gorgeousness of life which the world seems to be constituted to develope, when it is made the best of. The band was playing some <splendid> passages of brilliant music at the time, and the music blended so thoroughly with Veronese's splendour; the beautiful notes seeming to form one whole with the lovely forms and colours, and powerful human creatures. Can it be possible that all this power and beauty is adverse to the honour of the maker of it. Has God made faces beautiful and limbs strong – and created these strange, fiery, fantastic energies, and created the splendour of substance and the love of it – created gold & pearls, and crystal and the sun that makes them gorgeous; and filled human fancy with all splendid thoughts; and given to the human touch its power of <Setting> placing, and brightening and perfecting, only that all these things may lead his creatures away from him. and [*sic*] is this mighty Paul Veronese, in whose soul there is a strength as of the snowy mountains – and within whose brain all the pomp and majesty of humanity floats in a marshalled glory, capacious & serene like clouds at sunset – this man whose finger is as fire, and whose eye is like the morning – is *he* a servant of the devil, and is the poor little wretch in a tidy black tie to whom I have been listening this Sunday morning expounding Nothing with a twang – is *he* a servant of God?

It is a great mystery. I begin to suspect we are all wrong together; Paul Veronese in letting his power waste into wantonness – and the religious people in mistaking their weakness and dulness <by> for seriousness & piety – It is all very well for people to fast, who can't eat; and to preach, who cannot talk nor sing – and to walk barefoot who cannot ride, and then think themselves good. Let them learn to master the world before they abuse it.[41]

This note is written in a similar vein to other Sunday letters and diary entries by Ruskin. The 'one day' to which he refers was, however, prior[42] to the Sunday on which he heard the preacher and recorded these reflections, which is not the impression that Ruskin gives in later, published accounts. The questions he puts in the note are grounded in belief in God's wisdom as the creator. The description of Veronese is again reminiscent of earlier paeans of praise on Turner, but here the association between the 'mighty' Catholic artist and the 'snowy mountains' has the effect of further diminishing the 'little' Protestant preacher who might more naturally be associated

---

[41] Ibid., pp. 5–6; cf.7.xli.   [42] The 'one day' could have been as early as Monday 18 August.

with the Alps,[43] but who seems merely to be crushed under the weight of the paragraph's rhetoric of celebration. The short concluding paragraph begins in the same vein as Ruskin's criticism of the various churches in his letter to the Brownings, but it ends with a sharp critique of nineteenth-century Pharisaism.

Perhaps fearing his father's reaction to an immediate and therefore uninhibited description of the Sunday service itself, Ruskin deferred it until the following Wednesday, 4 August:

> I went to the Protestant church last Sunday . . . and very sorry I was that I did go. Protestantism persecuted or pastoral in a plain room, or a hill chapel whitewashed inside and ivied outside, is all very well; but Protestantism clumsily triumphant, allowed all its own way in a capital like this, & building itself vulgar churches with nobody to put into them, is a very disagreeable form of piety. Execrable sermon; – cold singing. A nice-looking old woman or two of the Mause Headrigg type – three or four decent french families – a dirty Turinois here and there spitting over large fields of empty pew – and three or four soldiers who came in to see what was going on and went out again, very wisely, after listening for ten minutes, made up the congregation.
>
> I really don't know what we are all coming to; but hope for something better from the Vaudois. Monte Viso looks very inviting, but by the maps, he seems terribly difficult to get at.[44]

The church that Ruskin describes as vulgar and unnecessarily large was neo-Gothic in design. It was consecrated on 15 December 1853, and soon had a congregation amounting to several hundred, including many communicants, led by the minister, M. Meille.[45] The clue to the thinness of the congregation when Ruskin attended may lie in his reference to three or four French families as, assuming that the pattern of services established in 1853 continued five years later, the 10.30 a.m. service was conducted in French, unlike the three others which were in Italian.[46]

As in the note of 1 August, Ruskin ends this letter with a sense of a general falling off – 'I really don't know what we are all coming to' –

---

[43] 'They pointed their children to the heights towering above them in unchanging majesty, and spoke to them of Him with whom there is no variableness nor shadow of turning, whose word is as enduring as the everlasting hills': Jane Louisa Willyams, *A Short History of the Waldensian Church in the Valleys of Piedmont, from the Earliest Period to the Present Time* (London: Nisbet, 1855), p. 66.

[44] Hayman, *Letters from the Continent*, p. 115–16. Mause Headrigg is a zealous covenanter in Scott's *Old Mortality* (1816).   [45] Willyams, *Waldensian Church*, pp. 241, 246.

[46] Ibid., p. 247. On 9 October 1853, according to the Revd W. S. Gilly, Mr Bert 'performed' the service in French 'for a mixed congregation' at 10.30 a.m. (in his sermon he was 'fluent, animated, and close to Scripture'), Mr Meille the Italian services for the young at 9.00 a.m. and for adults at 2.00 p. m., and M. de Sanctis the Italian service at 8.00 p. m.: Gilly, *Piedmont*, p. 3.

rather than a wish to blame any one tradition or individual for failing. Nevertheless, preaching is usually the main topic in correspondence between father and son when they are discussing church services, and behind Ruskin's comments on the 'poor little wretch in a tidy black tie' and his 'execrable sermon' lies their shared interest in Spurgeon's extraordinary power as a preacher. Writing from Baveno on 13 July, Ruskin had argued that cathedrals were best used for 'singing services' rather than preaching, and that if Spurgeon were to preach in York Minster, cast-iron galleries and a refreshment room would have to be installed.[47] Later, on 16 August, John James Ruskin was to describe how he had taken a guest to hear Spurgeon the day before, adding that she had found him 'Simple & not at all so eccentric as she expected.'[48] The extent to which Spurgeon was now part of the Ruskin circle is revealed in John James's letter of 27 August, in which he asked his son – who was in the public eye – whether he would prefer a donation to 'decayed Actors' to be anonymous, and commented that the gift 'may incur the surprise & wrath of Canon Dale Mr Moore & Spurgeon'.[49] Ruskin, whose own gift to a Turin actress neatly matched his mother's to the Vaudois shepherds,[50] replied that he was 'quite delighted' that his father should subscribe publicly, and then revealed how he regarded his public image:

I shall like your name being to that charity – because the very severity of my reputation helps my enemies to hurt it. They say – that man *must* be a knave – he pretends to be such a Puritan. (If ever I succeed in making myself able to draw the figure – I'll show them some Puritanism that will astonish them – the idiots.)[51]

The depth of feeling associated with his Puritan image in England, following the breakdown of his marriage, helps to explain the intensity of his revaluation of a revered Continental Puritan tradition during his stay in Turin.

Ruskin again tried the 'Protestant affair of a church' on his fourth Sunday in Turin, reporting that it was 'really too bad': 'Church as large as Camden chapel, and precisely 18 people in it besides myself, when service began.'[52] Meanwhile he felt that his copy of Veronese's Solomon was making good progress, and compared his copy and the original with two of his most admired masters of 'true sacred art'. His drawing, he

[47] Hayman, *Letters from the Continent*, p. 82.
[48] Lancaster L 4, Letters from John James Ruskin to John Ruskin.
[49] Ibid. On Dale and Moore see pp. 12–13, 44 above.
[50] See Hayman, *Letters from the Continent*, p. xxii.   [51] Ibid., p. 154.   [52] Ibid., p. 120.

told his father, required patience, 'like Hunt's work'.[53] On the Monday (9 August) he wrote, in a passage which later formed the basis of a passage in *Modern Painters* v (7.293):

I am very glad you like the notion of the negress, for I am pretty sure you will like Solomon too, and therefore both. I find these great Venetians, as I study them more, are all as full of mischief as an egg's full of meat; there's no knowing what they've got in their heads; or what they'll be up to next; – I have called Veronese 'thoughtless' in the end of the chapter on Purism in 3rd M. P. [5.122] but he's nearly as full of dodges as Tintoret. The way I took a fancy to this Solomon was especially on account of a beautiful white falcon on a falconer's fist, which comes against his dark purple robe. I thought it was only a pretty trick of colour; but as I worked on, I saw that the white falcon was put exactly and studiously under the head of one of the Lions which sustains the throne, so that the sitting figure is sustained by the Lion & eagle; who were the types of the Divine & Human power in Christ; and to show that he really meant to indicate thus Solomon's typical character, he has made one of the elders on the steps of the throne point to Solomon with a jewelled cross; (a tremendous licence by the way, as I imagine the Jews at that period would have avoided any crosslet ornament as much as after the time of Christ, but it answers his purpose.)[54]

Unlike in his troubled relationship with Puritan tradition, the outer or aesthetic eye not only co-operated with the inner or spiritual eye as Ruskin 'worked on', but actually stimulated it. 'This Solomon' was first attractive to the eye of the art critic, and the falcon seemed to be there for reasons of colour. In the act of copying, however, Ruskin 'saw' that the bird had been placed there for iconographic purposes. Visual delight leads to spiritual revelation, as Solomon mediates between the glory of the material world and the glory of Christ, of whom he is a type.[55] Thus a sacred art which celebrates the 'gorgeousness' of the material world and the orientalism of the young Solomon himself (plate 18) is legitimated, freeing Ruskin from his earlier and narrower ideas on the subject.

Having visited S. Ambrogio on the fifth Sunday of his stay in Turin, Ruskin finally encountered the Vaudois shepherds of La Tour on the sixth – 22 August. In a letter written to his father the following day, back in Turin, the silence on the subject of the quality of the sermon and the subsequent conversation with the Vaudois 'Professor' is deafening:

[53] Ibid., pp. 116–17. Also see p. 145. Plate 18 reproduces Ruskin's sketch of Solomon, presumably made in preparation for a more ambitious copy, the whereabouts of which are unknown.

[54] Ibid., p. 123.

[55] 'The queen of Sheba, hearing Solomon's wisdom, said, *Blessed are those thy servants, that always stand before thee, and hear thy wisdom:* if she was so taken with Solomon, remember that *a greater than Solomon is here.* And shall we deprive ourselves of that blessedness, which we might enjoy by standing always in the presence of Christ, to hear his wisdom, and to behold his glory?': Isaac Ambrose, *Works* (London: Tegg, 1835), p. 149.

Plate 18. John Ruskin, copy of Solomon, detail from Veronese,
The Presentation of the Queen of Sheba to Solomon, 1858

I am so much accustomed, now, to be disappointed in going to any new place that I was pleasantly surprised at not being very much disappointed with those Protestant vallies. La Tour itself, indeed, is a most disagreeable place . . . But the little side ravines are very beautiful; and, after sermon, I pursued one of the lateral ridges with Coutet for four hours and a half of steady climb . . . just underneath us lay the whole valley of Angrogna, celebrated in Vaudoise tradition . . . my theological Professor was to come at 7 . . .

I shall go back some day (*not* this year), to see that Viso; – and a little more of the shepherds – but I think I have a very fair idea of the kind of thing, even as it is . . . [56]

Ruskin seems to have been prepared for the disappointment, having already become disillusioned with the monks of the Grande Chartreuse, for example (35.476); and in reality he was not alone.[57] His response to the contrast between the Vaudois and the gorgeousness of Veronese led him away from a close affiliation with organized religion of any kind for the following sixteen years; which is not to say that he no longer believed in God.

The following Sunday (his last in Turin, 29 August) Ruskin made his third visit to the Protestant church, but this time attended the afternoon service after listening to the band in the public gardens, 'The Band gratis – the Sermon two francs (poor-box) – and very dear at the money.'[58] Earlier in the day he had written to his father at length on the evils of the nineteenth century – a favourite topic – in response to newspaper reports that he had been reading. This led to a long section on the need for the young to be properly taught – the result of which would be 'the Love of God and our Neighbour' (Matthew 22.37–40)[59] – and to important observations on the main 'mistakes which bring about the evil of the world':

1. Teaching religious doctrines and creeds instead of simple love of God & practical love of our neighbour. This is a terrific mistake – I fancy the fundamental mistake of humanity.

2. Want of proper cultivation of the beauty of the body and the fineness of its senses – a modern mistake chiefly.[60]

---

[56] Hayman, *Letters from the Continent*, pp. 143–5. The Vaudois had defended this valley from attack in the seventeenth century. In *Præterita* Ruskin recalls 'some pious talk of a mild kind with the person I gave my mother's five pounds to; but an infinitely pleasanter feeling from the gratitude of the overworn ballerina at Turin, for the gift of as many of my own' (35.497–8).

[57] Even in Evangelical circles it was felt that the Vaudois were not what they once were. See, for example, 'The Vaudois Christians', *The Evangelical Magazine and Missionary Chronicle*, NS 10 (March 1832), 110–11.   [58] Hayman, *Letters from the Continent*, p. 153.

[59] Compare p. 24 above.   [60] Hayman, *Letters from the Continent*, p. 152.

The first he had come to recognize gradually over a number of years; the second he had learned mainly during the six weeks in Turin. Both were in Ruskin's eyes characteristic of Evangelicalism.

On his return to England, Ruskin was to develop his ideas on education in his inaugural address to the Cambridge School of Art, part of which was based on observations originally made in a letter to his friend Mrs Hewitt on his last Sunday in Turin, where he complained about even the highest class of tourists generally giving the Veronese 'from three to four seconds' of their time, and attentive ones, 'who are really seeking for information, from seven to ten', when 'about three months' would be required to examine and appreciate it 'properly'.[61] It was by minutely copying parts of the painting that Ruskin saw it for what it was, and by applying his 'analytic mind' to what he saw that he developed some new principles of art, religion and education. As in the Evangelical tradition from which he now distanced himself, in which the converted person gave a personal testimony of the great change that he or she had undergone, Ruskin's published teaching on these subjects was to include striking personal testimony over the following thirty years – testimony which he himself came to regard as that of an un-converted man.

III

Having travelled home via Paris, where he 'thought more of' Veronese's great *Marriage of Cana* than ever, even though it was 'worse arranged than ever' in the Louvre,[62] Ruskin settled back into the quiet routine of Denmark Hill, and in October 1858 visited Spurgeon, who had continued to preach all over the country in his absence and was now ill. Forty years later Susannah Spurgeon was to give a graphic account of Ruskin's visit to her husband on his first day downstairs:

How well I remember the intense love and devotion displayed by Mr. Ruskin, as he threw himself on his knees by the dear patient's side, and embraced him with tender affection and tears. "My brother, my dear brother," he said, "how grieved I am to see you thus!" His sorrow and sympathy were most touching and comforting. He had brought him two charming engravings . . . and some bottles of wine of a rare vintage, which he hoped would prove a cordial to the sufferer's much-weakened frame. My husband was greatly moved by the love and consideration so graciously expressed, and he very often referred to it afterwards in grateful appreciation; especially when, in later years, there came a

---

[61] Ibid., p. 178. Compare a similar passage in a diary notebook, probably of 1859: Lancaster MS 11, Diaries, fol. 259; *D*, 537.   [62] Hayman, *Letters from the Continent*, p. 170.

change of feeling on Mr. Ruskin's part, and he strongly repudiated some of the theological opinions to which Mr. Spurgeon closely clung to the end of his life.[63]

The passage unsettles the assumption that Ruskin was incapable of expressing powerful emotion in this way.[64] Furthermore, Mrs Spurgeon believed that the 'change of feeling on Mr. Ruskin's part' took place 'in later years', although this could suggest that her husband did not report his private conversations with Ruskin to her in 1857 and 1858, and that Ruskin's promise made to Mrs La Touche in 1861, that he would not refer to his religious views for ten years, had its effect.

Ruskin was also catching up with his correspondence in the autumn of 1858, and describing to friends the changes that his views had undergone in Turin. On 14 October, for example, he wrote to Elizabeth Barrett Browning, 'I begin to think nobody can be a great painter who isn't rather wicked – in a noble sort of way' (36.292), and to Charles Eliot Norton ten days later, 'to be a first rate painter – you *must'nt* [sic] be pious; – but rather a little wicked – and entirely a man of the world. I had been inclining to this opinion for some years; but I clinched it at Turin.'[65] On 29 November he responded to Norton's reply by saying that Veronese and Titian were 'much deeper' than Norton knew yet – 'immensely deeper' than Ruskin had 'the least idea of till this last summer':

P's as full of mischief as an egg's full of meat – always up to some dodge or other – just like Tint. – In his Solomon receiving Queen of Sheba one of the golden lions of the throne is put into full light – and a falconer underneath holds a white falcon – as white as snow – just under the lion so as to *carry* Solomon on the lion and eagle – and one of the elders has got a jewel in his hand with which he is pointing to Solomon, of the form of a Cross. – The Queen's fainting – but her Dog *is'nt*, [sic] – a little King Charles Spaniel – about seven inches high – thinks it shocking his mistress should faint – stands in front of her on all his four legs apart – snarling at Solomon with all his might – Solomon all but drops his sceptre stooping forward eagerly to get the Queen helped up – such a beautiful fellow – all crisped golden short hair over his head and the fine Arabian arched brow, – and I believe after all – you'll find the subtlest & grandest *expression* going is hidden under the gold & purple of those vagabonds of Venetians.[66]

---

[63] Spurgeon, *Autobiography*, I, 501; compare 34.659.

[64] Ruskin's gift of wine was in the spirit of Thomas Scott's commentary on the chapter of Proverbs that had been Ruskin's text in his first lecture on *The Political Economy of Art* (1857; 16.20, 48, 55, 56) – 'strong drink should be administered as a cordial to those, who are ready to faint through weakness or weariness': Scott, *The Holy Bible*, III, Proverbs 31.4.

[65] *The Correspondence of John Ruskin and Charles Eliot Norton*, ed. John Lewis Bradley and Ian Ousby (Cambridge University Press, 1987), p. 46; compare 36.293.

[66] Ibid., p. 47. 'Tint.' refers to Tintoretto.

It would be tedious to rehearse the small differences between this summary made for Norton and the fuller observations that Ruskin had recorded in Turin.[67] The significance of the letter lies in the fact that the drama of the Veronese and the 'expression' of 'those vagabonds of Venetians' continued to excite and interest Ruskin a month after he had lectured on the subject on 29 October, in his inaugural address to the Cambridge School of Art.

As in his letter to Mrs Hewitt, Ruskin focused in the lecture upon his love of the material and patterns of the silk, and bemoaned the fact that none of the lady tourists who passed through the Turin gallery while he was working there admired the dresses in the Veronese (16.185). Having argued that good art is the result of enjoyment (16.183), he teasingly contradicted himself by stating that we must also restrain our love for art (16.188). This led to a discussion of simplicity, in which he explicitly related the strength of a 'rude and simple nation' to their lack of art and literature, taking the ancient Vaudois as an admirable example (16.189). The most powerful section of the lecture, however, summarized his newfound understanding of the importance of colour and the truthful portrayal of the human body – the highest form of creation – in Titian, Veronese and Tintoretto: 'The Venetians alone, by a toil almost superhuman, succeeded at last in obtaining a power almost superhuman; and were able finally to paint the highest visible work of God with unexaggerated structure, undegraded colour, and unaffected gesture' (16.198).

Having tested his ideas on his father and his friends, and applied them to art education in a lecture, the 'Author of *Modern Painters*' was still not ready to address his large and expectant readership on the subject of the Venetians. Volume v did not appear until 14 June 1860, and Ruskin apologized in the preface, explaining that it was when working on 'Veronese's Queen of Sheba' that he had seen the necessity of further work in the winter of 1858–9 on the 'moral power of the Venetians', thus delaying the writing of the book (7.6). (In fact he was already more interested in other, economic and social, topics, and completed the final volume mainly to please his father (7.lvi.).) In chapter 2 we saw how Ruskin's treatment of Turner in this final volume was based upon contrasts between Venetian Catholicism and English Protestantism. We can now see how the argument, in 'The Lance of Pallas', that Christian art 'erred

---

[67] In Turin, for example, Ruskin had been amused to find that Veronese forgot to paint in the dog's fourth leg: see Hayman, *Letters from the Continent*, p. 207. This letter to Norton contains the only reference to the 'fine Arabian arched brow' which Ruskin accentuated in his own sketch of Veronese's Solomon (plate 18), itself a gift to Norton.

by pride in its denial of the animal nature of man' and, 'in connection with all monkish and fanatical forms of religion, by looking always to another world instead of this' (7.264), grew out of his observations in the 'Notes on the Turin Gallery' written on Sunday 1 August 1858. It was in the subsequent chapter, 'The Wings of the Lion', that he focused upon the Veronese itself.

Ruskin's work on the Venetians had convinced him that they were 'the *last believing* school of Italy'. As he had already pointed out in *The Stones of Venice*, a further attraction of the city to the anxious northern Protestant reader was its history of 'quarrelling with the Pope' (7.286). Ruskin's readers, however, might still need to be convinced:

> Perhaps when you see one of Titian's splendidly passionate subjects, or find Veronese making the Marriage in Cana one blaze of worldly pomp, you imagine that Titian must have been a sensualist, and Veronese an unbeliever.
> Put the idea from you at once, and be assured of this for ever; it will guide you through many a labyrinth of life, as well as of painting, – that of an evil tree, men never gather good fruit [Matthew 7.18] – good of any sort or kind; even good sensualism. (7.287)[68]

He then developed the contrast between the Venetians who liked to be portrayed on their knees and the English gentry who would never have chosen such a pose. On the other hand, whereas in the rest of Italy 'piety had become abstract, and opposed theoretically to worldly life', in Venice the madonnas 'are on our own plain ground – nay, here in our houses with us' (7.290). The question that Ruskin resolved in his own mind in Turin concerning Veronese's 'pet dogs at Christ's very feet' led to analysis, first of the *Madonna and Child, with the Cuccina Family* in the Dresden gallery (visited in the summer of 1859), in which Hope is veiled in black (7.290–3), and then of *The Presentation of the Queen of Sheba to Solomon*:

> This picture is at Turin, and is of quite inestimable value. It is hung high; and the really principal figure the Solomon, being in the shade, can hardly be seen, but is painted with Veronese's utmost tenderness, in the bloom of perfect youth, his hair golden, short, crisply curled. He is seated high on his lion throne: two elders on each side beneath him, the whole group forming a tower of solemn shade . . . This column of noble shade is curiously sustained. A falconer leans forward from the left-hand side, bearing on his wrist a snow-white falcon, its wings spread, and brilliantly relieved against the purple robe of one of the elders. It touches with its wings one of the golden lions of the throne, on which the light also flashes strongly; thus forming, together with it, the lion and eagle

---

[68] Compare Ruskin on the 'labyrinth' with Thomas Scott on John 7.17: see note 15 above.

symbol, which is the type of Christ throughout mediæval work. In order to show the meaning of this symbol, and that Solomon is typically invested with the Christian royalty, one of the elders, by a bold anachronism, holds a jewel in his hand in the shape of a cross, with which he (by accident of gesture) points to Solomon; his other hand is laid on an open book. (7.293)

While in Turin, Ruskin had associated Veronese's painting with the work of Tintoretto, and his own copies with Holman Hunt. Now, in refining the reference he had made to 'Solomon's typical character' in the letter of 9 August 1858, and writing the carefully weighted statement that 'Solomon is typically invested with the Christian royalty', Ruskin celebrated Veronese's Catholic treatment of the type of which the Protestant Hunt's Christ figure in *The Light of the World* is the antitype – the Christ who wears 'the white robe, representing the power of the Spirit upon him; the jewelled robe and breastplate, representing the sacerdotal investiture; the rayed crown of gold, inwoven with the crown of thorns' (12.329).[69] Ruskin regarded Hunt's painting as 'true sacred art' because it portrayed the risen Christ in an English orchard. Veronese, whose madonnas are 'here in our houses with us', portrays Solomon enthroned in a Venetian palace, and the Queen of Sheba and her retinue, with the dog and the negro girl's 'two toy-birds', 'as they were likely to have occurred, down to trivial, or even ludicrous detail' (7.293–94).

Ruskin's third significant reference in print to *The Presentation of the Queen of Sheba to Solomon* came nineteen years later, in *Fors Clavigera*, Letter 76 (April 1877). Its context – Ruskin's discussion of the 'much more distinctly Christian' tone of *Fors* that year – will be considered in a later chapter.[70] His recollections of events in 1858 should, however, be examined here, being the first of two autobiographical accounts of his break with Evangelicalism:

My work on the Venetians in that year not only convinced me of their consummate power, but showed me that there was a great *worldly* harmony running through all they did – opposing itself to the fanaticism of the Papacy; and in this worldly harmony of human and artistic power, my own special idol, Turner, stood side by side with Tintoret; so also Velasquez, Sir Joshua, and Gainsborough, stood with Titian and Veronese; and those seven men – quite demonstrably and indisputably giants in the domain of Art . . . – stood, as heads of a great Worldly Army, worshippers of Worldly visible Truth, *against* (as it seemed then to me), and assuredly distinct from, another sacred army, bearing the Rule of the Catholic Church in the strictest obedience, and headed by Cimabue, Giotto, and Angelico; worshippers not of a worldly and visible Truth, but of a visionary one, which they asserted to be higher; yet under the (as they asserted – supernatural) teaching of the Spirit of this Truth, doing less perfect work than their unassisted opposites!

All this is entirely so; fact tremendous in its unity, and difficult enough as it stands to me even now; but as it stood to me then, wholly insoluble, for I was still in the bonds of my old Evangelical faith; and, in 1858, it was with me, Protestantism or nothing: the crisis of the whole turn of my thoughts being one Sunday morning, at Turin, when, from before Paul Veronese's Queen of Sheba, and under quite overwhelmed sense of his God-given power, I went away to a Waldensian chapel, where a little squeaking idiot was preaching to an audience of seventeen old women and three louts,* that they were the only children of God in Turin; and that all the people in Turin outside the chapel, and all the people in the world out of sight of Monte Viso, would be damned. I came out of the chapel, in sum of twenty years of thought, a conclusively *un*-converted man – converted by this little Piedmontese gentleman, so powerful in his organ-grinding, inside-out, as it were. "Here is an end to my 'Mother-Law' of Protestantism anyhow! – and now – what is there left?" You will find what was left, as, in much darkness and sorrow of heart I gathered it, variously taught in my books, written between 1858 and 1874. It is all sound and good, as far as it goes: whereas all that went before was so mixed with Protestant egotism and insolence, that, as you have probably heard, I won't republish, in their first form, any of those former books.

* Counted at the time; – I am not quite sure now if seventeen or eighteen. (29.88–90)

This would appear to be the first time that Ruskin referred to the content of the sermon, which epitomized all that he hated in the Puritan tradi-tion of his birth, and which, for his immediate purposes in *Fors*, strongly contrasted with the broader Catholicism that he now embraced (29.92). Ruskin seems to have written this passage without consulting his letters and notes from Turin, as it was on his second visit to the Vaudois church that he counted the eighteen members of the congregation, whereas it was on the first that the contrast between the preacher and the Veronese struck him so forcibly. The dramatic impact in the narrative of his going straight from the gallery to the church is also achieved at the expense of historical accuracy, and prepares for a fictional 'un-conversion' that is as sudden as a classic Pauline conversion. His purpose is to subvert Evangelicalism by adopting its own terminology and frame of reference. In what could be described as anti-Evangelical testimony, however, Ruskin has no sooner described himself as a 'conclusively *un*-converted man – converted by this little Piedmontese gentleman, so powerful in his organ-grinding, inside-out, as it were', than he is narrating a more recent and equally dramatic reversal of his religious and artistic views that took place at Assisi in 1874, again on a scaffold while copying a work of art – in this case a Giotto fresco (29.90–1). As in his writings as a cultural historian, Ruskin the autobiographer constructs narrative turning-points which dramatize rites of passage from which there can be no return – a habit of mind which suggests that in some respects at least he was still 'in the bonds of [his] old Evangelical faith' in 1877.

Ruskin's letters from the Continental tour of 1858 indicate that changes which had been going on in him for years were now crystallizing, but they give no hint of a sudden and total un-conversion experience. It was not until later that, for narrative purposes, he shaped events into a sharply defined pattern. Indeed, even in later accounts the record is complicated, for how can the account in *Fors* be reconciled with that note of 1868 on a diary entry of May 1858 in which he described the first Sunday on which he made a drawing: 'henceforward the beginning of total change in habits of mind' (*D*, 535; 35.493)? In 'The Grande Chartreuse' chapter of *Præterita* (1888), which ends dramatically with the last and best-known account of events in Turin, Ruskin – sometimes his own best critic – acknowledges the over-determined nature of hindsight while maintaining the sense of a permanent change having taking place:

So I settled at Turin for the autumn.

There, one Sunday morning, I made my way in the south suburb to a little chapel which, by a dusty roadside, gathered to its unobserved door the few sheep of the old Waldensian faith who had wandered from their own pastures under Monte Viso into the worldly capital of Piedmont.

The assembled congregation numbered in all some three or four and twenty, of whom fifteen or sixteen were grey-haired women. Their solitary and clerk-less preacher, a somewhat stunted figure in a plain black coat, with a cracked voice, after leading them through the languid forms of prayer which are all that in truth are possible to people whose present life is dull and its terrestial future unchangeable, put his utmost zeal into a consolatory discourse on the wickedness of the wide world, more especially of the plain of Piedmont and city of Turin, and on the exclusive favour with God, enjoyed by the between nineteen and twenty-four elect members of his congregation, in the streets of Admah and Zeboim [Deuteronomy 29.23].

Myself neither cheered nor greatly alarmed by this doctrine, I walked back into the condemned city, and up into the gallery where Paul Veronese's Solomon and the Queen of Sheba glowed in full afternoon light. The gallery windows being open, there came in with the warm air, floating swells and falls of military music, from the courtyard before the palace, which seemed to me more devotional, in their perfect art, tune, and discipline, than anything I remembered of evangelical hymns. And as the perfect colour and sound gradually asserted their power on me, they seemed finally to fasten me in the old article of Jewish faith, that things done delightfully and rightly were always done by the help and in the Spirit of God.

Of course that hour's meditation in the gallery of Turin only concluded the courses of thought which had been leading me to such end through many years. There was no sudden conversion possible to me, either by preacher, picture, or dulcimer. But, that day, my evangelical beliefs were put away, to be debated of no more. (35.495–6)

The sequence of the narrative follows more closely that of his original letters and notes, reflecting the fact that while writing *Præterita* he reviewed the accumulated private papers of a lifetime, marking them up and adding comments in preparation for composition.[71] Thirty years after the event, Ruskin puts slightly more flesh on his account of the sermon, and implies that he can recall a particular text that was quoted by the preacher, who is himself described in rather more detail.

The most significant new material, however, is in the description of his return to the gallery, 'where Paul Veronese's Solomon and the Queen of Sheba glowed in full afternoon light'. In his letter to his father dated Friday 30 July 1858 it was only the Queen of Sheba who 'glowed', and whose beauty defeated any attempt at copying, while Solomon presented problems of his own, being 'in the dark'.[72] Some of the glow of the whole painting, recorded in 1888, was that imparted by the working of Ruskin's memory, not only nostalgically – *Præterita* avoids unpleasant subjects for therapeutic reasons – but also with real intellectual and spiritual content; for, since the period in Turin, Solomon had been an important *alter ego* for him, and had helped him to sustain his belief in a God of Wisdom. During the first sixteen of those thirty years, Solomon, traditionally regarded as the author of the wisdom books in the Old Testament, presided over Ruskin's economic writings and the foundation of the Guild of St George, together with Athena and Neith, the Greek and Egyptian goddesses of wisdom. In the fourteen years that followed the rite of passage into 'Catholicism' at Assisi in 1874, Solomon again played a central role in Ruskin's rewriting of earlier histories and his preparations for writing the history of Christendom. Here are some of the subjects to be discussed in the second part of this study.

When Ruskin claimed in *Præterita* that his 'evangelical beliefs were put away' in 1858, 'to be debated of no more' he can only have meant inner debates, as on his return to London that year he continued his

---

[71] See, for example, Lancaster MS 11, Diaries, fols. 53, 79, 87, *et passim*. The church that he originally thought too large has, however, become a 'little chapel' in his memory.

[72] See p. 136 above.

discussions with Spurgeon and others, and argued with Evangelical friends and enemies for the rest of his life.[73] These dramatic statements, however, like the subsequent reference to 'the Queen of Sheba crash' (35.497), throw into sharper relief the other important addition to the paragraph describing Ruskin's return to the gallery after church – its final sentence: 'And as the perfect colour and sound gradually asserted their power on me, they seemed finally to fasten me in the old article of Jewish faith, that things done delightfully and rightly were always done by the help and in the Spirit of God [Genesis 1.2].' Far from being a narrative of loss, the *Præterita* account, like all its predecessors, is one of gain. Nowhere in the Old Testament is anything done more delightfully and rightly than Solomon's building of the temple, after which the prophet king says, in a verse that Ruskin learned by heart as a boy: 'Lord God of Israel, there is no God like thee, in heaven above, or on earth beneath, who keepest covenant and mercy with thy servants that walk before thee with all their heart' (1 Kings 8.23). And when the Queen of Sheba has 'seen all Solomon's wisdom', and the house that he has built, she says to the King:

Howbeit I believed not the words, until I came, and mine eyes had seen it: and, behold, the half was not told me: thy wisdom and prosperity exceedeth the fame which I heard. Happy are thy men, happy these thy servants, which stand continually before thee, and that hear thy wisdom. Blessed be the Lord thy God, which delighted in thee, to set thee on the throne of Israel: because the Lord loved Israel for ever, therefore made he thee king, to do judgment and justice. (I Kings 10.7–9)

---

[73] Contrary to the impression he gave later, Ruskin still did not work on Sundays when on a Continental tour with W. J. Stillman in 1860, and discussed Sabbatarianism with him (17.xxiv). Compare Tim Hilton, *John Ruskin: The Early Years, 1819–1859* (New Haven and London: Yale University Press, 1985), p. 254.

PART TWO

Victorian Solomon

CHAPTER 7

Solomon's 'maxims concerning wealth'

> Some centuries before the Christian era, a Jew merchant, largely engaged in business on the Gold Coast, and reported to have made one of the largest fortunes of his time (held also in repute for much practical sagacity), left among his ledgers some general maxims concerning wealth, which have been preserved, strangely enough, even to our own days.
>
> 'Qui Judicatis Terram', *Unto this Last* (17.57)

I

Between 1858 – the year of the 'Queen of Sheba' crash in Turin and Ruskin's introduction to Rose La Touche – and 1860, when *Unto this Last* appeared in parts in the *Cornhill Magazine* and was then prematurely terminated, Ruskin became convinced that his mission was to change people's way of life, rather than their way of looking at pictures, buildings and landscapes. In taking the Book of Proverbs as his inspiration at the beginning of the third essay in *Unto this Last*, quoted above, Ruskin invoked a tradition of Old Testament wisdom literature which informed his writing on political economy. This chapter examines the relationship between that tradition and Ruskin's critique of Victorian capitalism – a critique that was to have a profound influence upon a wide range of reformers, including Arnold Toynbee, Mahatma Gandhi and Martin Luther King – and considers his deepening interest in wisdom in other religions. Solomon proves to be Ruskin's crucial point of reference here, not only as the wealthy 'Jew merchant' divinely endowed with great wisdom, but also as the author of 'maxims' in Proverbs which anticipate the parables of one greater than Solomon, and which figure divine wisdom as a woman spinning, thus offering 'threads' connecting the Judæo-Christian tradition with Greek and Egyptian religion.

Insisting that Christ's most important teaching is on the use and misuse of money, Ruskin reads the expulsion of those who buy and sell in the temple in relation to Solomon and his temple, and to the 'temple' of the Christian soul – all signs of 'life', the key word of his writing on political economy. He also comes to see that divine wisdom is the originating power worshipped in Egyptian and Greek religion, as well as in Judaism and Christianity. In exploring the attributes associated with the female deities of Neith and Athena, Ruskin focuses upon the life-giving qualities associated with their spinning, which is also to be found in Proverbs.

Ruskin's theology of works developed in reaction to Evangelical teaching on 'salvation by faith alone'. In a letter probably written in the mid-1850s, addressed to the artist J. J. Laing who sought his advice on spiritual matters, Ruskin wrote:

I never met with but one book in my life that was clear on the subject of faith and works, and that book is the Bible. Read *it* only on this subject. And I think you will come to the conclusion that though works are not the *price* of salvation, they are assuredly the *way* to it, and the only way . . . Read the Sermon on the mount. It is work, work, work, from beginning to end . . . Strive always to *do* – acknowledge continually that it is Christ which worketh in you, both to will and do. And you will soon know the doctrine whether it be of God. (36.179–80)

On his way to Germany with his parents, on 18 May 1859, he wrote more in anger than sorrow to the Revd Daniel Moore, explaining that he believed 'the entire modern church system' of ministration to be 'a dream – & worse', and the 'whole Evangelical system a mere poetical absurdity':

The plain words & plain dealing of Christ are all I accept – & by those I stand – Thou *shalt* Love thy neighbour as thyself.
. . . If people believed the Atonement – they would'nt [sic] want it explained.
No words are strong enough to express my contempt for the common evangelical religion of the day – I think it the most despicable lie the devil has yet invented . . . [1]

Ruskin's rejection of the otherworldliness of Evangelicalism in favour of a this-worldly perspective is in some respects similar to George Eliot's. As he explained to his father on 29 September 1861, in a Sunday letter from Bonneville,

It is a difficult thing, to live without hope of another world, when one has been used to it for forty years. But by how much the more difficult, by so much it makes one braver and stronger. (17.xxxviii)

---

[1] Ruskin–Moore correspondence, Morgan MA 2186 (3). (Ruskin habitually punctuated contractions in this way.)

Six days later, when referring to the form of Christianity 'that is coming' (36.384), he sounded more like Tennyson. In fact this was a train of thought that he had explained to Rose La Touche in the one extant letter to her, written in Boulogne on 21 June 1861, where, in a manner reminiscent of Carlyle, he developed the biblical analogy of an ear of wheat: 'The Jewish dispensation enclosed the Christian as the blade does the ear: the Christian itself, blossoming partly, partly blighted, has yet to undergo the winnowing by Him whose Fan is in His hand; who will gather the grain into His garner and burn the chaff with fire' (36.370; Mark 4.28).

Ruskin spent most of his time abroad between the summer of 1861 and the end of 1863, frequently plagued by depression, and in flight from his tormented love for Rose la Touche[2] and from his exasperating elderly parents.[3] These relationships were made more problematic by his religious difficulties, which were now acute.[4] Even his regular Bible reading was affected: on Monday 7 July 1862, when he was in Milan, he recorded in his diary that he had read the first chapter of Jeremiah that morning, and commented, 'long since I looked at Bible, – the fresh eye and ear very useful'.[5]

One of the most immediate effects of the change in Ruskin's religious position was his revaluation of the works he had published as the 'Author of *Modern Painters*' – an appellation that he now dropped from his title-pages. He wrote to Margaret Bell, Headmistress of Winnington Hall, from Mornex, on 16 October 1862:

Early & rightly taught, it is perfectly possible to live happy . . . with no hope of another world . . .

But for us who have been long deceived, and who have all to forget & forsake, and desecrate – and darken it is dreadful – The world is an awful mystery to me now – but I see that is because I have been misled, not because it need be so . . .

I have to rewrite all my books – at least to take out the little good there's in

---

[2] See *John Ruskin and Rose la Touche: Her Unpublished Diaries of 1861 and 1867*, ed. Van Akin Burd (Oxford: Clarendon; New York: Oxford University Press, 1979), pp. 62–89.

[3] Years later he considered his absence from Denmark Hill to have been 'Cruel!': see Burd, ibid., p. 82.

[4] In February 1862 William Michael Rossetti found 'the whole tone of his thought on religious subjects changed, and the ardent, devout Protestant figured as a total disbeliever in any form of Christian or other defined faith': *Some Reminiscences*, 2 vols. (London: Brown, 1906), I, 183. Ruskin's response to the Higher Criticism of the Bible at this period, and to controversial books such as *Essays and Reviews* and Bishop Colenso's study on the Pentateuch, is discussed in chapter 8 below.

[5] Lancaster MS 12, Diaries, fol. 237v–236v (the numbering is reversed in this part of the diary notebook); compare *D*, 564. Ruskin is interested in Jeremiah's meekness in saying, 'I cannot speak: for I am a child' (Jeremiah 1.6): see fol. 235.

them . . . It is very difficult, at 43, to live a quite desolate life – believing that God cares for one precisely as much as He does for a midge – or a leach – or an ape – or an archangel – or what you will – Read Pope's essay on man; and universal prayer – again and again – and again. It is the only true divinity ever written in *English* by *way* of divinity . . .[6]

Pope's emphasis upon order, submission and reason met Ruskin's need at a time when he was embarrassed by his former Evangelical 'insolence' (8.15). For Ruskin, Pope was one of the 'good, wise, and happy men' (16.344), though 'intensely obnoxious to evangelical divines' (28.75), and his biography was one of Ruskin's unfulfilled projects. Significantly, Pope described God as 'Eternal Wisdom' in the second Epistle of the *Essay on Man*,[7] and ended his 'Universal Prayer' with these words:

> To thee, whose Temple is all Space,
> Whose Altar, Earth, Sea, Skies,
> One Chorus let all Being raise!
> All Nature's Incense rise!

Ruskin's search for secure moorings at this period is also reflected in his return to primary sources rather than modern scholarship in a number of different fields. In the later 1850s he noted the 'evangelical' texts in Isaiah and Matthew, in the sense of texts which proclaim the good news, when his struggle with Evangelicalism was intensifying.[8] A whole library of books had been written on political economy by the mid-nineteenth century, and its religious ramifications were complex;[9] yet Ruskin made detailed notes on Aristophanes' comedy, the second *Plutus*,[10] and years later announced that his political economy was 'all in Xenophon and Marmontel' (37.381). Biblical sources were still of supreme importance to him, however, on the subject of political economy. On the Continental tour of 1858, he transcribed verses from Isaiah in notes towards an essay on poverty.[11] Later in the same diary notebook he added the following entry to his notes on the *Plutus*:

---

[6] *The Winnington Letters: John Ruskin's Correspondence with Margaret Alexis Bell and the Children at Winnington Hall*, ed. Van Akin Burd (London: Allen, Unwin, 1969), p. 381.

[7] 'Go, teach Eternal Wisdom how to rule – / Then drop into thyself, and be a fool!' (II, 29–30); 'See! and confess, one comfort still must rise, / 'Tis this, Tho' Man's a fool, yet GOD IS WISE' (II, 294–5). Ruskin added this note to his diary entry of 22 May 1866: 'Pope's birthday. 1688. In London, "of parents whose rank or station were never ascertained!" The Essay on Criticism was written in 1709, when he was 21!': Lancaster MS 14, Diaries, fol. 4v.

[8] See Lancaster MS 11, Diaries, fols.17–19, 111, 126, 165, 283.

[9] See Boyd Hilton, *The Age of Atonement: The Influence of Evangelicalism on Social and Economic Thought, 1795–1865* (Oxford: Clarendon, 1988).

[10] See Lancaster MS 11, Diaries, fols. 98, 113, 119–23, 127.   [11] Ibid., fol. 96.

'Political economy. The whole of the 22nd of Jeremiah is important, especially v. 13th.'[12]

The published writings themselves, however, reveal that his most important source was the Book of Proverbs, traditionally ascribed to Solomon. It is important to emphasize at the outset that this is a deeply religious text. Archdeacon Julius Hare, whose nephew Augustus was to see Ruskin at work in Turin in 1858, said of Proverbs in a sermon of 1841: 'It is not a collection of mere prudential aphorisms, inculcating the business of this life, and the art of dealing with mankind, looking wholly at worldly gain and loss; but the fear of God is the beginning and the end of it, and runs through every precept, and is the principle of every maxim.'[13] The God of Proverbs is a God of justice and retribution who is closely involved in the lives of human beings.[14] Nevertheless, like the other wisdom books of the Old Testament, and like parts of the Sermon on the Mount, the Proverbs are more palatable to agnostics than most other books in the Bible because they can be received as ahistorical practical ethics,[15] and read alongside material from other cultures and creeds.[16] As Thomas Scott wrote in the commentary that we know Ruskin used, Solomon excelled in 'morality, politicks, and economicks; for he spake three thousand proverbs, [I Kings 4.32] of which such as were most suited for general utility have come down to us in the book of Proverbs'.[17]

Mashal, the Hebrew word that is translated 'proverb', more accurately signifies a similitude or parable.[18] Christopher Wordsworth stated that the Proverbs 'are like our Blessed Lord's own Parables . . . words of profound wisdom, which concern "the mysteries of the kingdom of heaven," and, like other divine utterances of the prophetic Scriptures, as St. Peter affirms, they were not revealed in their full meaning to those who first heard them'.[19] For Ruskin, who liked to remind his readers of

[12] Ibid., fol. 126. The text is: 'Woe unto him that buildeth his house by unrighteousness, and his chambers by wrong; that useth his neighbour's service without wages, and giveth him not for his work.'   [13] Julius Charles Hare, *Sermons* (London: Parker, 1846), p. 311.

[14] See Lennart Boström, *The God of the Sages: The Portrayal of God in the Book of Proverbs*, Coniectanea Biblica, Old Testament Series, 29 (Stockholm: Almqvist, 1990), p. 113.   [15] Ibid., p. [iv].

[16] See, for example, Christopher Tolley, *Domestic Biography: The Legacy of Evangelicalism in Four Nineteenth-Century Families*, Oxford Historical Monographs (Oxford: Clarendon, 1997), p. 52.

[17] *The Holy Bible*, with explanatory notes, practical observations, and copious marginal references by Thomas Scott, 9th edn, 6 vols. (London: Seeley, 1825), II, I Kings 4.30–4.

[18] See, for example, *The Holy Bible*, with Notes and Introductions by Chr[istopher] Wordsworth, 6 vols. (London: Rivingtons, 1864–70), IV, Pt III, xi. Compare [Robert Boswell], *The Book of Parables commonly entitled the Book of Proverbs, paraphrased in Metre; from the Original, compared with many Versions in different Languages* (Pinang: Mission, 1840).

[19] Christopher Wordsworth, *Holy Bible*, IV, Pt III, p. 18. For Ruskin's notes on 'Topics in Proverbs' and on 'Passages in Proverbs concerning Secresy', see Beinecke, Miscellaneous Notebook 3, fols. 1–13, and Beinecke, Architectural Notebook, Italy, 1850–1, fols. 57v – 59r, 65r.

Christ's teaching on money, and that the Sermon on the Mount is 'work – work – work – from beginning to end', it was the combination of the prophetic and the practical in Proverbs that proved to be particularly helpful in the 1850s and 1860s. Work, and especially manual labour, is highly respected in Proverbs,[20] although for all its teaching on wealth and poverty there is no sense in the book of the notion of social reform.[21] In mid-Victorian Britain, however, parallels were drawn between the nation's increasing wealth and that of Solomon's Jerusalem, as in Christopher Wordsworth's commentary:

> Wealth flowed from all sides into Jerusalem, and strangers flocked to it from all quarters. It became an emporium of commerce. It was also, especially after the building of the Temple, the centre of intellectual light and of religious life to the Hebrew Nation and to the World . . .
>
> But these benefits were accompanied with countervailing temptations . . . the Holy Spirit, in inspiring Solomon to write the Book of Proverbs, supplied an antidote for the poison of those influences, and has given to the world in this Book a moral and spiritual Manual, which has its special uses for those who dwell in populous towns and cities, and who are busily engaged in worldly traffic, and are exposed to such temptations as are rife in an age and country like our own, distinguished by commercial enterprise and mechanical skill, and by the production of great works of human Industry . . . [22]

More broadly, good conduct and the maintenance of order are highly valued in Proverbs,[23] and indeed, the values that Ruskin admired in Pope originated partly there, where 'ostentation and loudness are shunned, but taste and elegance are appreciated', and where a 'premium is placed on reserve, self-control, and propriety'.[24]

Although the Book of Proverbs has a discernible structure and coherence as a whole work, each maxim is quotable and applicable in isolation from its context, and this is how it is generally used in later writings, including Ruskin's, which itself became more fragmented and aphoristic in this middle period. Whereas the 'Author of *Modern Painters*' published book-length studies on art and architecture, subsidised by his

---

[20] See Claus Westermann, *Roots of Wisdom: The Oldest Proverbs of Israel and Other Peoples* (Edinburgh: Clark, 1995), p. 17.

[21] See R. N. Whybray, *Wealth and Poverty in the Book of Proverbs*, Journal for the Study of the Old Testament Supplement Series, 99 (Sheffield: JSOT, 1990), p. 113.

[22] Christopher Wordsworth, IV, Pt III, *Holy Bible*, pp. ix-x. Ruskin hardly needed to 'convert' Proverbs into an 'economic treatise' in the way that is suggested in Paul L. Sawyer, *Ruskin's Poetic Argument: The Design of the Major Works* (Ithaca and London: Cornell University Press, 1985), p. 208.

[23] See James L. Crenshaw, *Old Testament Wisdom: An Introduction* (London: SCM, 1982), p. 19.

[24] J. C. Rylaarsdam, 'Hebrew Wisdom', in *Peake's Commentary on the Bible*, ed. Matthew Black and H. H. Rowley (London: Nelson, 1962), p. 387.

father, the plain 'John Ruskin' who wrote on political economy, against his father's will, published collections of essays, letters, dialogues and lectures, some of which were prematurely terminated in their original, serial form. The grand narrative of Christian redemption that underpins his earlier work now gives way, first, to fragments of wisdom from Proverbs which provide him with texts for his essays and lectures, as in a sermon (the subject of section II in this chapter), and then, in the later 1860s, to wisdom literature from Greek and Egyptian religion, as well as from the Bible (the subject of section III). Ruskin's response to Greek mythology has been thoroughly examined;[25] the emphasis here falls upon Ruskin's exploration of the nature of divine wisdom in different religions. In a letter to his friend Henry Acland, written in the autumn of 1864, Ruskin reported that he was 'trying to understand what religions hitherto [had] been worth understanding, in some *impartial* manner', and 'endeavouring to make out how far Greeks and Egyptians knew God', adding, with reference to his godson, Harry Acland: 'that Church font by which I held Harry had Nile water in it, if we could have seen clearly' (18.xxxiv–xxxv).

II

In accepting an invitation to lecture in Manchester during the Art Treasures Exhibition of 1857, Ruskin entered the citadel of the dominant 'Manchester School' at a time of national economic crisis, when a number of banks stopped payment (17.xxiv, 137). The first of his lectures on *The Political Economy of Art* (later renamed *'A Joy for Ever'*) was entitled 'The Discovery and Application of Art' and delivered on 10 July. In the manner of a lay sermon, it took as its text (though not at the beginning) verses from Proverbs 31, the well-known final chapter of the book – an acrostic poem in praise of the virtuous woman, beginning 'The words of king Lemuel, the prophecy that his mother taught him.'[26] The chapter has been interpreted both as practical wisdom on the role of women,[27] and as prophetic writing inspired by divine wisdom, taught by

---

[25] Dinah Birch argues that Ruskin 'never lost his faith in the Bible as a repository of human and divine wisdom, as others had lost or were losing such faith; indeed he grew yet closer to the Bible during these years. The change in his position was not that he came to value the Bible less, but that he grew to revere mythology more': *Ruskin's Myths* (Oxford: Clarendon, 1988), p. 48. See also her article, 'Ruskin's "Womanly Mind"', *Essays in Criticism*, 38 (1988), 308–24.

[26] For Ruskin's use of the chapter see 6.70, 16.20, 55, 56, 18.40, 176, 297.

[27] See, for example, Matthew Henry, *An Exposition of the Old and New Testament*, stereotype edn, 3 vols. (London: Robinson, 1828), II, 578; and Scott, *The Holy Bible*, III, Proverbs 31.

the 'mother' of the Hebrew Church, and describing the Christian Church as the spouse of Christ.[28] Ruskin, engaged in redefining 'economics' and 'wealth' for his audience, sets Old Testament wisdom against the Manchester School of Political Economy, and, by implication, the divinely ordained, life-giving feminine principle against the death-dealing masculine principle.

Ironically addressing what he called the 'just and wholesome contempt in which we hold poverty' (16.15), Ruskin commented that nobody in the modern world was 'empty-purse proud' as in former ages, and reminded his audience that the Greeks and Romans mocked at the rich (16.16), that Dante reserved special punishment for usurers and that the 'Spirit of Poverty' was reverenced in the Middle Ages (16.17). Set in the context of Manchester's recognition that 'this great gathering of British pictures' was, he supposed, 'part and parcel of the real wealth of the country', his theme was 'certain commercial questions connected with this particular form of wealth'. His argument is a classical one – that providence supplies our needs:

To begin, then, with one of these necessary truisms: all economy, whether of states, households, or individuals, may be defined to be the art of managing labour. The world is so regulated by the laws of Providence, that a man's labour, well applied, is always amply sufficient to provide him during his life with all things needful to him, and not only with those, but with many pleasant objects of luxury; and yet farther, to procure him large intervals of healthful rest and serviceable leisure. (16.18)

There is nothing unusual in a writer on political economy seeing the workings of a divine hand. Adam Smith's *The Wealth of Nations* provides the most obvious precedent,[29] while Richard Whateley, the 'Oriel Noetic', is of particular interest here, as he places a heavy emphasis upon divine wisdom in his treatise on political economy.[30]

[28] See, for example, Christopher Wordsworth, *Holy Bible*, IV, Pt III, pp. 69–70.

[29] Adam Smith 'was concerned to identify the natural order first ordained by a benevolent Prime Mover as a guide to the arrangement of social and political conventions most conducive to human welfare . . . behind the apparently random transactions of the market place, there lay a "hidden hand" which . . . automatically directed resources to their most productive use': *Critics of Capitalism: Victorian Reactions to 'Political Economy'*, ed. Elisabeth Jay and Richard Jay, Cambridge English Prose Texts, ed. Graham Storey (Cambridge University Press, 1986), pp. 4–5.

[30] 'Anatomy and Physiology . . . throw more and more light on the stupendous wisdom of contrivance which the structure of organized bodies displays; – in short, to furnish a most important portion of Natural Theology. And it might have been anticipated, that an attentive study of the constitution of Society, should bring to light a no less admirable apparatus of divinely-wise contrivances, directed no less to beneficial ends; – that as the structure of a single bee is admirable, and still more so that of a hive of bees, instinctively directing their efforts towards a common object, so, the Divine Maker of the human body, has evinced no less benevolent wisdom in his

Ruskin's argument, however, then takes a turn which places the responsibility for the regulation of an economy firmly upon man:

It is not accident, it is not Heaven-commanded calamity, it is not the original and inevitable evil of man's nature, which fill your streets with lamentation, and your graves with prey. It is only that, when there should have been providence, there has been waste; when there should have been labour, there has been lasciviousness; and wilfulness, when there should have been subordination.*

*Proverbs xiii.23: 'Much food is in the tillage of the poor, but there is that is destroyed for want of judgment.' (16.19)[31]

Following the rejection in the opening sequence of negatives of three possible explanations, including Calvinist Evangelicalism's belief in the 'total depravity of man', Ruskin's secondary and secular use of the word 'providence' captures the spirit of the Book of Proverbs, with its emphasis upon appropriate human conduct in a world in which 'grace played no role'.[32]

'Economy', far from meaning 'sparing or saving', means 'the administration of a house; its stewardship' – applying labour rationally, preserving produce carefully, and distributing produce seasonably (16.19):

so fulfilling in all ways the Wise Man's description, whether of the queenly housewife or queenly nation: 'She riseth while it is yet night, and giveth meat to her household, and a portion to her maidens. She maketh herself covering of tapestry, her clothing is silk and purple. Strength and honour are in her clothing, and she shall rejoice in time to come.' [Proverbs 31.15, 22, 25][33]

Now, you will observe that in this description of the perfect economist, or mistress of a household, there is a studied expression of the balanced division of her care between the two great objects of utility and splendour: in her right hand, food and flax, for *life* and clothing; in her left hand, the purple and the needlework, for honour and for beauty. [Proverbs 3.16] (16.20; our emphasis)

Having run three separate verses of chapter 31 together, Ruskin alludes to a verse that he learnt at his mother's knee, and with which he is to end

provisions for the progress of society; – and that though in both cases the designs of Divine Wisdom are often counteracted by human folly . . . and by mistake or fraud . . . still, in each case, attentive study may enable us to trace more and more the designs of a wise Providence, and devise means for removing the impediments to their completion': Richard Whateley, *Introductory Lectures on Political Economy, being part of a Course delivered in Easter Term, MDCCCXXXI* (London: Fellowes, 1831–2), pp. 96–7. Also compare pp. 110, 111, 198.

31 Thomas Scott glosses this verse: 'The poor and industrious, who labour to cultivate a little spot of land, often live in a plentiful though homely manner: while those who have inherited large estates, are reduced to poverty by negligence, indiscretion, ostentation, and extravagance': Scott, III, Proverbs 13.23.   32 Crenshaw, *Old Testament Wisdom*, p. 19.

33 The Authorized Version reads: 'She riseth also while it is yet night, and giveth meat to her household, and a portion to her maidens . . . She maketh herself coverings of tapestry; her clothing is silk and purple . . . Strength and honour are her clothing; and she shall rejoice in time to come.'

his second lecture on the political economy of art: 'Length of days is in her right hand; and in her left hand riches and honour' (Proverbs 3.16).

The word 'life' occurs more frequently in Proverbs than in any other book in the Bible. Held in wisdom's right hand, life stands in opposition to what Ruskin calls 'the "Let-alone" principle' which is, 'in all things which man has to do with, the principle of death' (16.26). Speaking in Manchester, the home town of his friend Elizabeth Gaskell, author of *Ruth* (1853), Ruskin pricks the consciences of his audience by encouraging them not to use labour selfishly, and suggesting that if the veil could be lifted from their sight, they would see – 'the angels do see' – signs of death on their white dresses: 'strange dark spots, and crimson patterns' (16.51).

Ruskin ends the lecture with commentary on the figures of Faith, Hope and Charity in Ambrogio Lorenzetti's fresco in the Palazzo Pubblico at Siena, portraying 'Good Civic Government'. Government, he argues, should be 'hopeful still of more wisdom and power', and 'hopeful chiefly, and active, in times of national trial or distress, according to those first and notable words describing the queenly nation: "She riseth, *while it is yet night*"' (16.55; Proverbs 31.15). Finally he asks the audience to guess to which of the virtues in the fresco the public revenues are entrusted. The answer is surprising:

a virtue of which we hear too little in modern times, as distinct from others; Magnanimity: largeness of heart . . . that character, in fine, which, in those words taken by us at first for the description of a Queen among the nations, looks less to the present power than to the distant promise; "Strength and honour are in her clothing, – and she shall rejoice IN TIME TO COME." [Proverbs 31.25] (16.56)

In his first lecture, then, Ruskin presents his Manchester audience with a vision of the queenly nation in which wisdom presides, holding life in her right hand and, through magnanimity, drawing upon her store of wealth for the common good. In the second lecture, entitled 'The Accumulation and Distribution of Art' and delivered three days later, on 13 July 1857, he works towards a more direct appeal to the wealthy merchants who are present, again invoking the Book of Proverbs. Addressing issues such as the accessibility of art to ordinary people, the need for Britain to help rescue scandalously neglected masterpieces of Italian art and architecture, but also itself to acquire great art for the nation, he teases his listeners by praising the medieval guild system and mocking what they would consider to be signs of progress in the modern world:

So that the time and powers of the nation are wasted, not only in wretched struggling against each other, but in vain complaints, and groundless discouragements, and empty investigations, and useless experiments in laws, and elections, and inventions; with hope always to pull wisdom through some new-shaped slit in a ballot-box, and to drag prosperity down out of the clouds along some new knot of electric wire; while all the while Wisdom stands calling at the corners of the streets, [Proverbs 1.20] and the blessing of Heaven waits ready to rain down upon us, deeper than the rivers and broader than the dew, if only we will obey the first plain principles of humanity, and the first plain precepts of the skies: "Execute true judgment, and show mercy and compassion, every man to his brother; and let none of you imagine evil against his brother in your heart."* [Zechariah 7.9,10]

* It would be well if, instead of preaching continually about the doctrine of faith and good works, our clergymen would simply explain to their people a little what good works mean . . . (16.96)

This passage anticipates *Fors Clavigera* in its lively Carlylean juxtaposition of traditional values drawn from ancient sources – in this case Proverbs and Zechariah – and the new values of a modern democracy, symbolized by the ballot box and the electric wire.

Far from wishing to redistribute the wealth of his Manchester audience through changes in direct taxation, the deeply anti-democratic Ruskin challenges them and, through the publication of the lecture in *The Political Economy of Art*, the other 'rich men of England', to follow Solomon's maxims on the use of their wealth:

What less can we hope from your wealth than this, rich men of England, when once you feel fully how, by the strength of your possessions – not, observe, by the exhaustion, but by the administration of them and the power, – you can direct the acts – command the energies – inform the ignorance – prolong the existence, of the whole human race; and how, even of worldly wisdom, which man employs faithfully, it is true, not only that her ways are pleasantness, but that her paths are peace; and that, for all the children of men, as well as for those to whom she is given, Length of days is in her right hand, as in her left hand Riches and Honour? [Proverbs 3.16–17] (16.103)[34]

In January 1858 George Eliot recommended Ruskin's books to Sarah Hennell. The third and fourth volumes of *Modern Painters*, she believed, contained 'some of the finest writing of the age' (5.lx). His 'little book on *The Political Economy of Art*' also contained 'some magnificent passages',

---

[34] Ruskin was addressing some of the new patrons of art – philanthropic cotton lords who had contributed to the exhibition, and whose wealth he also wished to see used wisely in this respect: see Dianne Sachko Macleod, *Art and the Victorian Middle Class: Money and the Making of Cultural Identity* (Cambridge University Press, 1996), p. 102.

but these were 'mixed up with stupendous specimens of arrogant absurdity on some economical points' (16.xxiii). George Eliot's radical political affiliations, reflected in her former editorship of the *Westminster Review*, founded by Jeremy Bentham and James Mill, put her firmly in the opposition camp on questions of political economy – a subject on which she had read widely. Some reviewers of the new *Cornhill Magazine*, owned by Ruskin's publisher, Smith, Elder, were also to accuse him of arrogance in their vehement attacks upon *Unto this Last*, when it appeared as monthly essays two years later.[35] The first essay, entitled 'The Roots of Honour' and signed 'J. R.', was printed between chapters of Trollope's *Framley Parsonage* and a paper on 'Physiological Riddles: II. Why we Grow'.[36] In the second, 'The Veins of Wealth', Ruskin developed his theme of the supreme value of human life, arguing that 'the true veins of wealth are purple – and not in Rock, but in Flesh' (17.55–6). It was after the publication of the third essay, entitled 'Qui Judicatis Terram', that Thackeray, as editor, asked Ruskin to end the serialization prematurely with a final, fourth essay – 'Ad Valorem' – in November 1860 (17.xxviii).

Ruskin explains the title of his third essay in a passage in which Dante is invoked as Solomon's greatest interpreter. Starting with the 'small word', 'just', in the ordinary political economist's definition of his own 'science' – 'getting rich by legal or just means' – Ruskin both explains and imitates Dante by taking the mundane up into the supramundane in a passage of commentary on the *Paradiso*, canto 18:

For then it will follow that in order to grow rich scientifically, we must grow rich justly; and, therefore, know what is just; so that our economy will no longer depend merely on prudence, but on jurisprudence – and that of divine, not human law. Which prudence is indeed of no mean order, holding itself, as it were, high in the air of heaven, and gazing for ever on the light of the sun of justice; hence the souls which have excelled in it are represented by Dante as stars forming in heaven for ever the figure of the eye of an eagle; they having been in life the discerners of light from darkness; or to the whole human race, as the light of the body, which is the eye; [Matthew 6.22] while those souls which form the wings of the bird (giving power and dominion to justice, "healing in its wings" [Malachi 4.2]) trace also in light the inscription in heaven: "DILIG-ITE JUSTITIAM QUI JUDICATIS TERRAM." [Wisdom of Solomon 1.1, Vulgate], "Ye who judge the earth, give" (not, observe, merely love, but) "diligent love to justice": the love which seeks diligently, that is to say, choosingly, and by preference to all things else. (17.62–3)

[35] See J. L. Bradley, *Ruskin: The Critical Heritage*, Critical Heritage series, ed. B. C. Southam (London: Routledge, 1984), pp. 273–89.
[36] *The Cornhill Magazine*, 2 (July–December 1860), 155–66.

Ruskin, a close student of Plato's *Laws*,[37] reminds his readers of eternal truths against which the new science of political economy should be tested. In choosing the first verse of the Wisdom of Solomon for his own title, he implicitly draws upon that work's teaching on the conflict between the creative forces that make for life and the godless men who ask for death (Wisdom 1.14–15). Dante, whose commentary on the Wisdom of Solomon takes the form of this paradisal vision, epitomizes the Christian understanding of wisdom which flourished in the Middle Ages, and to which Ruskin refers at the beginning of his essay.

In the opening paragraph of 'Qui Judicatis Terram', Ruskin defamiliarizes the story of Solomon and his great wealth by relating it in modern, mercantile terms:

Some centuries before the Christian era, a Jew merchant, largely engaged in business on the Gold Coast, and reported to have made one of the largest fortunes of his time (held also in repute for much practical sagacity), left among his ledgers some general maxims concerning wealth, which have been preserved, strangely enough, even to our own days. (17.57)

From the political economist's perspective, Solomon's Proverbs are secondary to his reputation as a wealth creator: his wisdom is mentioned parenthetically, and his teaching is said to be 'left among his ledgers'. This reference to ledgers provides a clue to Ruskin's private identification with Solomon, as many of the diaries and literary manuscripts, including that of *Unto this Last*, are written either in ledgers or on vertically ruled accounts paper of the kind used by his father – a constant reminder of the profit-and-loss economy of both the wine trade and Evangelical Christianity.[38] As a published statement, the reference has the effect of 'making strange' Solomon's prophetic teaching in the modern world.

[37] See, e.g., 8.28, 17.18, 17.210, 17.371, 19.178, 20.295, and in the later Letters in *Fors, passim*.

[38] Brought up amongst ledgers, Ruskin was 'Entered, Filed, and Registered, according to the custom in use among Protestant Dissenters', at the age of 18 (see p. 4 above). His father pasted favourable reviews of his works into large ledgers (Ashmolean Library of Western Art). In the final Appendix to *The Stones of Venice* I (1851) he stated his belief that 'accounts have been literally kept for all of us' by God in 'the account-book' (9.473). Many of the diary notebooks have the vertical rules of the account book (Lancaster). The Brantwood Diary is written in a handsomely bound ledger which has 'LEDGER' embossed on the spine (Morgan). For a reproduction of a sample page of the MS of *Unto this Last* (Huntington), see 17.74–5. More practical reasons for Ruskin's using ledgers and account books were their availability (several of the diary notebooks contain London stationers' labels) and the high quality of their paper. (On 31 November 1873 he wrote in one of his larger diary notebooks, *not* ruled up in this way, 'How I spoil these pretty pages by writing on them': Lancaster MS 16, Diaries, fol. 143.) They may also have been of sentimental value to Ruskin: see Lancaster MS 16, Diaries, fol. 67r, where he refers to continuing his diary in his father's 'diary book'.

Continuing the paragraph with a comparison between modern and medieval responses to Solomon's 'maxims', Ruskin refers to the Ducal Palace:

They were held in considerable respect by the most active traders of the Middle Ages, especially by the Venetians, who even went so far in their admiration as to place a statue of the old Jew on the angle of one of their principal public buildings. Of late years these writings have fallen into disrepute, being opposed in every particular to the spirit of modern commerce. (17.57)

Ruskin still finds it convenient to ignore the fact that the statue of the Judgment of Solomon is Renaissance work.[39] Nevertheless, his broader point is supported by the fact that the Christian understanding of wisdom which flourished in the Middle Ages gave way to a classical humanist understanding in the Renaissance, today conceived of as the early modern period.[40]

Casting himself, then, in his characteristic prophetic role of a man out of tune with his times, he develops the subject of the Jew merchant's maxims:

Nevertheless I shall reproduce a passage or two from them here, partly because they may interest the reader by their novelty; and chiefly because they will show him that it is possible for a very practical and acquisitive tradesman to hold, through a not unsuccessful career, that principle of distinction between well-gotten and ill-gotten wealth, which, partially insisted on in my last paper, it must be our work more completely to examine in this.

He says, for instance, in one place: "The getting of treasures by a lying tongue is a vanity tossed to and fro of them that seek death"; [Proverbs 21.6] adding in another, with the same meaning (he has a curious way of doubling his sayings): "Treasures of wickedness profit nothing: but justice delivers from death." [Proverbs 10.2] . . .

Again: the merchant says, "He that oppresseth the poor to increase his riches, shall surely come to want." [Proverbs 22.16] And again, more strongly: "Rob not the poor because he is poor; neither oppress the afflicted in the place of business. For God shall spoil the soul of those that spoiled them." [Proverbs 22.22] (17.57–8)

Ruskin's *faux-naïf* comment in parenthesis on the doubling structure of the Proverbs signals the fact that he is offering informal biblical commentary. Like Thomas Scott's commentary, Ruskin's offers not only 'explanatory notes' but also 'practical observations' on Solomon's maxims:[41]

[39] Compare *The Seven Lamps of Architecture* (8.230): see p. 79 above.
[40] See Eugene F. Rice Jr., *The Renaissance Idea of Wisdom* (Cambridge, Mass.: Harvard University Press, 1958), p. 3.   [41] See note 163 above.

But the two most remarkable passages in their deep general significance are the following:-

"The rich and the poor have met. God is their maker." [Proverbs 22.2]

"The rich and the poor have met. God is their light." [Proverbs 29.13, Vulgate]

They "have met": more literally, have stood in each other's way (*obviaverunt*). That is to say, as long as the world lasts, the action and counteraction of wealth and poverty, the meeting, face to face, of rich and poor, is just as appointed and necessary a law of that world as the flow of stream to sea, or the interchange of power among the electric clouds: – "God is their maker." (17.58–9)

Nevertheless, Ruskin insists, whether the stream 'shall be a curse or a blessing' depends upon 'man's labour' (17.60). The traditions surrounding Solomon, like those associated with his father David, were arranged by the Deuteronomist historian around what is known as the 'blessing-curse scheme' – 'Solomon under the blessing – Solomon under the curse'[42] – a scheme that was to become increasingly significant in Ruskin's own work, and to be the subject of Letter 20 of *Fors Clavigera* – 'Benediction' – in 1872.[43] For the moment he completes the stream analogy by returning to his key text from Proverbs:

In like manner this wealth "goes where it is required". No human laws can withstand its flow. They can only guide it: but this, the leading trench and limiting mound can do so thoroughly, that it shall become water of life – the riches of the hand of wisdom;* or, on the contrary, by leaving it to its own lawless flow, they may make it, what it has been too often, the last and deadliest of national plagues: water of Marah [Exodus 15.23] – the water which feeds the roots of all evil.

* "Length of days in her right hand; in her left, riches and honour." [Proverbs 3.16] (17.61)

Ruskin's gloss on the first half of Proverbs 3.16 in *The Political Economy of Art* was 'in her right hand, food and flax, for life and clothing' (16.20).[44] In the fourth and final essay of *Unto this Last*, where he was forced to distil what he had planned to develop in further essays in the *Cornhill*, Ruskin's own most famous maxim summarizes Solomon's teaching on 'life' in the Book of Proverbs:

THERE IS NO WEALTH BUT LIFE. Life, including all its powers of love, of joy, and of admiration. That country is the richest which nourishes the greatest number of noble and happy human beings; that man is richest who, having perfected the functions of his own life to the utmost, has also the widest helpful

---

[42] J. Alberto Soggin, 'The Davidic–Solomonic Kingdom', in John H. Hayes and J. Maxwell Miller, eds., *Israelite and Judaean History* (London: SCM, 1977), pp. 332–80 (p. 366).

[43] See chapter 9 below.   [44] See p. 163 above.

influence, both personal, and by means of his possessions, over the lives of others. (17.105)[45]

In *Unto this Last* Ruskin adopts the role of a Victorian Solomon, and both this work and much of his subsequent writing can be described as Victorian wisdom literature.

III

'Life' is a crucially important word not only in Proverbs but also in the gospel to which, for Christian commentators, Solomon's maxims point – John's gospel. Thus Proverbs 8.35 – 'For whoso findeth me findeth life, and shall obtain favour of the Lord' – anticipates John 3.36 – 'He that believeth on the Son hath everlasting life: and he that believeth not the Son shall not see life'.[46] The link between wisdom and life is also implicit in some of Christ's most important *logoi*, such as 'I am come that they might have life, and that they may have it more abundantly' (John 10.10) and 'I am the resurrection, and the life' (John 11.25), in that Christ himself *is* wisdom (1 Corinthians 1.30).[47] A third example – 'I am the bread of life' (John 6.35) – is cited in Ruskin's final paragraph in *Unto this Last*, where he draws out the eschatological meaning of the words addressed to the labourers in the vineyard, which he takes as his title:

Raise the veil boldly; face the light; and if, as yet, the light of the eye can only be through tears, and the light of the body [Matthew 6.22] through sackcloth, go thou forth weeping, bearing precious seed [Psalm 126.6], until the time come, and the kingdom, when Christ's gift of bread, [John 6.35] and bequest of peace, [John 14.27] shall be "Unto this last as unto thee"; [Matthew 20.13] and when, for earth's severed multitudes of the wicked and the weary, there shall be holier reconciliation than that of the narrow home, and calm economy, where the Wicked cease – not from trouble, but from troubling – and the Weary are at rest. [Job 3.17] (17.114)

Following the hostile critical reception given to *Unto this Last*, however, Ruskin recognized the danger of being accused of hypocrisy if he quoted the Bible in his work,[48] which might explain the comparative paucity of biblical allusions in the *Essays on Political Economy* (*Fraser's*

---

[45] In the rider Ruskin nods to Wordsworth by echoing 'We live by Admiration, Hope, and Love': *The Excursion* (1814), IV, line 763.

[46] See Christopher Wordsworth, *Holy Bible*, IV, Pt III, p. 22.   [47] See p. 116 above.

[48] He wrote to his father from Lucerne on 15 November 1861: 'There is . . . little use and much harm in quoting Bible now; it puts religious people in a rage to have anything they don't like hammered into them with a text, and the active men of the world merely think you a hypocrite or a fool' (17.l).

Magazine, 1862–3), later entitled *Munera Pulveris*. Yet even in the mid-1860s, when his agnostic side was in the ascendant and his imagination inhabited Greek and Egyptian temples, Ruskin explored the significance for political economy of the typological relationship between Solomon and his temple and Christ's driving out those who bought and sold in Herod's temple, and between Christ's declaration that his body was the temple and New Testament teaching on Christ's followers treating their own bodies and souls as temples.

As in Manchester in 1857, the Bradford audience to which Ruskin delivered the lecture he called 'Traffic', on 21 April 1864, would have included some of the town's industrialists and merchants; and, as in *The Political Economy of Art*, some of his audience's cherished ideas of modernity and progress were held up for ridicule through contrasts drawn with ancient traditions. Instead of an art exhibition, the context for 'Traffic' was architectural: no design for the new Exchange at Bradford had been accepted when he delivered the lecture, and in the published version he distanced himself from the Venetian Gothic design that had by that time been chosen (18.lxxv). His way into the subject of the 'three distinct schools of European architecture' is through religion. 'We Europeans,' he argues,

have had three great religions: the Greek, which was the worship of the God of Wisdom and Power; the Mediæval, which was the worship of the God of Judgment and Consolation; the Renaissance, which was the worship of the God of Pride and Beauty: these three we have had – they are past, – and now, at last, we England have got a fourth religion, and a God of our own, about which I want to ask you. (18.445)

His analysis of Greek religion focuses upon Athena, daughter of 'Jupiter the revealer' and of 'the Intellect, springing armed from the head' (18.445). Acknowledging the recent research which was beginning to 'penetrate the depth of meaning couched under the Athenaic symbols',[49] he relates her divine perfection to the ideals of Greek architecture:

. . . from perfect knowledge, given by the full-revealed Athena, strength and peace, in sign of which she is crowned with the olive spray, and bears the resistless spear.

[49] Compare Ruskin's analysis of Athena with, for example, Carl Otfried Müller, *Ancient Art and its Remains; or, A Manual of the Archæology of Art*, new edn, with additions by F. G. Welcker, trans. John Leitch (London: Bohn, 1852), pp. 460–1. W. E. Gladstone writes at length on Minerva (changed in his corrections copy at St Deiniol's Library, Hawarden, to Athena) in the section on 'The Religion of the Homeric Age' in his *Homer and the Homeric Age*, 3 vols. (Oxford University Press, 1858), II, 39–172, which Ruskin knew.

This, then, was the Greek conception of purest Deity; and every habit of life, and every form of his art developed themselves from the seeking this bright, serene, resistless wisdom . . . And the Greek architecture rose unerring, bright, clearly defined, and self-contained. (18.446)

Both Greek religion and Medieval Christianity were in time corrupted, and so was their architecture; but what, Ruskin asks his audience, do '*we* worship, and what *we* build?' Answering his own question, he states that while we may 'dispute a great deal about the nominal religion' of Christianity, we are 'all unanimous' about the 'practical' religion to which we devote 'nine-tenths of our property, and six-sevenths of our time', and which is ruled over by the 'Goddess of Getting-on', or 'Britannia of the Market', to whom the great architectural works of the day, such as 'railroad stations, vaster than the temple of Ephesus', are built (18.448).

Now as Trollope recognized, Athena and 'Getting-on' are 'goddesses' in quite different senses. [50] Ruskin's purpose, however, is homiletic, and this comic treatment of the 'practical religion' of Victorian England makes the specific reference that follows to an aspect of its 'nominal religion' all the more powerful:

On his temples, the Greek put contests of great warriors in founding states, or of gods with evil spirits. On his houses and temples alike, the Christian put carvings of angels conquering devils; or of hero-martyrs exchanging this world for another: subject inappropriate, I think, to our direction of exchange here. And the Master of Christians not only left His followers without any orders as to the sculpture of affairs of exchange on the outside of buildings, but gave some strong evidence of His dislike of affairs of exchange within them. [Matthew 21.12] (18.449)

Whereas the 'favoured votaries' of the Goddess of Getting-on tend to assume that captains of industry should enrich themselves, generals, Ruskin points out, do not take the land they win, and kings do not 'consume all the profits of the nation's work'. If 'the crowned creature' covers his body with jewels he is probably not a real king:

It is possible he may be, as Solomon was; but that is when the nation shares his splendour with him. Solomon made gold, not only to be in his own palace as stones, but to be in Jerusalem as stones.[51] But, even so, for the most part these splendid kinghoods expire in ruin, and only the true kinghoods live, which are of royal labourers governing loyal labourers; who, both leading rough lives, establish the true dynasties. (18.454)

[50] Bradley, *Ruskin*, p. 313.
[51] In fact it was silver that Solomon 'made to be in Jerusalem as stones' (I Kings 10.27), as Ruskin knew (4.156–7).

The 'Author of *Modern Painters*' wrote as an Evangelical of the 'luxury and idolatry of the reign of Solomon' (34.483), referring to the king's love of many 'strange women' and his sacrifices to their gods (1 Kings 11.1–8). Now Ruskin's Puritanism expresses itself in relation to the use of wealth.

In characteristically homiletic manner, Ruskin draws his lecture to a close by first asking his audience to choose between 'change of growth, or change of death' (18.455); then invoking the teaching of Christ – 'our great Master' – on doing the best for others, and of Plato, in 'the last words of the chief wisdom of the heathen', speaking of 'this idol of riches';[52] and finally sending his audience out into the world with good news, in the conditional mode that was to become a feature of such endings:

if you can fix some conception of a true human state of life to be striven for – life, good for all men, as for yourselves; if you can determine some honest and simple order of existence; following those trodden ways of wisdom, which are pleasantness, [Proverbs 3.17] and seeking her quiet and withdrawn paths, which are peace;* – then, and so sanctifying wealth into "commonwealth", all your art, your literature, your daily labours, your domestic affection, and citizen's duty, will join and increase into one magnificent harmony. You will know then how to build, well enough; you will build with stone well, but with flesh better; temples not made with hands, [Acts 7.48] but riveted of hearts; and that kind of marble, crimsonveined, is indeed eternal.
* I imagine the Hebrew chant merely intends passionate repetition, and not a distinction of this somewhat fanciful kind; yet we may profitably make it in reading the English.[53] (18.458)

In his testimony, or 'apology', before his martyrdom, St Stephen summarizes the story of God's covenant with Israel: our fathers 'had the tabernacle of witness in the wilderness'; but Solomon built God 'an house'; 'Howbeit the most High dwelleth not in temples made with hands' (Acts 7.44, 47, 48).[54] Like the preachers of his day, Ruskin used this

---

[52] Ruskin's own translation of a long passage from the *Critias* includes Plato's description of the early Athenians: 'in *all meekness of wisdom, they dealt with each other*' and they '*bore lightly the burden* of gold and of possessions' (18.456–7).

[53] The Authorized Version reads: 'Her ways are ways of pleasantness, and all her paths are peace.'

[54] In Samuel Lee's frontispiece (plate 9), Acts 7.47 is inscribed on the curtain held by Solomon and Zadok. In the main text, however, Lee writes: 'King *Solomon* declined in his latter dayes, to shew that he was but a man, although a most glorious and admirable Type of Jesus Christ: Yet herein our blessed Lord as he did farre out-bid all other prefigurations of himself; so also this personal Type of King': *Orbis Miraculum; or, The Temple of Solomon* (London: Streater, 1659), p. 188. On St Stephen's apology, see p. 61 above.

typological sequence in his teaching on ethics.[55] His imaginative use, however, of the visual similarity between marble and the human heart which the cathedral-builders, sculptors and poets of the Middle Ages exploited is particularly bold, and leaves his audience with the sense that eternal life is attainable not in heaven but on earth, and not in death but in life.[56]

Building with stone is also the subject of the second chapter ('The Pyramid Builders') in *Ethics of the Dust* (1865), a dialogue based on Ruskin's talks with the girls of Winnington Hall, Cheshire (18.lxxi-lxxii). *Ethics* is one of Ruskin's scientific books, and concerns crystallography. It also addresses issues related to political economy,[57] and was greeted enthusiastically by Carlyle, if not by the reading public. Carlyle was particularly impressed by Ruskin's use of dreams as a poetic medium for teaching. The Lecturer tells 'Isabel' that in one of his dreams he and 'Egypt' had difficulty moving through the passages inside one of the pyramids, and was glad that she was not with them:

But after all this, I suppose the imagination of the heavy granite blocks and the underground ways had troubled me, and dreams are often shaped in a strange opposition to the impressions that have caused them; and from all that we had been reading in Bunsen about stones that couldn't be lifted with levers, I began to dream about stones that lifted themselves with wings. (18.225)

As well as studying Greek coins and vases and Egyptian antiquities in the British Museum, when he was living at Denmark Hill, caring for his mother, from the beginning of 1864 to the spring of 1866 (18.xxxiii), Ruskin had studied books on ancient Egypt by J. Gardner Wilkinson and Chevalier Bunsen among others, which shed new light on Old Testament chronology before the building of Solomon's temple.[58] In a

---

[55] See, for example, Archdeacon Julius Hare, in 'The Worth of Knowledge, or the Judgement of the Queen of Sheba: A Sermon Preacht in the Cathedral Church of Chichester, on Thursday, June 9th, 1841, in Behalf of the Chichester Central Schools': 'the great purpose for which Solomon was endowed with all his wisdom, was, that he might build the temple of God in the beauty of holiness: and we should tell our children that they too have the same glorious work to accomplish, – that they too have a temple of God to build, even in their own hearts and souls . . . and that, poor and lowly as it may seem, if it be but clean and simple, the Holy Ghost will dwell in it, and it will endure for ever': Hare, *Sermons*, p. 317.

[56] See, for example, Dante, *Purgatorio*, IX, 94–106.

[57] The first lecture was 'meant for a metaphorical description of the pleasures and dangers in the kingdom of Mammon, or of worldly wealth', but Ruskin later came to regard it as 'both obscure and dull' (18.206).

[58] 'the study of Scripture had long convinced me, that there is in the Old Testament no connected chronology prior to Solomon': Christian von Bunsen, *Egypt's Place in Universal History: An Historical Investigation in Five Books*, trans. Charles H. Cottrell, 2 vols. (London: Longmans, 1848), I, viii. In his second volume Bunsen writes on the Great Pyramid's 'vast blocks of fine Turah limestone'

letter to Henry Acland in the autumn of 1864 he expressed the hope that Edward Burne-Jones would 'do some Egyptian things', and then revealed how far he had travelled away from organized religion:

I can tell you in few words what I am mainly about. You know when I was last with you, on the last walk together, you said, pointing from above Hincksey to St. Mary's Spire – "So the men who built that were all wrong!" to which the proper answer – if it had come definitely into my head at the time – would have been, "If those who built the Parthenon were, probably also, and *a fortiori*, these, but neither *All* wrong, only one at least as much as the other." But you may suppose, from what we talked of then, that I was not likely to stay quiet in the mess I was in. So I am trying to understand what religions hitherto have been worth understanding, in some *impartial* manner – however little of each – and as I have strength and time, am endeavouring to make out how far Greeks and Egyptians knew God; or how far anybody ever may hope to know Him. (18.xxxiv)

The letter also indicates the range of his reading in this investigation which, in contrast to Mr Casaubon's fruitless search for 'the key to all mythologies' in George Eliot's *Middlemarch* (1871–2), is both theological and spiritual in purpose:

If you know – and I think you know – much of Bunsen, you may guess how pleasant it is to me to have to wade and work through his masses of misarranged material; and if you know the state of Egyptian science in general – and contemplate a little the fact that the only two works of value on Rome and Greece are by a polished infidel, Gibbon, and a vulgar materialist, Grote – you may wonder that I have not had fever of the very scarletest, long ago. However, one thing I *know*, that nothing can ever be done unquietly. So I do what I can – of course *my* hold on all these races is through their art, and so I am cast perforce into figure work . . . (18.xxxiv)

Ruskin is often most dismissive when he is actually appropriating useful material for his own purposes, as is the case here with Bunsen.

To return to the text, Sibyl then insists that the Lecturer tells them 'all about' his dream about stones with wings, to which he replies that a vast form, like a pillar of sand, changed into the shape of a beautiful woman:

L. . . . She was robed to the feet with a white robe; and above that, to her knees, by the cloud which I had seen across the sun; but all the golden ripples of it had become plumes, so that it had changed into two bright wings like those of a vulture, which wrapped round her to her knees. She had a weaver's shuttle hanging over her shoulder, by the thread of it, and in her left hand, arrows, tipped with fire.

(II, 162). His appreciation of the 'casing', 'fastened together with such nicety, that the blade of a penknife cannot be inserted between the joints of the enormous layers of stone' (II, 163), is similar to Ruskin's comments on Lucca's masonry in *Præterita* (35.350).

ISABEL (*clapping her hands*). Oh ! it was Neith, it was Neith! I know now.
L. Yes; it was Neith herself; and as the two great spirits came nearer to me, I saw they were the Brother and Sister – the pillared shadow was the Greater Pthah. And I heard them speak, and the sound of their words was like a distant singing. (18.226)

Drawing upon recent Egyptology,[59] Ruskin describes Neith, who declares herself to be 'the Lady of wisdom' in the dream (18.227), constructing a pyramid which is then reduced in size by the lower Pthah, and becomes the piece of crystal of rose Fluor which the Lecturer had shown the girls a few days previously (18.230–1):

EGYPT. But how you *do* puzzle us! Why do you say Neith does it? You don't mean that she is a real spirit, do you?
L. What *I* mean, is of little consequence. What the Egyptians meant, who called her "Neith," – or Homer, who called her "Athena," – or Solomon, who called her by a word which the Greeks render as "Sophia," you must judge for yourselves. But her testimony is always the same, and all nations have received it: "I was by Him as one brought up with Him, and I was daily His delight; rejoicing in the habitable parts of the earth, and my delights were with the sons of men." [Proverbs 8.31]
MARY. But is not that only a personification?
L. If it be, what will you gain by unpersonifying it, or what right have you to do so? Cannot you accept the image given you, in its life; and listen, like children, to the words which chiefly belong to you as children; 'I love them that love me, and those that seek me early shall find me'? [Proverbs 8.17] (18.231–2)

In returning to the Book of Proverbs, Ruskin harmonizes Egyptian, Jewish and Greek religion under the unifying testimony of wisdom, and adds a note on Neith as 'the Egyptian spirit of divine wisdom; and the Athena of the Greeks' (18.364).

It is through the symbolism of the weaver's shuttle, however, that the figures of wisdom in the Book of Proverbs, Neith and Athena are most strongly linked by Ruskin,[60] and here again he could have drawn upon

---

[59] See, for example, images of women weaving and of 'Ptah', and reference to 'Neith, the Egyptian Minerva', in Sir J. Gardner Wilkinson, *The Manners and Customs of the Ancient Egyptians*, new edn, ed. Samuel Birch, 3 vols. (London: Murray, 1878), I, 317; III, 21, 39 (1st edn, 1837–41). The Lecturer and the girls read Wilkinson on 'the lower Pthah' in *Ethics* (18.240–1). Compare 'The name of Athene would appear to be formed by transposition from the Egyptian Neith': Gladstone, *Homer*, II, 134. Also 'This is Neith, Athena': Bunsen, *Egypt's Place*, I, 386.

[60] In his Dublin lecture of 1868 entitled 'The Mystery of Life and its Arts', published in the revised and enlarged edition of *Sesame and Lilies*, Ruskin wrote on 'Weaving; the art of queens, honoured of all noble Heathen women, in the person of their virgin goddess [Athena] – honoured of all Hebrew women, by the word of their wisest king – "She layeth her hands to the spindle, and her hands hold the distaff; she stretcheth out her hand to the poor . . . "' [Proverbs 31] (18.176). In 1876 he was to write in a note on Botticelli's *Zipporah* in the Sistine Chapel, of which he himself

modern scholarship which suggested that weaving probably signified creating to the Egyptians.[61] In December 1864, in his lecture 'Of Queens' Gardens' (published the following year in *Sesame and Lilies*), he had spoken of how 'that great Egyptian people, wisest then of nations, gave to their Spirit of Wisdom the form of a Woman; and into her hand, for a symbol, the weaver's shuttle; and how the name and the form of that spirit, adopted, believed, and obeyed by the Greeks, became that Athena of the olive-helm, and cloudy shield, to faith in whom you owe, down to this date, whatever you hold most precious in art, in literature, or in types of national virtue' (18.118). Interestingly, Ruskin's younger friend James Smetham, himself an artist and a devout Methodist, testified to the help he found in imagining wisdom as a beautiful female figure of the kind Ruskin describes.[62] Thus men like Ruskin and Smetham could substitute feminine wisdom for the Catholics' Madonna or the political economist's 'Goddess of Getting-on'.[63]

By the later 1860s, Ruskin regarded the Bible as one among several important, divinely inspired but humanly produced wisdom texts,[64] as he made clear in his letters to the Sunderland cork-cutter Thomas Dixon, later published as *Time and Tide, by Weare and Tyne* (1867):

The fourth, and last possible, theory is that the mass of religious Scripture contains merely the best efforts which we hitherto know to have been made by any of the races of men towards the discovery of some relations with the spiritual world; that they are only trustworthy as expressions of the enthusiastic visions or beliefs of earnest men oppressed by the world's darkness, and have no more authoritative claim on our faith than the religious speculations and histories of the Egyptians, Greeks, Persians, and Indians; but are, in common with all these, to be reverently studied, as containing a portion, divinely appointed,

made one of his most careful copies: 'Botticelli, trained in the great Etruscan Classic School, retains in his ideal of the future wife of Moses every essential character of the Etrurian Pallas, regarding her as the Heavenly Wisdom given by inspiration to the Lawgiver for his helpmate; yet changing the attributes of the goddess into such as become a shepherd maiden' (23.478–9). He also comments upon the reed in which Zipporah carries her wool and spindle.

[61] See, for example, John Kenrick, *Ancient Egypt under the Pharaohs*, 2 vols. (London: Fellowes, 1850), I, 388–9.

[62] See *The Letters of James Smetham, with an Introductory Memoir*, ed. Sarah Smetham and William Davies (London and New York: Macmillan, 1891), p. 95.

[63] Compare 'When in the Holy Scriptures we find wisdom personified in the feminine, we regard this only as a mode of speech, though as one evidently tending to account for the sex of Minerva. But the Jewish traditions went far beyond this. The two natures of our Lord would appear from the Sohar to have been distinguished under the figure of mother and daughter. The Shechina, or "glory of God", is of the feminine gender: and the relation of His divinity to His humanity is set forth under the figure of a marriage': Gladstone, *Homer*, II, 51–2. See also Birch, 'Ruskin's "Womanly Mind"'.

[64] Compare 'The personality of Athena and the personality of biblical wisdom are now of comparable weight and value in Ruskin's eyes': Birch, *Ruskin's Myths*, p. 90.

of the best wisdom which human intellect, earnestly seeking for help from God, has hitherto been able to gather between birth and death. (17.349)

Remote as this is from his former Evangelical position, his literalism survived the change. The failure of the Revd Capel Molyneux to accept a literal reading of the parable of the Prodigal Son had contributed to Ruskin's rejection of Evangelicalism in the 1850s.[65] Now, in Letter xxv of *Time and Tide*, 'Hyssop', he asks Dixon whether he has ever observed that 'all Christ's main teachings, by direct order, by earnest parable, and by His own permanent emotion, regard the use and misuse of *money*?' (17.458), and, having cited other examples, he turns to the same parable, clearly with the Revd Molyneux in mind:

the first thing I want you to notice in the parable of the Prodigal Son (and the last thing which people usually *do* notice in it), is – that it is about a Prodigal! He begins by asking for his share of his father's goods; he gets it, carries it off, and wastes it . . .

Now, I do not doubt but that I shall set many a reader's teeth on edge by what he will think my carnal and material rendering of this "beautiful" parable. But I am just as ready to spiritualise it as he is, provided I am sure first that we understand it. If we want to understand the parable of the sower, we must first think of it as of literal husbandry; if we want to understand the parable of the prodigal, we must first understand it as of literal prodigality. And the story has also for us a precious lesson in this literal sense of it, namely this, which I have been urging upon you throughout these letters, that all redemption must begin in subjection, and in the recovery of the sense of Fatherhood and authority, as all ruin and desolation begin in the loss of that sense. The lost son began by claiming his rights. He is found when he resigns them. He is lost by flying from his father, when his father's authority was only paternal. He is found by returning to his father, and desiring that his authority may be absolute, as over a hired stranger. (17.459–61)

Again, for Ruskin as for Thomas Scott, 'practical observations' follow naturally from 'explanatory notes' in his biblical commentary.

In order to clinch the point, however, he returns, as so often, to the temple and its associated typology:

Nor while the desire of gain is within your heart, can any true knowledge of the Kingdom of God come there. No one shall enter its stronghold, – no one receive its blessing, except, "he that hath clean hands and a pure heart;" [Psalms 24.4] clean hands that have done no cruel deed, – pure heart, that knows no base desire. And, therefore, in the highest spiritual sense that can be given to words, be assured, not respecting the literal temple of stone and gold, but of the living temple of your body and soul, that no redemption, nor teaching, nor hal-

[65] See p. 126 above.

lowing, will be anywise possible for it, until these two verses have been, for it also, fulfilled: –

"And He went into the temple, and began to cast out them that sold therein, and them that bought. And He taught daily in the temple." [Luke 19.45, 47] (17.464)

As Christ's parables complete Solomon's Proverbs, so his cleansing of and teaching in the temple fulfil Solomon's pious aim in the building of the temple: a greater than Solomon is here (Matthew 12.42). Solomon's 'maxims', however, provide Ruskin with both the main ethical source for his own writing on political economy and a model for his own modern version of wisdom literature.

While Solomon the author of Proverbs and Christ the teacher of parables presided over Ruskin's economic writings and the foundation of the Guild of St George in the years between his self-styled 'un-conversion' in 1858 and his recovery of something approaching orthodox Christian belief in 1874, Athena and the Holy Spirit presided over his study of myth. It is to Ruskin's use of myth in response to his contemporaries' 'scientific' analysis of both the Bible and nature that we now turn.

CHAPTER 8

Science, myth and a creative wisdom

And this forming power has been by all nations partly confused with the breath or air through which it acts, and partly understood as a creative wisdom, proceeding from the Supreme Deity; but entering into and inspiring all intelligences that work in harmony with Him.

'Athena Keramitis', *The Queen of the Air* (19.378)

I

Mr Gradgrind's demand for 'facts' at the beginning of Dickens's *Hard Times* (1854) has come to epitomize not only Utilitarian educational methods but also everything that Carlyle demonized as 'mechanical' in nineteenth-century politics and economics, science and technology.[1] Yet 'facts' had always been a positive term in both revealed and natural theology, where they were regarded as 'evidences' of Christianity, either in the Bible or in nature. Hence the value that the 'Author of *Modern Painters*' placed upon facts gleaned from his own early scientific work and his daily Bible reading; hence, too, his veneration for Turner as the supreme observer of facts and messenger of divinely inspired truth in nature. By the 1860s, as new questions posed by science and historical biblical criticism converged,[2] Ruskin, no longer an Evangelical, found Bishop Colenso on the Pentateuch reassuring, being similar to his own private findings; whereas Darwin, although hugely impressive as a naturalist, failed in his view to relate the facts to larger truths, and the life of animals and plants to the work of 'a creative wisdom, proceeding from the Supreme Deity'. Following the completion of *Modern Painters* in 1860

---

[1] Raymond Williams's classic study on *Culture and Society 1780–1950* (1958) was particularly influential in this respect. *Hard Times* was dedicated to Carlyle and was regarded by Ruskin as being in several respects Dickens's greatest novel (17.31n.).

[2] See John Hedley Brooke, *Science and Religion: Some Historical Perspectives*, Cambridge History of Science, ed. George Basalla (Cambridge University Press, 1991), p. 271.

and the death of his father four years later, the 'Victorian Solomon' who offered a powerful if idiosyncratic critique of the new social sciences and natural sciences placed less emphasis in his creation theology upon God the Father and more upon God the Holy Spirit – for Ruskin the New Testament antitype of divine wisdom not only in the Old Testament, but also in Greek and Egyptian religion.

Revealed theology in the late eighteenth and early nineteenth centuries explored the relationship between the truth of the gospel and the facts of the gospels – facts concerning the life, death and resurrection of Jesus Christ. Thomas Scott wrote on Matthew 3.16–17 (the Baptism of Jesus) in his famous commentary: 'Here, as in every part of the gospel, *facts* are simply related, without any studied remarks to awaken our attention: but what *facts* are they!'[3] William Paley concluded in his frequently reprinted *Evidences of Christianity* (1794) that the 'truth of Christianity depends upon its leading facts, and upon them alone'.[4] Victorian biblical scholars were to investigate the origins of these 'leading facts', and to highlight the discrepancies between the four gospels. In the face of new 'evidences' emerging from the Higher Criticism and historical research, attempts to harmonize the gospels became increasingly futile, as Ruskin saw, and the need to return to the primary sources with an open mind became increasingly urgent.

Meanwhile scientific challenges to the traditional arguments from design on which natural theology had been based led Victorian commentators from different Christian traditions to attempt to harmonize scientific and scriptural 'facts'. In the opening pages of his last book, *Natural Theology* (1802), Paley had developed the famous analogy of finding a watch in a field and realizing that it must have had a maker who had a purpose in mind when he made it. By 1880 the Christian Evidence Committee of the Society for Promoting Christian Knowledge thought it necessary to commission an edition 'revised to harmonize with modern science', with 'such alterations in the illustrative part of the text as are required by the progress of science since the

---

[3] *The Holy Bible*, with explanatory notes, practical observations, and copious marginal references by Thomas Scott, 9th edn, 6 vols. (London: Seeley, 1825), v.

[4] William Paley, *A View of the Evidences of Christianity, in Three Parts*, 12th edn, 2 vols. (London: Faulder, 1807), II, 376. The Ruskins' friend the Revd George Croly further argued that 'the leading facts of Christian history have been the leading facts of the two former dispensations, Judæism and the Patriarchal religion': *Divine Providence; or, The Three Cycles of Revelation . . . being a new Evidence of the Divine Origin of Christianity* (London: Duncan, 1834), p. xi. Ruskin himself described the Resurrection as the 'cardinal fact of Christianity' (23.368).

author's time' and with the natural history revised.[5] Science and religion were now frequently discussed together: in referring to Darwin's *The Origin of Species* (1859), clerical contributors to *Essays and Reviews* (1860) set the agenda for religious debate in Britain for a decade; *The Descent of Man* (1871) appeared in the middle of the period in which Ruskin investigated most closely the relationship between science and myth.

In the 1830s Ruskin's scientific studies had been carried out in the spirit of the Bridgewater Treatises, and under the tutelage of the Revd Dr Buckland of Christ Church, who introduced him to Darwin when he was a guest in college.[6] (In a more uncanny anticipation of Victorian cultural crisis, Ruskin recorded in 1835 that he had found 'a fragment or two of cornelian on Dover beach' (*D*, 3).) By the late 1860s and early 1870s he was acknowledging the progress of *science* while questioning the value of *progress*. In opposing Darwinism he emphasized the traditional view, based upon Genesis, of humankind as the highest form of creation, while also acknowledging, and indeed celebrating the God-given limits of the human observer – for him a further sign of divine wisdom. When the Revd George Henslow, a Lecturer in Botany in London, examined the theory of evolution as illustrative of the 'Wisdom and Beneficence of the Almighty' in 1873, he argued that

to bring forward instances of advantages or even blessings to one being, even if we select Man, as proofs of the wisdom and beneficence of God, is, and must be, a partial and one-sided view of Creation: and this, if I understand them aright, is an unmistakeably weak point in the arguments of the writers of the *Bridgewater Treatises*, and of Natural Theologians in general.[7]

Although Ruskin always guarded against taking a narrowly anthropocentric view of the creation, and constantly encouraged his audiences and readers to study the glories of the natural world, his own writings of this period continued to emphasize humankind's unique ability to receive and value those glories through observation and reflection, and still argued that this gift is indeed illustrative of the wisdom and beneficence of the Almighty.

Darwin begins *The Origin of Species* with these words:

[5] *Paley's Natural Theology*, revised to harmonize with modern science by F. le Gros Clark (London: SPCK, 1880), p. v.

[6] *The Ruskin Family Letters: The Correspondence of John James Ruskin, his Wife, and their Son, John, 1801–1843*, ed. Van Akin Burd, 2 vols. (Ithaca and London: Cornell University Press, 1973), p. 463.

[7] Henslow, *The Theory of Evolution of Living Things and the Application of the Principles of Evolution to Religion, considered as Illustrative of the "Wisdom and Beneficence of the Almighty"* (London: Macmillan, 1873), p. 161.

When on board H. M. S. 'Beagle,' as naturalist, I was much struck with certain facts in the distribution of the organic beings inhabiting South America, and in the geological relations of the present to the past inhabitants of that continent. These facts . . . seemed to throw some light on the origin of species . . . [8]

The crucial issue, however, was the method that he adopted in arranging the facts when developing his theory. A modern commentator has observed of Darwin:

The order which he seeks in the data . . . must be manifest in the facts themselves but not manifested in such a way as to display the operations of any transcendental power. In order to establish this notion of nature's plan, he purports, first, simply to entertain "objectively" all of the "facts" of natural history provided by field naturalists – in much the same way that the historian entertains the data provided by the archives. But his entertainment of the record is no simple reception of the facts; it is an entertainment of the facts with a view toward the discrediting of all previous taxonomic systems in which they had previously been encoded. [9]

Three years after the publication of *The Origin of Species*, Bishop Colenso balanced scriptural authority with topical relevance in his choice of epigraphs for *The Pentateuch and Book of Joshua Critically Examined:*

'We can do nothing against the Truth, but for the Truth.' – *St. Paul*, 2 Cor.xiii.8.

'Not to exceed, and not to fall short of, facts, – not to add, and not to take away, – to state the truth, the whole truth, and nothing but the truth, – are the grand, the vital, maxims of Inductive Science, of English Law, and, let us add, of Christian Faith.' – *Quarterly Review* on 'Essays & Reviews,' Oct. 1861, p. 369.[10]

His aim was to show that the books of the Pentateuch contain such 'remarkable contradictions' that they cannot be regarded as 'true narratives of actual, historical, matters of fact'.[11] What most upset Colenso, however, was the immorality of characters of whom the Old Testament itself approved and the dishonesty of modern traditionalists who presented what he called 'fiction' as truth.[12] Ruskin informed Sir John Murray Naesmyth that he was greatly relieved when the first part of Colenso's book appeared, as he himself had been working on the Bible

---

[8] Charles Darwin, *The Origin of Species by means of Natural Selection*, popular impression (London: Murray, 1902), p. 1.

[9] Hayden White, 'The Fictions of Factual Representations', in *The Literature of Fact: Selected Papers from the English Institute*, ed. Angus Fletcher (New York: Columbia University Press, 1976), pp. 21–44 (pp. 37–8).

[10] John William Colenso, *The Pentateuch and Book of Joshua Critically Examined*, 7 parts (London: Longman, 1862–79), I, [iii].   [11] Ibid., I, 17.

[12] See Peter Hinchliff, *John William Colenso, Bishop of Natal* (London: Nelson, 1964), pp. 87, 91.

in the 'same direction alone' for four years but had been 'quite unable
to tell any one' what he was about (36.424).[13] He saw that there would
be 'fair war directly', and told Naesmyth that he was happy to 'stand
with the bishop' (36.425), whose daughter, Frances Colenso, became one
of his Winnington 'pets' and later a founding Member of the Guild of
St George. Bishop Colenso was to be present at one of Ruskin's Oxford
lectures in 1874,[14] and the following year Ruskin took the Bishop of
Oxford to task for preventing Colenso from preaching at Carfax, asking
whether Dr Mackarness himself believed 'every statement in the Bible'
(28.244–5).

　　Colenso's book is less significant as a contribution to biblical scholarship than as a focus for controversy, for on the basis of it and his commentary on Romans he was deposed from his bishopric in Natal in 1863.
In terms of the present discussion its significance lies in the convergence
of science and biblical criticism in the argument. Colenso stated in the
Preface that he 'knew for certain, on geological grounds, a fact' – that 'a
Universal Deluge . . . could not possibly have taken place in the way
described in the Book of Genesis'.[15] He regarded modern biblical criticism as being 'scientific', arguing that the 'results of scientific criticism,
applied to the examination of the letter of the Scriptures will also soon
be acknowledged as *facts*, which must be laid as the basis of all sound
religious teaching'.[16] Like other commentators, he invoked Galileo as an
example of a scientist whose findings had been rejected by the religious
authorities of his day, but were now 'recognised as *facts*'.[17] Where
Colenso diverged from Darwin was in his theological understanding of
what he called 'the Light of Modern Science' as a 'gift of God', a position similar to that later held by Ruskin.[18]

　　We have seen that in 1851 Ruskin held a Christocentric view of Old
Testament prophecy, thinking of certain Psalms as 'the clearest speakings in the person of Christ'.[19] Ten years later his views were utterly
different, and his satirical treatment of Evangelical exegesis on the
Psalms was that of a 'scientific' biblical critic. His 'perverters', he wrote
to his father from Lausanne on 13 December 1861, were not people like
Carlyle and Emerson, as his mother believed, but Evangelicals –

---

[13] Ruskin had been working on questions of chronology in the Old Testament since 1851–2: see
　　Lancaster MS 8, Diaries, fol. 44.
[14] *The Correspondence of John Ruskin and Charles Eliot Norton*, ed. John Lewis Bradley and Ian Ousby
　　(Cambridge University Press, 1987), p. 348.　　　[15] Colenso, *The Pentateuch*, I, vii–viii.
[16] Ibid., 151–2.　　　[17] Ibid., 151.　　　[18] Ibid., IV, 82.　　　[19] See p. 112 above.

'Mr. Moore and Mr. Bayne and the Bishop of Oxford, and Lord Shaftesbury':[20]

I name Mr. Moore first, however, for the most damaging thing to Christianity I ever yet heard in my life was a sermon of his on a verse in Psalms, "Thou hast magnified *thy word* above all thy name", [Psalms 138.2] in which, applying the phrase "thy word" to the Bible, he sent, or endeavoured to send, his congregation away with the impression that David had a neatly bound volume in the Bible Society's best print always on his dressing-table, with a blue string at his favourite chapter of St. John, and I fully expected to hear, before the sermon finished, how Masters Amnon and Absalom were good boys and always learned their texts correctly, but little Solomon had to have a Watts' hymn to learn besides, for having made a mess of his pinafore in Bathsheba's back garden. (36.396–7)

Noting in passing Ruskin's implicit personal identification with the 'little Solomon', the more important feature of the passage is Ruskin's witty analysis of the Revd Daniel Moore's lack of historicism in wrenching an Old Testament text from its context and sanitizing it for his pious congregation.

By the end of the 1860s Ruskin was regretting the 'want of faith in God shown by most of our scientific men' and the 'want of courage and common-sense among the clergy', although he did admire Kingsley, Maurice, Stopford Brooke and Tyrwhitt (18.lii-liii). Modern science, he complained in *Fors Clavigera*, Letter 5 (May 1871),

gives lectures on Botany, of which the object is to show that there is no such thing as a flower; on Humanity, to show that there is no such thing as a Man; and on Theology, to show there is no such thing as a God. No such thing as a Man, but only a Mechanism; no such thing as a God, but only a series of forces. The two faiths are essentially one . . . (27.83)

The strength of feeling in this passage reflects the fact that Ruskin had been there, or thereabouts, himself. Five years earlier he wrote to his friend Mrs Cowper, later Lady Mount-Temple, from the Hotel of the Giesbach:

If I thought it my duty to fancy anything, I *could* fancy it – and get into passionate states of reverence or affection – or anything else – for my imaginary God. But I do *not* think it my duty – it seems to me I am bound to act only on what I know to be fact – and that is little enough. But I shall come out of this state – for good or evil – some day, – so it is of no use talking about it . . .[21]

20 The Revd Daniel Moore succeeded Melvill at Camden Church in 1844, and the Rt Revd Samuel Wilberforce was Bishop of Oxford from 1845 to 1869.

21 *The Letters of John Ruskin to Lord and Lady Mount-Temple*, ed. John Lewis Bradley ([Columbus]: Ohio State University Press, 1964), p. 72.

A pragmatic emphasis upon the facts remained central to Ruskin's religious and scientific thought. 'What we call theology, if true, is a science', he wrote in *The Eagle's Nest* (1872), and 'if false, is not true' (22.169–70). Following Dickens's death in 1870 Ruskin acknowledged the novelist's 'entire superiority to [him] in every mental quality but one – the desire of truth without exaggeration', adding: 'It is my stern desire to get at the pure fact and nothing less or more, which gives me whatever power I have.'[22] His quarrel, however, with what he called 'the scientific people' in the 1870s and 1880s was that they were materialists who interpreted facts 'mechanically', in the Carlylean sense, whereas his kind of science interpreted them 'dynamically' – with a sense of wonder, love and worship. All 'true science', he argued in *Fors*, Letter 5, is ' "savoir vivre" ': 'But all your modern science is the contrary of that. It is "savoir mourir" ' (27.85). For Ruskin, the spirit that gives life to natural forms could be apprehended and venerated through myth.

A myth, Ruskin stated in *The Queen of the Air* (1869), is 'a story with a meaning attached to it, other than it seems to have at first; and the fact that it has such a meaning is generally marked by some of its circumstances being extraordinary, or, in the common use of the word, unnatural' (19.296). Ruskin's choice of particular myths for close analysis and contemporary application was based upon his conviction that 'moral and physical law are ultimately the same, and together form a law of light in perpetual conflict with anarchic forces of destruction'.[23] In the autumn of 1875, when staying with the Cowper-Temples at Broadlands, Ruskin studied the Wisdom of Solomon, and reflected upon the destruction of a universe created by divine wisdom.[24] He interpreted the 'precious' thirteenth chapter as a 'condemnation of people who believe the world governed only by the forces of nature', and quoted Wisdom 7.7 in the subsequent December issue of *Fors* – Solomon's 'I willed, and sense was given to me. I prayed and the Spirit of Wisdom was given to me' (28.464).

Ruskin's thinking on wisdom and science took him back not only to

[22] Bradley and Ousby, *Correspondence of John Ruskin*, p. 197.
[23] Jeffrey L. Spear, ' "*These* are the furies of Phlegethon": Ruskin's set of mind and the creation of *Fors Clavigera*', in *The Ruskin Polygon: Essays on the Imagination of John Ruskin*, ed. John Dixon Hunt and Faith M. Holland (Manchester University Press, 1982), pp. 137–58 (p. 145); see also Robert Hewison, *John Ruskin: The Argument of the Eye* (London: Thames, Hudson; Princeton: Princeton University Press, 1976), p. 141.
[24] Lancaster MS 20, Diaries, fols. 50–1; compare *Christmas Story: John Ruskin's Venetian Letters of 1876–1877*, ed. Van Akin Burd, with an Introductory Essay on Ruskin and the Spiritualists, His Quest for the Unseen (Newark, NJ and London: University of Delaware Press and Associated University Press, 1990), pp. 119–20. See also p. 224 below.

first principles, but also to what he regarded as the origins of life and light themselves. Characteristically, he had much earlier examined the etymology of 'science' during a stay at Bonneville in 1862, like Solomon leaving 'among his ledgers some general maxims concerning wealth' when he interspersed 'Economy' notes among diary entries inscribed on notebook pages printed with vertical red lines, for use as a cash-book. One page of these notes, which comes between diary entries and some Latin constructions, has the marginal heading 'Wisdom', and explores the difference between 'sapi-entia' and 'sci-entia': 'Wisdom is not knowledge – but the Dom. or government by what we know of the moral nature.'[25] A modern commentator on the distinction in Alexander of Hales between *scientia*, 'a speculative knowledge of the true', and *sapientia*, 'a perfection of the will moving it toward the good', writes: 'The learned man knows the truth; the wise man loves and does the good.'[26] Whereas the 'Author of *Modern Painters*' sought only the truth, the 'Victorian Solomon' who set himself a new agenda after 1860 also strove to love and do the good. In *The Queen of the Air* (the subject of section II), he developed his thinking on 'life' through an analysis of Athena, the Greek goddess of wisdom, whom he found to be akin to the Holy Spirit. Freed from the contraints of narrower Christian doctrinal issues, Ruskin answered Darwin by focusing upon the 'creative wisdom' of the Spirit.[27] The further development of these ideas in the 1870s – in *The Eagle's Nest*, *Deucalion* (1875–83) and *Proserpina* (1875–86) – is discussed in section III.

II

Some of the weapons that Ruskin had used in his attacks upon the political economists, such as defamiliarization, the juxtaposition of the venerable with the modish, and a typological progression from the temple of the money-changers in Jerusalem to the temple not made with hands were brought out again when he confronted that other increasingly

---

[25] Lancaster MS 12, Diaries, fol. 203. His reference to 'Dominatus' leads him to query whether 'Duomo' comes from 'Domum, or Home knowledge', and whether 'Kingdom' means 'Kinghome' and 'Wisdom' means 'Knowledge-Home'. The note ends: 'Janus – connected'.

[26] Eugene F. Rice Jr., *The Renaissance Idea of Wisdom* (Cambridge, Mass.: Harvard University Press, 1958), p. 2.

[27] A. S. Mories wrote, 'It seems as though, *pari passu* with the crumbling of the dogmatic edifice, there rose within him more potent, more insistent, and more wide-reaching than ever, the conviction of external spiritual Power, at the fulness of Whose nature man can but grope, but of Whose wisdom and beneficence he cannot rest in doubt': 'The Sophia of Ruskin: What was it? and How was it Reached?', *Saint George: The Journal of the Ruskin Society of Birmingham*, 4, 14 (January 1901), 150–71 (p. 157).

influential manifestation of Victorian modernity, science. The battle was now waged across a broader front, as in Ruskin's view the materialism of Darwin and Tyndall represented a threat to belief in a teleological universe, created and sustained by God. As in the case of political economy, however, Ruskin chose to take the battle to the enemy.

Whereas the lectures on *The Political Economy of Art* had been delivered in Manchester, and that on 'Traffic' in Bradford, Ruskin gave the first lecture in *The Queen of the Air* on 6 March 1869 at University College London, an institution founded in 1826 by Utilitarians (including Jeremy Bentham and James Mill) and Dissenters for the education of middle-class boys.[28] As the college foundation included neither a chapel nor a theology faculty, its first students had been known as the 'godless young men of Gower Street'. In 1869 Grote, the historian of Greece and one of the founding members of Council, was still the President. Ruskin considered him to be a 'vulgar materialist' (18.xxxiv). Thus the playful irony of his opening remarks on Greek mythology was pointed, and although the preface which he added to the printed volume two months later addressed a wider readership, his comments on Professor Tyndall's lecture 'On Chemical Rays, and the Light of the Sky', delivered on 15 January that year at the Royal Institution, had an equally sharp contemporary focus (19.268). Tyndall had demonstrated that a blue could be produced in a flask which 'no sky-blue could exceed in its richness and purity'.[29] On 1 May, Ruskin the amateur scientific observer recorded in his preface that on Lake Geneva, 'half a mile from the shore', he could scarcely see the blade of his oar under the polluted (or 'defiled') water,[30] and concluded with an appeal that was again similar in style to those he had made to the political economists and northern manufacturers in earlier lectures:

Ah, masters of modern science, give me back my Athena out of your vials, and seal, if it may be, once more, Asmodeus therein. You have divided the elements, and united them; enslaved them upon the earth, and discerned them in the stars. Teach us, now, but this of them, which is all that man need know, – that the Air is given to him for his life; and the Rain to his thirst, and for his baptism; and the Fire for warmth; and the Sun for sight; and the Earth for his meat – and his Rest. (19.294)

---

[28] See H. Hale Bellot, *University College London: 1826–1926* (University of London Press, 1929), pp. 20, 25, 56, 305.

[29] John Tyndall, 'On Chemical Rays, and the Light of the Sky', 15 January 1869, *Notices of Proceedings of the Royal Institution*, 5 (1869), 429–50; rpt. in *Fragments of Science: A Series of Detached Essays, Lectures, and Reviews*, 4th edn (London: Longmans, 1872), pp. 241–83 (p. 268).

[30] In fact the opacity of the water in the lake is partly dependent upon the weather.

In Ruskin's treatment of the opposition between Athena and the demon Asmodeus[31] the words 'vials' and 'seal' hint at the Last Judgment (Revelation 5.1, 15.7); and he makes Tyndall's science seem Faustian when contrasted with the humility of his own analysis of the elements, where he quietly rehearses the most ancient and fundamental relationships between humankind and the creation, the most significant here being 'that the Air is given to him for his *life*'.

In his first lecture, 'Athena Chalinitis' (the Restrainer) – Athena in the Heavens – Ruskin asks permission of his audience to approach the subject of Greek mythology in an unusual way, and craves their forgiveness for not always calling the creeds of the past 'superstition' and those of the present 'religion' (19.295). Having then defined a myth, he works towards the myth that is to be his 'subject of closer inquiry' – the story of Athena and of the 'deities subordinate to her'. As in *Sesame and Lilies* and *Ethics of the Dust*,[32] he equates the Greek goddess of wisdom with deities in other traditions:

This great goddess, the Neith of the Egyptians, the Athena or Athenaia of the Greeks, and, with broken power, half usurped by Mars, the Minerva of the Latins, is, physically, the queen of the air; having supreme power both over its blessings of calm, and wrath of storm; and spiritually, she is the queen of the breath of man, first of the bodily breathing which is life to his blood, and strength to his arm in battle; and then of the mental breathing, or inspiration, which is his moral health and habitual wisdom; wisdom of conduct and of the heart, as opposed to the wisdom of imagination and the brain; moral, as distinct from intellectual; inspired, as distinct from illuminated. (19.305–6)

This passage contains the seeds of several ideas that are to germinate later in this lecture and to flower in the next. Ruskin's distinction between the physical and the spiritual anticipates his important reference to St Paul on the resurrection of the body – teaching which itself refers to the account of the creation of Adam in Genesis, when God breathes life into the clay, or dust. Creation is to be Ruskin's subject in the second lecture, where he emphasizes that the Greek *pneuma* means 'wind', 'breath' and 'life', as well as 'spirit'. Finally, the references to

---

[31] In Le Sage's *Diable Boiteux* (1707), the demon Asmodeus is released from a bottle and lifts the roofs off houses to show his benefactor what is going on inside; in the end he announces that his captor will soon be calling him back to his imprisonment. The name is taken from the evil spirit in Tobit 3.8, referred to by Milton in *Paradise Lost*, IV, 168. Max Müller had recently cited Bréal's work on the influence of Persian ideas on the writers of the Old Testament, which showed that a name like Asmodeus could only have been borrowed from Persia: 'Genesis and the Zend-Avesta', in *Chips from a German Workshop*, 3 vols. (London: Longmans, Green, 1867–70), I, 143–59 (pp. 147–8).

[32] See pp. 173–7 above.

Mars, Athena and the wisdom of conduct and the heart anticipate
Ruskin's other crucial reference to St Paul, this time preaching in Athens,
on 'Mars' hill' (Acts 17.22), on the Unknown God who does not live in
temples made by hands.

Unlike the 'scientific people' who focused exclusively upon physical
phenomena that could be recorded and analysed, Ruskin celebrated the
way in which the Athena myth treats the physical as spiritual, and vice
versa. Take, for example, this vivid passage on the city of Edinburgh and
its topography:

> It is curious that the British city which has somewhat saucily styled itself the
> Modern Athens, is indeed more under her especial tutelage and favour in this
> respect than perhaps any other town in the island. Athena is first simply what
> in the Modern Athens you so practically find her, the breeze of the mountain
> and the sea; and wherever she comes, there is purification, and health, and
> power. The sea-beach round this isle of ours is the frieze of our Parthenon,
> every wave that breaks on it thunders with Athena's voice; nay, whenever you
> throw your window wide open in the morning, you let in Athena, as wisdom
> and fresh air at the same instant; and whenever you draw a pure, long, full
> breath of right heaven, you take Athena into your heart, through your blood;
> and with the blood, into the thoughts of your brain. (19.329)

Shrugging off the dualism of the Judæo-Christian distinction between
body and soul, and of the metaphoric and the literal, Ruskin can affirm
within the frame of Greek myth that Athena *is* the breeze, and that she
is also wisdom and fresh air, at the same instant.

These ideas are developed towards the end of the lecture, when
Ruskin focuses upon the two kinds of spiritual power associated with
Athena, and then, with an ironic apology, refers to parallels between her
and the Holy Spirit:

> first, she is the Spirit of Life in material organism; not strength in the blood only,
> but formative energy in the clay; and, secondly, she is inspired and impulsive
> wisdom in human conduct and human art, giving the instinct of infallible deci-
> sion, and of faultless invention . . .
>
> You would, perhaps, hardly bear with me if I endeavoured farther to show
> you – what is nevertheless perfectly true – the analogy between the spiritual
> power of Athena in her gentle ministry, yet irresistible anger, with the ministry
> of another Spirit whom we also, believing in as the universal power of life, are
> forbidden, at our worst peril, to quench or to grieve. [Matthew 12.31, I
> Thessalonians 5.19, Ephesians 4.30] (19.346)

Athena in her 'gentle ministry' is analogous to the Holy Spirit
bequeathed by Christ as the 'Comforter' (John 15.26), and her 'irresis-

tible anger' to 'our worst peril' – the judgment awaiting the unforgiveable sin against the Holy Spirit.[33] The Greek gods may be 'vain to us',
but for Ruskin there was a nobility in the very absence of hope in a future
life in ancient Greek religion. Whereas 'the modern Christian', he
reminds his audience at the end of the lecture, can hope for treasure in
heaven if the order 'sell that thou hast' is obeyed (Matthew 19.21), the
'poor Greeks of the great ages expected no reward from heaven but
honour, and no reward from earth but rest' – a position that Ruskin
himself shared with George Eliot in the 1860s.

Ruskin glossed the title of his second lecture (which was never delivered), 'Athena Keramitis (Athena in the Earth)', as 'Athena, fit for being
made into pottery' (19.351). Before, however, discussing the power of
Athena in giving life, he insists upon the importance of clarifying what
we mean 'when we translate the Greek word for "breathing" into the
Latin-English word "spirit"'. Seven years earlier he had asked his friend
the Revd Tyrwhitt how many clergymen who lectured on 'spiritualities'
he supposed knew the meaning of either 'Holy' or 'Ghost'.[34] Now, in
challenging his readers directly, Ruskin offers exegesis of his own which
avoids the danger of elevating the concept of 'spirit' until it loses its true
meaning, and which emphasizes the relationship between the 'Spirit' as
a creative force and 'life':

This very word, which is so solemn in your mouths, is one of the most doubtful. In Latin it means little more than breathing, and may mean merely accent;
in French it is not breath, but wit, and our neighbours are therefore obliged,
even in their most solemn expressions, to say "wit" when we say "ghost". In
Greek, "pneuma", the word we translate "ghost", means either wind or breath,
and the relative word "psyche" has, perhaps, a more subtle power; yet St. Paul's
words "pneumatic body" [*soma pneumatikon*, spiritual body AV, 1 Corinthians
15.44] and "psychic body" [*soma psychikon*, natural body AV] involve a difference
in his mind which no words will explain. But in Greek and in English, and in
Saxon and in Hebrew, and in every articulate tongue of humanity, the "spirit
of man" truly means his passion and virtue, and is stately according to the
height of his conception, and stable according to the measure of his endurance.

Endurance, or patience, that is the central sign of spirit; a constancy against
the cold and agony of death; and as, physically, it is by the burning power of
the air that the heat of the flesh is sustained, so this Athena, spiritually, is the
queen of all glowing virtue, the unconsuming fire and inner lamp of life.
(19.352)

[33] See, for examples, Scott, *The Holy Bible*, v, Matthew 12.31.
[34] 1 October 1862, Mornex: HRC, Letters of John Ruskin, letters to Revd Richard St John
Tyrwhitt.

Typically, Ruskin is highly selective in this etymological survey of a word which has twenty-two senses in the *OED*, and privileges those meanings which best suit his argument.[35] Thomas Scott read Paul's 'natural' body as the 'animal' body which returns to the dust, whereas the 'spiritual body' is 'capable of the spiritual employment, worship, and happiness of heaven'.[36] However, as Dean Alford's reference in his Victorian commentary to 'animal *life*' and 'spiritual *life*' may indicate,[37] the problem with *psyche* is that it tends to be restricted to the physical sphere instead of 'embracing within this sphere the gift of God that transcends death', whereas the problem with *pneuma* is that it tends to be seen as the 'inner spiritual life that we are given'.[38] While Ruskin acknowledged the problem of translation, he also exploited it: the fact that 'no words will explain' the difference in Paul's mind allowed him to fill the space thus opened up with his own gloss on the 'spirit of man', which he related to Athena, the 'unconsuming fire and inner lamp of life'.

He uses a similar technique in his subsequent comments upon Ezekiel's vision of the valley of dry bones, where indeterminacy in a famous but difficult prophetic text allows him to make an affirmation of his own within the horizon of the present, based upon a Johannine text traditionally associated with the passage from Ezekiel:[39]

What precise meaning we ought to attach to expressions such as that of the prophecy to the four winds that the dry bones might be breathed upon, and might live, [Ezekiel 37.9–10] or why the presence of the vital power should be dependent on the chemical action of the air, and its awful passing away materially signified by the rendering up of that breath or ghost, we cannot at present know, and need not at any time dispute. What we assuredly know is that the states of life and death are different, and the first more desirable than the other, and by effort attainable, whether we understand being "born of the spirit" [John 3.5] to signify having the breath of heaven in our flesh, or its power in our hearts. (19.354)

---

[35] The *OED* definitions which come closest to Ruskin's are: I.I.a. 'The animating or vital principle in man (and animals); that which gives *life* to the physical organism, in contrast to its purely material elements; the breath of *life*' [our emphasis]; II.6.a. 'the active essence or essential power of the Deity, conceived as a creative, animating, or inspiring influence'; III.13.a. 'Mettle; vigour of mind; ardour; courage; disposition or readiness to assert oneself or to hold one's own.' The philological school, headed by Max Müller, dominated the study of mythology in 1869: see 19.lxvii, and Dinah Birch, *Ruskin's Myths* (Oxford: Clarendon, 1988), pp. 107–8.

[36] Scott, *The Holy Bible*, vi, 1 Corinthians 15.44.

[37] Henry Alford, *The Greek Testament: With a Critically Revised Text*, 7th edn, 4 vols. (London: Rivingtons, 1877), ii, 617 (our emphasis).

[38] *Theological Dictionary of the New Testament*, ed. Gerhard Kittel and Gerhard Friedrich, trans. and abridged Geoffrey W. Bromiley (Grand Rapids: Eerdmans; Exeter: Paternoster, 1985), p. 1351.

[39] See, for example, Scott, *The Holy Bible*, iv, Ezekiel 37.9; *The Holy Bible*, with Notes and Introductions by Chr[istopher] Wordsworth, 6 vols. (London: Rivingtons, 1864–70), v, Pt ii, 244.

Like Paul's teaching in 1 Corinthians 15.44–5, the early chapters of John's gospel draw upon the account in Genesis of God forming man of the 'dust of the ground' and 'breathing into his nostrils the breath of life': 'and man became a living soul' (Genesis 2.7). Increasingly in this 'lecture', Ruskin is to replace commentary on Athena Keramatis with commentary on creation in relation to wisdom in the Bible, as he moves towards a description of the decline of Greek religion and the birth of Christianity.

All this work on the word 'spirit' provides Ruskin with material with which first to tease the scientists, and then to answer them. 'What is heat? or what, motion?' he muses: 'What is this "primo mobile," this transitional power, in which all things live, and move, and have their being?' (19.356; Acts 17.28). St Paul's preaching in Athens on the 'Unknown God' who 'made the world' (Acts 17.24) is going to be brought fully into play later. First, however, Ruskin teases the scientists by pointing out that this power is 'by definition something different from matter', but that we can 'show no scientific proof of its not being personal, and coinciding with the ordinary conception of a supporting spirit in all things'. There are problems, he suggests, with applying the word 'spirit' or 'breathing' to this power, 'while it is only enforcing chemical affinities'. He can, however, affirm that this 'force, now properly called life, or breathing, or spirit, is continually creating its own shells of definite shape out of the wreck around it'; and, taking the 'Spirit in the plant' as his example, he argues that it is strongest at the moment of its flowering: 'The flower is the end or proper object of the seed, not the seed of the flower' (19.356–7). In both its teleology and in its anthropocentrism, Ruskin's botany conflicts directly with Darwin (to whose work he makes a graceful reference in a footnote).[40] For the presence of the strongest life is in his view 'asserted by characters in which the human sight takes pleasure, and which seem prepared with distinct reference to us', and these characters he presents as 'facts':

And we are led to feel this still more strongly, because all the distinctions of species, both in plants and animals, appear to have similar connection with human character. Whatever the origin of species may be, or however those species, once formed, may be influenced by external accident, the groups into which birth or accident reduce them have distinct relation to the spirit of man.

[40] See 19.358. When Ruskin exchanged visits with Darwin in 1868 he found him 'delightful' (19.xlv). Huxley, Darwin's disciple and popularizer, was among the other eminent contributors to the Tuesday evening series of public lectures held in University College between 1867 and 1871: see Bellot, *University College*, p. 354.

It is perfectly possible, and ultimately conceivable, that the crocodile and the lamb may have descended from the same ancestral atom of protoplasm . . . but the practically important fact for us is the existence of a power which creates that calcareous earth itself . . . and that . . . crocodiles and lambs, may be, the one repellent to the spirit of man, the other attractive to it, in quite inevitable way, representing to him states of moral evil and good, and becoming myths to him of destruction or redemption, and, in the most literal sense, "Words" of God.

And the force of these facts cannot be escaped from by the thought that there are species innumerable, passing into each other by regular gradations, out of which we choose what we most love or dread, and say they were indeed prepared for us. (19.358–9)

Thus in the midst of his comparative study on myth, nature remains God's culture for Ruskin – a system of signs designed to be read by humankind. The bird, 'little more than a draft of the air brought into form by plumes . . . *is* the air, conscious of itself, conquering itself, ruling itself', and becomes, 'through twenty centuries, the symbol of Divine help, descending, as the Fire, to speak, but as the Dove, to bless' (19.360–2; Acts 2.3; Genesis 1.2); while the serpent, 'the clothed power of the dust', becomes the symbol of the 'grasp and sting of death' (19.353; 1 Corinthians 15.56; Genesis 3.14). It is at this crucial point in his argument that Ruskin explains his theory of myth by relating the power of the Holy Spirit to the 'creative wisdom' of God. What, he asks, makes plants grow in a particular way, searching for water or light?

There is no answer. But the sum of all is, that over the entire surface of the earth and its waters, as influenced by the power of the air under solar light, there is developed a series of changing forms, in clouds, plants, and animals, all of which have reference in their action, or nature, to the human intelligence that perceives them; and on which, in their aspects of horror and beauty, and their qualities of good and evil, there is engraved a series of myths, or words of the forming power, which, according to the true passion and energy of the human race, they have been enabled to read into religion. And this forming power has been by all nations partly confused with the breath or air through which it acts, and partly understood as a creative wisdom, proceeding from the Supreme Deity; but entering into and inspiring all intelligence that work in harmony with Him. (19.378)

The phrase 'creative wisdom' had been used by Buckland in his Bridgewater Treatise of 1837,[41] and although Ruskin's reference to

[41] On the megatherium: 'through all their deviations from the form and proportion of the limbs of other quadrupeds, affording fresh proofs of the infinitely varied, and inexhaustible contrivances of Creative Wisdom': William Buckland, *Geology and Mineralogy Considered with Reference to Natural Theology*, 2 vols. (London: Pickering, 1837), I, 164.

'many nations' maintains the comparative religious dimension of his analysis, his emphasis three decades after Christ Church still falls upon the Judæo-Christian tradition. In his discussion of the 'crocus-colour and the purple', for example, he invokes God's instructions to Moses on the 'sacred chord of colours' to be used in the tabernacle, 'from the day when the cloud descended on a Rock more mighty than Ida' (19.384), and in closing, Ruskin uses St Paul's preaching in Athens to indicate the eventual decline of Greek religion, marked by the Athena of Phidias being 'in very fact, not so much the deity, as the darling of the Athenian people' (19.384). Having first encouraged his readers to explore for themselves the connections between the myth of Athena and 'the now recognized facts of existent nature', he gathers these facts together 'in brief sum' by describing the 'deep of air that surrounds the earth' in one of the most beautiful passages in all Ruskin, which deserves to be quoted in full.[42] For in invoking the true spirit of Athena who inspired the Greeks before she became more a darling in a temple than a deity in the air, Ruskin breaks his self-denying ordinance and again writes the kind of lyric prose for which 'the Author of *Modern Painters*' was famous:

It gives its own strength to the sea; forms and fills every cell of its foam; sustains the precipices, and designs the valleys of its waves; gives the gleam to their moving under the night, and the white fire to their plains under sunrise; lifts their voices along the rocks, bears above them the spray of birds, pencils through them the dimpling of unfooted sands. It gathers out of them a portion in the hollow of its hand: dyes, with that, the hills into dark blue, and their glaciers with dying rose; inlays with that, for sapphire, the dome in which it has to set the cloud; shapes out of that the heavenly flocks: divides them, numbers, cherishes, bears them on its bosom, calls them to their journeys, waits by their rest; feeds from them the brooks that cease not, and strews with them the dews that cease. It spins and weaves their fleece into wild tapestry, rends it, and renews; and flits and flames, and whispers, among the golden threads, thrilling them with a plectrum of strange fire that traverses them to and fro, and is enclosed in them like life.

It enters into the surface of the earth, subdues it, and falls together with it into fruitful dust, from which can be moulded flesh; it joins itself, in dew, to the substance of adamant; and becomes the green leaf out of the dry ground; it enters into the separated shapes of the earth it has tempered, commands the ebb and flow of the current of their life, fills their limbs with its own lightness, measures their existence by its indwelling pulse, moulds upon their lips the words by which one soul can be known to another; is to them the hearing of the ear, and the beating of the heart; and, passing away, leaves them to the peace that hears and moves no more. (19.386)

---

[42] Among his own books, *The Queen of the Air* was one of his favourites (19.lxxi).

Ruskin then contrasts this living spirit with the numerous temples and sculptures which surrounded St Paul when he preached on Mars' hill in the city to which Athena leant her name, with the Acropolis above him and the temple of the Eumenides below:

This was the Athena of the greatest people of the days of old. And opposite to the temple of this Spirit of the breath, and life-blood, of man and of beast, stood, on the Mount of Justice, and near the chasm which was haunted by the goddess-Avengers, an altar to a God unknown; – proclaimed at last to them, as one who, indeed, gave to all men, life, and breath, and all things; and rain from heaven, filling their hearts with food and gladness; – a God who had made of one blood all nations of men who dwell on the face of all the earth, and had determined the times of their fate, and the bounds of their habitation. (19.386–7; Acts 17.19, 23, 25, 26; 14.17)[43]

Paul told the men of Athens that God who 'made the world, and all things therein, seeing that he is Lord of heaven and earth, dwelleth not in temples made with hands' (Acts 17.24).[44] Ruskin preaches to the modern world which is even less ready than the Greeks for the Lord who will suddenly come to his temple:

We ourselves, fretted here in our narrow days, know less, perhaps, in very deed, than they, what manner of spirit we are of, or what manner of spirit we ignorantly worship. [Acts 17.23] Have we, indeed, desired the Desire of all nations? [Haggai 2.7] and will the Master whom we meant to seek, and the Messenger in whom we thought we delighted, confirm, when He comes to His temple, [Malachi 3.1] – or not find in its midst, – the tables heavy with gold for bread, and the seats that are bought with the price of the dove? [Matthew 21.12] Or is our own land also to be left by its angered Spirit; – left among those, where sunshine vainly sweet, and passionate folly of storm, waste themselves in the silent places of knowledge that has passed away, and of tongues that have ceased?

This only we may discern assuredly: this, every true light of science, every mercifully-granted power, every wisely-restricted thought, teach us more clearly day by day, that in the heavens above, and the earth beneath, there is one continual and omnipotent presence of help, and of peace, [Psalms 46.1, 10] for all men who know that they Live, and remember that they Die.

The spiritual impoverishment of the age, Ruskin argues, is caused, not by God's absenting himself, but by humankind – including not only materialist scientists who bottle the sky but also clergy who wrangle over

---

[43] Compare the chapter entitled 'St. Paul at Athens' in Frederick William Farrar, *The Life and Work of St. Paul* (1879).

[44] Generally assumed to be a reference to the sermon of the first martyr, St Stephen (Acts 7.48): see p. 173 above.

the 'letter' – losing its ability to receive the free gifts of the Spirit, and to understand the nature of the Spirit which 'giveth life' (2 Corinthians 3.6).[45] Following up the first lecture he delivered in a classical temple of secular learning in Gower Street, Ruskin, a latter-day St Paul, now preaches on the Unknown God who 'dwelleth not in temples made with hands', but in the heavens above and the earth beneath, and in the temple of the human heart.

III

Less than twelve months later, on 16 February 1870, Ruskin used the same text from Acts in his second lecture as Slade Professor of Fine Art at Oxford, where the summary of his argument sounded one of the solemn keynotes of his professorship:

That we *may* have splendour of art again, and with that, we may truly praise and honour our Maker, and with that set forth the beauty and holiness of all that He has made: but only after we have striven with our whole hearts first to sanctify the temple of the body and spirit of every child that has no roof to cover its head from the cold, and no walls to guard its soul from corruption, in this our English land. (20.71)

Privately, Ruskin described 'The Relation of Art to Religion' as a 'sermon-lecture'[46] and the inaugural series as his 'life's most earnest work'.[47] The religious content of the Oxford lectures as a whole cannot be explained away as Ruskin's attempt to help his young listeners to keep the faith which he had lost, or as a complex response to Rose La Touche's neurotic anxieties about his religious position. For over the four years between his Inaugural and his formative visit to Assisi in 1874, the spirit of reverence that he invoked at the end of his second lecture (19.72), and that had never left him, again found a specifically Christian

---

[45] Four years later Ruskin was to write in *The Nature and Authority of Miracle*: 'for the last thousand years, miraculous powers seem to have been withdrawn from, or at least indemonstrably possessed, by a Church which, having been again and again warned by its Master that Riches were deadly to Religion, and Love essential to it, has nevertheless made wealth the reward of Theological learning, and controversy its occupation' (34.124–5).

[46] Letter to Joan Agnew, Saturday [22 January 1870?], Lancaster L 35, Letters of John Ruskin to Joan Severn. Ruskin thought that this 'sermon-lecture' would be 'really the best of all'.

[47] The private dedication that he intended to put in Rose La Touche's copy of these Oxford lectures read: 'To the woman, / Who bade me trust in God, and her, / And taught me / The cruelty of Religion / And the vanity of Trust, / This – my life's most earnest work / Which – without her rough teaching, / Would have been done in ignorance of these things / Is justly dedicate': *Letters of Ruskin to Mount-Temple*, p. 273.

focus in his life and work.[48] As his desire for revenge faded along with Rose herself, religion again became a 'source of hope, so changing the whole bent of Ruskin's views on Christian art'.[49]

Wisdom, however, remained the central divine attribute for Ruskin in this period, and in *The Eagle's Nest* (1872) – ten Oxford lectures 'On the Relation of Natural Science to Art' – his discussion of *sophia* (or *sapientia*) in classical sources still led him back to the wisdom of Solomon in Proverbs and the workings of the Holy Spirit in the New Testament. In the first lecture, for example, entitled 'The Function in Art of the Faculty called by the Greeks σοφια', he rendered Aristotle's five faculties in the *Ethics*, in 'simplest English, – art, science, sense, wisdom, and wit' (22.129), and explained *sophia* by means of a homely analogy from rowing. At the end of the short lecture, however, Aristotle gave way to Solomon on wisdom as 'life', when Ruskin returned to what he privately called his mother's chapter of Proverbs, declaring that

over these three kingdoms of imagination, art, and science, there reigns a virtue or faculty, which from all time, and by all great people, has been recognized as the appointed ruler and guide of every method of labour, or passion of soul; and the most glorious recompense of the toil, and crown of the ambition of man. "She is more precious than rubies, and all the things thou canst desire are not to be compared unto her. Lay fast hold upon her; let her not go; keep her, for she is thy life." [Proverbs 3.15, 4.13] (22.135–6)[50]

Announcing that his next lecture will show how, contrary to Aristotle's view, wisdom regards nothing but the sources of happiness, he ends with a quotation from another chapter of Proverbs that he learnt by heart with his mother:

[48] Shortly before Joan Severn was delivered of a child, Ruskin wrote to her saying that this was 'one of those periods of life which are intended to make us look with closer trust to Him in whom we live, and move, and have our Being' (28 January 1873): Lancaster L 38, Letters of John Ruskin to Joan Severn. As an Honorary Fellow of Corpus Christi College he was a 'constant attender at early chapel' from 1877 to 1879, and kept an open Bible and a pair of silver candlesticks on his desk: 'My seat in chapel was next to his. When I read of his "attitude as to religion, constantly shifting," I think of these eight o'clock services, and of talks which sometimes followed, and how easy it is for mental attitudes to change, and to leave unchanged the spirit of reverence within.' 'Peter' [Barrow], 'Recollections of Ruskin at Oxford', *St George*, 6, 22 (April 1903), 103–15 (p. 111); 20.xxxvii–xxxviii. Plate 19 shows Ruskin, in the right foreground, listening to Pusey preaching in St Mary's, Oxford. Appropriately he sits *facing* most of the Oxford Anglican establishment, including the Heads of Houses and his fellow Professors, who are listed in the Appendix below.

[49] Jeanne Clegg, 'Modes of Opposition: Tuscany in the Oxford Lectures', in Jeanne Clegg and Paul Tucker, *Ruskin and Tuscany*, Ruskin Gallery, Collection of the Guild of St. George (Sheffield and London: Ruskin Gallery / Humphries, 1993), pp. 139–52 (p. 139).

[50] Ruskin wrote in his diary on 31 March 1874, at Meurice's hotel, Paris: 'Think of my mothers [sic] chapter in Proverbs "It shall be Life to thy soul, and grace to thy neck" [Proverbs 3.22]': Lancaster MS 16, Diaries, fol. 178; compare *D*, 782.

Plate 19. Fred Hill, *Pusey Preaching in St. Mary's*, from *Caricatures published by Thomas Shrimpton & Son*, 1877

we are permitted to conceive her [Wisdom] as the cause even of gladness to God – "I was daily His delight, rejoicing always before Him". – and that we are commanded to *know* her as queen of the populous world, "rejoicing in the habitable parts of the Earth, and whose delights are with the sons of Men". [Proverbs 8.30–1] (22.136)

It is significant that Ruskin explains the Blakean source of his book title, *The Eagle's Nest*, in the second lecture, 'The Function in Science of the Faculty called by the Greeks σοφια', as it was in his view the scientists of his day who most needed to learn the lessons of *sophia* which Blake, like Bacon and Pope before him, had taught.[51] Wisdom, his audience had heard in the previous lecture, is our 'life', and now Ruskin developed the theme that was central to *The Queen of the Air*:

Sophia is the faculty which recognizes in all things their bearing upon life, in the entire sum of life that we know, bestial and human; but, which, understanding the appointed objects of that life, concentrates its interest and its power on Humanity, as opposed on the one side to the Animalism which it must rule, and distinguished on the other side from the Divinity which rules it, and which it cannot imagine.

It is as little the part of a wise man to reflect much on the nature of beings above him, as of beings beneath him. It is immodest to suppose that he can conceive the one, and degrading to suppose that he should be busied with the other. To recognize his everlasting inferiority, and his everlasting greatness; to know himself, and his place; to be content to submit to God without understanding Him; and to rule the lower creation with sympathy and kindness, yet neither sharing the passion of the wild beast, nor imitating the science of the Insect; – this you will find is to be modest towards God, gentle to His creatures, and wise for himself.

I think you will now be able to fasten in your minds, first the idea of unselfishness, and secondly, that of modesty, as component elements of sophia; and having obtained thus much, we will at once make use of our gain, by rendering more clear one or two points respecting its action on art, that we may then see more surely its obscurer function in science. (22.144)

When Ruskin finally took aim at his main target, the contrast between the virtues he had been expounding and the 'demand of a sensual economy for originality in science' (22.246) was stark. In his paper addressed to the Metaphysical Society on *The Nature and Authority of Miracle* (1873) he was to write of 'the tendency to parade our discoveries of the laws of Nature, as if nobody had ever heard of a law of Nature before' (34.115). Ruskin was perfectly well aware that many scientists

---

[51] Ruskin asked the undergraduates to memorize two lines which are reminiscent of Proverbs: 'Doth the Eagle know what is in the pit, / Or wilt thou go ask the Mole?' (22.138).

were modest, God-fearing individuals, who shared his sense of humankind's place in a divinely ordered world.[52] In order, however, for his rhetoric of opposition to Darwinist materialism to work on his audience, he set such complexities and ambiguities aside, frequently referring in later lectures in *The Eagle's Nest* to the wisdom that is Solomon's subject in Proverbs.[53]

As in *The Queen of the Air*, the logic of Ruskin's argument based upon wisdom leads to his reminding his audience in *The Eagle's Nest* of the unforgiveable sin against the Holy Spirit, the 'Lord and Giver of Life':

> Disbelieve that; and your own being is degraded into the state of dust driven by the wind; and the elements of dissolution have entered your very heart and soul.
>
> All Nature, with one voice – with one glory, – is set to teach you reverence for the life communicated to you from the Father of Spirits. The song of birds, and their plumage; the scent of flowers, their colour, their very existence, are in direct connection with the mystery of that communicated life: and all the strength, and all the arts of men, are measured by, and founded upon, their reverence for the passion, and their guardianship of the purity, of Love. (22.237)

This passage helps to explain Ruskin's plan two years later, in 1874, to work at Assisi and write a monograph of it.[54] For, as we shall see in the next chapter, St Francis epitomized the kind of reverence for wisdom and the Holy Spirit that Ruskin sought to inculcate in his undergraduates, and drew him to Assisi just as much as Giotto's frescoes.

Like Ruskin's work on Greek and Egyptian deities in the 1860s, his deepening interest in the Christian saints in the 1870s reflects both the idealist and the realist in him. As he became increasingly convinced that the world is an arena in which a cosmic battle between good and evil is being fought out, he developed a rhetoric of opposition and conflict in which ideal figures from myth and legend could be shown to epitomize traditional values and beliefs which modernity seemed to threaten or ignore. In this respect the figure of Solomon was actually problematic, in that his whoring after strange gods in later life represented for the Church a classic fall into worldliness and sin. Indeed, for the Venerable Julius Charles Hare, Archdeacon of Lewes, the 'type of the history of Science' was not Frankenstein, as one might expect in early Victorian culture, but Solomon, who fell into idolatry and, like scientists, forgot the

---

[52] For a lucid account of the relationship between Victorian religion and science, see *Science and Religion in the Nineteenth Century*, ed. Tess Cosslett (Cambridge University Press, 1984), pp. 1–24.

[53] See 22.167, 169–70, 175–82 *passim*, 197, 251, 252, 260, 263.

[54] Bradley and Ousby, *Correspondence of John Ruskin*, p. 301.

creator 'while gazing on the creature'.[55] Although Ruskin refers to
Solomon's idolatry in other contexts,[56] it suits his anti-materialist agenda
to represent the author of Proverbs as the founding father of natural
science, informed by divine wisdom. In 1853 he had referred to Solomon
as 'the first great naturalist the world ever saw', who, 'at the central point
of Jewish prosperity', showed us that 'heavenly wisdom is manifested as
much in the knowledge of the hyssop that springeth out of the wall
[1 Kings 4.33] as in political and philosophical speculation' (12.106).[57]
Twenty-two years later, at the end of Letter 59 of *Fors Clavigera*, Ruskin
cited the same text when explaining the purpose of St George's
Museum, which he had established at Walkley, Sheffield. Museums, he
argues, like schools, are to enable people to 'devote a certain portion of
secluded laborious and reverent life to the attainment of the Divine
Wisdom, which the Greeks supposed to be the gift of Apollo, or of the
Sun; and which the Christian knows to be the gift of Christ' (28.450). He
adds that under 'St. George's rule, when none but useful work is done',
some British workmen may devote the equivalent of two or three days a
week to 'the contemplation and study of the works of God, and the
learning that complete code of natural history which, beginning with
the life and death of the Hyssop on the wall, rises to the knowledge of
the life and death of the recorded generations of mankind, and of the
visible starry Dynasties of Heaven' (28.450–1).

As Ruskin could have read in his copy of Smith's *Dictionary of the Bible*,
the identification of the hyssop had probably given rise to more
differences of opinion than any other plant in scripture – something that

---

[55] 'as Science is ever mainly employed about the things of the creation, in contemplating the wonderful proofs of wisdom which the universe displays by the symmetry and harmonious adjust-
ment and working together of all its parts, there has been a constant aptness in Science to forget
the Creator, while gazing on the creature. Indeed the story of the life of Solomon may be
regarded as in some measure a type of the history of Science, in most nations in which it has
flourisht. As every good gift comes from above, Science, also like every other higher intellectual
exercise, has always sprung at the first from some sort of perception of a Divine Unity pervad-
ing the multitudinous objects presented to our minds by our senses, from some perception of a
Divine Cause, of a Divine Ruler, of a Divine Order, from a faith in something invisible. But here
again the visible things in course of time have mostly eclipst the invisible; and the same dismal
and appalling degradation, which we deplore in the old age of Solomon, has been exemplified
again and again in the history of Philosophy and Science. They have fallen from the worship of
the Creator to the idolatry of the creature'. . .: Julius Charles Hare, 'The Worth of Knowledge,
or the Judgement of the Queen of Sheba: A Sermon Preacht in the Cathedral Church of
Chichester, on Thursday, June 9th, 1841, in Behalf of the Chichester Central Schools', *Sermons*
(London: Parker, 1846), pp. 299–319 (pp. 311–12).   [56] See p. 173 above.
[57] See p. 39 above, and note 24. In referring to the Book of Job and the Psalms, John Drury makes
the broader point that 'these Old Testament scribe-naturalists were Ruskin's tutors': 'Ruskin's
Way: *Tout a Fait Comme un Oiseau*', in the forthcoming *festschrift* for John Burrow.

might have been avoided had Solomon's botanical works survived.[58] Ruskin's own emphasis, however, falls upon the hyssop's being regarded as the lowliest of plants, at the opposite end of the scale from 'the cedar tree that is in Lebanon' in I Kings. He thus suggests an alternative route – humble, devout and anthropocentric – to a 'complete code of natural history' from that proposed by the Darwinians. It corresponds to the gifts of wisdom, and leads from the study of botany, through history (a different kind of 'descent of man'), to astronomy.[59]

Ruskin's contribution to botany, entitled *Proserpina: Studies of Wayside Flowers*,[60] was published in parts between 1875 and 1886 – years in which he was dogged by mental illness – and was never completed. Here he directly criticized *The Descent of Man* for its failure to address the true nature of colour and our love of colour, arguing that 'even Mr. Darwin' must be often ranked among those whose 'one-sided intensity' leads them into 'materialisms, in their unclean stupidity' (25.263). One strand of Ruskin's argument is based upon what he calls 'the divinity of the mind of man' (25.268). Another directly challenges scientific 'facts' in a chapter entitled 'Genealogy', where he argues that the naming of plants should be based, not upon their forms, but upon 'historic fact':

For instance, – and to begin, – it is an historical fact that for many centuries the English nation believed that the Founder of its religion, spiritually, by the mouth of the King who spake of all herbs, had likened Himself to two flowers, – the Rose of Sharon, and Lily of the Valley [Song of Solomon 2.1]. The fact of this belief is one of the most important in the history of England, – that is to say, of the mind or heart of England: and it is connected solemnly with the heart of Italy also, by the closing cantos of the *Paradiso* [30–2] (25.347)

Ruskin's use of the past tense in his reference to Solomon as Christ's mouthpiece marks his own and his generation's fall into critical knowledge, and points to the fact that he valued traditional beliefs and associations more highly than recent scientific discoveries.[61]

---

[58] [William Aldis Wright], 'Hyssop', in *A Dictionary of the Bible, comprising its Antiquities, Biography, Geography, and Natural History*, ed. William Smith, 3 vols. (London: Murray, 1863), I, 845–6 (p. 845).

[59] 'In addition to the subjects on which Solomon wrote (Songs, Proverbs: Plants, Beasts, Fowls, Creeping Things, Fishes), Cosmology, Meteorology, Astronomy, Psychology, and even the elements of history (viii.8), are included among the gifts of Wisdom': [Brooke Foss Westcott], 'The Wisdom of Solomon', in Smith, *Dictionary of the Bible*, III, 1778–84 (p. 1782).

[60] The full title is *Proserpina: Studies of Wayside Flowers, while the Air was yet Pure among the Alps, and in the Scotland and England which my Father knew.*

[61] Compare *Fors* Letter 53, May 1875: 'whatever chemical or anatomical facts may appear, to our present scientific intelligences, inconsistent with the Life of God, the historical fact is that no happiness nor power has ever been attained by human creatures unless in that thirst for the presence of a Divine King' (28.328).

Ruskin's other main criticism of Darwinian science was that it lacked imagination, a faculty with which Solomon, he had argued in *Modern Painters* II, was richly endowed.[62] In his Introduction to *Deucalion: Collected Studies of the Lapse of Waves, and Life of Stones* (1875–83), Ruskin answered the 'pious modern reader' who might have asked why he did not focus upon Genesis:

Because I think it well that the young student should first learn the myths of the betrayal and the redemption, as the Spirit which moved on the face of the wide first waters, [Genesis 1.2] taught them to the heathen world. And because, in this power, Proserpine and Deucalion are at least as true as Eve or Noah; and all four incomparably truer than the Darwin Theory. And in general, the reader may take it for a first principle, both in science and literature, that the feeblest myth is better than the strongest theory: the one recording a natural impression on the imaginations of great men, and of unpretending multitudes; the other, an unnatural exertion of the wits of little men, and half-wits of impertinent multitudes. (26.98–9)

Later, when lamenting the increasing separation of the 'man of science' from the artist in the chapter entitled 'The Three Æras', he turns to Solomon's Proverbs to strengthen his case:

And it is at once the wisdom, the honour, and the peace, of the Masters both of painting and literature, that they rejoice in the strength, and rest in the knowledge, which are granted to active and disciplined life; and are more and more sure, every day, of the wisdom of the Maker in setting such measure to their being; and more and more satisfied, in their sight and their audit of Nature, that "the hearing ear, and the seeing eye, – the Lord hath made even both of them". (26.116; Proverbs 20.12)

Whereas the wisdom tradition which Ruskin sought to revive for the nineteenth century celebrated the harmony and coherence of creation, modern science seemed to be based upon separation and division. Indeed, Ruskin's excuse for resigning from the Slade Chair for the second time, in 1885, was his protest against vivisection, a highly controversial subject in Oxford at the time. The final paragraph of one of his most engaging lectures, entitled 'Yewdale and its Streamlets', delivered before the Members of the Literary and Scientific Institution, Kendal on 1 October 1877 and later reprinted in *Deucalion*, included words which Canon Rawnsley was to inscribe on his monument at Friar's Crag, Derwentwater, after his death:

[62] See p. 65 above. Ruskin would have endorsed George Macdonald's view that imagination 'is aroused by facts, is nourished by facts, seeks for higher and yet higher laws in those facts; but *refuses* to regard science as the sole interpreter of nature, or the laws of science as the only region of discovery': 'The Imagination: its Functions and its Culture', in Macdonald, *Orts* (London: Sampson Low, 1882), p. 2.

All true science begins in the love, not the dissection, of your fellow-creatures; and it ends in the love, not the analysis, of God. Your alphabet of science is in the nearest knowledge, as your alphabet of morals is in the nearest duty. "Behold, it is nigh thee, even at the doors". [Mark 13.29] The Spirit of God is around you in the air that you breathe, – His glory in the light that you see; and in the fruitfulness of the earth, and the joy of its creatures. He has written for you, day by day, His revelation, as He has granted you, day by day, your daily bread. [Matthew 6.11] (26.266)

For Ruskin the amateur scientist and opponent of the 'scientific people', God is a spirit (John 4.24). When establishing the Guild of St George in the 1870s (the subject of the next chapter) he reflected upon the command to worship Him 'in spirit and in truth' and upon the exemplary lives of the saints who obeyed that command.

CHAPTER 9

St George, St Francis and the rule of love and wisdom

> If *anything* is true of what all good and noble Christians have believed, it is true that we not only may, but should pray to the saints, as simply as we should ask them to do anything for us while they were alive. Do but Feel that they ARE alive and love us still, and that they have powers of influencing us by their love and wisdom, and what else *can* we do?
>
> Letter to Sara Anderson, Aylesbury, 17 August 1876 (24.xxiv)

I

During a brief stay in Aylesbury, on a visit to his printers, Ruskin was replying to a letter from his friend in which she had spoken of 'feeling the angels nearer' her (24.xxiv). It was strange, he commented, that her letter should have come to him and been read in the room in which he had received the news of Rose La Touche's death in May 1875.[1] His subsequent remarks about praying to the saints, quoted above, drew upon new and formative experiences during the intervening fifteen months, including a period at Broadlands, home of the Cowper-Temples, who had first introduced him to Spiritualism twelve years earlier. During this stay Ruskin had briefly been persuaded that Rose had been present during a séance – an event which was to shape his strange experiences in Venice at Christmas 1876.[2] Even before Rose's death, Ruskin had been ready to receive an increasingly wide variety of 'signs', as he wrote month by month to the 'Workmen and Labourers of Great Britain' on

---

[1] For an account of these and subsequent events, see *John Ruskin and Rose la Touche: Her Unpublished Diaries of 1861 and 1867*, ed. Van Akin Burd (Oxford: Clarendon; New York: Oxford University Press, 1979), pp. 131–3, and *Christmas Story: John Ruskin's Venetian Letters of 1876–1877*, ed. Van Akin Burd, with an Introductory Essay on Ruskin and the Spiritualists, His Quest for the Unseen (Newark, New Jersey and London: University of Delaware Press and Associated University Press, 1990).

[2] Ruskin wrote in his copy of *Fors*, alongside a comment on 'spiritual lies, and lasciviousness': 'Explain; spiritualism, music, painting, etc.' (27.674).

the workings of the three 'Forses' (Force, Fortitude and Fortune) in his own life, in *Fors Clavigera* (1871–8; sporadically 1880–4), where he adapted a schema derived from Horace and other classical sources (27.xix-xxiii) to overtly Christian ends, when it suited him. He had also been able to write privately to his cousin Joan Severn in January 1873, shortly before the birth of her first child, that this was 'one of those periods of life which are intended to make us look with closer trust to Him in whom we live, and move, and have our Being' (Acts 17.28).[3]

Ruskin's comments to Sara Anderson reveal how much further he had travelled in his spiritual journey away from Evangelicalism – the last links with which had been broken when his mother died in 1871 and Rose in 1875[4] – and beyond the 'religion of Humanity' (29.90) of the 1860s. Later in the letter he developed his theme:

> Do not permit yourself to be disturbed by the so often repeated foolish saying that we should never go to any one but God . . . It is the greater sanctity and power of the 'Cloud of Witnesses' [Hebrews 12.1] which makes simple people fancy they are idolatrous in addressing them instead of Christ. But they are all as the Angel who *talked* with John – but when he would have worshipped him, said, 'See thou do it not.' [Revelation 19.10][5]

The word 'foolish' is full of significance to the author of *Fors*. In earlier works this 'Victorian Solomon' had ridiculed aspects of modernity – the Manchester School of political economy, Darwinism, the Goddess of Getting-on, the ballot box and the electric wire – by measuring them against wisdom. In *Fors*, the monthly 'letters' which he used as the vehicle for formulating, developing and reporting upon St George's 'Society', later 'Company', and finally 'Guild', he took this analysis a stage further, presenting the modern world as the site of a battle between heavenly wisdom and hellish folly, and turning for inspiration and direction to the soldier saint George and the 'seraphical saint of love',[6] Francis, both of whom, he believed, influenced him 'by their love and wisdom'.

---

[3] Lancaster L 38, Letters from John Ruskin to Joan Severn, 28 January 1873. For uses of the text in the published works, see 4.133, 19.356, 20.270, 28.739, 33.498, 34.156; also see p. 234 below.

[4] Ruskin recorded a conversation with his mother five weeks before her death, in which her last words were 'remember that there are other worlds. God bless my child': Lancaster MS 91, Adams Bequest. When he visited Rose for the last time in February 1875 she lay in his arms and made him promise that he 'would never let her stand between [him] and God': Burd, ed., *Ruskin and Rose La Touche*, p. 131.

[5] Ruskin had written on the 'insolent Evangelical notion' that one should not pray to the saints in *Fors*, Letter 27 (March 1873), 27.493. In 1869, when his Christian faith was at a low ebb, he had described Jesus as 'the dearest saint of humanity': *The Correspondence of John Ruskin and Charles Eliot Norton*, ed. John Lewis Bradley and Ian Ousby (Cambridge University Press, 1987), p. 175.

[6] See p. 209 below.

Ruskin began to be aware of the help of the saints in his own spiritual life in the early 1870s, although at this stage he was rather casual
about it. Writing to his mother from Siena on 25 June 1870, for example,
he described how on the previous day – 'St. John's day' – he had seen a
painting of the Baptist, and was 'really beginning', for the first time in
his life, to be glad that his name was John, adding: 'Many thanks for
giving it me' (20.liii). Increasingly alienated from Victorian culture in the
1860s and 1870s, Ruskin regarded himself as 'one crying in the wilderness' (Luke 3.4). In 1873 he started to record saints' days in his diary, after
missing St George's day on 23 April; but he did not keep it up.[7] The following year he wrote to Norton on 11 April, 'Is it not *absurd* that in all my
St George plans, *I* never remembered Turner was born on St George's
day';[8] but he still had to record in his diary for 24 April, 'Y[esterday] S[t]
George's day; Amy [Yule] reminded me in time.'[9] He could also be
vague about hagiography, even when it came to his own adopted patron
saint, Antony of Padua (27.328) – a Franciscan who, like him, took up
residence in the sacristan's cell in Assisi (35.391–2). As with Ruskin's
exploration of Spiritualism, his deepened interest in the saints seems to
have been something of a phase.

Ruskin was more interested in the reverence which the saints inspired
in Catholics, both past and present, and which in his view outweighed
the credulity of the devout with respect to the more absurd legends of
hagiography. In a passage of *Fors*, Letter 41 (May 1874), written on the
way to Italy, he argued that

the worship of the Madonna has been one of [Catholicism's] noblest and most
vital graces, and has never been otherwise than productive of true holiness of
life and purity of character. I do not enter into any question as to the truth or
fallacy of the idea; I no more wish to defend the historical or theological position of the Madonna than that of St. Michael or St. Christopher; but I am
certain that to the habit of reverent belief in, and contemplation of, the character ascribed to the heavenly hierarchies, we must ascribe the highest results
yet achieved in human nature, and that it is neither Madonna-worship nor
saint-worship, but the evangelical self-worship and hell-worship . . . which have
in reality degraded the languid powers of Christianity to their present state of
shame and reproach . . . every brightest and loftiest achievement of the arts and
strength of manhood has been the fulfilment of the assured prophecy of the
poor Israelite maiden, "He that is mighty hath magnified me, and Holy is His
name." [Luke 1.49, Book of Common Prayer] What we are about to substitute

---

[7] See Lancaster MS 16, Diaries, fol. 74r, f., and *D*, 745f. Ruskin clearly used French sources for saints'
    days at this period.   [8] Bradley and Ousby, *Correspondence*, p. 314.
[9] Lancaster MS 16, Diaries, fol. 184; *D*, 785

for such magnifying in our modern wisdom, let the reader judge from two slight things that chanced to be noticed by me in my walk round Paris. (28.82)

('Our modern wisdom' is reflected in two advertisements: one, fastened to the back of an empty niche near the north-west door of Notre Dame, is for excursions, the other for a fur sale – an 'Apotheosis'.)[10]

During the 1874 tour of Italy, which extended from April to October and included periods of hard copying work in Rome, Assisi and Florence, Ruskin changed his views on religious art and deepened his understanding of and respect for the mendicant tradition of St Francis in particular, and for Catholicism in general; meanwhile he also developed his plans for St George's work. Dante, Ruskin's guide in his exploration of the spirituality of medieval Catholicism, explicitly links the great mendicant saints with wisdom in the *Paradiso*, where the poet's contribution to the debate concerning the salvation of Solomon is to place him in the fourth heaven – the sun – among twelve blessed saints, doctors and teachers, including some of the brightest lights of the monastic orders. In Canto x, St Thomas Aquinas introduces him thus, in Cary's translation, which Ruskin used:

> The fifth light,
> Goodliest of all, is by such love inspired,
> That all your world craves tidings of his doom:
> Within, there is a lofty light, endow'd
> With sapience so profound, if truth be truth,
> That with a ken of such wide amplitude
> No second hath arisen.[11]

The following canto is devoted to St Francis, the 'seraphical saint of love', and St Dominic, the 'cherubical saint of wisdom', but relates only the legend of the former at length, focusing upon the marriage between Francis and the Lady Poverty, widowed of her first husband, Christ[12] –

[10] Compare his comments in a letter dated 14 April 1874 on the value of a relic at Assisi being in the fact that St Louis had 'poured out his soul' before it: Lancaster L 39, Letters of John Ruskin to Joan Severn.

[11] Dante, *The Divine Comedy*, trans. Henry Francis Cary, ed. Edmund Gardner, Everyman's Library, 1308 (London: Dent; New York: Dutton, 1967), p. 338. On Ruskin's journeys in the late 1870s, Cary was 'always on the carriage seat', or in his pocket (26.224); see note 00 below, on Dante's later reference to St Francis.

[12] Dante, *Divine Comedy*, p. 341. 'For Dante, with his fixed idea of human cupidity as the root of current evil, Francis is the saint who revived that basic apostolic virtue lost to the Church since the time of Christ': Vincent Moleta, *From St. Francis to Giotto: The Influence of St. Francis on Early Italian Art and Literature* (Chicago: Franciscan Herald, 1983), p. 87. For a photogravure of Giotto's fresco see 28.164, and for a slightly clearer photograph see Harry Quilter, *Giotto* (London: Sampson Low, 1880), p. 105.

the subject among Giotto's frescoes at Assisi to which Ruskin paid closest attention in the summer of 1874.

Changes in earlier generations' responses to the saints provided Ruskin with a helpful index to that 'fall' which followed his idealized Middle Ages – one of his subjects in 'The Flamboyant Architecture of the Valley of the Somme', for example, delivered on 29 January 1869 at the Royal Institution, immediately before writing *The Queen of the Air*. In Flamboyant Gothic, he argued, 'the niche becomes as important as the statue':

> As people began to gain more civilized domestic habits, each man's house became of greater importance to him: each statue has a house of its own . . . people began to think solitude more sacred . . . So each holy statue has its own oratory, and every saint has his special tabernacle; and at last the saintship disappears in the seclusion; and all over England and France you have tabernacle work instead of sculpture, Shrines instead of Saints, and Canopies instead of Kings. (19.254)

In one of those apparently effortless transitions from architectural analysis to political commentary which make Ruskin one of the finest writers on the history of social space, he ends the lecture by challenging his audience to rediscover the true meaning of sainthood through the 'tabernacle work' of caring for the London poor: 'let the air and sun in among them . . . and bringing back the true Saints to their shrines, and building a tabernacle work that shall keep out the wind and the rain from shivering bodies, – carve a victorious St. George and a prostrate Flamboyant Dragon over every poor man's door' (19.267).

As well as continuing to criticize the clergy in general for failing to lead exemplary lives like the saints, and instead looking after their 'livings' and seeking preferment, Ruskin was soon berating the London clergy in particular for preaching against almsgiving to the 'lower poor' of the metropolis in the winter of 1870–1 (27.67). His diary entries and letters of the early 1870s reveal that church-going had not only become a rare event for him, but also sometimes a depressing one.[13] Later, in *Fors*, Letter 49 (January 1875), he reflects upon a visit to a 'ritualistic church' in the West End of London, commenting, punningly, that 'the particular kinds of folly . . . which lead youths to become clergymen, uncalled, are especially intractable' (28.238). Any man's becoming a clergyman, he concludes, implies that, at best, 'his sentiment has overpowered his intel-

---

[13] See, for example, Lancaster MS 16, Diaries, fols. 1870.48–9; L 36 and 37, Letters of John Ruskin to Joan Severn, 28 May 1871, 26 February 1872, Sunday [n.d.] 1872. For his views on the clergy later in the decade see *Letters to the Clergy on the Lord's Prayer and the Church* (1879–80; 34.191–230).

lect', and that he is gratified by being 'regarded as an oracle, without the trouble of becoming wise, or the grief of being so' (28.238–9).[14] In the battle between wisdom and folly, the saints and the clergy often seemed to be on opposite sides.

Fors Clavigera, described by Frederic Harrison as Ruskin's 'Apocalypse' (27.xxiii), often reads more like a modern version of wisdom literature, in the form of a lay sermon or pastoral epistle.[15] Preaching salvation by works, Ruskin set out to challenge some of the doctrine being taught in the pulpits of England, and each December his 'Christmas *Fors*' expounded an incarnational theology. If the clergy were unwilling to ride out and fight the dragons of folly, sensuality, materialism, usury and laissez-faire economics in the name of the saints and their 'love and wisdom', Ruskin was, and the Guild of St George (the subject of section IV) can be seen as an attempt to fill a gap left by the Established Church.[16] He also wished the Guild to be open to honest members of other faiths. In planning and financing the Guild, Ruskin was inspired by the eastern wisdom of Solomon and the Magi (discussed in section II) and by the love of St Francis (examined in section III). (St Ursula, whose influence over Ruskin intensified in the winter of 1876–7, in Venice, is treated in the next chapter.) That the project was Utopian is obvious, and it is all too easy to dwell upon the absurdity of some of Ruskin's quirkier schemes. His visionary idealism, however, like his practical tithing and (often impractical) social action, was grounded in the New Testament teaching on which he believed Catholic Christendom had been established, and to which the modern Church of England appeared to pay only lip-service.

II

Ruskin's vision of what was to become the Guild of St George perhaps seems less quixotic today than it did in May 1871: 'the buying and securing of land in England, which shall not be built upon, but cultivated by Englishmen, with their own hands, and such help of force as they can find in wind and wave' (27.95). *Fors*, Letter 5, which is nailed down to 'Denmark Hill, 1st May, 1871', begins with a quotation from the Song of

[14] Compare 28.364–5, 28.413–16.
[15] John Rosenberg compares *Fors* to the pastoral epistles, and considers Ruskin to be 'like a quixotic St Paul who stayed at all the best hotels': 'Ruskin's Benediction: A Reading of *Fors Clavigera*', in *New Approaches to Ruskin: Thirteen Essays*, ed. Robert Hewison (London: Routledge, 1981), pp. 125–41 (p. 127).
[16] For Ruskin's challenge to Bishop Fraser of Manchester on the subject of usury, see 34.401–25.

Solomon (2.11–13) – 'For lo, the winter is past, / The rain is over and gone . . .' (27.89) – and ends with a reference to the Magi, of whom the Queen of Sheba was an antitype:[17]

We will have some music and poetry . . . We will have some art . . . and feeble rays of science may dawn for us. Botany, though too dull to dispute the existence of flowers; and history, though too simple to question the nativity of men; – nay – even perhaps an uncalculating and uncovetous wisdom, as of rude Magi, presenting, at such nativity, gifts of gold and frankincense. (27.96–7)

(In his own copy, Ruskin noted: 'As opposed to modern University money wisdom.')

Ten days earlier Ruskin had received a sign when he set to work on this number of *Fors* – 'hoping it may be a Good Friday' to him, 'for such work as may be useful' – and opened his manuscript Greek Testament.[18] The first words that he read were τον προφητον (the prophet) in Matthew 24.15: 'When ye therefore shall see the abomination of desolation, spoken of by Daniel the prophet, stand in the holy place, (whoso readeth, let him understand)'. It is, he records in his diary, if he 'chose to take it so – absolutely the work I am about now, preaching against the βδελυγμα, εστος εν τοπω αγιω' (abomination, stand in the holy place). Ruskin associates himself with the prophetic role of Daniel in a tradition which culminates in the Book of Revelation, or Apocalypse (from the Greek, meaning uncovering, or manifestation), to which Christ refers after prophesying the destruction of the temple at Jerusalem in a passage summarized in the Authorized Version as 'The signs of Christ's coming to judgment'. St George's land is to be the 'holy place' from which Ruskin can prophesy on the abomination of desolation, and to which, like Solomon and the Magi before him, he will bring riches.

Indeed, a promised 'Christmas gift' was duly delivered seven months later, as announced at the beginning of the first Christmas *Fors* (Letter 12) – '£7000 Consols', a 'fair tithe' of what Ruskin had (27.199). Having confessed his own doubts about the Nativity story, he then asked his readers what it was to them, before launching into commentary on this other kind of manifestation, and attempting to explain what it had been to 'the people of its time' (27.201). Again, his interest is in the affective power of the story, rather than the question of its historical veracity:

It relates either a fact full of power, or a dream full of meaning. It is, at the least, not a cunningly devised fable, but the record of an impression made, by some

---

[17] See p. 96 above. Ruskin wrote further notes on Solomon's 'receiving of the Queen of Sheba', and on the meaning of the names Solomon, Salma, Sheba and Saba in the autumn of 1871: see Lancaster MS 17, Diaries, fol. 106.   [18] Lancaster MS 16, Diaries, fol. 1871.7r; compare *D*, 711.

strange spiritual cause, on the minds of the human race, at the most critical period of their existence: – an impression which has produced, in past ages, the greatest effect on mankind ever yet achieved by an intellectual conception; and which is yet to guide, by the determination of its truth or falsehood, the absolute destiny of ages to come.

Ruskin argued that J. S. Mill's ideas on 'independent womanhood', education and class conflicted with the wisdom of the Magi, and that we should 'simply trust' God (and therefore his messengers) rather than have opinions about Him (27.207, 211). The lesson of the Magi is that the 'wisest men that could be found on earth at that moment' were, together with the simple local shepherds, called to 'do reverence' (27.219) – also the key to Ruskin's hagiography.[19]

Called to do reverence, the Wise Men had shown obedience – for Ruskin the most important aspect of 'religion', from the Latin meaning obligation, bond and reverence (28.156), and an essential attribute of those who would follow St George.[20] Writing on Good Friday 1875 in *Fors*, Letter 53, Ruskin describes his childhood Bible study, and his love as an adult of Psalm 119, before setting out 'some principles respecting the use of the Bible as a code of law, which are vital to the action of the St. George's Company in obedience to it' (28.319). If we 'rule the earth rightly' we will know God, and 'on doing what is plainly ordered, the wisdom and presence of the Orderer become manifest' (28.328–9). In answer to his 'supremely sagacious correspondent' who believed that the Jewish monarchy was a total failure, Ruskin ended the Letter with a long quotation of sixteen verses from chapters 15 and 16 of the Wisdom of Solomon: the words of 'that king whose political institutions' appeared to him to 'reach the roots of these, and of many other hitherto hidden things' (28.333). Like Christ's apocalyptic words in the temple and the Magi's response to the Nativity, this third kind of manifestation of 'hitherto hidden things' in the words of Solomon inspires St George's work: 'But thy sons not the very teeth of venomous dragons overcame: for thy mercy was ever by them, and healed them' (28.334; Wisdom 16.10).

---

[19] The importance of the particular historical moment is underlined in the second Christmas *Fors* (Letter 24), when Ruskin observes of the constellations that 'there is not a space of heaven with a Christian story in it; the star of the Wise Men having risen but once, and set, it seems, for ever' (27.419).

[20] When his faith was at a low ebb, in Verona in 1869, he wrote to Susan Scott: 'All beauty is now dreadful to me – I have no sense of any help coming to me – from the Maker of it – other than He gives to any worm cut through by the spade – which seems to me – nearly zero – There is help only in the discovery of his Laws and obedience to them – and in my own *activity* when possible. – I am always content and well while at work – the Deadly thing to me is Rest': Lancaster BV, Letters of John Ruskin to the Family of the Revd A. J. Scott, 21 June 1869.

Ruskin's personal identification with Solomon deepened in the 1870s, as he reflected upon the disposition of his own inherited wealth. In 'Traffic', his Bradford lecture of 1864, he had encouraged captains of industry to emulate Solomon's enrichment not only of his own palace, but also of Jerusalem.[21] Now Ruskin himself could enrich Oxford, through his endowment of a Drawing School, and Sheffield, through St George's Museum at Walkley. Solomon and the temple were in his mind in the autumn of 1875, as he looked forward to the publication of his fifth Christmas *Fors*, where he planned to tell his readers 'something about marbles, and beads, and coral, and pearls, and shells; and in time . . . you may be able to draw . . . a Parthenon, and a Virgin in it; and a Solomon's Temple, and a Spirit of Wisdom in it; and a Nehemiah's Temple, and a Madonna in it' (*Fors*, Letter 59 (November 1875), 28.447).[22] He also reminded his readers that a 'Museum', meaning 'Belonging to the Muses', is to enable people to 'devote a certain portion of secluded laborious and reverent life to the attainment of the Divine Wisdom, which the Greeks supposed to be the gift of Apollo, or of the Sun; and which the Christian knows to be the gift of Christ' (28.450).[23]

Ruskin reserved his ideas on the contents of St George's Museum, however, for the shortened Christmas *Fors* itself, where these practical matters are discussed within a mystical framework in which divine wisdom is the creative spirit.[24] He thinks that it is now appropriate to return to the subject, 'already opened in *Fors* 12th, of the Three Wise Men', but immediately vents his spleen on the subject of an awful pantomime entitled 'Three wise men of Gotham', and other modern horrors (28.462). Through his own 'laborious work among real magi', he has discovered things concerning 'Magi and their doings' that he wants to pass on to his readers. Using the old magical powers of his descriptive prose with the economy that characterizes *Fors*, Ruskin contrasts the mystery of the creation of light – still discernible daily to those who rise early enough to hear, with their spirit, 'the Morning Star and his fellows sing together' (Job 38.7), and 'their Master say, Let there be light – and there is light; to see the world made, that day, at the word' (Genesis 1.3) – with the counter-order of darkness issued each morning by the nearby

---

[21] See p. 172 above.

[22] In fact Ruskin could not finish the Christmas *Fors* that he had planned (see 28.460).

[23] See also Michael Wheeler, *Ruskin's Museums and Galleries: The Treasury, the Storehouse and the School – A Lecture delivered at the National Gallery, London, 21 November 1994* (London: Pilkington, 1994).

[24] A. S. Mories considered that Ruskin was '*intellectually an Agnostic, and spiritually a Mystic*': 'The Sophia of Ruskin: What was it? and How was it Reached?', *Saint George: The Journal of the Ruskin Society of Birmingham*, 4, 14 (January 1901), 150–71 (p. 158).

'United Grand Steam Percussion and Corrosion Company, Limited (Offices, London, Paris, and New York)', in the form of smoke and pollution (28.463).

In October 1875, the month in which he wrote the Christmas *Fors*, Ruskin had published the third of his *Mornings in Florence* (1875–7), entitled 'Before the Soldan', where he had praised Giotto for his sympathetic treatment of the Sultan as the noblest figure in this 'picture of Christian missionary work' – one of the frescoes in the Bardi Chapel of Sta Croce in Florence (23.353). Giotto's Sultan is 'the type of all noblest religion and law, in countries where the name of Christ has not been preached', and, Ruskin emphasizes, 'the religion and morality of Zoroaster were the purest, and in spirit the oldest, in the heathen world' (23.353–4). In August 1874 Ruskin had prolonged his stay in Italy in order to copy parts of *The Triumph of St Thomas Aquinas* – a fresco now attributed to Andrea di Bonaiuto in the Spanish Chapel of Sta Maria Novella in Florence – including what he described to Norton as 'the daring and divine heresy of Zoroaster under Astronomy', 'quite exquisite',[25] which he praised at length in *Mornings in Florence* (23.394–6).

Ruskin's receptiveness to eastern as well as western wisdom was to be reflected in St George's Creed. Meanwhile, in the Christmas *Fors* of 1875, Ruskin moved on from the wisdom of the Magi to the apocryphal Wisdom of Solomon – itself associated with the East[26] – as he invited his readers to

hear the word of God, spoken to you by the only merchant city that ever set herself to live wholly by His law.†
"I willed, and sense was given to me.
I prayed, and the Spirit of Wisdom was given to me.
I set her before Kingdoms and Homes,
And held riches nothing, in comparison of her." [Wisdom 7.7–8]

† See Fourth Morning in Florence. 'The Vaulted Book.' (28.464)

When he examined this text in detail in the fifth *Morning in Florence* ('The Strait Gate'), it was as the inscription on the book held open by the

---

[25] Ousby and Bradley, *Correspondence*, pp. 323–4; see also Jeanne Clegg and Paul Tucker, *Ruskin and Tuscany*, Ruskin Gallery, Collection of the Guild of St. George (Sheffield and London: Ruskin Gallery / Humphries, 1993), pp. 100–2; *D*, 805–7. Ruskin wrote that the Spanish Chapel 'contains the entire system of Fors politics and morals, superbly painted': Lancaster L39, Letters of John Ruskin to Joan Severn, 24 August 1874. In *Fors*, Letter 45 (September 1874), Ruskin argues that when Turner said 'The Sun is God' '*He* meant it, as Zoroaster meant it; and was a Sun-worshipper of the old breed' (28.147).

[26] See, for example, [Thomas Harmer], *The Outlines of a New Commentary on Solomon's Song, Drawn by the help of Instructions from the East* (London: Buckland, 1768). Harmer argues that the work may be denominated, 'in the Eastern Style, a *Song of Loves*', p. 3.

saint in *The Triumph of St Thomas Aquinas*, which in Ruskin's view 'informs us of the meaning of the whole picture' (23.383).[27] In *Fors*, Letter 60 he concentrated upon Solomon's teaching that riches are nothing in comparison to wisdom: 'Not so much as *mention* shall be made "of coral, nor of pearls, for the price of wisdom is above rubies"' (28.465; Job 28.18). In an ironic *volte-face*, however, Ruskin then teasingly justified his wish to endow the Workmen and Labourers of Great Britain with exotic riches from his own fine collection of minerals, through St George's Museum, and again invoked Solomon, as well as St George:

> You have not had the chance, you think, probably, of making any particular mention of coral, or pearls, or rubies? Your betters, the Squires and the Clergy, have kept, if not the coral, at least the pearls, for their own wives' necks, and the rubies for their own mitres; and have generously accorded to you heavenly things, – wisdom, namely, concentrated in your responses to Catechism. I find St. George, on the contrary, to be minded that you shall at least know what these earthly goods are, in order to your despising them in a sensible manner; – for you can't despise them if you know nothing about them.
>
> I am going, under His orders, therefore, to give you some topazes of Ethiopia, – (at least, of the Ural mountains, where the topazes are just as good), – and all manner of coral . . . and, indeed, all the things that Solomon in his wisdom sent his ships to Tarshish for, – gold, and silver, ivory, and apes, and peacocks, [I Kings 10.22] – you shall see in their perfection and have as much of as St. George thinks good for you . . . (28.465–6)

Ruskin plays the role of a 'Victorian Solomon' not only in writing a form of wisdom literature, but also in his use of his private wealth for the public good.

During his stay in Assisi in the summer of 1874, Ruskin had studied Ecclesiasticus ('The Wisdom of Jesus the Son of Sirach')[28] – another apocryphal wisdom book, and one that, earlier in the year, he had believed to contain personal revelations of God for him.[29] He had also

---

27 Ruskin thought that the 'common translation in our English Apocrypha loses the entire meaning of this passage', and took the opportunity to correct his own translation in *Fors*, substituting 'came upon me' for 'was given to me' (23.384–5). He also referred to 'Hagia Sophia' (Divine Wisdom, Jesus Christ) in Constantinople: 'The *personal* power of Wisdom: the "σοφια" or Santa Sophia, to whom the first great Christian temple was dedicated.'

28 Lancaster MS 19, Diaries, fol. 9f.; *D*, 798–9. Ruskin sent the books of the Apocrypha to St George's Museum. He considered that they should be included in the 'bound Bible' as useful 'books of historical reference', although this would spoil the flow of the 'memorable scriptures': Rosenbach, Unpublished Letters from John Ruskin to Henry and Emily Swan, 77 (Venice, 25 January 1877).

29 He wrote to his cousin Joan from Brantwood on 23 February 1874: 'Have you those letters, still, I wrote you about the opening sky in St John's vale? The same thing happened to me yesterday as I was walking through Miss Beever's wood, after calling there; – but I can't tell you about it; – only it led me this morning to find my entry, <for> {on} my birth-day last year of opening on

reflected upon what he called the 'contingent promises to Solomon' in I Kings 9.2, 4 and 11.38, and 'chanced upon' the prophet Jeremiah on the 'Uncreation by folly, of what had been created by wisdom.'[30] In *Fors*, Letter 46 (October 1874), he stated that there were 'six main heads of God's and the Devil's work':

> And as Wisdom, or Prudentia, is with God, and with His children in the doing, – "There I was by Him, as one brought up with Him, and I was daily His delight", [Proverbs 8.30] – so Folly, or Stultitia, saying, There is no God, [Psalms 14.1] is with the Devil and his children, in the *un*doing. "There she is with them as one brought up with them, and she is daily their delight."
>
> And so comes the great reverse of Creation, and wrath of God, accomplished on the earth by the fiends, and by men their ministers, seen by Jeremy the Prophet: "For my people is foolish, they have not known me; they are sottish children, and they have none understanding: they are wise to do evil, but to do good they have no knowledge. (Now note the reversed creation.) I beheld the Earth, and, lo, it was without form, and void; and the Heavens, and they had no light. I beheld the mountains, and, lo, they trembled, and all the hills moved lightly. I beheld, and, lo, there was no man, and all the birds of the heavens were fled. I beheld, and, lo, the fruitful place was a wilderness, and all the cities thereof were broken down at the presence of the Lord, and by His fierce anger." [Jeremiah 4.22–6] (28.177–8)

Ruskin also found Jeremiah 9 to be full of meaning to him at Assisi – a chapter which includes the prophecy, 'And I will make Jerusalem heaps, and a den of dragons.' Ruskin wrote his account of 'what the St. George's Company [had] to do', as he put it in *Fors*, in Assisi (28.171–3), where he drew upon the divine wisdom mediated not only through Solomon and the Magi, but also through the seraphical saint of love, St Francis.

III

When Charles Eliot Norton learned that Ruskin was reading Jeremiah at Assisi, he wrote back to suggest that his friend had 'too much of the old Scotch Covenanting blood' in him to make Jeremiah 'healthy reading', and that perhaps he might turn to works such as *The Little Flowers of St Francis*, St Bonaventura's *Life*, or, better still, the seventh

Ecclesiasti*cus*, (not *tes*) L, 17, 18, and then chancing to look back to v.8, of the same chapter': Lancaster L 39, Letters of John Ruskin to Joan Severn; *D*, 738. Both incidents related to Rose La Touche, and the second to the temple in Jerusalem. Simon the high priest is described as being 'as the flower of roses in the spring of the year' in Ecclesiasticus 50.8. On 'St John's vale', see Burd, *A Christmas Story*, pp. 71–6.   [30] Lancaster MS 19, Diaries, fols. 11, 3; *D*, 799, 795.

chapter of the Rule of St Francis.[31] Ruskin himself, however, already
had a 'strong leaning' towards religious communities: he had happy
memories of helping the Franciscans with the hay harvest at Fésole in
1845 (18.304), and recalled a prophetic dream when convalescing from
his illness at Matlock in 1871, in which he was told that he was a 'brother
of St. Francis' (22.446).[32]

It is hardly surprising that the author of the Preface to *The Queen of the
Air* ('the Air is given to him for his life; and the Rain to his thirst, and for
his baptism') and of the final paragraph of 'Yewdale and its Streamlets'
('The Spirit of God is around you in the air that you breathe') should be
drawn to St Francis, author of the *Canticle of the Sun* and inspiration of
Giotto and his followers, and thus the origins of modern western art.[33]
It was, however, the Rule of St Francis that attracted Ruskin most. The
abruptness and finality with which the saint embraced a life of poverty,
chastity and obedience was to Ruskin both admirable and enviable,
while the theological basis of the Rule was attractive, being in his view
'the gospel of Works, according to St. Francis' (23.300).[34] In 1867 Ruskin
had told his Manchester audience of the reverence in which the 'Spirit
of Poverty' was held in the Middle Ages (16.17),[35] and as early as May
1869 had privately expressed the wish to 'form a society – no matter how
small at first, which shall vow itself to simple life in what is called poverty,
that it may clothe & cleanse, and teach habits of honour and justice – to
as many as will receive its laws among the existing poor'.[36] Ruskin considered that St Dominic 'taught Christian men what they should think',
whereas St Francis – his role model in this regard – taught them 'how

---

[31] Ousby and Bradley, *Correspondence*, p. 320. The seventh chapter of the Rule of 1222 is on 'Work
and the service of others': see St Francis of Assisi, *Writings and Early Biographies: English Omnibus
of the Sources for the Life of St. Francis*, trans. Raphael Brown, *et al.*, ed. Marion A. Habig (Chicago:
Franciscan Herald, 1973), pp. 37–8.

[32] Compare 'For indeed, from the midst of the tumult and distress of nations, fallen wholly Godless
and lordless, perhaps the first possibility of redemption may be by cloistered companies, vowed
once more to the service of a divine Master, and to the reverence of His saints': *Fors*, Letter 27
(March 1873), 27.492.

[33] 'He was the first major poet to write in Italian, and his feeling for humanity and for nature is
usually regarded as a formative influence on the new, realistic, art of Giotto and his followers,
and hence on the whole course of Western art': Peter and Linda Murray, *The Oxford Companion
to Christian Art and Architecture* (Oxford and New York: Oxford University Press, 1996), p. 187. The
Ruskin passages are discussed on pp. 188–9 and 205 above.

[34] Obedience, which is at the heart of Ruskin's religious thought, occupies a significantly greater
space in St Francis's writings than those about poverty: see M. D. Lambert, *Franciscan Poverty: The
Doctrine of the Absolute Poverty of Christ and the Apostles in the Franciscan Order, 1210–1323* (London:
SPCK / Church Historical Society, 1961), p. 36.   [35] See p. 162 above.

[36] Letter to Susan Scott, Verona, 14 May 1869: Lancaster BV, Letters of John Ruskin to the Family
of the Revd A. J. Scott. See also letter of 27 May.

they should behave' (23.299). The convent at Assisi proved to be a fitting place in which to work on the Rule of St John Ruskin *manqué*, whose copy of Cimabue's St Francis is something of a self-portrait.[37]

When Ruskin arrived in April 1874, he stayed only for a few days in order to supervise Edward Kaiser's work copying Giotto's frescoes for the Arundel Society.[38] Following a stay with a friend in Sicily, Ruskin settled in Rome. Here he copied Botticelli's *Zipporah*, knelt 'a long while, by St. Paul's grave' (23.xxxvii), and reflected upon the attraction of Roman Catholicism for those who are sensitive to the 'intense reality of the Past', where to step into a newly excavated subterranean basilica, built by the 'King Solomon of that time' (37.104), is to find oneself 'standing – suddenly – in the 2nd Century instead of the 19th'. If he were 'a Christian at all – instead of a Turk', he joked with his cousin Joan, Rome would make a Romanist of him in a fortnight.[39]

Ruskin returned to Assisi on 8 June and stayed until 11 July, sending vivid accounts to friends of life in the sacristan's cell, within 30 yards of the tomb of St Francis, of his debates with the friars and thoughts about Catholicism, and of the copying work he carried out in the Upper and Lower Churches. Meanwhile St George's work was never far from his mind, and, as throughout the Italian tour, *Fors* still had to be written, as did Oxford lectures. Ruskin's complex response to the religious environment in which he lived cannot be separated from his thoughts on St George's Company. He wondered, for example, why Mrs Cowper-Temple, who guided him in his excursions into Spiritualism, 'could'nt [sic] believe in Utopia', and whether she really, since she did not '*see Him* either', believed in Christ.[40] He told Carlyle that no readers of *Past and Present* knew precisely what sympathy its author had 'with the faith of Abbot Samson' (37.116). In his private correspondence Ruskin was to describe his 'discovery' of Cimabue's fresco of *The Virgin and Child Enthroned, with St Francis* in the Lower Church with the same intensity that

---

[37] Spear states of Ruskin's copy from *The Virgin and Child Enthroned, with St. Francis*: 'His elongation of the face and treatment of the lips heighten the already remarkable likeness of the saint to Ruskin who began to see himself as "a brother of the third order of St. Francis"': Jeffrey L. Spear, *Dreams of an English Eden: Ruskin and His Tradition in Social Criticism* (New York: Columbia University Press, 1984), p. ix. Curiously, however, an anonymous copy of the sixteenth or the seventeenth century also elongates the face: see *La Basilica Patriarcale di S. Maria degli Angeli, Assisi* (Assisi: Edizioni d'Arte Porziuncola, 1970), p. 129. Perhaps the most striking feature of Ruskin's copy is the deathly greyness of the flesh tints, perhaps emphasizing the austerity of St Francis's marriage to poverty.   [38] See Clegg and Tucker, *Ruskin and Tuscany*, p. 94.

[39] Lancaster L 39, Letters of John Ruskin to Joan Severn, 5 and 31 May 1874.

[40] See *The Letter of John Ruskin to Lord and Lady Mount-Temple*, ed. John Lewis Bradley ([Columbus]: Ohio State University Press, 1964), p. 355.

he had that other formative moment in Turin sixteen years earlier (37.112–14). In his diary, however, 'Giottino's' *St. George* is mentioned in the same entry, and a copy of this fresco, rather than of the Cimabue, was begun immediately.[41] In *Fors*, Letter 45 (September 1874), which he described in his diary as 'the great central *Fors*,[42] he examines in detail Giotto's *The Marriage of St Francis and Poverty*, which he has 'just been drawing, or trying to draw', before closing the Letter with a rebuke to his lady readers for not joining St George's Company, to which he adds a jocular reference to George's white cloak (28.163–5). He takes up where he left off in the following *Fors*, explaining that it is in the sacristan's cell at Assisi that he writes his 'steady explanation of what the St. George's Company have to do', which he bases upon the six days of creation and the opposing forces of 'Wisdom, or Prudentia' and 'Folly, or Stultitia' (28.173–7).

Ruskin had always been sensitive to the associations of particular times and places, and to their degree of appropriateness or 'fitness' to his project. In later life he looked for more, wanting active 'help' from his surroundings, different aspects of which should, ideally, 'help' each other.[43] The juxtaposition in the diary entry of his discovering the Cimabue and noticing the *St. George* is an example of this, and behind it is the history of St Francis's help from St George. Francis's earliest education was from the canons of S. Giorgio, whose simple church and house stood near the Porta Nuova in Assisi.[44] Following the recognition of Francis' Rule by Pope Innocent III, it was the canons of S. Giorgio who first offered the saint a pulpit.[45] The associations in *Fors* between St George's Company and St Francis's Rule, and between St George's work and the wisdom of the Magi, were graphically represented in the iconography of Assisi's churches, for one who had eyes to see them. In Sta Chiara, for example, on the wall behind the altar, the Virgin is sur-

[41] The entry for 20 June begins: 'Yesterday discovered Cimabue in lower church, altering my thoughts of all early Italian art. St George, also, by Giottino': Lancaster MS 19, Diaries, fol. 3; *D*, 796. The next day he writes: 'Read Jeremiah IX, compare entry on 18th. Began St. George yesterday, successfully.' In a letter of 20 June, written in babytalk, he describes his 'nice morning' painting St George, who is 'such a darlin booby of a Georgyporgy': Lancaster L 39, Letters from John Ruskin to Joan Severn. See also the letters of 'St Johns day', 24 June, and 25 June, and 10 July (which lists all his Assisi drawings).　　[42] *D*, 802.

[43] See 'The Law of Help' (7.203–16) and 'St George's vow' (27.95–6, compare 27.44, 28.656–67). See also Ruskin's account in *Præterita* of the Veronese in Turin: 'And as the perfect colour and sound gradually asserted their power on me, they seemed finally to fasten me in the old article of Jewish faith, that things done delightfully and rightly were always done by the help and in the Spirit of God' (35.496) – see pp. 150–1 above.

[44] See Mrs Robert Goff, *Assisi of Saint Francis* (London: Chatto, Windus, 1908), p. 25.

[45] See ibid., p. 84.

rounded by St Francis, St Michael the Archangel, St Jerome, and St Clare (head of the Second Order of St Francis). On the north wall, beneath the Annunciation, are represented St George slaying the dragon, the Nativity, and the Adoration of the Magi.[46]

Whereas the young Evangelical had scorned what he saw as the bric-à-brac of Catholic relics, his response to St Francis's coat, which Father Antonio showed him during this stay in 1874, was profound.[47] His reflections upon its austere roughness, which at once impressed and appalled him, were those of a troubled intellectual who himself took up extreme positions on religious as on other matters, but who could not himself take the final step of faith into a complete rejection of the world and its comforts which he considered the gospel to command.[48] As a radical, Ruskin admired St Francis and St Dominic for having 'turned the world upside down and saved Italy and Christianity for the time', and he wished to emulate them: 'I don't know what I can do – but assuredly, if I can do anything great – it will be by sudden and fierce effort at the *fitting* time. No quiet or middle measures can be now waited for.'[49] In order to determine the 'fitting time' for St George's work, Ruskin continued to open the Bible at random for guidance, as St Francis did.[50] He also encouraged manual labour and ordered that their houses be humble, as St Francis did.[51] He liked to think of himself as a secular tertiary of the Third Order of St Francis – the epitome for him of the social structure of medieval Europe which the Order helped to create – and in his own mind associated the Guild of St George with Franciscan tradition.[52] Members of the Third Order were to

---

[46] See ibid., p. 205.

[47] Ruskin mentioned to his cousin on 14 April 'St. Francis' sackcloth – very rough indeed': Lancaster MS 39, Letters of John Ruskin to Joan Severn; 23.xlvii. The following day he referred to it in his draft of *Fors*, Letter 41 (May 1874), contrasting it with the fur trade in Paris: 'I don't like the look of it at all' (28.89). He 'fondly' kept a 'little "pinch"' of St Francis's cloak in a reliquary at Brantwood (25.125).

[48] In a proof of *Fors*, Letter 89 (September 1880), Ruskin added this note to his characteristic criticism of the clergy: 'In not delivering the primary command of Christianity by the Mouth of the Baptist. "The *people* asked him, saying, What shall we do, then? He answereth and saith unto them, He that hath two coats, let him impart to him that hath none . . ."' Lancaster MS 58/A, *Fors Clavigera* proofs; compare 29.409.

[49] Ruskin to Blanche Atkinson, Lucca, 11 August 1874, cited in Burd, *Christmas Story*, p. 105.

[50] See Ernest Raymond, *In the Steps of St. Francis* (London: Rich, Cowan, 1938), p. 83.

[51] Habig, ed., Assisi, *Writings*, p. 37; *The Life of St. Francis of Assisi from the "Legenda Santa Francisci" of St. Bonaventure*, ed. [Henry Edward] Manning, 8th edn (London: Burns, n.d.), p. 65 (1st edn 1868).

[52] In *Deucalion*, Ruskin describes a drive in the Alps in the autumn of 1876 on which he opened his copy of Cary's Dante at a passage of the *Paradiso*, canto 21 which refers to the decline of the Franciscans: 'I stopped at this (holding myself a brother of the third order of St. Francis), and began thinking how long it would take for any turn of the tide by St. George's work' (26.225; compare 23.xlvii).

live honourably in their residences and to busy themselves with pious actions and to flee from the vanities of the world. And among them thou seest noble knights and others of the great ones of the world in humble costume acting so beautifully with the poor and the rich that thou canst well see that they are truly God-fearing.[53]

Although the Rule of the Third Order was too strict for Ruskin to have followed in its entirety without becoming a Roman Catholic and changing his style of life, the pattern of his days at Brantwood and Oxford was closer in spirit to the Rule than those at Denmark Hill or when staying at the best hotels abroad.[54] One of the most remarkable features of the story of St Francis is the fact that several of his first followers were rich men. Ruskin found that he could not follow them into the life of a mendicant friar. He could, however, encourage other wealthy people to help him in creating a Company which would try to 'turn the world upside down'.

IV

The story of the Guild of St George has been told more than once, and its outline is well known.[55] By August 1871 Ruskin was referring to investments and two trustees and the St George's fund (27.141). He then worked over several years to achieve legal status for the 'St George's Company', to which friends donated some land and some property, and which came to be known as the 'Guild of St George'. The first meeting of the Guild took place on 21 February 1879 in Birmingham; Ruskin was too ill to attend in person, but remained 'Master' until his death. The

---

[53] Bernard of Bessa, cited in Raymond, *In the Steps of St. Francis*, p. 172.

[54] Ruskin's editors wonder whether it was because he considered himself to be a member of the Third Order of St Francis that he liked to have even the domestic animals present when he led family prayers at Brantwood around 1880 (33.xxii).

[55] See Janet Barnes, *Ruskin in Sheffield*, The Ruskin Gallery, Guild of St George Collection (Sheffield: Sheffield Arts Department, 1985); Philip Barnes, *St. George, Ruskin and the Dragon*, The Ruskin Gallery, Collection of the Guild of St George (Sheffield: Sheffield Arts Department, 1992); Anthony Harris, *Why Have Our Little Girls Large Shoes?: Ruskin and the Guild of St George*, Ruskin Lecture, 1985 (London: Brentham / Guild of St George, 1985); Anthony Harris, 'The Guild of St George', in *The Dominion of Daedalus: Papers from the Ruskin Workshop held in Pisa and Lucca, 13–14 May 1993*, ed. Jeanne Clegg and Paul Tucker (St Albans: Brentham / Guild of St George, 1994), pp. 19–27; Robert Hewison, *Art and Society: Ruskin in Sheffield, 1876*, Guild of St George Ruskin Lecture 1979 (London: Brentham / Guild of St George, 1981); Catherine W. Morley, *John Ruskin, Late Work, 1870–1890: The Museum and Guild of St George, An Educational Experiment* (New York: Garland, 1984); Paul L. Sawyer, 'Ruskin and St. George: The Dragon-Killing Myth in "Fors Clavigera"', *Victorian Studies*, 23 (1979), 5–28; Judith Stoddart, 'Ruskin's St George and the Cult of Community', *Victorians Institute Journal*, 20 (1992), 230–59; P. Wardle and Cedric Quayle, *Ruskin and Bewdley* (St Albans: Brentham / Guild of St George, 1989).

only meeting that he managed to attend, in fact, was at Oxford in 1884 when a resolution was passed authorising the setting up of a museum at Bewdley. This never materialized, though the Guild owns an estate and farm there to this day.[56] The Guild also still continues its quiet work of supporting projects relating to 'good husbandry and craftsmanship' (30.5), and to education in these and related areas.

The planning work that Ruskin put into the Guild in the 1870s bore fruit in the most tangible way in the creation of a museum in the North of England. Ruskin had a high regard for the guild tradition associated with metal-workers, and was acutely aware of the fact that skilled craftsmen in Victorian Sheffield worked in a poor environment and would never enjoy the privileges of connoisseurship and Continental travel that he himself did. In 1876 he forwarded St George's work by enabling the acquisition of a small house at Walkley, on a hill overlooking the city, to serve as a museum exhibiting material donated by him or acquired under his direction.[57] From his own collection at Brantwood Ruskin gave drawings of plants, rock formations and architectural studies; his first and last love is reflected in a remarkable collection of minerals; he endowed a library, which he considered to be of great significance; and in order for the people of Sheffield to see the architectural details on which he based his arguments in his writings, he commissioned others to record them in Italy and France, in drawings, plaster casts and photographs which were then exhibited at the Sheffield museum.

Many of the principles embodied in the Guild, especially those relating to the care of the land and the sea-coast, were passed on to the founders of the National Trust. Some of Ruskin's campaigns, such as the Defence of the Lake District, which he thought of as St George's work, were taken up by disciples like Canon Hardwicke Rawnsley, and these provided the political and cultural context of the foundation of the Trust. The National Trust was, however, 'less radical, ambitious and demanding towards its members than was the Guild',[58] and this helps to explain the failure of the Guild to become a national movement and the extraordinary success of the Trust in this regard in our own time. The Trust was also more practical and secular in outlook, and the radical, ambitious and demanding qualities of the Guild can be related to the

[56] See Wardle and Quayle, *Ruskin and Bewdley.*

[57] See Hewison, *Art and Society*; Janet Barnes, *Ruskin in Sheffield*; Philip Barnes, *St. George, Ruskin and the Dragon.*

[58] John Walton, 'The National Trust: preservation or provision?', in *Ruskin and Environment: The Storm-Cloud of the Nineteenth Century*, ed. Michael Wheeler (Manchester and New York: Manchester University Press, 1995), pp. 144–64 (p. 157).

radical, ambitious and demanding qualities of religion in general, Christianity in particular, and, within historical Christianity, both the Rule of St Francis, discussed earlier, and the soldier-martyr tradition of St George.

Consider, for example, among the official statements and documents relating to the Guild, St George's Creed, which 'every person received into the St. George's Company' was to write with their own hand and sign 'with the solemnity of a vow' (28.419). Ruskin sketched the first article of the Creed in the autumn of 1875, when staying with the Cowper-Temples at Broadlands, where he briefly believed that Rose La Touche was present, studied the Wisdom of Solomon, and reflected upon the destruction of a universe created by divine wisdom.[59] Ruskin published the Creed in *Fors*, Letter 58 (October 1875), which begins with an attack upon the 'adulteration' of the 'great' Catholic prayer, '*Deus, a quo sancta desideria*', in the Second Collect for Evening Prayer in the Prayer Book, and upon the hypocrisy of the millions who recite it each week in 'this deadest of all dead languages' (28.417–18). He then offers commentary on the 'peace which the world cannot give' – the nature of which is 'not to be without war, but undisturbed in the midst of war' – and suggests that those who use the Collect 'understandingly' are 'already, consciously or not, companions of all good labourers in the vineyard of God', while those who have not sought to 'find out what the commandments of God are' should now do so. He believes that, having searched them out, 'no sincerely good and religious person would find, whatever his own particular form of belief might be, anything which he could reasonably refuse, or which he ought in anywise to fear to profess before all men' (28.419). The Creed follows:

1.   I trust in the Living God, Father Almighty, Maker of heaven and earth, and of all things and creatures visible and invisible.
      I trust in the kindness of His law, and the goodness of His work. And I will strive to love Him, and keep His law, and see His work, while I live.

---

[59] See p. 186 above. Ruskin's diary for 19 October 1875 includes an interesting deletion: 'For Xmas Fors. <The entirely accursed and abominable wickedness of the Evangelical school of clergymen, in calling the Bible the Word of God, and so making void the Word of God by their tradition> that Word having been from everlasting'. On 22 October he writes: 'A First article of St G. Creed. Believe in Almighty ie. in a Law, ascertainable, as the will of a Governor. Compulsion according to that is a duty They who refuse to compel confess they know not God. All is of a piece . . . B John Mill Liberty – nobody to be guided. conf Wisdom of Solomon XIII': Lancaster MS 20, Diaries, fols. 50–1. Frederic Myers's account of Ruskin in his obituary notice is that of a Spiritualist: 'it was on the stately lawns of Broadlands, and in that air as of Sabbatical repose, that Ruskin enjoyed his one brief season, – since the failure of his youthful Christian confidence, – of blissful trust in the Unseen' (24.xxii).

II.   I trust in the nobleness of human nature, in the majesty of its faculties, the
fulness of its mercy, and the joy of its love.

      And I will strive to love my neighbour as myself, and, even when I
cannot, will act as if I did.

III.   I will labour, with such strength and opportunity as God gives me, for my
own daily bread; and all that my hand finds to do, I will do with my might.

IV.   I will not deceive, or cause to be deceived, any human being for my gain
or pleasure; nor hurt, or cause to be hurt, any human being for my gain or
pleasure; nor rob, or cause to be robbed, any human being for my gain or
pleasure.

V.   I will not kill nor hurt any living creature needlessly, nor destroy any beautiful thing, but will strive to save and comfort all gentle life, and guard and
perfect all natural beauty, upon the earth.

VI.   I will strive to raise my own body and soul daily into higher powers of duty
and happiness; not in rivalship or contention with others, but for the help,
delight, and honour of others, and for the joy and peace of my own life.

VII.   I will obey all the laws of my country faithfully; and the orders of its
monarch, and of all persons appointed to be in authority under its
monarch, so far as such laws or commands are consistent with what I
suppose to be the law of God; and when they are not, or seem in anywise
to need change, I will oppose them loyally and deliberately, not with malicious, concealed, or disorderly violence.

VIII.   And with the same faithfulness, and under the limits of the same obedience, which I render to the laws of my country, and the commands of its
rulers, I will obey the laws of the Society called of St. George, into which
I am this day received; and the orders of its masters, and of all persons
appointed to be in authority under its masters, so long as I remain a
Companion, called of St. George. (28.419–20)

The Creed is based upon the two great commandments of Christ, as
Ruskin himself pointed out in a later *Fors* (Matthew 22.35–40; 28.517),
and is non-sectarian. Ruskin had stated in an earlier *Fors* – Letter 37
(January 1874) – that the St George's Company would be 'consistently
monastic in its principles of labour' and that its land would be worked
by families 'accustomed to obey orders, and live in the fear of God'
(28.19). Crucially, however, he added: 'Whether the fear be Catholic, or
Church-of-England, or Presbyterian, I do not in the least care, so that
the family be capable of any kind of sincere devotion.' More radically,
Ruskin's inclusiveness in the Creed also extended beyond Christianity, as
when he had criticized the wording of the Third Collect for Good Friday
in *Fors*, Letter 30 (June 1873):

I think that our common prayer that God "would take away all ignorance, hard-
ness of heart, and contempt of His word, from all Jews, Turks, infidels, and

heretics", is an entirely absurd one. I do not think all Jews have hard hearts; nor that all infidels would despise God's word, if only they could hear it; nor do I in the least know whether it is my neighbour or myself who is really the heretic. But I pray that prayer for myself as well as others; and in this form, that God would make all Jews honest Jews, all Turks honest Turks, all infidels honest infidels, and all Evangelicals and heretics honest Evangelicals and heretics; that so these Israelites in whom there is no guile, [John 1.47] Turks in whom there is no guile, and so on, may in due time see the face, and know the power, of the King alike of Israel [i.e. Jacob] and Esau. (27.547)

In place of the exclusive 'Evangelical theology' to which he no longer adhered (27.546), Ruskin based his teaching upon an inclusive theology which recognized the common frailty of members of all faiths and the Kingship of the one God who rules over all.

When Ruskin again deprecated the Third Collect for Good Friday in *Fors*, Letter 49 (January 1875) – one of his fiercest attacks upon the bishops of the Established Church – his criticism of the Bishop of Oxford was particularly pointed, as Dr Mackarness had inhibited Bishop Colenso of Natal from preaching at Carfax the previous year (28.243–5).[60] Drawing upon his experience in South Africa, Colenso had argued in his controversial study on the Pentateuch and Joshua that children must be taught

to recognise the voice of God's Spirit, in whatever way, by whatever ministry, He vouchsafes to speak to the children of men; and to realise the solid comfort of the thought, that, – not in the Bible only, but also out of the Bible, – not to us Christians only, but to our fellow-men of all climes and countries, ages and religions, – the same Gracious Teacher is revealing, in different measures, according to His own good pleasure, the hidden things of God.[61]

Ruskin, who befriended Colenso and his daughter, seems to have agreed.

In the 1870s, dialogue between members of different faiths, and discussion on the question of revelation through traditions outside Christianity, intensified. Reporting on the meeting of the Metaphysical Society at which Ruskin delivered his essay on miracles in 1873, Dr Magee, the Bishop of Peterborough, wrote: 'We only wanted a Jew and a Mahometan to make our Religious Museum complete' (34.xxx). In 1875, the year in which Ruskin published St George's Creed, and Anglican, Catholic and Orthodox delegates met in Bonn for their

---

[60] On the Colenso affair, see pp. 183–4 above.

[61] John William Colenso, *The Pentateuch and Book of Joshua Critically Examined*, 7 parts (London: Longman, 1862–79), I, 154. Rowland Williams had written in a similar vein in his equally controversial essay on 'Bunsen's Biblical Researches', in Frederick Temple, *et al.*, *Essays and Reviews*, 12th edn (London: Longmans, Green, 1869), p. 60.

second Reunion Conference, Monier Williams, the Boden Professor of Sanskrit at Oxford, published his lectures on *Indian Wisdom*, expressing the hope in his Preface that 'points of contact between Christianity, Brahmanism, Buddhism, and Islam become better appreciated, and Christians while loyally devoting themselves – heart and soul, body and mind – to the extension of the one true faith, are led to search more candidly for the fragments of truth, lying buried under superstition and error'.[62] Ruskin went further than this, and found the article on 'Islam' by the Jewish scholar Emanuel Deutsch – George's Eliot's model for Mordecai in *Daniel Deronda* – 'wonderfully interesting' when it appeared in 1869.[63] Deutsch's exegesis on the 'Word' as a surrogate for the divine name in different traditions would hardly have escaped Ruskin's notice,[64] nor his reminder that Goethe and Carlyle had shown that 'Mohammedanism is a thing of vitality.'[65] Deutsch's essay begins with these momentous words:

The Sinaitic Manifestation, as recorded in the Pentateuch, has become the theme of a thousand reflections in the Talmud and the Haggadah generally. Yet, however varied their nature – metaphysical, allegorical, ethical – one supreme thought runs through them all – the catholicity of Monotheism, its mission to all mankind.[66]

The opening of St George's Creed is to be read, not as a Unitarian statement, but as an affirmation of monotheism and the one creator God. In *Fors*, Letter 58, Ruskin stated that he would never ask anyone to sign this 'creed and vow' whom he did not know to be 'capable of understanding and holding it in the sense in which it is meant'. In a cancelled passage in the first draft he added:

Only lest I should be accused of any subtlety or reticence in vital points, I beg the reader to observe that the form is deliberately constructed so that Jews and Mahometans may sign it, no less frankly than Christians; that it absolutely excludes only atheists (and of these, there are some whom I am grieved to exclude), but not materialists, for it makes no statement whatever respecting the immortality of the Soul, though most distinct statements of its dignity. And the most faithful believers in Christ will do well to observe that many of the basest

[62] Monier Williams, *Indian Wisdom; or, Examples of the Religious, Philosophical, and Ethical Doctrines of the Hindus* (London: Allen, 1875), p. ix.

[63] Ruskin L 34, Letters of John Ruskin to Joan Severn, n.d..

[64] 'Milla=Memra=Logos, are identical: being the Hebrew, Chadee (Targum, Peshito in slightly varied spelling), and Greek terms respectively for "*Word,*"- that surrogate for the Divine Name used by the Targum, by Phil, by St. John': Deutsch, p. 130.   [65] Deutsch, p. 64.

[66] [Emanuel Deutsch], 'Islam', *Quarterly Review*, 127 (October 1869), 293–353; rpt. in *Literary Remains of the late Emanuel Deutsch, with a Brief Memoir* (London: Murray, 1874), pp. 59–134 (p. 59).

men, while they are content to lead a brute's life, found only upon insolence and ignorance their claims to the duration of a God's; while some of the noblest who have ever glorified the Earth were content in leading such life as their God taught them, to accept gratefully at His hand, if He so willed it, the duration of His earthly creatures. . . . (28.420–1)

Ruskin was right to omit the passage, which then rambles into an embarrassingly wayward reading of mothers' responses to infant mortality. It is worth citing, however, for its characteristically forthright puncturing of human pomposity and self-deceit in religious matters; for its emphasis upon striving to fulfil God's will in the present reality of our earthly lives (a message which in Ruskin's view was not taught by the Church in his generation); and for its inclusiveness in terms of at least two other world religions – Judaism and Islam.

Two years later, on 20 December 1877, Ruskin drew up an abstract of the 'Objects and Constitution of St. George's Guild'. Far from being stiff and legalistic, the draft smacks of *Fors*, as in this, the first paragraph:

The St. George's Guild consists of a body of persons who think, primarily, that it is time for honest persons to separate themselves intelligibly from knaves, announcing their purpose, if God help them, to live in godliness and honour, not in atheism and rascality; and who think, secondarily, that the sum which well-disposed persons usually set aside for charitable purposes (namely, the tenth part of their income), may be most usefully applied in buying land for the nation, and entrusting the cultivation of it to a body of well-taught and well-cared-for peasantry. (30.3)

'To live in godliness and honour, not in atheism and rascality': here is the bedrock of Ruskin's Guild, and indeed of his whole critique of Victorian Britain. A further two years later, in his Master's Report for 1879, dated 12 February, from Brantwood, we find him condoling with his fellow members of the Guild for the smallness of their numbers, and finding the 'radical cause of this general resistance to St. George's effort' in the doctrine, 'preached for the last fifty years as the true Gospel of the Kingdom, that you serve your neighbour best by letting him alone; except in the one particular of endeavouring to cheat him out of his money' (30.15). Yet Ruskin ends his report on a hopeful note, writing: 'The St. George's Guild may be able to advance but slowly, but its every step will be absolute gain, and the eternal principles of right, on which it is founded, make its failure impossible' (30.22).

Ruskin's later 'General Statement explaining the Nature and Purposes of St. George's Guild' (1882) vividly illustrates his sharp distinction between the truth claims of Christianity and the teaching and practices of the Victorian Church. What we need is more museums, he argues, not more churches, for which subscriptions seem to be everywhere: 'a good clergyman never wants a church' (30.52). Yet, like so many pieces by the writer who in his father's view missed his vocation, the statement ends on a high note from a preacher who himself needs no pulpit, and wants no church:

> The promise to be honest, industrious, and helpful (that is to say, in the broadest sense charitable) is . . . required from all persons entering the Guild; and as, on the one hand, I trust that the prejudices of sectarian religion may turn aside from us none who have learned in their hearts that "Christ is all in all", [1 Corinthians 15.28; Colossians 3.11] so, on the other hand, I trust that the cause of true religion may be, even yet by modern sciolists,[67] so far identified with that of useful learning as to justify me in taking the first article of the Apostles' Creed for the beginning, the bond, and the end of our own. (30.58–9)

Why, then, was St George Ruskin's choice as patron of the Guild, and why was the saint such an important *alter ego* for him?

In 1876, the year after Rose La Touche's death, Ruskin spent the autumn and following winter in Venice, with its own little island, great church and smaller churches dedicated to S. Giorgio, and reflected upon a problem relating to St George's work in England. For technical legal reasons he had to change the name of the 'Company', and it was during this disturbed winter that he thought of calling it the Guild, even though he did not announce this until August the following year (19.181–2).[68] A particular thematic focus for part of the St George's Museum was Venice, where St George was highly venerated,[69] and of special interest were the studies from Carpaccio's St George series,[70] painted between 1501 and 1511 for the Confraternity of the Sclavonians, and still housed today in the chapel which Ruskin describes in *St. Mark's Rest* (1877–84) as 'The Shrine of the Slaves'.[71] These studies were executed by Ruskin and his assistants in Venice in 1876–7, when he planned but abandoned a

---

[67] Superficial pretenders to knowledge.

[68] Michael Wheeler, 'Carlyle and Ruskin', *Carlyle Society Newsletter*, NS 7 (1993–4), 2–13 (p. 13).

[69] Today the visitor to the Guild of St George's Ruskin Gallery at Sheffield, opened in 1985, will see on one wall casts of architectural details from St Mark's and the Ducal Palace exhibited next to John Bunney's laboriously detailed copy of the façade of St Mark's.

[70] See the listing of the 'St George Series' (30.197).

[71] In *Fors*, Letter 26 (February 1873), Ruskin had quoted Peter Heylyn's history of St George, printed in 1631; argued that the kernel of the legend of St George was 'that a young soldier, in early days of Christianity, put off his armour, and gave up his soul to his Captain, Christ'; and then added that it would be the 'best work' he had ever done in his 'broken life', if he could 'some day show you, however dimly', how Victor Carpaccio had painted St George in the humblest of the churches dedicated to him in Venice – 'the little chapel of St. George on the "Shore of the Slaves"' (27.479–83).

revision of *The Stones of Venice*, and instead published serially his guide-book, *St. Mark's Rest.*

In the opening chapter of *St. Mark's Rest* (24.208–9), Ruskin encourages the reader to be rowed across to S. Giorgio Maggiore, where it is possible to read in the shade, looking up in comfort at the pillars of St Mark and St Theodore in the Piazzetta across the lagoon – part of Doge Michael's spoils of war with Tyre and Byzantium, and the subject of detailed analysis in the second chapter. Part I of *St. Mark's Rest* was issued as a conveniently small maroon 'leatherette' booklet in April 1877, and contained three chapters. Part II followed in October and began with a chapter entitled 'St. Theodore the Chair-Seller'. Here Ruskin uses Venetian sculpture of widely separated dates as indicators of the city's artistic and spiritual development, from the 'childish art' of the representation of the Lamb and the holy Apostles on the north wall of St Mark's (24.242); through the early thirteenth-century sculpture of St George on his portable throne, on the west front of St Mark's, which, Ruskin explains, shows the saint *sheathing* his sword (24.244); to the late fifteenth-century 'literal realization' of St George and the dragon on a house above the Ponte de' Baratteri ('Rogue's Bridge'), the sculptor of which is 'half-way to infidelity', with all his 'dainty chiselling', in that he does not care whether St George did or did not kill a dragon in that manner, but 'is more bent, in the heart of him, on making a pretty bas-relief than on anything else' (24.248).

It is in 'The Shrine of the Slaves', issued as the First Supplement to *St. Mark's Rest*, three months later, in December 1877, that Ruskin rhapsodizes over the Carpaccio series in the little chapel of the brotherhood of St George of the Sclavonians. 'No dragon that I know of', he writes, 'pictured among mortal worms; no knight I know of, pictured in immortal chivalry, so perfect, each in his kind, as these two' (24.340). As well as the copy of the whole scene in the Carpaccio (plate 20), presented to St George's Museum, Sheffield, Ruskin also drew the 'upper part' of the painting, to illustrate that St George rode without a helmet, in order to be able to see the dragon in time on the ground, in contrast to the St George on the coin of the realm dated 1818 (when old King George was still alive) who is naked except for an improbable helmet (*Fors*, Letter 26, February 1873: 27.475). He also commissioned copies of Carpaccio's St George series for the Sheffield museum from the young artist Charles Fairfax Murray (30.197).

'The Place of Dragons' was issued as the Second Supplement to *St. Mark's Rest*, in April 1879, the publication having been delayed by

Plate 20. John Ruskin, copy of Carpaccio's, *St. George and the Dragon*, 1870/72

Ruskin's serious illness in 1878. Ruskin describes the chapter as the analysis by his 'fellow-worker, Mr. James Reddie Anderson, of the mythological purport of the pictures' described in 'The Shrine of the Slaves'. Here Anderson examines the parallels between St George and Perseus, and then offers a minutely detailed analysis of Carpaccio's *St George and the Dragon* which makes connections with other key paintings in the Ruskinian canon, including Turner's *Apollo and Python* (24.387; plate 4).[72]

It is not necessarily in the details of the Carpaccio, however, or in Ruskin's own published comments on St George, that the most significant aspects of the legend for him and for the Guild are revealed. If we turn to Richard Johnson's *Seven Champions of Christendom* (1616), for example, to which Ruskin refers in *St. Mark's Rest* (24.246) and a copy of which he owned (35.23), we find a story which might interest the psychoanalytic critic or biographer of Ruskin, in which a Christian knight rescues the virgin Sabra from a dragon of massive proportions with his trusty sword Ascalon, and is later lulled to sleep by her chastely playing on the melodious strings of her lute.[73] Later, Sabra witnesses seven of the queen's virgins being raped and then eaten by a lustful giant, but escapes their fate by making herself physically repulsive to the giant, who wanders discontentedly away, repenting himself of his wicked crime.[74]

More relevant to the present discussion, however, are certain other details of the legend of St George, who was said to have been martyred in Palestine around 303 AD. First, St George has traditionally been venerated by Christian and Muslim alike,[75] making him a fitting patron for Ruskin's inclusive Guild, the Creed of which was 'deliberately constructed so that Jews and Mahometans may sign it'. Secondly, St George's Greek name means 'earth-worker', or 'husbandman' (*ge*, earth; *ergon*, work), the true model for Members (later Companions) of the

---

[72] Ruskin wrote to the widow of the Revd A. J. Scott from Herne Hill on 31 December 1873: 'Every one fails me; and the tremendous power of self-deceived mammon worshippers, blasting the life of all humanity, is something too horrible to *face*. I go against it without looking at it – the putrefying Dragon is so much more ghastly than the old Living one. – It is curious that Turner is the only <living> man in Europe, who fully understood this battle. – If you are ever able to drive as far as the National gallery in any of these sunny days, – look at his picture of Apollo and the Python. – *He* only saw the terror of Corruption, in body and soul.' Lancaster MS BV, Letters from John Ruskin to the Scott Family.

[73] [Richard Johnson], *The Renowned History of the Seven Champions of Christendom, St. George of England, St. Denis of France, St. James of Spain, St. Anthony of Italy, St. Andrew of Scotland, St. Patrick of Ireland, and St. David of Wales; and their Sons* (London: Baynes, 1824), pp. 23–7.

[74] Johnson, *Renowned History*, p. 147.

[75] See E. O. Gordon, *Saint George: Champion of Christendom and Patron Saint of England* (London: Sonnenschein, 1907), p. 3.

Guild.[76] Thirdly, St George is associated with the rose – symbol of England, and for Ruskin of much more in his private life – and sacred rosebushes have been grown next to his churches.[77] Fourthly, King Arthur established The Order or Society of St George and the Round Table which itself had a moral code based upon a series of oaths, some of which are not dissimilar from Ruskin's Creed.[78] Finally, this soldier-saint went out to do battle against a fire-breathing dragon which had laid waste the land,[79] fit symbol for the furnaces and steam-engines of industrial England which inspired Ruskin's Utopian vision of men cultivating the land with 'such help of force as they can find in wind and wave'.

Unlike the National Trust, the Guild of St George carried heavy symbolic freight, both in its conception and its development. The many different 'signs' which came to Ruskin as he formulated St George's work by Fors were, like *Fors Clavigera* itself, less random and disparate than might at first appear. In opening himself to eastern as well as western wisdom, Ruskin revived his interest in Solomon and the Magi, and saw the relationship between St Francis and that much older and legendary saint who became the patron of his beloved Guild. At Turin in 1858 he had come to understand the 'old article of Jewish faith, that things done delightfully and rightly were always done by the help and in the Spirit of God' (35.496). At Assisi in 1874 he came to understand that, if he was to encourage a return to godliness and honour in an England that seemed to have sold its soul to atheism and rascality, it would be through the 'help' of the saints, in their 'love and wisdom'.

---

[76] See ibid., p. 6. (Also compare Athena Keramatis – 'fit for being made into pottery', from 'clay intact' (19.351): see p. 191 above.)   [77] Gordon, *Saint George*, pp. 10, 126.
[78] Ibid., pp. 53–4.   [79] Johnson, *Renowned History*, p. 25.

CHAPTER 10

Fragments of Christendom in Venice and Amiens

But there was yet, in the Feudal System, one Seventh and Final Authority, of which the imagination is like to be also lost to Protestant minds. That of the King of Kings, and Ruler of Empires; in whose ordinances and everlasting laws, and in 'feudom' or faith and covenant with whom, as the Giver of Land and Bread, all these subordinate powers lived, and moved, and had their being. [Acts 17.28]

. . . the Feudal System, with all consequences and members thereof, is verily at an end.

Fors Clavigera, Letter 71 (28.739)

I

Ruskin's description of the feudal system, written in Venice on 4 October 1876, prepares the ground for his assistant James Reddie Anderson's collation of the legends of St Ursula, which the reader 'may guess to be in some close connection with the proposed "practice" of St. George's Company' (28.740). Two months earlier Ruskin had written a letter to Anderson's cousin, Sara, which is quoted at the head of chapter 9: 'Do but Feel that [the saints] ARE alive and love us still, and that they have powers of influencing us by their love and wisdom . . .'. Now, in *Fors*, he points out that Carpaccio produced only three small pictures of the 'quite real' St Jerome, three more important ones of the 'disputable' St George, but of the 'entirely aerial' St Ursula 'a splendid series, the chief labour of his life' (28.733–4). Even if Carpaccio 'did not actually believe that the princess and angel ever were, at least he heartily wished there had been such persons, and could be':

Now this is the first step to real faith. There may never have been real saints: there may be no angels, – there may be no God. Professors Huxley and Tyndall are of opinion that there is no God: they have never found one in a bottle. Well: possibly there isn't; but, my good Sheffield friends, do you wish there was? (28.735)

Ruskin had corresponded with his father on Pascal back in 1848, when travelling in revolutionary France and reflecting upon the difficulty of believing in 'God's government' of such a world (36.90). In *The Seven Lamps of Architecture* (1849) he had argued that his natural sympathy for the 'principles and forms of the Romanist Church' should earn him all the more respect for stating that the 'entire doctrine and system of that Church is in the fullest sense anti-Christian; that its lying and idolatrous Power is the darkest plague that ever held commission to hurt the Earth' (8.267–8).[1] By the mid- to late 1870s he wished to set the record straight by expunging from his popular early works what he now regarded as their 'Protestant egotism and insolence' (29.90). The attempt to produce new versions of *The Stones of Venice* and *The Seven Lamps* failed. In *St. Mark's Rest* (1877–84) and *The Bible of Amiens* (1880–5), however, English Protestant tourists were challenged to reflect upon not only the feudal system, which they had read about in Carlyle, but also Catholic Christendom, fragments of which had survived the depredations of the restorers and revolutionists of modern Italy and France.

In the middle of Ruskin's disturbed winter of 1876–7 in Venice, he recorded encounters with a gondolier's daughter who looked like the Madonna, and with the spirit of Rose La Touche, then confused in his mind with Carpaccio's St Ursula. Amidst these personal impressions, however, he also thought of founding a 'St Ursula, St George and Carpaccio scholarship' in the city.[2] By the end of the winter he was explaining to his readers the 'much more distinctly Christian' tone which they would have noticed in *Fors* over the previous two years (Letter 76, 29.86). Apart from a desire to 'contradict the idiot teaching of Atheism', the main reasons for this change were, first, formative personal experiences to which he would not refer at present, and secondly, the impact of his work at Assisi in 1874 upon the theory of art which he had been teaching since the crisis in Turin in 1858.[3] The 'sixteen full years with "the religion of Humanity" for rough and strong and sure foundation of everything' which followed his work on a scaffold in Turin ended when another scaffold was raised for him, for the first time in history, above the high altar at Assisi, and therefore above the body of St Francis (29.90).

Ruskin was also aware, however, that his English Protestant readers

---

[1] See p. 76 above.

[2] Ruskin MS 21, Diaries, fol. 62; compare *D*, 929. In a letter dated 2 January 1878 and on Windsor Castle letterhead, Ruskin described how St Ursula had guided him to St George's Chapel, Windsor, and made him sit in Prince Leopold's own stall: Lancaster L 42, Letters from John Ruskin to Joan Severn.

[3] For analysis of Ruskin's description of the Turin crisis in *Fors*, Letter 76, see pp. 148–50 above.

may have drawn other conclusions from the much more distinctly
Christian tone of *Fors* in recent years. Privately he had revealed to those
close to him that 'the religion of Venice' was virtually now his own
(37.216).[4] Publicly he wrote:

> Meantime, don't be afraid that I am going to become a Roman Catholic,
> or that I am one, in disguise. I can no more become a *Roman*-Catholic, than
> again an Evangelical-Protestant. I am a "Catholic" of those Catholics, to
> whom the Catholic Epistle of St. James is addressed – "the Twelve Tribes
> which are scattered abroad" [James 1.1] – the literally or spiritually wandering
> Israel of all the Earth. The St. George's creed includes Turks, Jews, infidels,
> and heretics; and I am myself much of a Turk, more of a Jew; alas, most of
> all, – an infidel; but not an atom of a heretic: Catholic, I, of the catholics;
> holding only for sure God's order to His scattered Israel, – "He hath shown
> thee, oh man, what is good; and what doth the Lord thy God require of thee,
> but to do justice, and to love mercy, and to walk humbly with thy God?"
> [Micah 6.8] (29.92)[5]

The Revd Frederick Meyrick's article on 'The General Epistle of
James' in Smith's *Dictionary of the Bible*, which we know Ruskin used,
states that the Jewish Christians, whether living in Jerusalem or 'scattered among the Gentiles' and only visiting the city occasionally, were
the 'especial charge' of James the Just, the son of Alphaeus.[6] Like
Ruskin's own writing, the epistle aims not to teach doctrine but to
'improve morality': it pleads for patience, and warns against formalism,
fanaticism, fatalism, meanness, falsehood, partizanship, evil-speaking
and boasting.[7] Meyrick argues that the much debated verse on
justification – 'Ye see then how that by works a man is justified, and not
by faith only' (James 2.24) – does not in fact contradict St Paul. Whereas
St Paul argued against the Judaizing party, which claimed to earn acceptance through good works, by stating that acceptance cannot be earned
by man at all, St James was opposing the 'old Jewish tenet that to be a

[4] Ruskin kissed the feet of a crucifix for the first time in Venice on Christmas Day 1876, and in a
letter to Joan Severn dated 25 January 1877 commented that both she and Mrs Cowper-Temple
would be 'quite seriously alarmed lest after all I should become so *practically* a Roman Catholic
that the Unpractical Protestantism left would'nt [sic] much matter!': *Christmas Story: John Ruskin's
Venetian Letters of 1876–1877*, ed. Van Akin Burd, with an Introductory Essay on Ruskin and the
Spiritualists, His Quest for the Unseen (Newark, New Jersey and London: University of
Delaware Press and Associated University Press, 1990), pp. 256, 248.

[5] On 1 April 1887 Ruskin was to write to the press denying rumours that he had converted to
Roman Catholicism (29.92), and to write to Kathleen Olander on 26 February 1888: 'It is *only*
their doctrine of the Mass that separates me from them – and *that* is certainly by my own fault':
The Gulf of Years: Letters from John Ruskin to Kathleen Olander, commentary by Kathleen Prynne, ed.
Rayner Unwin (London: Allen, Unwin, 1953), p. 33.

[6] *A Dictionary of the Bible*, ed. William Smith, 3 vols. (London: Murray, 1863), I, 926.

[7] Ibid., 927.

child of Abraham was all in all; that godliness was not necessary, so that the belief was correct'.[8]

For the moment, Ruskin's emphasis falls upon the 'Catholic' nature of the epistle. Whereas St Paul's epistles are written to particular people, he explains, the Catholic (or 'General') epistles of James, Peter, John and Jude are written to all, including the 'Sheffielders' to whom he writes – every word 'vital' for them, and particularly II Peter and Jude (29.93). The reader must choose, guided by St George, whether to fight in God's heavenly army or the Devil's worldly army; must learn from St James that 'true Religious service' has nothing to do with current rows over Ritualism, but is to 'visit the Fatherless and Widows in their affliction, and to *keep himself unspotted from the world*' (29.94–5; James 1.27); and must base education in St George's schools upon a command in another Catholic epistle: 'Fear God. Honour the King' (29.97; I Peter 2.17).

Other aspects of Ruskin's catholicity are revealed in his gloss on the text from Micah, where he emphasizes the command to 'walk humbly with thy God' – '*your's*, observe, and your Fathers', as revealed to you otherwise than a Greek's and *his* Fathers', or an Indian's and his Fathers' (29.92). Having sown a seed for his later project of writing the history of Christendom, to be entitled *Our Fathers have Told Us*,[9] Ruskin then asks his readers whether they have 'ever taken the least pains to know what kind of Person the God of England once was'. In the first Christmas *Fors*, Letter 12 (December 1871), Ruskin had tried to explain what the Nativity was to 'the people of its time' (27.201). Now he wants his readers to reflect upon what religion had been to their fathers when England was part of Catholic Christendom. In both cases, a lesson on the religion of the past is meant to be applied in the present.

Ruskin also displayed a much broader kind of catholicity in expressing his respect for religious traditions other than Christianity – what Emanuel Deutsch called the 'catholicity of monotheism'.[10] His comments in *Fors*, Letter 76 on the inclusion of 'Turks, Jews, infidels, and heretics' in St George's Creed coincided with a deepening sense of crisis in England concerning the Eastern Question.[11] They also reflected

---

[8] Compare Ruskin's remarks of c.1883 in *Valle Crucis*: 'The essentially British heresy, the Pelagian – that men can save themselves by the exertion of their own will, and do not need the calling or grace of God – is also the essentially practical one – an extremely healthy heresy, to my thinking, and one half of it quite true' (33.210).

[9] 'We have heard with our ears, O God, our fathers have told us, what work thou didst in their days, in the times of old' (Psalms 44.1).   [10] See p. 227 above.

[11] In December 1876 Ruskin was named as one of the convenors of the London conference on the Eastern Question (24.xxxviii), and while watching the sun rise over S. Giorgio Maggiore on Christmas Day he felt the 'clue' to the whole Eastern Question flash upon him, 'all of a sudden' – 'the Restoration of the Greek & the Jew': Burd, ed, *Christmas Story*, p. 253.

Ruskin's own belief in particular revelation, as reflected in differences between the great monotheistic faiths. His books, he was later to tell Kathleen Olander, were meant to 'define laws of art and work for everybody, – Christian or Jew, Cretan or Arabian'; and he added, 'if I appeal continually to the text of the Bible, it is simply because it is the religious code of England – just as I should appeal to the Koran in writing for Turks'.[12] Ironically, however, it seems to have been only after the death of Rose La Touche that Ruskin was also willing and able to make public confessions of the more orthodox aspects of his faith. On 21 December 1877, for example, only two months before his first major psychotic episode, he told his readers in *Fors*, Letter 86, that he would 'take henceforward happier, if not nobler, ground of appeal, and write as a Christian to Christians: that is to say, to persons who rejoice in the hope of a literal, personal, perpetual life, with a literal, personal, and eternal God' (29.336).

St. Mark's Rest and *The Bible of Amiens* were written immediately before and between the periods of dementia which, in the absence of modern medicines, gradually destroyed Ruskin's mind, the first beginning on the night of 22–23 February 1878 and later described by Ruskin as the 'Dream'. As he pieced together fragments of Christendom and recorded his longing for unity and order in a divided and chaotic world, the boundaries between external reality and internal delusion became harder to define. In moments of psychological crisis, Ruskin turned to the Old Testament wisdom literature on which he had always relied. His personal faith, his understanding of divine wisdom, and indeed his sense of divine peace, deepened, and biblical texts which had formerly meant nothing now spoke to him for the first time. At the same time his sense of evil, experienced in direct encounters with the Devil in his madness, intensified.

As a tortured religious psycho-drama was played out in Ruskin's mind, this lifelong diarist and keenest of observers managed to record some of it, and even tried to involve the readers of *Fors* in it. Writing in Letter 87 (March 1878) only seven days before the Dream, he explained that confused messages had arrived in the post. In order to hold on to his sanity he invited readers to join him in his morning study of the first chapter of Proverbs, known from his 'mother's knee' but not understood until 'this very hour' (29.376):

It can't be the end of this *Fors*, however, I find (15th February, half-past seven morning), for I have forgotten twenty things I meant to say; and this instant, in

[12] Letter dated 26 February 1888: Unwin, ed., *The Gulf of Years*, p. 32.

my morning's reading, opened and read, being in a dream state, and not knowing well what I was doing, – of all things to find a new message! – in the first chapter of Proverbs.

I was in a dreamy state, because I had got a letter about the Thirlmere debate, which was to me, in my purposed quietness, like one of the voices on the hill behind the Princess Parizade. And *she* could not hold, without cotton in her ears, dear wise sweet thing. But luckily for me, I have just had help from the Beata Vigri at Venice, who sent me her own picture and St. Catherine's, yesterday, for a Valentine; and so I *can* hold on:- only just read this first of Proverbs with me, please.

"The Proverbs of Solomon, the son of David, king of Israel."

"To *know* wisdom and instruction."

(Not to "opine" them.)

"To *perceive* the words of understanding."

(He that hath eyes, let him read – he that hath ears, hear. And for the Blind and the Deaf, – if patient and silent by the right road-side, [Matthew 20.30] – there may also be some one to say "He is coming.")

"To receive the instruction of WISDOM, JUSTICE, and JUDGMENT, and EQUITY."

Four things, – oh friends, – which you have not only to *perc*eive, but to *rec*eive. And the species of these four things, and the origin of their species, – you know them, doubtless, well, – in these scientific days? (29.374–5)[13]

And so the commentary continues, including a gloss on verse 9 ('For they shall be an ornament of grace unto thy head') in which he harks back to *Fors* Letter 77 and his reference to the breaking off of Solomon's head from a capital of the Ducal Palace 'by recent republican movements in Venice', which he read as a sign of the times (29.166, 377). In his diary entry for 15 February he recorded that his copy of the *Solomon and the Queen of Sheba* which he believed to be by Carpaccio was on his chimney-piece, adding, in words later scored through: 'I *must* get to work, – or I shall get utterly – into dreamland.'[14]

Divine wisdom, mediated through the Book of Proverbs and the figure of Solomon, provided temporary defence against incipient madness, and also against Satan, with whom Ruskin felt himself to be engaged in mortal combat. On 17 February he opened a dialogue with

[13] The references are to the second reading of Manchester Corporations's Thirlmere Bill on 13 February, the *Arabian Nights*, and the 'Beata Catherine Vigri's St. Ursula' (see 24.185).

[14] *The Brantwood Diary of John Ruskin, together with selected related letters and sketches of persons mentioned*, ed. Helen Gill Viljoen (New Haven and London: Yale University Press, 1971), pp. 91–2. The panel paintings in the Church of S. Alvise which include *The Meeting of Solomon and the Queen of Sheba* were later attributed to Lazzaro Bastiani or his school: see Pompeo Molmenti and Gustav Ludwig, *The Life and Works of Vittorio Carpaccio*, trans. Robert H. Hobart Cust (London: Murray, 1907), p. 13.

the Devil in his diary;[15] the pathetic entry for 22 February 1878 ended with references to 'the Horses of St Marks' and to Athena;[16] the following morning he was discovered in a state of dementia. Ruskin's own remarkable account of the Dream was recorded and eventually published, possibly by his friend Dr George Harley:

During my first illness of wild delirium . . . the voice of the fowls was an inexpressible terror to me. Ridiculous as it may seem, my madness took the form of my ever being in conflict, more or less personal, with the Evil One. I had at that time an old peacock who was good for nothing – and bad for very much; for at that season of the year the weather was abominable, and he was for ever foretelling rain with his ugly, croaking voice. I was lying ill upstairs, and so quickly flew my thoughts (I have since in my subsequent attacks, which were much less severe, been able to verify this extraordinary psychological fact, which proves how the Creator of all can subdivide time infinitesimally) that every time he croaked I thought I was in a farmyard and that I was impelled by the tyrant Devil to do some fearful wrong, which I strove with all my might and main to resist. But my passionate efforts were to no avail; and every time I did the wrong I heard the voice of the Demon – that is, the peacock – give forth a loud croak of triumph. And this was more terrible than I can express in words. (38.172)[17]

In the Christmas *Fors* of 1875 Ruskin had promised to send St George's Museum 'all the things that Solomon in his wisdom sent his ships to Tarshish for, – gold, and silver, ivory, and apes, and peacocks' (28.465–6; 1 Kings 10.22).[18] Having further emulated Solomon by introducing peacocks to Brantwood, Ruskin now found that the bird which signified Resurrection, and which he himself associated with St Mark's, Venice, became demonic in delusions which echoed St Peter's denial of Christ, and which he interpreted within the framework of his belief in 'the Creator of all'.[19] Indeed, his classic narrative of manic-depressive psychosis continues with accounts not only of hellish darkness, but also of heavenly light and colour. Walking up and down his room all night, naked, in 'a state of greater and greater exaltation', waiting for the Devil, he had grappled with a black cat at dawn; and during the two weeks of dementia that followed, articles in the room had turned into imps, devils and witches. Yet Ruskin's twenty or so Turner drawings on his bedroom

[15] Viljoen, *Brantwood Diary*, p. 92. Looking back on the Dream a year later, Ruskin was to quote I Thessalonians 2.18 in the Greek: 'and Satan hindered us' (24.400).
[16] Viljoen, *Brantwood Diary*, p. 102.
[17] Reprinted from 'H', 'Mr. Ruskin's Illness described by himself', *British Medical Journal*, 27 January 1900, p. 225.   [18] See p. 216 above.
[19] Ruskin wrote to Joan Severn in an undated letter written on Corpus Christi College letterhead, possibly in 1877, 'Oh please di ma, I forgot – let the peacocks come down directly – I shall like so if they'll stay': Lancaster L 41, Letters from John Ruskin to Joan Severn.

walls seemed 'a thousand times more lovely, the colours brighter', and 'more like pictures of Heaven than of earth', the same applying to 'pretty patterns' in the furnishings of the room (38.173).

Like Ruskin's reading of his paranoid delusions, his interpretation of the fragments of Christendom represented by the tesserae of Venice in *St. Mark's Rest* (the subject of section II) and the sculptures of the cathedral in *The Bible of Amiens* (discussed in section III) is informed by belief in the wisdom of 'the Creator of all', and a sense of urgency in St George's fight against the (modern) world, the flesh and the Devil.

II

Ruskin refrained from describing to his friend Susan Beever the 'many lovely things' that happened to him in Venice over Christmas 1876, as he thought she would be frightened and think that he was going to be a Roman Catholic (37.217). 'I'm writing *such* a Catholic history of Venice', he added, 'and chiselling all the Protestantism off the old *Stones*, as they do here the grass off steps'. The title of *St. Mark's Rest* offers a clue to its hidden meaning, for it is in meditating upon the serenity of the Doges that a restless Ruskin comes to understand a theological scheme which offers alternative models both of divine judgment and of redemption through the 'Kinghood and its Sorrow' of Christ, signified in the 'Byzantine "purple"' in which David and Solomon, as types of Christ, are also adorned in the mosaics (24.301–2).[20]

Ruskin gloried in the richness of association which the very indeterminacy of 'purple' made possible, and references to the colour abound in both the published works and private papers.[21] He knew that 'Tyrian purple', the dye obtained from the species of gastropod molluscs *purpura* and *murex*, and the imperial or royal colour, was originally a crimson.[22]

---

[20] Ruskin wrote to his friend Mrs Scott from Verona on 21 June 1869, 'I am always content and well while at work – the Deadly thing to me is Rest': Lancaster BV, Letters from John Ruskin to the Family of the Revd A. J. Scott. Ruskin's full title was *St. Mark's Rest: the history of Venice, written for the help of the few travellers who still care for her monuments*.

[21] In one of the 1845 diary notebooks used on his formative first trip to Italy without his parents, for example, the word 'purple' recurs frequently, and is capitalized in the margins of his descriptions of the art and sculpture of Genoa: Lancaster MS 5a, Diaries, fols 1,2. See also, for example, 3.418–19, quoted on p. 35 above; 6.140;19.379–80. He argued that 'the true veins of wealth are purple – and not in Rock, but in Flesh' (17.55–6; see p. 166 above), and changed 'the dark leaves' to 'the purple leaves' in the final paragraph of *Præterita*, dated 19 June 1889 (35.562).

[22] In Byzantine aesthetics, according to Gervase Mathew, the Imperial 'purple' was probably a dark red, at least by the twelfth century: *Byzantine Aesthetics* (London: Murray, 1963), p. 147. Ray Haslam kindly points out that the first edition of Ruskin's Oxford *Lectures on Art* (1870), which included his Inaugural, was published in purple cloth with gold embossed rules – 'purple' in the modern bluish-purple sense.

Its most important associations for him were always biblical, as in his
description in *Modern Painters* I of the trees of La Riccia as 'purple, and
crimson, and scarlet, like the curtains of God's tabernacle' (3.279),[23] and
in his definition of 'purpure', the 'third of the three secondary colours',
in *Deucalion*, chapter VII, published in the year (1876) in which he began
the long stay in Venice which gave rise to *St Mark's Rest*:

VI. Purpure. The true purple of the Tabernacle, "blue, purple, and scarlet"
[Exodus 25.4] – the kingly colour, retained afterwards in all manuscripts of the
Greek Gospels; therefore known to us absolutely by its constant use in illumina-
tion. It is rose colour darkened or saddened with blue; the colour of love in
noble or divine sorrow; borne by the kings, whose witness is in heaven [Job
16.19], and their labour on the earth. Its stone is the Jacinth, Hyacinth, or
Amethyst, – "like to that sanguine flower inscribed with woe." (36.186)[24]

In *The Stones of Venice* II (1853), Ruskin had read St Mark's as a
Byzantine Venetian version of Solomon's temple – a sign of mediation
between earth and heaven, and of a present hope of future (spiritual)
restoration. The appallingly crude physical restoration of St Mark's
which now so alarmed Ruskin takes on added significance when one
considers the moral and religious freight which the building's encrusted
symbolism carried for him. His richest sign of salvation from ruin was
being ruined. During his stay in Venice in 1876–7 Ruskin was introduced
to Count Zorzi and became involved in the campaign to save St Mark's
from further damage. In a letter to Zorzi, published in the Count's book
on the subject (1877), Ruskin lamented recent developments, recalling
how in 1876 he had taken back to London for teaching purposes, to his
'bitter sorrow', pieces of the 'white and purple veined alabasters, more
than a foot square, bought here in Venice out of the wrecks of restoration' (24.408).[25]

Ruskin also remembered nostalgically 'the bright recess of your
Piazzetta, by the pillars of Acre' where he once spent so many 'happy
and ardent days' (24.405–6). The mosaics of the south side, which had
been 'restored',

[23] See p. 37 above.

[24] See Exodus 26.1, 39.1–3. For an explanation of the colour purple in the Priests' Code see James
Hastings, *Dictionary of the Bible*, 2nd edn, rev. by Frederick C. Grant and H. H. Rowley
(Edinburgh: Clark, 1963), p. 170. The closing quotation is from Milton, *Lycidas*, line 106. For anal-
ysis of the mosaic depicting 'Mary receiving the true Purple and Scarlet for the Temple Veil',
see Alexander Robertson, *The Bible of St. Mark: St. Mark's Church – The Altar & Throne of Venice*
(London: Allen, 1898), p. 215.

[25] In Ruskin's sixth Oxford lecture in the 'Readings in *Modern Painters*' series (17 November 1877),
he showed images of St Mark's – his favourite building (22.525).

especially were of such exquisite intricacy of deep golden glow between the courses of small pillars, that those two upper arches had an effect as of peacock's feathers in the sun, when their green and purple glitters through and through with light. But now they have the look of a peacock's feather that has been dipped in white paint. (24.407–8).[26]

(Here, perhaps, is material for the Dream of 1878.) As if to compensate for this loss of colour, Ruskin was later to make a number of drawings on purple paper, including one of the pillars of Acre.[27] He had commented on the peacock as a favourite symbol of Resurrection in Byzantine art in *The Stones of Venice* (10.171), and had contributed to the design of the book cover (plate 21). In 1879 he was to write to T. M. Rooke: 'The real *fact* is that all Byzantine mosaic (and all Eastern colour) has splendour for its first object – and its type is the peacock's tail. If your drawings glow and melt like that you are right' (30.lviii). In July 1872 John Bunney – another of Ruskin's copyists – had given Ruskin a box, 2 7/8" in diameter, containing fragments of mosaic and labelled, 'One of the Eyes of the Peacock's tail from old pavement in North Aisle of St Mark's Venice destroyed when the pavement was removed in April 1872' – literally the stones of Venice.[28]

By January 1877 Ruskin's plans for the revised version of *The Stones of Venice* had been abandoned in favour of the new project, *St. Mark's Rest*, which he began at the same time as his finest architectural drawing – a large drawing of what he called the 'gold and purple' northwest portico (24.xxxvi). 'Throughout the whole façade of St. Mark's', he was to write in 1879, 'the capitals have only here and there by casualty lost so much

---

[26] John Unrau compares the present structure of St Mark's with a photograph of the early 1860s, and identified 'particular slabs of the purple-veined marbles which were removed': *Ruskin and St. Mark's* (London: Thames, Hudson, 1984), p. 127.

[27] *The Pillars of Acre and Southwest Portico of St. Mark's* (reversed image), 1879; pencil and watercolour heightened with white on purple paper, 152 x 89, British Museum. The drawing figured in an 'Exhibition of Drawings and Sketches' in the British Museum in 1901. The Guide read (p. 61): 'A very characteristic example of Mr. Ruskin's remarkable power of eye and hand in expressing the detail and character of scultured ornaments. He loved the colour purple, and has translated the material of these columns into that colour for his pleasure' (38.298). Hewison notes that 'Ruskin's works on purple-tinted paper form a distinct group; some of them are dated 1879, and it is reasonable to attribute the whole group to that year. It is likely that Ruskin made the series as an indirect consequence of the request from Norton to copy the large drawing of the northwest portico of St Mark's': Robert Hewison, *Ruskin and Venice* (London: Thames, Hudson, 1978), p. 90. The British Museum has another drawing on purple paper: *Jean d'Acre Pillar, Venice*, watercolour, with white (280 x 222). A drawing of *Palazzo Bernardo a S. Polo* (Lancaster, 1996 p1578), is on purple-coated paper, and is based on Lancaster Daguerreotype 24. (Daguerreotypes themselves have been said to have a purple tint, and this is certainly pronounced where the copper plate is exposed through deterioration, as in this case.)

[28] Hewison, *Ruskin and Venice*, p. 96.

Plate 21. John Ruskin, cover design for *The Stones of Venice*, 1851–3

as a volute or an acanthus leaf, and whatever remains is perfect as on the day it was set in its place, mellowed and subdued only in colour by time, but white still, clearly white; and grey still, softly grey; its porphyry purple as an Orleans plum, and the serpentine as green as a greengage' (24.419).

The first seven chapters of *St. Mark's Rest*, and chapter 10, appeared in 1877; chapters 8 and 11 in 1879 (following the first terrible period of dementia in 1878); the remainder in 1884. It is in chapter 5, 'The Shadow on the Dial', that Ruskin defines the third period in the history of Venice (1301 to 1530) as being 'that of religious meditation, as distinct, though not withdrawn from, religious action' (24.255). He adds: 'The entire body of her noble art-work belongs to this time.' He then describes the craft guilds:

> Protected and encouraged by a senate thus composed, distinct companies of craftsmen, wholly of the people, gathered into vowed fraternities of social order; and, retaining the illiterate sincerities of their religion, laboured in unambitious peace, under the orders of the philosophic aristocracy; – built for them their great palaces, and overlaid their walls, within and without, with gold and purple of Tyre, precious now in Venetian hands as the colours of heaven more than of the sea. (24.257)

The 'social order' of medieval Venice – for Ruskin the Book of Proverbs put into practice – and the association of 'gold and purple of Tyre' with Solomon's temple, also find expression for Ruskin in Gentile Bellini's *Procession in St. Mark's Place,* in which serried ranks of blooming Venetians parade in front of the porches of St Mark's.[29]

St. Mark's Rest itself is far being from a restful, ordered text: its confusions and disappointments reflect Ruskin's state of mind during this stay in Venice. On Sunday 20 May 1877, however, towards the end of his work on St Mark's, the discovery of a particular mosaic brightened him – 'a mosaic of upright figures in dresses of blue, green, purple, and white, variously embroidered with gold' (24.294). Ruskin made his own watercolour copy, the *Study of Mosaic of the Doge and his People* (plate 22), on the spot, and four days later was homeward bound, his head full of

[29] 'From the Sinai desert, from the Sion rock, from the defiles of Lebanon, met here the ghosts of ancient builders to oversee the work, – of dead nations, to inspire it: Bezaleel and the maids of Israel who gave him their jewels; Hiram and his forgers in the vale of Siddim – his woodmen of the Syrian forests; – David the lord of war, and his Son the Lord of Peace, and the multititudes that kept holyday when the cloud filled the house they had built for the Lord of All; [Exodus 36.1, 35.22; 2 Samuel 5.11; I Kings 5, and 7.13,14; Genesis 14.10; Psalms 42.4; I Kings 8.10] – these, in their myriads stood by, to watch, to guide; – it might have been, had Venice willed, to bless': *Guide to the Academy at Venice* (1877), 24.164.

Plate 22. John Ruskin, *Study of Mosaic of the Doge and His People,* 1877

it. Ruskin had asked Charles Fairfax Murray to join him in the gallery and to bring his drawing materials:

I am going up into the gallery, behind organ at St Mark's, to study a mosaic plainly visible, and of extreme beauty and importance. A sketch of it . . . will be the most important work you or I have yet done in Venice. (24.xl)

Two years later he was to record in chapter 8 of *St. Mark's Rest,* 'The Requiem', that this remained the 'most precious "historical picture"' to his mind 'of any in worldly gallery, or unworldly cloister, east or west' (24.296). The mosaic was so important to Ruskin because it depicts not only the harmony between Church, people and Doge that was so sadly lacking in the modern world, but also a Doge who is 'serene of mind'. Ruskin comments: 'Most Serene Highnesses of all the after Time and World, – how many of you knew, or know, what this Venice, first to give the title, meant by her Duke's Serenity! and why she trusted it?' (24.296).

Ruskin's private intention of 'chiselling all the Protestantism off the old *Stones*' is stated publicly in the opening paragraph of 'The Requiem', where he confesses that in re-reading the 'St. Mark's' chapter in volume II and remembering his first visits to Venice he is 'struck, almost into silence, by wonder' at his own 'pert little Protestant mind, which never thought for a moment of asking what the Church had been built for', or who was 'lying dead therein' (24.277). Having reassured his good Protestant reader that he is not a Roman Catholic, but a 'mere wandering Arab', if that is less alarming, he returns to his central religious theme at this period, arguing against Protestant objections that St Mark is not in fact buried there: 'Whether God ever gave the Venetians what they thought He had given, does not matter to us; He gave them at least joy and peace in their imagined treasure, more than we have in our real ones' (24.278). In order to emphasize the fact that he is revising the 'St. Mark's' chapter in 'The Requiem', Ruskin again invites the reader to enter the building via the baptistery, as he did 'many a day since' (24.282).[30] Whereas in 1853 his description of the Baptistery focused upon choice and the convert's 'baptism' by fire, in a passage crammed with favourite Evangelical types of Baptism and appropriate biblical texts, his typology now encompasses the Greek origins of the Christian iconography, and particularly that associated with wisdom. Having explained the structure of the 'little chamber', he asks the reader to pass on into the 'farther chapel under the darker dome', and to admire it as the Greek precursor of 'all those golden-domed backgrounds' of Bellini, Cima and Carpaccio. That ten-winged cherub in the recess behind the altar, 'once a Greek Harpy', has 'written on the circle of its breast, "Fulness of Wisdom"' ('Plenitudo Scientie'): it is the 'type of the Breath of the Spirit' (24.283–4).[31] Ruskin reinforces the point in his later treatment of the 'Greek' spirals that decorate the façade of St Mark's, 'under the power of the Queen of the Air', and the leaves that are 'only the amplification of the cornice over the arches of the Holy Sepulchre at Jerusalem' (24.288).

Moving back into the church through 'the real porch of the temple', Ruskin then guides the Protestant reader to a point on the gallery from which the central dome can be viewed, in readiness for a lesson in Catholic theology:

Round the circle enclosing Christ is written, "Ye men of Galilee, why stand ye at gaze? This Son of God, Jesus, so taken from you, departs that He may be the arbiter of the earth: in charge of judgment He comes, *and to give the laws that ought to be.*"

---

[30] On Christmas Day 1876 Ruskin's own route through the building was precisely that which he had avoided for fear of encountering Catholic idolatry in the 'St. Mark's' chapter of 1853: see Burd, ed., *Christmas Story*, p. 254, and p. 92 above.

[31] See Unrau, *Ruskin and St Mark's*, plate xxx.

Such, you see, the central hope of Venetian worship. Not that we shall leave the world, but that our Master will come to it: and such the central hope of Venetian worship, that He shall come to *judge* the world indeed; not in a last and destroying judgment, but in an enduring and saving judgment, in truth and righteousness and peace. Catholic theology of the purest, lasting at all events down to the thirteenth century; or as long as the Byzantines had influence. (24.292)

Ruskin finds in the Latin inscription an attractive emphasis upon the covenant promised in Jeremiah 31.33 and fulfilled in Hebrews 8.10 ('I will put my laws into their mind, and write them in their hearts') which contrasts with the usual reading of the Ascension account in Acts 1.11 ('shall so come in like manner') as a prophecy of Jesus's return in the end-time to preside over the Last Judgment (represented elsewhere by the mosaicists).

For Ruskin this 'Catholic theology of the purest' helps to explain the serenity of the group in the mosaic of *The Doge and his People*, towards which he now directs the reader, along the gallery above the transept (24.295). He then brings the chapter to a climax by turning attention to the mosaic of the eastern dome, viewed better from here than from below. Having first identified the figures who surround Christ Emmanuel ('God with us') and transcribed their scrolls, he writes:

The decorative power of the colour in these figures, chiefly blue, purple, and white, on gold, is entirely admirable, – more especially the dark purple of the Virgin's robe, with lines of gold for its folds; and the figures of David and Solomon, both in Persian tiaras, almost Arab, with falling lappets to the shoulder, for shade; David holding a book with Hebrew letters on it and a cross (a pretty sign for the Psalms); and Solomon with rich orbs of lace like involved ornament on his dark robe, cusped in the short hem of it, over gold underneath. And note in all these mosaics that Byzantine "purple", – the colour at once meaning Kinghood and its Sorrow, – is the same as ours – not scarlet, but amethyst, and that deep. (24.301–2)

In August 1858 Ruskin had written to his father from Turin describing the 'dark purple robe' of Veronese's Solomon, and admiring the bold use of a jewelled cross to indicate Solomon's 'typical character' (16.xxxix).[32] Now he emphasizes the fact that 'Byzantine "purple"' signifies both 'Kinghood and its Sorrow': robed in purple, Solomon is the type of the Man of Sorrows who is also King of Kings.[33] The copy

---

[32] See p. 141 above.

[33] 'When they had mocked him, they took off the purple from him, and put his own clothes on him, and led him out to crucify him' (Mark 15.20). In 1875 Ruskin had criticized young clergymen for enjoying the gratification of being 'regarded as an oracle, without the trouble of becoming wise, or the grief of being so' (28.238–9; see pp. 210–11 above).

Plate 23. T. M. Rooke, *Christ Surrounded by Prophets on the Eastern Cupola of St. Mark's*, 1879

of the mosaic which Ruskin commissioned for St George's Museum from Rooke in 1879 (plate 23; 30.lvii) places at the centre of the drawing, not the Virgin Mary in the eastern axis, which would be the normal practice, but Solomon, whose inscription Ruskin translates as 'Who is this that ascends as the morning?' (Song of Solomon 6.10), and David, whose scroll prophesies the kingship of his son: 'Of the fruit of thy body will I set upon thy throne' (Psalms 132.11).[34] Like the dominant figure of the Virgin, the prophet kings and their scrolls emphasize the Incarnation – for Ruskin the central subject of St Mark's.[35]

The Christ figures depicted in St Mark's are for Ruskin the same 'King of Kings, and Ruler of Empires' whose 'ordinances and everlasting laws' shaped the feudal system. *St. Mark's Rest* was as much a relig-

[34] The finished drawing disappointed him only in its inevitable failure to convey the subtle gradations of purples and blues in the mosaics: Unrau, *Ruskin and St Mark's*, p. 208. Ruskin also asked Bunney to 'make a sketch . . . of the David and Solomon, of the apse cupola', not in competition with or opposition to Rooke, but in order to get the 'facts' of the colours in a way that was more habitual to him (Lancaster 1996 p0127).

[35] See Otto Demus, *The Mosaic Decoration of San Marco, Venice*, ed. Herbert L. Kessler (Chicago and London: University of Chicago Press / Dumbarton Oaks, 1988), p. 58.

ious as an aesthetic project, and Byzantine 'purple' was not only a colour of great 'charm' for Ruskin, but also the colour of kinghood and of sorrow, and thus, read typologically, of redemption through the (purple) blood of Christ.

III

At the end of his writing career, in the final paragraph of *Praeterita* (1885–9), Ruskin was to reflect upon the mysterious workings of Fors in bringing disparate people and events together in our lives, and of memory in bringing those people and events back into consciousness in new and meaningful patterns: 'How things bind and blend themselves together!' (33.561). Seven years earlier, in the third chapter of *The Bible of Amiens*, he used the same binding metaphor when discussing his scattered comments on biblical interpretation, claiming that 'the fragmentary expressions of feeling or statements of doctrine', which from time to time he had been able to give, 'will be found now by an attentive reader to bind themselves together into a general system of interpretation of Sacred literature' (33.119). This verbal parallel raises the question whether the plan to write the series entitled 'Our Fathers have Told Us' was, as in the case of *Praeterita*, partly therapeutic in purpose, following shattering periods of illness? More significantly, to what extent did Ruskin's plan to write the history of Christendom reflect a personal need to bind the fragments of his own religion together, as against a more overt and public purpose related to the search for unity between Christian sects, and even between different faiths, in the later decades of a century wearied by internecine strife on matters of doctrine and tradition, and now aware of an increasing secularization in many areas of public and private life? 'Our Fathers have Told Us' was to 'consist of ten parts, each taking up some local division of Christian history, and gathering, towards their close, into united illustration of the power of the Church in the Thirteenth Century' (33.186). *The Bible of Amiens*, together with a few other fragments, is all that we have of an ambitious scheme which would have worked from the parts to the whole, tracing in its hermeneutics the contours of Christendom in Ruskin's understanding.[36]

---

[36] Ruskin's successive volumes were to examine (2) Verona, (3) Rome, (4) Pisa, (5) Florence, (6) the Monastic Architecture of England and Wales, (7) Chartres, (8) Rouen, (9) Lucerne, and (10) Savoy, Geneva and the Scottish border: see 33.lxv, 186–7. For fragments of these later volumes see 'Chapters for Later Parts of "Our Fathers"' (33.189–254) and Lancaster MS 46, Our Fathers have Told Us. Ruskin's full title for the series was '"Our Fathers have Told Us": sketches of the history of Christendom for boys and girls who have been held at its fonts'.

Even in the weakest parts of *The Bible of Amiens*, which are character-
ized by a sense of world-weariness and a loss of intellectual grip, there
is a sustained attempt to explain how the unity of Christendom,
achieved over a period of three centuries (from the eleventh to the thirteenth), provided lessons for a divided world at the end of the nineteenth
century. Could the Christian faith, stripped of the corrupting accretions
of years, both Catholic and Protestant, find common cause with other
religions stemming from our father Abraham in proclaiming the will of
God – an aim reflected in Ruskin's frequent use of symbolism associated
with division and unity, separation and bonding, fragmentation and
binding, the parts and the whole?[37] In wishing to arrest the drift towards
secularization in British society, Ruskin flirted with what we would now
call ecumenism and inter-faith dialogue. His heart, however, was with
the medieval sculptors of Amiens, who lived in an age when, as Hardy's
Angel Clare puts it, 'faith was a living thing'.[38]

Ruskin revisited Northern France with his secretary Laurence
Hilliard and Hilliard's sister Connie in the late summer of 1880. He then
returned to Amiens in October with Arthur Severn and Hercules
Brabazon Brabazon to write chapter I, on which the lecture he delivered
at Eton on 6 November was also based. The Preface to *The Bible of
Amiens*, published with the first chapter on 21 December, touches upon
the central theme of unity when Ruskin cites his own apothegm from
The Laws of Fésole, that 'all great Art is Praise', and adds:

So is all faithful History, and all high Philosophy. For these three, Art, History,
and Philosophy, are each but one part of the Heavenly Wisdom, which sees not
as man seeth [I Samuel 16.7], but with Eternal Charity; and because she rejoices
not in Iniquity, *therefore* rejoices in the Truth [1 Corinthians 13.6]. (33.23–4)

For Ruskin, the 'Heavenly Wisdom' remained the 'creative spirit', mediating between the Creator and the creature, and witnessed not only in
the Jewish and Christian traditions, but also in Greek religion and Islam.
(In lecture IV of *The Pleasures of England* series, delivered in November
1884, he was to argue that the 'most mythic' of early saints is St Sophia,
'the shade of the Greek Athena, passing into the "Wisdom" of the
Jewish Proverbs and Psalms, and the Apocryphal "Wisdom of

---

[37] For an example of Ruskin's thinking in mid-career on the subject of separation, see 'The
Mountain Gloom' – the penultimate chapter of *Modern Painters* IV – where he writes of Martin
Schöngauer's 'Betrayal' (fig. 113): 'This tendency to dismember and separate everything is one
of the eminent conditions of a mind leaning to vice and ugliness; just as to connect and harmonize everything is that of a mind leaning to virtue and beauty' (6.401).

[38] *Tess of the d'Urbervilles* (1891), chapter 17.

Solomon'" (33.486).) Three other elements of Ruskin's later intellectual
and religious life shape *The Bible of Amiens*, as they do *St. Mark's Rest*: his
conception of himself as an interpreter; his belief in divine judgment;
and his interest in the Greek sources of Christian symbolism. More
significantly in terms of this study, the final chapter, 'Interpretations',
uncannily 'binds together' each of the religious themes in Ruskin's
earlier works that were the subject of part one.

In 'The Lamp of Obedience', from *The Seven Lamps*, Ruskin used the
river flowing between banks as a metaphor for order (8.250), and he
begins the first chapter of *The Bible of Amiens* – 'By the Rivers of Waters'
(Song of Solomon, 5.12) – by celebrating the way in which the river
Somme divides as it passes through what was once 'the Venice of
France', and then reunites (33.25). The medieval city divided the water
only to control and utilise it, as in Eden, and without disturbing its
natural course through the open countryside of Picardy, which Ruskin
also admired.[39] The 'intelligent English traveller' journeys not by river
or road, but by train, and is in a hurry to get to Paris. Ruskin, however,
encourages him or her to look back as the train gathers speed, and to see
amidst the fifty or so smoking factory chimneys near the station 'one, a
little taller than any, and more delicate, that does not smoke', and to see
amidst 'fifty masses of blank wall, enclosing "works"',

. . . *one* mass of wall – not blank, but strangely wrought by the hands of foolish
men of long ago, for the purpose of enclosing or producing no manner of
profitable work whatsoever, but one –
"This is the work of God; that ye should believe on Him whom He hath
sent!" (33.28; John 6.29)

The Somme moves from unity to division to unity restored; the many
different factories achieve the unity only of blank uniformity; the
'oneness' of the cathedral, with its 'flèche' or 'minaret', makes its unique
claim to attention and interpretation through its difference. Ruskin
would indeed seem to be working in the domain of hermeneutics.

In late nineteenth-century Britain the imperial ideal represented the
ultimate expression of unity in difference, the unification of different
peoples and nations under the Crown, which was itself under God – the
Christian God, three in one and one in three. The reality was somewhat
different, and new challenges arose in the mind of the established
Church of England through an increased awareness of other world

---

[39] A deleted section of paragraph 2 in the manuscript reads, 'by groves of aspen and glades of
poplar, surpassed perhaps, in grace and gladness by the trees of Paradise; but no where by any
rooted in our common Earth': Lancaster MS 46, Our Fathers have Told Us.

faiths – a contributory factor in the liberalization of Protestant teaching on hell in the 1870s, for example, as it became increasingly difficult to imagine the vast majority of the world's population being condemned to everlasting torment. Ruskin's interest in the validity of true worship in traditions other than his own had been evident since the 1840s in his treatment of 'Romanist idolatry', and had later broadened in works such as *The Queen of the Air* and in St George's Creed. In his notes to chapter I in *The Bible of Amiens* he quotes an intriguing passage from a contemporary travel book entitled *Far Out: Rovings Retold* (1880), in which Colonel Butler's views on the English traveller on 'A Trip to Cyprus' seem to chime with Ruskin's own: 'Of the features of English character brought to light by the spread of British dominion in Asia, there is nothing more observable than the contrast between the religious bias of Eastern thought and the innate absence of religion in the Anglo-Saxon mind' (33.49). As a result, he argues, 'our rule in the East has ever rested, and will ever rest, upon the bayonet'. For Colonel Butler the Empire represents division rather than unity, separation rather than assimilation. Yet in the East, for all its history of bloody religious conflict, there is a shared respect for 'the worship of the Creator by the created' – words which summarize Ruskin's own practice through all the twists and turns of his own religious pilgrimage, and specifically his recognition in later life of Catholicism's profound sense of the sacred.

Chapter II was to follow twelve months later, in December 1881, after a second period of dementia (from late February to late March). There continued to be close links between his spiritual life and his mental state at this time; indeed, Ruskin himself believed that this illness was brought on by the longing for contact with Rose La Touche interrupting his devotions.[40] Entitled 'Under the Drachenfels',[41] the chapter discusses European history, and again some of its most striking passages are meditations upon either unity or separation and division (33.59–60, 62). Yet another attack, in March 1882, preceded the publication of chapter III, during a European tour which Ruskin made with his secretary, W. G. Collingwood.[42] (They did not stay in Amiens.) Geography, history and

---

[40] See *The Correspondence of John Ruskin and Charles Eliot Norton*, ed. John Lewis Bradley and Ian Ousby (Cambridge University Press, 1987), p. 444.

[41] The subject of a Prout drawing reproduced in 1879, together with a drawing of Amiens among others, in Ruskin's *Notes on Prout and Hunt*.

[42] From Champagnole Ruskin wrote to his cousin on 3 August 1882: 'Get a "Seven lamps" from Allen and read the opening of the Lamp of Memory. That's where I took Collie this morning – and curiously – we saw a hawk hovering as we came back.' Lancaster L 44, Letters of John Ruskin to Joan Severn.

religion come together in the chapter entitled 'The Lion Tamer' (but up
until proof stage 'Monte Cassino'), as Ruskin reminds the reader of his
discussion in the previous chapter of the 'division' of Europe on the basis
of climate (33.90). He offers a tabular scheme of countries by zones,
from north to south (33.93), and then, at last taking up the thread of the
note in chapter I, compares the practices of Arab and Jew:

> Using therefore the terms "Gothic" and "Classic" for broad distinction of the
> northern and central zones of this our own territory, we may conveniently also
> use the word 'Arab' for the whole southern zone. The influence of Egypt van-
> ishes soon after the fourth century, while that of Arabia, powerful from the
> beginning, rises in the sixth into an empire whose end we have not seen.[43] And
> you may most rightly conceive the religious principle which is the base of that
> empire, by remembering, that while the Jews forfeited their prophetic power by
> taking up the profession of usury over the whole earth, the Arabs returned to
> the simplicity of prophecy in its beginning by the well of Hagar [Genesis
> 21.17–20], and are not opponents of Christianity; but only to the faults or follies
> of Christians. They keep still their faith in the one God who spoke to Abraham
> their father; and are His children in that simplicity, far more truly than the
> nominal Christians who lived, and live, only to dispute in vociferous council, or
> in frantic schism, the relations of the Father, the Son, and the Holy Ghost.
> (33.95–6)[44]

It is as if Ruskin, yearning for simplicity, has felt the full dismissive force
of the Muslim description of the Jews as the 'people of the book', and
has seen, as Kierkegaard does in one of his parables, that the interpretation of the Bible can become so engaging that no time is left for acting
upon its message.[45]

The fit does not last, however, as Ruskin is soon immersed in the
history of biblical interpretation and its patron saint, Jerome. While he
knows that 'the real meaning, in its first power, of the word 'Bible' is not
'book, merely', but '"Bibliotecha," Treasury of Books' (33.108–9), he
argues, in one of his most resonant statements, that Jerome's translation
resolved multiplicity into unity: 'the severity of the Latin language was
softened, like Venetian crystal, by the variable fire of Hebrew thought;
and the "Book of Books" took the abiding form of which all the future
art of the Western nations was to be an hourly enlarging interpretation'
(33.109–10). The unity in Christendom that this melting of Hellenism by

---

[43] A reference to the Mahdi and the death of General Gordon.
[44] For Ruskin's prolonged debate with Bishop Fraser of Manchester on usury, see especially 'Usury:
A Reply and a Rejoinder' (1880; 34.401–25).
[45] See David Lyle Jeffrey, *People of the Book: Christian Identity and Literary Culture* (Grand Rapids,
Michigan, and Cambridge MA: Eerdmans, 1996), pp. 13–14.

Hebraism made possible can be explained not only by the translation of the 'Hebrew and Greek Scriptures' into the Latin – 'an easier and a common language' – but also 'in their *presentation to the Church as of common authority*'. The context in which Jerome worked was one of fragmentation, as for example among the Gnostics, who had 'insidiously effaced the authority of the Evangelists by dividing themselves, during the course of the third century, "into more than fifty numerably distinct sects, and producing a multititude of histories, in which the actions and discourses of Christ and His Apostles were adapted to their several tenets"' (33.110).[46]

Ruskin, then, admired the way in which St Jerome contributed to the 'fixing' of the 'canons of Mosaic and Apostolic Scripture' (24.111), rather as George Herbert, one of his favourite poets, had admired Solomon, who '*finished* and *fixed* the old religion' by building the temple in Jerusalem.[47] Ruskin also recognized the global nature of Jerome's achievement:

All that the younger reader need know is, that when Jerome died at Bethlehem, this great deed was virtually accomplished: and the series of historic and didactic books which form our present Bible, (including the Apocrypha) was established in and above the nascent thought of the noblest races of men living on the terrestial globe, as a direct message to them from its Maker, containing whatever it was necessary for them to learn of His purposes towards them; and commanding, or advising, with divine authority and infallible wisdom, all that was best for them to do, and happiest to desire. (33.111)

Ruskin takes up the theme of 'infallible wisdom' later in the chapter, writing that 'only the Eternal Sophia, the Power of God and the Wisdom of God', can be depended upon for the interpretation of scripture (33.115).

The problem, however, was that in Evangelical circles such as that in which Ruskin had been brought up, interpretation could lead to accommodation with Mammon:

You see I have connected the words "charity" and "labour" under the general term of "bearing the cross". "If any man will come after me, let him deny himself, (for charity) and take up his cross (of pain) and follow me."

The idea has been *exactly* reversed by modern Protestantism, which sees, in

---

[46] Ruskin quotes Gibbon's *Decline and Fall*, chapter 15.
[47] Keble quotes Herbert: '"King Solomon *finished* and *fixed* the old religion." He *finished, by* fixing it: by determining once for all the metropolis of the religion': John Keble, 'The Character and History of Solomon, with a View Especially to the Question of his Final Penitence', unpublished MS in *Occasional Papers and Reviews* (Oxford and London: Parker, 1877), pp. 392–434 (p. 411).

the cross, not a furca to which it is to be nailed; but a raft on which it, and all its valuable properties,* are to be floated into Paradise.

* Quite one of the most curious colours of modern Evangelical thought is its pleasing connection of Gospel truth with the extension of lucrative commerce! (33.112)[48]

and to the randomness associated with individualism:

The Protestant reader, who most imagines himself independent in his thought, and private in his study, of Scripture, is nevertheless usually at the mercy of the nearest preacher who has a pleasant voice and ingenious fancy; receiving from him thankfully, and often reverently, whatever interpretation of texts the agreeable voice or ready wit may recommend: while, in the meantime, he remains entirely ignorant of, and if left to his own will, invariably destroys as injurious, the deeply meditated interpretations of Scripture which, in their matter, have been sanctioned by the consent of all the Christian Church for a thousand years; and in their treatment, have been exalted by the trained skill and inspired imagination of the noblest souls ever enclosed in mortal clay. (33.113)

Having offered a 'Catholic' critique of some of the worst aspects of the religion of his birth, Ruskin pays homage at the end of this second passage to the 'great arts of Europe' which represent 'national commentaries' upon the Bible.[49]

Ruskin's own journey from the Evangelical chapels and churches of south London, where the early Church fathers such as Jerome were the subject of suspicion, to the sacristan's cell in Assisi had been tortuous, and he soon offered some personal testimony. Having again striven for unity in difference by referring to the Bible as an incomparable 'literature' (33.118) – a term which itself unites many parts in one whole – he explains that he is 'no despiser of profane literature', and that it was from the Bible that he learned the 'symbols of Homer, and the faith of Horace' (33.118–19). Again, his argument turns upon the continuity between the wisdom of East and West:

That there *is* a Sacred classic literature, running parallel with that of the Hebrews, and coalescing in the symbolic legends of mediaeval Christendom, is shown in the most tender and impressive way by the independent, yet similar

---

[48] On Evangelicalism and wealth creation see Boyd Hilton, *The Age of Atonement: The Influence of Evangelicalism on Social and Economic Thought, 1795–1865* (Oxford: Clarendon, 1988).

[49] On 9 December 1882, Francesca Alexander told Lilly Cleveland in a letter from Florence that Ruskin 'spoke with much sadness of the enmity between different Christian sects, saying that he had known . . . equally good Christians, in all of them': Lucia Gray Swett, *John Ruskin's Letters to Francesca and Memoirs of the Alexanders*, with an introduction by William Clyde De Vane (Boston: Lothrop, 1931), p. 376.

influence of Virgil upon Dante, and upon Bishop Gawaine Douglas.[50] At earlier dates, the teaching of every master trained in the Eastern schools was necessarily grafted on the wisdom of the Greek mythology; and thus the story of the Nemean Lion, with the aid of Athena in its conquest, is the real root-stock of the legend of St. Jerome's companion, conquered by the healing gentleness of the Spirit of Life. (33.119–20)

Characteristically, Ruskin ends his chapter in homiletic mode, bringing the legend of St Jerome home to the conscience of the individual reader through a 'Catholic' reworking of the kind of point he had made often enough in *Modern Painters*: 'the Kingdom is God is already come to those who have tamed in their own hearts what was rampant of the lower nature, and have learned to cherish what is lovely and human, in the wandering children of the clouds and fields' (33.120).

Chapter IV was published in October 1883, by which time Ruskin had resumed the Slade Professorship. Its title, 'Interpretations', is at once ambiguous and explicit, like a parable, announcing what was implicitly the subject not only of the earlier chapters of *The Bible of Amiens*, but also of Ruskin's project throughout his career: the interpretation of interpretations. The iconography of Amiens is a supreme example of what he had described in 'The Lion Tamer' as that 'art of the Western nations' which was an 'hourly enlarging interpretation' of the 'Book of Books', or 'national commentary' upon the Bible (33.109–10, 113); and as Ruskin begins his own interpretation of the cathedral, he returns to the themes which had been central to his religious thought as the 'Author of *Modern Painters*'.

In his analysis of Tintoretto's *Annunciation* in *Modern Painters* II, Ruskin echoed the description of Solomon's temple, 'built of stone made ready before it was brought thither: so that there was neither hammer nor axe nor any tool of iron heard in the house, while it was in building' (1 Kings 6.7).[51] Now, in 'Interpretations', his continued interest in the theme of unity and separation is expressed in an early note that at Amiens, as at other French cathedrals, the 'natural blocks were never sawn, only squared into fitting, the whole native strength and crystallization of the stone being thus kept unflawed' (33.122). In *The Stones of Venice* II he described St Mark's as 'the Book-Temple' (10.141).[52] Now he sees the external sculpture of Amiens as an 'alphabet and epitome' of the religion which inspired an 'acceptable worship' to the 'Lord whose Fear was in His Holy Temple, and whose seat was in Heaven' (33.123; Psalms 11.4,

---

[50] Translator of the *Aeneid* into English, c.1513.   [51] See p. 67 above.   [52] See p. 73 above.

Book of Common Prayer).[53] Now, in his description of the unified culture of thirteenth-century Amiens, he shows how natural it was for the people to think of the Christ who was a 'Jew among Jews, and a Galilean among Galileans' as also the 'Beau Christ d'Amiens' – 'as true a compatriot to them as if He had been born of a Picard maiden' (33.122). In *Modern Painters* 1 Ruskin celebrated God's presence in the 'Shechinah of the blue' (3.381).[54] Now he describes how God was housed in the glorious enclosed choir of Amiens, where the medieval carpenter made his 'Master-carpenter' comfortable in the part of the building 'in which the Divine presence was believed to be constant, as in the Jewish Holy of Holies' (33.122–3).

And what trace is there in 'Interpretations' of Ruskin's earlier readings of Solomon's 'Christian royalty'? On the central pillar of the central porch of the great west front at Amiens is the statue of 'Christ Immanuel, – God *with* us' (33.143; Matthew 1.23), while the Madonna and St Firmin preside over the 'minor porches':

> As you look full at the façade in front, the statues which fill the minor porches are either obscured in their narrower recesses or withdrawn behind each other so as to be unseen. And the entire mass of the front is seen, literally, as built on the foundation of the Apostles and Prophets, Jesus Christ Himself being the chief corner-stone [Ephesians 2.20]. Literally *that*; for the receding Porch is a deep "angulus", and its mid-pillar is the "Head of the Corner".
>
> Built on the foundation of the Apostles and Prophets, that is to say of the Prophets who foretold *Christ*, and the Apostles who declared him. Though Moses was an Apostle, of *God*, he is not here – though Elijah was a Prophet, of *God*, he is not here. The voice of the entire building is that of the Heaven at the Transfiguration, "This is my beloved Son, hear ye Him [Matthew 17.5, 21.7]." (33.144)

A *single* 'voice'; *one* 'cornerstone': Ruskin is here celebrating not unity between faiths but the unity of medieval iconography, based upon the unique truth claims of Christianity.

He continues:

> There is yet another and a greater prophet still, who, as it seems at first, is not here. Shall the people enter the gates of the temple, singing "Hosanna to the Son of *David*"; and see no image of His father, then? – Christ Himself declare,

---

[53] Amiens contrasts with Rheims in this respect. When staying in Rheims on 14 August 1882 he wrote: 'This is a nasty, worldly – modern milliner and banker sort of place – I've got the whole cathedral front opposite my window – (and the big bells are cleaving air at this moment –) but it's no good the filthy modern houses built all about it would have taken the good out of the temple of Jerusalem'. Lancaster L 44, Letters of John Ruskin to Joan Severn.

[54] See p. 29 above.

Plate 24. 'The Central Pedestal', central porch, Amiens Cathedral, from *The Works of John Ruskin*, ed. E. T. Cook and Alexander Wedderburn, Library Edition, 39 vols (London: Allen, and New York: Longmans, Green, 1903–12), vol. 33, Plate XIII

"I am the root and the offspring of David"; and yet the Root have no sign near it of its Earth?

Not so. David and his Son are together. David is the pedestal of the Christ. (33.144–5)

As he examines the statue of David, a sceptre in his right hand, a scroll in his left (plate 24), Ruskin finds harmony in the typology of 'one of the noblest pieces of Christian sculpture in the world': 'King and Prophet, type of all Divinely right doing, and right claiming, and right proclaiming, kinghood, for ever' (33.145). Like others before and after him, however, Ruskin may have misconstrued the king, for Durand, author of a voluminous study on the cathedral, was to come down on the side of Jourdain and Duval, who believed that the statue depicts Solomon.[55] Ironically, such a reading would have strengthened rather than diminished Ruskin's sense of unity in the iconography of this central porch, as above the main pedestal is a minor one bearing an idealized lily which, he writes, 'fulfils, together with the rose and vine, its companions, the

[55] Georges Durand, *Monographie de l'Église Notre-Dame Cathédrale d'Amiens*, 2 vols. (Amiens and Paris: Yvert, Picard, 1901–3), I, 316–17.

triple saying of Christ, "I am the Rose of Sharon, and the Lily of the Valley." [Song of Solomon, 2.1] "I am the true Vine" [John 15.1]'.[56] Instead, his discussion of Solomon is restricted to commentary upon the statues in the southern (Madonna) porch, where he contrasts the king's reception of the Queen of Sheba with Herod's 'driving out the Madonna into Egypt' (33.167).

By this point in the chapter, most of Ruskin's energy is devoted to identifying the large number of statues and related bas reliefs in the three porches, and briefly commenting upon them. As he concludes his examination of the bas reliefs in the Madonna's porch, however, the central theme of the 'Beau Christ d'Amiens' re-emerges strongly, as Ruskin focuses upon the same Christ Emmanuel of the Incarnation who presided in his St Mark's:

They were never intended to serve as more than signs, or guides to thought. And if the reader follows this guidance quietly, he may create for himself better pictures in his heart; and at all events may recognize these following general truths, as their united message.

First, that throughout the Sermon on his Amiens Mount, Christ never appears, or is for a moment thought of, as the Crucified, nor as the Dead: but as the Incarnate Word – as the present Friend – as the Prince of Peace on Earth [Isaiah 9.5], – and as the Everlasting King in Heaven. What His life *is*, what His commands *are*, and what His judgment *will be*, are the things here taught: not what He once did, nor what He once suffered, but what He is now doing – and what He requires us to do. That is the pure, joyful, beautiful lesson of Christianity; and the fall from that faith, and all the corruptions of its abortive practice, may be summed briefly as the habitual contemplation of Christ's death instead of His Life, and the substitution of His past suffering for our present duty.

Then, secondly, though Christ bears not *His* cross, the mourning prophets, – the persecuted apostles – and the martyred disciples *do* bear theirs. (33.169)

Here, as elsewhere in the late work,[57] Ruskin's somewhat unorthodox Christology seems unbalanced in its privileging of the immanent. His 'Catholic' theology of works also brings him close to stating a belief in conditional salvation: 'This *be*, and thou shalt live' – 'pure in heart' (33.170; Luke 10.28, Matthew 5.8). The 'notion of Justification by Faith, in the modern sense', has led to separation rather than unity, he argues: it 'remains now the basest of popular solders and plasters for every condition of broken law and bruised conscience which interest can provoke,

---

[56] Ruskin had written of the words from the Song of Solomon as those of Christ himself in volume I, chapter XI of *Proserpina* (1879): see p. 203 above.　　[57] See, for example, 20.64.

or hypocrisy disguise' (33.172). Yet Catholicism, with its quarrels about 'prayers for the Dead, Indulgences to the Living, Papal supremacies, or Popular liberties', has simply been one of 'two great sects of the corrupted church'. The 'Life, and Gospel, and Power' of Christianity are in the 'mighty works of its true believers', and most of all in the 'foundation stones of Amiens': 'Believe it or not, reader', Ruskin writes, 'as you will: understand only how thoroughly it *was* once believed' (33.172–3).

In conclusion, Ruskin argues that morality 'has nothing to do with religion', and that those who preach on the assumption that religion can patch up human failings are wasting their time:

> But if, loving well the creatures that are like yourself, you feel that you would love still more dearly, creatures better than yourself – were they revealed to you; – if striving with all your might to mend what is evil, near you and around, you would fain look for a day when some Judge of all the Earth shall wholly do right, and the little hills rejoice on every side [Genesis 18.25; Psalms 65.12]; if, parting with the companions that have given you all the best joy you had on Earth, you desire ever to meet their eyes again and clasp their hands, – where eyes shall no more be dim [Isaiah 32.3], nor hands fail; – if, preparing yourselves to lie down beneath the grass in silence and loneliness, seeing no more beauty, and feeling no more gladness – you would care for the promise to you of a time when you should see God's light again, and know the things you have longed to know, and walk in the peace of everlasting Love – *then*, the Hope of these things to you is religion, and Substance of them in your life is Faith [Hebrews 11.1]. And in the power of them, it is promised us, that the kingdoms of this world shall yet become the kingdoms of our Lord and of His Christ [Revelation 11.15]. (33.174)

The repeated 'if' drives home the conditional element of Ruskin's soteriology, and is strongly reminiscent of what he called the 'contingent promises to Solomon' in I Kings,[58] and of Solomon's own teaching in Proverbs.[59] It also draws the various strands of his theology together into one long, penultimate sentence, ending with the release through *'then'* into the hope and faith that flow from love, and the final sentence's homiletic affirmation of the ultimate sign of unity within the Judæo-Christian scheme, when Christ's kingdom comes. As in *St. Mark's Rest*, Ruskin's aim has been to apply a lesson on the religion of the feudal past ('it *was* once believed') to the present ('the Hope of these things to you is religion'), for our fathers, in their wisdom, have told us.

[58] See above p. 217.

[59] 'One of the dominant thought patterns in the book of Proverbs is that quality of life runs closely parallel to conduct': Lennart Boström, *The God of the Sages: The Portrayal of God in the Book of Proverbs*, Coniectanea Biblica, Old Testament Series, 29 (Stockholm: Almqvist, 1990), p. 90.

CHAPTER 11

The 'visible Heaven' and apocalyptic wisdom

I believe it will be an extreme benefit to my younger readers if I
write for them a little *Grammar of Ice and Air*, collecting the known
facts on all these matters, and I am much minded to put by my
ecclesiastical history for a while, in order to relate what is legible of
the history of the visible Heaven.

The Storm Cloud of the Nineteenth Century, Lecture II (34.59)

I

By 1884 Ruskin had resumed the Slade Professorship and was planning
to continue work on 'Our Fathers have Told Us'. That project, like the
proposed *Grammar of Ice and Air*, was never completed, as the precarious
state of Ruskin's mental health compelled him to concentrate upon
drawing together fragments of autobiography in *Præterita* (1885–9),
where he focused upon happy memories and tried to avoid topics which
excited or enraged him.[1] The desire, however, to collect the 'known
facts' remained as strong as it had been in *Modern Painters* – a work to
which Ruskin frequently referred in his late work, including the Slade
lectures.[2] His recent rewriting of the histories of Venice and Amiens had
recorded fragments rescued from the ruins of Christendom, and had

---

[1] A fourth period of mental illness occurred at the end of July 1885 and a fifth almost exactly a
year later (35.xxvii).

[2] The last lectures of Ruskin's first tenure of the Slade Professorship were the *Readings in 'Modern
Painters'*, the last of which was delivered on 1 December 1877 and published in the *Nineteenth
Century* in January 1878 as 'An Oxford Lecture'. Here he argued that a dead sheep in the polluted
Teviot was the 'work of your prayerless science' and the true modern symbol of the 'Lamb as it
had been slain' (22.534). On resuming the Chair in 1883 he intended to celebrate 'England's
Modern Painters' in *The Art of England* series (33.269), and said in the first lecture: 'I know that
fresh air is more wholesome than fog, and that blue sky is more beautiful than black, to people
happily born and bred' (33.273). Ruskin's notes in *The Storm Cloud*, Lecture II, frequently return
to *Modern Painters*: see 34, 44, 45, 47, 49, 55, 58, 68, 69, 78. Two chapters of *Coeli Enarrant: Studies
of Cloud Form and of its Visible Causes, collected and completed out of 'Modern Painters'* were published
with a preface and notes in 1885. Ruskin contributed an Epilogue to George Allen's Complete
Edition of *Modern Painters* in 1888: see p. 279 below.

challenged his readers to apply the lessons their fathers had told them in the modern world.[3] In the first version of his lecture on *The Storm Cloud of the Nineteenth Century* he revised his analysis of clouds in *Modern Painters* by arguing that the ruin of the 'visible Heaven' reflected moral decline associated with the industrial age. This first lecture ended in apocalyptic mode, drawing upon the late prophets of the Old Testament. In the ending for the revised second lecture a new note is added through commentary on what Ruskin calls the 'wisdom of Solomon' in the Book of Proverbs, and through a quotation from the Psalms (34.74). Ruskin is writing in a tradition coming down from early Judaism and from Christ's teaching, in which eschatology, which concerns the end-time and the inauguration of a new order, is held in tension with wisdom teaching, which assumes that the world will continue. In his Epilogue to *Modern Painters* (1888) and in the final paragraph of *Præterita*, this 'Victorian Solomon' emulated the prophet king whose name means 'peaceable'. In *The Storm Cloud* he also remembered that this *alter ego* was traditionally regarded as the founding father of natural science.

In *Modern Painters* IV (1856), Ruskin had encouraged his readers to understand the 'Heavens' as literally the 'veil of clouds above the earth' (6.109), and to recognize that 'in the midst of the material nearness of these heavens God means us to acknowledge His own immediate presence as visiting, judging, and blessing us' (6.113).[4] The clouds were also his favourite symbol of mediation between God and man in the first and fifth volumes of his *magnum opus*, the whole of which, he claimed, 'declares the perfectness and eternal beauty of the work of God; and tests all work of man by concurrence with, or subject to that' (7.9). The 'Author of *Modern Painters*' regarded nature as God's culture, and both nature and God were central to his later perception that aspects of the creation were ruined. He wrote to Charles Eliot Norton from Denmark Hill on 3 April 1871,

everything is infinitely sad to me – this black east wind for three months most of all. Of *all* the things that oppress me – this sense, of the evil-working of nature herself, – my disgust at her barbarity – clumsiness – darkness – bitter mockery of herself – is the most desolating[5]

and to Joan Severn from Palermo on 22 April 1874,

---

[3] Ruskin also advised his Oxford audience to 'transfer' the teaching of the Bible 'to modern need' (22.536).

[4] See p. 40 above. Subsequent quotations from *Modern Painters* are those discussed on pp. 30, 37. See also Blyth, p. 49 above.

[5] *The Correspondence of John Ruskin and Charles Eliot Norton*, ed. John Lewis Bradley and Ian Ousby (Cambridge University Press, 1987), p. 226; also 37.30.

Nothing is such a trial to me as this weather – That men – and things – and roses – should betray me – I can bear; But that God himself should spoil his own beautiful work – and bite his own tender spring-blossom to death – this is too horrible. ^ 23rd, morning. I've read the 1st and 2nd of Zephaniah, and understand better. ^ [6]

In the *Fors* for May 1875 he publicly cited Solomon – the king whose political institutions appeared to him to 'reach the roots of these, and of many other hitherto hidden things' – along lines similar to Zephaniah's: 'For the ungodly, that denied to know thee, were scourged by the strength of thine arm: with strange rains, hails, and showers, were they persecuted, that they could not avoid, for through fire were they consumed' (28.334; Wisdom of Solomon, 16.16). Gradually he was working his way towards the position he adopted in *The Storm Cloud*.

On the narrower question of pollution, for which only humankind could be blamed, *Fors* provided a vehicle for St George's work in bringing both the problems and possible solutions home to individual readers through personal address and testimony. In the early Letter 5 (May 1871) Ruskin wrote of his readers' 'infinite power over the rain and riverwaters' (27.92). Behind his comments on 'Folly', or 'Stultitia', as the reverse of 'Wisdom', or 'Prudentia', in Letter 46 (October 1874) lies a contrast between his own work of cleansing the 'springs of Wandel' at Carshalton, beside which he played as a child, and the 'correspondent Diabolic work' of 'poisoning fish, as is done at Coniston, with coppermining' (28.177).[7] In Letter 61 (January 1876) he argued that 'grievous changes and deterioration of climate' were among the 'great and terrible signs of supernatural calamity' which had flowed from the offences committed by 'all the nations of Christendom' against the 'law of Christ' in the nineteenth century (28.488).

Such readings of the signs of the times (Matthew 16.3) are generally described as 'apocalyptic' – a term which has been used so loosely in modern literary criticism that we must reconsider its meaning here. When Ruskin wrote in *Modern Painters* 1 of Turner's rendering of the 'neglected upper sky' as 'another apocalypse of Heaven' (3.363), he knew that 'apocalypse' meant revelation, from the Greek word meaning

---

[6] Lancaster L 39, Letters from John Ruskin to Joan Severn. From Zephaniah: 'I will utterly consume all things from off the land, saith the Lord . . . The great day of the Lord is near . . . That day is a day of wrath . . . a day of darkness and gloominess, a day of clouds and thick darkness . . . And I will bring distress upon men, that they shall walk like blind men, because they have sinned against the Lord . . . Surely Moab shall be as Sodom, and the children of Ammon as Gomorrah, even the breeding of nettles, and saltpits, and a perpetual desolation . . .' (1.2, 14–15, 17, 2.9).   [7] On Ruskin's treatment of wisdom and folly see p. 217 above.

uncovering, or unveiling.[8] In Robert Barr's short story, 'The Doom of London', published half a century later in *The Idler* in 1892, the narrator escapes from the heavily polluted city by train; he is one of only three passengers to survive the journey to Richmond, so little oxygen is there in the atmosphere. Barr's story is certainly representative of a particular late Victorian sub-genre, as is Richard Jefferies's novel, *After London*, published in 1885, which portrays the aftermath of some mysterious environmental disaster. To observe, however, that fog in Barr, Jefferies and Conan Doyle may be 'an element of an apocalyptic mood in literature and art that is to be found at the end of the nineteenth century', is to use the term in a purely negative modern sense.[9] For in our own age of the disaster movie, the science-fiction dystopia, and the nightmare scenario of a world destroyed by nuclear weapons or unfiltered solar rays, the term has come to mean simply the disastrous end of things. In English, 'apocalypse' was first associated exclusively with the last book in the Bible, a revelation of a divine scheme in which the world is brought to judgment and the glory of God is uncovered in the last days. Far from being a revelation, 'apocalypse' has, ironically, come to mean a covering over, or closing down, or dead end. This is a sign of our times, in which, predictably, environmental panic has seized the public mind as the second millennium closes. Historians, however, could argue that our times were either inaugurated or anticipated by a generation which included Gissing, Conrad and Wells.

Meanwhile some modern literary criticism, including Ruskin criticism, has sought to broaden the meaning of the term 'apocalypse', with the result that it can cease to be helpful.[10] One of the leading historians of Romantic thought has identified in 'Christian history and Christian

---

[8] See p. 37 above.

[9] Peter Brindlecombe, *The Big Smoke: A History of Air Pollution in London since Medieval Times* (London and New York: Methuen, 1987), pp. 127–8. The opening paragraphs of Dickens's *Bleak House* (1852–3) anticipate these late-Victorian works.

[10] Raymond Fitch, author of a massive study entitled *The Poison Sky: Myth and Apocalypse in Ruskin* (Athens, Ohio and London: Ohio University Press, 1982), seldom refers to the Revelation of St John the Divine. His canvas is wider. Referring to M. H. Abrams's use of the term 'apocalypse' in the restricted sense 'used in the Biblical commentary, where it signifies a vision in which the old world is replaced by a new and better world', he writes: 'The problem in this definition for us is that while Wordsworth and the earlier Romantics concentrate, in their poetic apocalyptics, on the *consummation* of the biblical Apocalypse (Rev.21:1–4), Ruskin's primary interest appears to be in those earlier chapters that speak of the coming of the red dragon, the worship of the Beast, and the pouring out of God's wrath upon the earth. Further, since Ruskin's revelations invoke other mythic symbols or schemes . . . we must liberalize the term apocalypse here to include not only literary revelations relating to the biblical Apocalypse, but also any personal revelation confirming the truth of myth or of providential intentions in natural phenomena' (pp. 11–12).

psycho-biography' the tendency, 'grounded in texts of the New Testament itself, to internalize apocalypse by transferring the theater of events from the outer earth and heaven to the spirit of the single believer, in which there enacts itself, metaphorically, the entire eschatological drama of the destruction of the old creation, the union with Christ, and the emergence of a new creation – not *in illud tempus* but here and now, in this life'.[11] The transferring of the theatre of events from the outer earth and heaven to the spirit of the single believer is certainly characteristic of the Evangelical tradition into which Ruskin was born. Theologically, however, he, like many of his contemporaries, grounded much of his thinking on belief in a literal, external divine judgment, as well as an understanding that the judgment of all mankind, as described in the Revelation of St John the Divine (otherwise known as the Apocalypse), is also literally enacted in the individual soul in the here-and-now, through the workings of the conscience. (It is helpful to recall here that the Greek root of the English word 'crisis' means judgment.) We have seen that Ruskin described Revelation 21 as 'one of the most important chapters' in the Bible and drew upon it in his famous description of St Mark's, Venice; that he claimed to have learnt 'most of the Apocalypse' by heart (27.168); and that his study of it in middle age enthralled and excited him.[12] His career began in the era of the 'apocalyptic sublime' (Turner, John Martin, Danby)[13] and ended in that of 'environmental apocalyptic'. At the mid-point between these decades – the period around the time of the Second Reform Act of 1867 – millenarian expectation was once again (and for the last time in the nineteenth century) both strong and widespread in Britain. While being acutely aware of all these readings of the signs of his times, however, and being himself an heir to the tradition upon which they draw, Ruskin sets himself apart by also maintaining an unwavering scientific interest in 'collecting the known facts on all these matters'.

As an undergraduate, Ruskin ended his 'Remarks on the Present State of Meteorological Science' in the *Transactions of the Meterological Society* with an appeal for data to be sent in from all quarters, so that the 'vast multitude of beautiful and wonderful phenomena, by which the wisdom and benevolence of the Supreme Deity regulates the course of the times and the seasons' could be reduced to 'principle and order' (1.210).[14] In

---

[11] M. H. Abrams, *Natural Supernaturalism: Tradition and Revolution in Romantic Literature* (New York and London: Norton, 1971), p. 47.   [12] See p. 89 above.

[13] See Morton D. Paley, *The Apocalyptic Sublime* (New Haven and London: Yale University Press, 1986).   [14] See p. 33 above.

stating in the fifth and final volume of *Modern Painters* (1860) that 'perhaps the best and truest piece of work done' in volume I was the 'account given in it of the rain-cloud' (7.175), the word 'truest' included the sense of that which was grounded in careful observation of the facts.[15] At Brantwood, which became something of an environmental field station in the 1870s and 1880s, as well as a home, he tried to draw together the many strands of his lifelong interests and concerns, writing in the study which contained not only his source material, such as his library, diaries, drawings and collection of minerals, but also afforded him a view of mountain, sky and lake. Geology interested him even more than meteorology, and the microscopic observation of the action of frost on particles of earth in the gardens at Brantwood, which he related to the formation of the Alps, complemented experiments in the kitchen with 'pie-paste' and ice-cream to test his theories for publication in *Deucalion: Collected Studies of the Lapse of Waves, and Life of Stones* (1875–83). By 1884 he had been taking note of the sky daily for fifty years, as had some of the contemporaries who validated his results, announced in *The Storm Cloud*.[16] At the same time Ruskin continued to castigate the 'scientific people' as inadequate observers of the 'facts' of the created world who then also ignored the received wisdom of 'our fathers'.

Meanwhile, in the autobiographical passages of a number of his later publications, Ruskin quoted extracts from the diaries which he had kept since the 1830s, and explored the effect upon his adult life and work of the conditions under which he had been brought up – precisely what his master, Carlyle, had meant when he translated a phrase of Goethe's in 1827 as an 'environment of circumstances'.[17] In these fragments of autobiography, Ruskin contrasts his memories of an old England of coach travel and clean rivers with his more recent observations of the railway age – the subject, *inter alia*, of many Letters in *Fors*, of some of the 'Outlines of Scenes and Thoughts perhaps Worthy of Memory in my Past Life' in *Præterita*, and of sections of *Fiction, Fair and Foul* (1880–1).

But then, how does the reader of Ruskin's late work break the hermeneutic circle and separate the observer from the observed, subject from object, inner from outer storm-cloud, autobiography (Ruskin's analysis of his own 'environment of circumstances') from documentary observa-

---

[15] See p. 34 above.

[16] G. D. Leslie, RA, confirmed that his 'description of what he calls the plague, or devil, wind' was 'singularly correct', and W. G. Collingwood made observations similar to Ruskin's (34.xxv-vi).

[17] *Environment*, OED 2b: *esp.* 'The conditions under which any person or thing lives or is developed; the sum-total of influences which modify and determine the development of life or character.'

tion (his analysis of the natural environment)? His later writing on environmental themes embodies an apocalyptic which is as deeply rooted in the Bible as the work on architecture; but the writing is more troubled, even tormented. The natural world – God's architecture, as celebrated in his earlier work – is being ruined in front of his eyes. Whereas the measurement of Venice had been an act of recovery or restoration for Ruskin, however, it now became difficult for him to separate object from subject, external from internal storm cloud: hence his obsessive need to 'collect the known facts'; hence, too, his reliance upon the biblical tradition of apocalyptic wisdom as a frame of reference.

II

Ruskin's lecture entitled *The Storm Cloud of the Nineteenth Century* was first delivered at the London Institution on 4 February 1884. He begins, tongue in cheek, by saying that, unusually, his title means what it says and that he intends simply to bring to his audience's notice 'a series of cloud phenomena', which, so far as he can weigh existing evidence, are 'peculiar to our own times' (34.9). As in Sterne, the more straightforward the proffered reader–narrator contract, the more complex the narrative that follows, and in *The Storm Cloud* the meteorological is soon interwoven into the narratological, autobiographical, psychological, soteriological and finally (perforce) the eschatological.

Ruskin first takes us back to the 'ancient observors', such as Homer and Virgil, and then up to the time of his own immediate precursors, such as Byron, whose descriptions of the sunrise and the sunset he quotes at length, indicating that the 'plague-wind' that is his subject is a recent phenomenon, observed by him for less than twenty years (34.9–13). Before developing his argument concerning the plague-wind, he explains that he 'had better define what every cloud is, and must be, to begin with' (34.14). Yet he has already begun. This is simply the first of several carefully crafted narrative blocks, whereby deferral heightens the audience's or reader's expectations. The Sternean parallels become more obvious when, following a little homely scientific writing, Ruskin announces that he must 'parenthetically' give his audience some advice about 'scientific people in general', and concludes: 'You will not, therefore, *so please you*, expect me to explain anything to you, – I have come solely and simply to put before you a few facts' (34.17–18; our emphasis). But it is not for another twenty-four pages of the first edition that he can 'at last' enter on his 'immediate subject' (34.30).

As the narrative thus moves undulatingly forward, Ruskin is also constantly referring back in time to the detailed observations recorded in his drawings, diaries and published works which together document the fieldwork on which he bases his argument. He produces for the audience an enlargement of a 'careful sketch' he made of the 'sunset of 1st October, 1868, at Abbeville, which was a beautiful example of what, in fine weather about to pass into storm, a sunset could then be, in the districts of Kent and Picardy unaffected by smoke' (34.21), and contrasts this with Arthur Severn's enlargement of his 'sketch of the sky in the afternoon of the 6th of August, 1880, at Brantwood, two hours before sunset' (34.23).

On finally entering on his immediate subject, he promptly moves back in time again, to an entry headed 'BOLTON ABBEY, 4th July, 1875' (34.30), in which the tremulous action of the trees is described; and then further back, to 'the year 1871', when he 'first noticed the definite character of this wind' (34.31). (He thus seems to contradict the dating of the phenomenon at the beginning of the lecture.) He now quotes from the opening of *Fors* for August 1871, written on 1 July in Matlock, Derbyshire, in which the grey cloud is 'a new thing' to him, 'and a very dreadful one':

> It looks partly as if it were made of poisonous smoke; very possibly it may be: there are at least two hundred furnace chimneys in a square of two miles on every side of me. But mere smoke would not blow to and fro in that wild way. It looks more to me as if it were made of dead men's souls – such of them as are not gone yet where they have to go, and may be flitting hither and thither, doubting, themselves, of the fittest place for them. (34.33)

This dead souls motif is then developed in a reminiscence of a more recent visit (in 1882) to Avallon in the South of France, when he was appalled by the Walpurgis Night scene in a production of *Faust* in a little country theatre (34.34).

Ruskin's 'Storm Cloud' has been read as a complex of antagonistic forces – psychological, environmental, philosophical.[18] That it also had powerful theological meaning for Ruskin becomes clear when his references to dead souls wandering the earth are bracketed with his earlier description of 'two different species of cloud' observed 'in those old days', when, if the weather was bad, 'it was often abominably bad, but it had its fit of temper and was done with it':

The beneficent rain-cloud was indeed often extremely dull and grey for days together, but gracious nevertheless, felt to be doing good, and often to be

---

[18] See Fitch, *The Poison Sky*.

delightful after drought . . . and continually traversed in clearing by the rainbow; – and, secondly, the storm-cloud, always majestic, often dazzlingly beautiful, and felt also to be beneficent in its own way, affecting the mass of the air with vital agitation, and purging it from the impurity of all morbific elements. (34.10)

Echoing the dualism of blessing and cursing in *Fors*, Letter 20, Ruskin describes what for him are old certainties: 'In the entire system of the Firmament, thus seen and understood, there appeared to be, to all the thinkers of those ages, the incontrovertible and unmistakable evidence of a Divine Power in creation.' An overt connection between the clouds and religion is also made in the more lighthearted reference to 'distinct monastic disciplines of cloud: Black Friars, and White Friars, and Friars of Orders Grey' (34.19). In contrast, the 'terrific and horrible thunderstorm' over Brantwood, described in Ruskin's diary on 13 August 1879, gives hardly any rain, but 'increasing to heavier rollings, with flashes quivering vaguely through all the air, and at last terrific double streams of reddish-violet fire, not forked or zigzag, but rippled rivulets' (34.37). The apocalyptic sublime that spoke of God's wrath – the 'lightnings and thunderings and voices' of Revelation 4.5 – is now dissipated into a thunderstorm which 'rolls incessantly, like railway luggage trains, quite ghastly in its mockery of them' (34.37).

For Ruskin, the clouds (signs of the sky) are actually signs of the times: he frequently cited Revelation 1.7 in his writings – 'Behold, he cometh with clouds; and every eye shall see him, and they also which pierced him: and all kindreds of the earth shall wail because of him.'[19] In the closing passages of the lecture, Ruskin declares that he cannot interpret these recent phenomena according to the audience's 'modern beliefs', but he can tell them 'what meaning it would have borne to the men of old time' (34.40). He thus at once distances himself from the lecture's final crisis of interpretation and denies the possibility of new ways through it. He then calls upon his audience to 'Remember, for the last twenty years, England, and all foreign nations, have blasphemed the name of God deliberately and openly' (34.40). This prophetic note makes explicit what has always been implicit in the structure of the lecture. For the pattern of deferral mentioned earlier is, structurally, not so much Sternean as imitative of a particular kind of literary work with which Ruskin would have been familiar in his youth (his personal 'old time'): the religious epic poem. Take, for example, Robert Pollok's hugely ambitious work, *The Course of Time* (1827).[20] Pollok's main narra-

---

[19] See, for example, *Modern Painters* IV, 6.109.
[20] Unknown today, *The Course of Time* earned Pollok the huge sum of £2,500 when it was first

tive strategies – themselves learnt from the last book in the Bible – are those of deferral and suspense combined with repetition, allowing the poet to dwell upon the sinfulness of man at great length, and thus to justify the sharp separation of the sheep from the goats at the last judgment, which is delayed until the final books.[21] Vestiges of such a structure can be detected in *The Storm Cloud*, through which Ruskin can both dwell upon the unfolding drama of the damning 'evidence' he has gathered over a long period and defer the crisis of interpretation of the final paragraphs, when he at last presents to his audience the very challenge that he has for years set himself. For 'the poetry of the prophecies', as he described it in a letter to his father of 1852, Ruskin has substituted 'one or two clearer dates'.[22] Now, himself a late prophet of the nineteenth century, he invokes the late prophets of the Old Testament:

Of states in such moral gloom every seer of old predicted the physical gloom, saying, "The light shall be darkened in the heavens thereof, and the stars shall withdraw their shining." [Joel 2.10] All Greek, all Christian, all Jewish prophecy insists on the same truth through a thousand myths; but of all the chief, to former thought, was the fable of the Jewish warrior and prophet, for whom the sun hasted not to go down, [Joshua 10.13] with which I leave you to compare at leisure the physical result of your own wars and prophecies, as declared by your own elect journal not fourteen days ago, – that the Empire of England, on which formerly the sun never set, has become one on which he never rises. (34.40–1)

Ruskin had stated in *The Queen of the Air* that great myths are made by great people: 'you cannot make a myth unless you have something to make it of. You cannot tell a secret that you don't know' (19.301). Having in the penultimate paragraph of *The Storm Cloud* brought his audience down to the nadir of this comparison between the story of the sun standing still for Joshua and the trifling ditty from a recent issue of the *Pall Mall Gazette*, he ends the lecture – as he ended *The Seven Lamps of Architecture* – no longer citing prophets but himself prophesying, in the manner of the preacher who takes his theme and thus his congregation up into the eschatological:

published. The poem ran into twenty-six editions over the subsequent forty years and was published in an attractive illustrated edition in 1857, for which Birket Foster and John Tenniel provided designs.

[21] See Michael Wheeler, *Death and the Future Life in Victorian Literature and Theology* (Cambridge University Press, 1990), pp. 86–90.

[22] 'When I was a boy, I used to read the poetry of the prophecies with great admiration – as I used to read other poetry. But now their poetry torments me. It seems to me trifling with what is all-important, and wasting words. I don't want poetry *there*. I want plain truth – and I would give all the poetry in Isaiah and Ezekiel willingly, for one or two clearer dates' (36.127).

What is best to be done, do you ask me? The answer is plain. Whether you can affect the signs of the sky or not, you can the signs of the times. [Matthew 16.3] Whether you can bring the sun back or not, you can assuredly bring back your own cheerfulness, and your own honesty. You may not be able to say to the winds, "Peace; be still", [Mark 4.39] but you can cease from the insolence of your own lips, and the troubling of your own passions. [Job 3.17] And all that it would be extremely well to do, even though the day were coming when the sun should be as darkness, and the moon as blood. [Joel 2.31] But, the paths of rectitude and piety once regained, who shall say that the promise of old time would not be found to hold for us also? "Bring ye all the tithes into my storehouse, and prove me now herewith, saith the Lord God, if I will not open you the windows of heaven, and pour you out a blessing; that there shall not be room enough to receive it." [Malachi 3.10] (34.41)

Far from suggesting 'doubt' – that much overused word in Victorian cultural history – the conditional mode manoeuvres the doubter into an uncomfortable position: 'who shall say that the promise of old would not be found to hold for us also?' Back in 1852, Ruskin had placed great emphasis upon works when writing to his father: 'Is it not rather apparent that God's purpose is to leave every man dependent upon his own conduct and choice for the discovery of truth, shutting it up in greater mystery as men depart from His ways, and revealing it more and more to each man's conscience as they obey Him . . . ?' (36.128–9). Speaking in a room frequented by the 'scientific people', Ruskin leaves his audience not with the secure sense that they have heard a rational argument condemning their generation for polluting the skies through the waste products of capitalist industrial production, but with the insecure sense that they have also been challenged to respond to a latter-day prophet whose 'discovery of truth' in revelation cannot finally be separated from his observation of the skies over fifty years.

Ruskin achieves this feeling of unsettlement partly through his complex use of tense within the conditional mode, as in the reference to Joel: 'And all that it would be extremely well to do, even though the day were coming when the sun should be as darkness, and the moon as blood.' In challenging his audience to respond to his teaching in the here-and-now through tithing, as in the Guild of St George, but also to remain aware of the imminent possibility of the end-time, Ruskin seems to follow the pattern of Jesus's teaching, which combined two apparently conflicting currents of Jewish tradition: an ethic grounded in wisdom, which assumes that the world continues, and an ethic grounded in eschatology, which assumes a radical transformation of the world.[23] New

[23] Gerd Theissen and Annette Merz, *The Historical Jesus: A Comprehensive Guide*, trans. John Bowden (London: SCM, 1998), p. 372.

Testament scholars have related Jesus' freedom from the Torah in his teaching to his use of these two traditions coming down from early Judaism, combined in what is known as 'apocalyptic wisdom':

> In the period of early Judaism, wisdom and eschatological traditions were combined. The Wisdom of Solomon presents an eschatologized wisdom: the wise and righteous who suffer tribulation in this world will rule in the new world. God will change the cosmos (Wisdom 1–5). The apocalyptic wisdom writings claim to be higher wisdom . . . What unites the two currents of tradition is the extension of the knowledge of revelation beyond the tradition: God become accessible through Wisdom and extra-normal visions independently of temple and Torah. Therefore both traditions were also available for Jesus in freely interpreting and transcending the Torah.[24]

Ruskin had taught 'independently of temple and Torah' since abandoning the Evangelicalism of his youth. In the changed ending of *The Storm Cloud* for its second delivery, on 11 February 1884, the associations between his lecture and apocalyptic wisdom become clearer.[25]

Ruskin had argued in the penultimate paragraph of Lecture I that for the previous twenty years England, and 'all foreign nations, either tempting her, or following her', had 'blasphemed the name of God deliberately and openly' (34.40). In Note 20 of Lecture II he developed these comments, thundering against the '*deliberate* blasphemy of science, the assertion of its own virtue and dignity against the always implied, and often asserted, vileness of all men and – Gods, – heretofore' (34.70). The wisdom of Homer, David and St John, he argues, was denigrated in a modern study in which science is said to have 'mastered the system of nature' and revealed the 'true method and order of the University' by adding fact to fact and law to law (34.73). There then follows text by Ruskin which was 'read in termination of the lecture on its second delivery, only with an added word or two of comment on Proverbs xvii'. In developing the point he makes in *Fors*, Letter 94 (March 1884) on the value of children's learning by heart (29.489), Ruskin comments:

> And of writings to be learned by heart, among other passages of indisputable philosophy and perfect poetry, I include certain chapters of the – now for the most part forgotten – wisdom of Solomon; and of these, there is one selected portion which I should recommend not only school-boys and girls, but

---

[24] Ibid., p. 373.
[25] Ruskin was forced to complete Lecture I under pressure of time, having discovered on 26 January that he was to lecture on 4 February, and not 24 February as he had thought (*D*, 1057). The week between his two deliveries of the lecture gave him time to refine it. The printed version of Lecture II takes the form of notes and additional passages for the benefit of the reader, as a supplement to Lecture I.

persons of every age, if they don't know it, to learn forthwith, as the shortest
summary of Solomon's wisdom; – namely, the seventeenth chapter of Proverbs,
which being only twenty-eight verses long, may be fastened in the dullest
memory at the rate of a verse a day in the shortest month of the year. Out of
the twenty-eight verses, I will read you seven, for example of their tenor, – the
last of the seven I will with your good leave dwell somewhat upon. You have
heard the verses often before, but probably without remembering that they are
all in this concentrated chapter. (34.74)

What follows is uncannily reminiscent of that passage in *Fors*, Letter
87 (March 1878) in which Ruskin had tried to hold on to his sanity by
inviting the reader to join him in his morning study of the first chapter
of Proverbs (29.374-5):[26]

1. Verse 1. – Better is a dry morsel, and quietness therewith, than a house full
of good eating, with strife.

(Remember, in reading this verse, that though England has chosen the strife,
and set every man's hand against his neighbour, her house is not yet so full of
good eating as she expected, even though she gets half of her victuals from
America.)

And so on through verses 3, 4, 5, 12 and 16, after which he turns to 'verse
7' – in fact a mistake for verse 24, missed by his editors:

7. Lastly, Verse 7. – Wisdom is before him that hath understanding, but the
eyes of a fool are in the ends of the earth.

"And in the beginnings of it"! Solomon would have written, had he lived in
our day; but we will be content with the ends at present. No scientific people,
as I told you at first, have taken any notice of the more or less temporary phenomena of which I have to-night given you register. But, from the constant
arrangements of the universe, the same respecting which the thinkers of former
time came to the conclusion that they were essentially good, and to end in good,
the modern speculator arrives at the quite opposite and extremely uncomfortable conclusion that they are essentially evil, and to end – in nothing. (34.75-6)

The wisdom of Solomon, who as we have seen was traditionally
regarded as the father of the natural sciences, is weighed against that of
modern science, and in the final sentence Ruskin offers a lucid reading
of apocalyptic ancient and modern.[27]

Modern scientific apocalyptic is immediately help up to ridicule in the
shape of *The Conservation of Energy* by the 'very foolish and very lugubri-
ous' Balfour Stewart, who likens the universe to a candle which is

---

[26] See p. 238 above.
[27] When rebinding his Cuvier, Ruskin described it as a 'beastly wretch of a modern scientific book
– ought to be bound in ass-skin': Lancaster L 43, *Letters of John Ruskin to Joan Severn*.

burning and will eventually cease to burn (34.76). Ruskin goes on to parry the disturbingly acute critique of Lecture I which had appeared in the *Daily News* on 6 February by answering its false objection that he had concealed his own opinions. Had the weather been as it is now when he was young, he declares, he could not have written *Modern Painters*, which was based upon the belief that over much of the world's surface 'the air and the earth were fitted to the education of the spirit of man': 'That harmony is now broken, and broken the world round: fragments, indeed, of what existed still exist, and hours of what is past still return; but month by month the darkness gains upon the day' (34.78). He ends the lecture, however, reaffirming a person's Wordsworthian instincts of hope, reverence (or admiration) and love:

Having these instincts, his only rational conclusion is that the objects which can fulfil them may be by his effort gained, and by his faith discerned; and his only earthly wisdom is to accept the united testimony of the men who have sought these things in the way they were commanded. Of whom no single one has ever said that his obedience or his faith had been vain, or found himself cast out from the choir of the living souls, whether here, or departed, for whom the song was written: –

"God be merciful unto us, and bless us, and cause His face to shine upon us;

That Thy way may be known upon earth, Thy saving health among all nations.

Oh let the nations rejoice and sing for joy, for Thou shalt judge the people righteously and govern the nations upon earth.

Then shall the earth yield her increase, and God, even our own God, shall bless us.

God shall bless us, and all the ends of the earth shall fear Him." (34.80; Psalms 67.1,2,4,6–7)

Ruskin presents this benediction as being freely available to all those who learn from tradition, and particularly from Solomon, and thus place wisdom above knowledge, and knowledge above facts.

The printing, however, of both the full text of Lecture I and the fragments of notes and additions that he called Lecture II in the published version of *The Storm Cloud*, thus keeping both endings in play, quietly confirmed Ruskin's argument that the harmony of the world was now broken. His late version of apocalyptic wisdom, grounded in faith in the God of Israel, was delivered amidst the encircling gloom of scientific materialism, and extended the hope of divine blessing in the context of a fragmented modernity that had been uncannily anticipated almost fifty years earlier, when he recorded in his diary that he had found 'a fragment or two of cornelian on Dover beach' (*D*, 3).

III

This literary-historical study has focused upon the impact of Ruskin's religious beliefs on his writings, and has tried to relate his whole project of interpretation and criticism to the religious agenda of his age. It is therefore appropriate briefly to recall what some of Ruskin's contemporaries thought of his religious teaching.

Dean Farrar's lecture to the Ruskin Society of Birmingham in October 1898, entitled *Ruskin as a Religious Teacher* and published in revised form in 1904, opens with a statement that typifies the panegyrics that were published before and after the death of the Grand Old Man in 1900:

> The religious character of Mr. Ruskin's mind is one of its most distinguishing features; and it has been one secret of his most powerful influence. Everything around us – all the glory of heaven, and all the furniture of earth – is to him one great scroll, on which he reads – not half-obliterated, as in a palimpsest, but in letters of light, radiant and unquenchable – the one word God. To him everything is a message to our souls by Him who is the Word of God.[28]

It would be easy to read such a statement as Farrar's contribution to the construction of the religious Sage of Brantwood, along with Hollyer's photographic portrait of Ruskin the patriarch (*Datur hora quieti*), Joan Severn's description of the deathbed scene in *The Times* and Canon Rawnsley's verses.[29] The lecture that follows is, however, substantial and carefully considered, and concludes that 'all the sources of Revelation on which Mr. Ruskin dwells – the Revelation by Nature; by Science; by Art; by Scripture; by the Constitution of Man; by History; by Mythology; by all great Books – is a revelation which bears on the two grand and universal spheres of Morality and of Religion'.[30] Moreover, others had written along similar lines, if less fulsomely, during Ruskin's lifetime.[31]

For example, the anonymous author of an article in the *Christian Observer* for September 1862 entitled 'John Ruskin as a Religious Writer' regarded him as 'boldly advancing opinions upon questions that come more properly within the province of the divine', and as introducing Christian ethics into Art by 'making war, persevering and relentless,

---

[28] [F. W.] Farrar, *Ruskin as a Religious Teacher* (London: Allen, 1904), pp. 3–4.
[29] See 35.frontispiece, xlv, xlvi.   [30] Farrar, *Ruskin as a Religous Teacher*, pp. 43–4.
[31] Mrs Louisa C. Tuthill added no commentary to her anthology of *Precious Thoughts: Moral and Religious, gathered from the Works of John Ruskin, A. M.* (New York: Wiley, 1866), which went into several editions. Mary and Ellen Gibbs later produced an anthology of *The Bible References of John Ruskin* (London: Allen, 1898), which was also reprinted.

upon whatever if false or factitious, showy and empty'.[32] Ruskin's bold-ness and freedom of approach was in this reviewer's opinion associated with the fact that he had no suspect sectarian affiliations or moderniz-ing tendencies; and in spite of his 'overweening confidence in his own judgment on *all subjects*' – his 'besetting infirmity' – he may 'truly be said to have baptized Art into Christianity'.[33]

The contrast between Ruskin's aims as the 'Author of *Modern Painters*' and as a 'Victorian Solomon' is reflected in the different emphasis that the Revd W. T. Moreton was to place upon Ruskin's teaching on the 'dignity of manual toil', the 'Christian use of wealth', and the 'Christian spirit of social and political brotherhood' twenty-six years later.[34] Ruskin's nature is described by Moreton as 'penetrated . . . with the very spirit of Christianity' and his words as a 'trumpet-call to God-like service in all departments of life'.[35] His parents may have regretted that he was not ordained, but 'God meant him to be a preacher of right-eousness without the laying on of hands'; and 'he who has intelligently spent a hundred and forty-thousand pounds in trying to fulfil the behests of Christian brotherhood may probably have something to teach us that we have not clearly seen, or that we have not entirely obeyed'.[36]

But what of Ruskin today, as we reflect upon the centenary of his death? In rediscovering him, our postmodern age has constructed a godless Ruskin, and yet one explanation for the current revival of inter-est in his writings – and indeed drawings – is the attractiveness of his 'spirituality'. Consider, for example, the way in which Ruskin's spiritual principles of architecture have been invoked by practitioners and critics alike in the exceptionally lively discussion on the subject during the 1990s in Britain, and indeed globally.[37] Yet without an understanding of the specifically biblical frame of reference in which Ruskin worked out those principles it is impossible to place him accurately in relation either to his contemporaries or to ourselves. Similarly, in our millennial times, 'envi-ronmental' issues have moved rapidly up the political agenda, and again Ruskin has been recognized as one of our most eloquent and persistent prophets on issues such as sustainability, pollution and mechanical

[32] Anon, 'John Ruskin as a Religious Writer', *The Christian Observer*, 62 (September 1862), 658–78 (pp. 660–1).   [33] Ibid., pp. 674–5.
[34] W. T. Moreton, 'The Religious Teachings of John Ruskin', *The Christian World Pulpit* (18 April–2 May 1888), 248–50, 266–8, 282–5.   [35] Ibid., p. 248.
[36] Ibid., pp. 266, 282–3.
[37] See *The Lamp of Memory: Ruskin, Tradition and Architecture*, ed. Michael Wheeler and Nigel Whiteley (Manchester University Press, 1992).

sources of power.[38] Only by attending closely to the anthropocentrism of his creation theology, however, can we avoid mistaking him for a proto-ecologist, or the first 'green man'.

More fundamental than Ruskin's contribution to continuing debates on particular issues is the prophetic quality of his foundational beliefs. His statement, born out of his reading of the Book of Proverbs, that 'There is no wealth but life' resonates in a culture in which materialism, now firmly established in the West as the main 'religion', fails to deliver more than fleeting consumerist gratification. His belief that religion is primarily about obedience speaks to a generation that has lost its spiritual moorings. His respect for monotheistic religions other than his own anticipates the challenges and opportunities facing today's multi-cultural societies. Within the Christian sphere, Ruskin's critique of the Church's failure to proclaim and live out a gospel which is too radical to be contained by institutions is more widely acceptable today than it was in the nineteenth century, while his rejection of Evangelical doctrines raises interesting questions concerning the main current growth area in the Church. As the arts are subsumed under the label of 'culture' (a term which in a secular society implies purely human agency), as postmodernity mimics consumerism's crisis of choice in the cultural hypermarket and as criticism of the arts is dominated by the hermeneutics of suspicion, Ruskin's affirmation that 'All great art is praise' merits the fresh attention it receives.[39] Finally, as the full implications of the information revolution begin to emerge, Ruskin's constant reference to a traditional hierarchy in which information is subservient to knowledge, which is in turn subservient to wisdom, and his personal struggle to relate facts to truth, and truth to God, seem even more relevant today than in the industrial age in which he lived.

The argument of this study has been that Ruskin's whole project is grounded in his belief in wisdom and in a God of peace, and that this belief is nurtured by his imaginative engagement with the peaceable Solomon and Old Testament wisdom literature. The still small voice of peaceful benediction that we heard in both endings of *The Storm Cloud* finds a distant echo in the famous final paragraphs of *Præterita*, dated 19 June 1889, where Ruskin writes of drawing back to his own home, twenty years earlier, 'permitted to thank Heaven once more for the

---

[38] See Jonathan Bate, *Romantic Ecology: Wordsworth and the Environmental Tradition* (London: Routledge, 1991); *Ruskin and Environment: The Storm-Cloud of the Nineteenth Century*, ed. Michael Wheeler (Manchester University Press, 1995).

[39] See Peter Fuller, *Theoria: Art, and the Absence of Grace* (London: Chatto, Windus, 1988).

peace, and hope, and loveliness of it', and of things binding and blend-
ing themselves together, and of the fireflies in Siena 'moving like fine-
broken starlight through the purple leaves' (35.560–2). A stronger echo,
however, is in the Epilogue which he wrote for George Allen's Complete
Edition of *Modern Painters*, and dated 'CHAMOUNI, Sunday, September
16th, 1888'. Here Ruskin states that the 'vital teaching and purpose' of
the work is 'the claim . . . of the Personal relation of God to man as the
source of all human, as distinguished from brutal virtue', on the (non-
doctrinal) assumption 'that man can love and obey a living Spirit' and
can be 'happy in the presence and guidance of a Personal Deity' (7.462).
Man is to advance God's glory by his obedience and happiness, not by
'lectures on the Divine wisdom, meant only to show his own' (7.463).
After the 'crowning of obedience, and fulfilment of joy, comes the joy of
praise'. The final paragraph serves as Ruskin's benediction to his own
generation, and to ours:

All that is involved in these passionate utterances of my youth was first
expanded and then concentrated into the aphorism given twenty years afterwards in my inaugural Oxford lectures, "All great Art is Praise";[40] and on that
aphorism, the yet bolder saying founded, "So far from Art's being immoral, in
the ultimate power of it, nothing but Art is moral: Life without Industry is sin,
and Industry without Art, brutality" (I forget the words, but that is their
purport): and now, in writing beneath the cloudless peace of the snows of
Chamouni, what must be the really final words of the book which their beauty
inspired and their strength guided, I am able, with yet happier and calmer heart
than ever heretofore, to enforce its simplest assurance of Faith, that the knowledge of what is beautiful leads on, and is the first step, to the knowledge of the
things which are lovely and of good report [Philippians 4.8]; and that the laws,
the life, and the joy of beauty in the material world of God, are as eternal and
sacred parts of His creation as, in the world of spirits, virtue; and in the world
of angels, praise. (7.463–4)

[40] In fact in *The Laws of Fésole* (15.351); the subsequent quotation is from the *Lectures on Art* (20.93).

Appendix

Pusey House, Oxford, owns a copy of Fred Hill, *Pusey Preaching in St. Mary's*, from *Caricatures Published by Thomas Shrimpton & Son*, 1877, together with a complete list of characters, kindly supplied by the Revd William Davage. Beginning on the left-hand side, under the gallery:

First row:

Revd Dr Bulley	*President of Magdalen*
Revd B. Jowett	*Master of Balliol, Regius Professor of Greek*
Revd Dr Sewell	*Warden of New College*
Revd Mark Pattison	*Rector of Lincoln*
Revd Dr Griffiths	*Warden of Wadham*

Second row:

Revd Dr Craddock	*Principal of Brasenose*
Revd Dr Cotton	*Provost of Worcester*
Revd G. G. Bradley	*Master of University*
Revd Dr Lightfoot	*Rector of Exeter*
Revd E. S. Talbot	*Warden of Keble*
Revd Dr Moore	*Principal of St Edmund Hall*
Professor Monier Williams	*(University) Boden Professor of Sanskrit*
Professor Bonamy Price	*(Worcester) Professor of Political Economy*
Revd C. H. G. Daniel	*Vice-Provost of Worcester*
Revd Dr Bellamy	*President of St John's*
Revd Dr Evans	*Master of Pembroke*

Third row:

Revd Dr Liddell	*Dean of Christ Church*
Revd Dr Leighton	*Warden of All Souls*
Dr Masham	*Warden of Merton*

Revd Dr Jackson	*Provost of Queen's*
Sir Henry W. Acland Bart.	*(Ch Ch: All Souls) Regius Professor of Medicine*
Revd Dr Macgrath	*Fellow of Queen's*
Revd Dr Michell	*Principal of Hertford College*
Revd Dr Williams	*Principal of Jesus*
Revd S. W. Wayte	*President of Trinity*
Revd Dr Cornish	*Principal of New Inn Hall*
Professor Rolleston	*(Merton) Professor of Physiology*

Fourth row:

Revd Dr King	*(Ch Ch) Regius Professor of Pastoral Theology*
Revd Dr Bright	*(Ch Ch) Regius Professor of Ecclesiastical History*
Revd C. A. Heurtley	*(Ch Ch) Lady Margaret Professor of Divinity*
Revd Dr Palmer	*(Ch Ch) Corpus Professor of Latin*
Revd T. Fowler	*(Lincoln) Wykeham Professor of Logic*
Revd Dr Liddon	*(Ch Ch) Professor of Exegesis of Holy Scripture*
Professor Montagu Burrows	*(All Souls) Chichele Professor of Modern History*
Revd W. Stubbs	*(Oriel) Regius Professor of Modern History*
Mr Thorold Rogers	*(Worcester) Sometime Professor of Political Economy*
Professor J. O. Westwood	*(Magdalen) Hope Professor of Zoology*
Revd T. L. Papillon	*Fellow of New*

Under the pulpit:

Professor Max Müller	*(All Souls) Corpus Professor of Comparative Philology*
Professor J. Ruskin	*(Ch Ch) Slade Professor of Fine Art*

Under the pulpit (facing lectern):

Mr Matthew Arnold	*(Oriel) Sometime Professor of Poetry*
Rt Hon. W. E. Gladstone	*(Ch Ch) Sometime Burgess of the University*
Rt Hon. J. R. Mowbray	*(Ch Ch) Burgess of the University*

Index

CAMBRIDGE STUDIES IN NINETEENTH-CENTURY
LITERATURE AND CULTURE

General editor
Gillian Beer, *University of Cambridge*

Titles published